ELECTRONIC RESOURCE MANAGEMENT : What, Why and How

Shiva Sukula

Ess Ess Publications

4837/24, Ansari Road, Darya Ganj,
New Delhi-110002
✆ : 23260807, 41563444
Fax : 011-41563334
E-mail: info@essessreference.com
url:http://www.essessreference.com

First Published 2007

Published by SUMIT SETHI
for Ess Ess Publications
4837/24, Ansari Road, Darya Ganj,
New Delhi - 110 002
Ph. : 23260807, 41563444
Fax : 011-41563334
E-mail: info@essessreference.com
url:http://www.essessreference.com

ISBN : 978-81-7000-608-4

Price : Rs. 1675/-

Laser Typesetting:
Mukesh Graphics
T-1264, Mangolpuri, New Delhi
Ph. : 9899079035, 20106135
E-mail:mukeshgraphics29@yahoo.com

Printed at :
Print Line

CONTENTS

Office 2760554
2760551
Fax 2762838
Resi. 2600066
Fax 2760577

चौ० चरण सिंह विश्वविद्यालय, मेरठ
CH. CHARAN SINGH UNIVERSITY, MEERUT

प्रो० शिबन किशन काक
पीएच०-डी० (इलैक्ट्रोनिक्स इन्जी०)
साल्ज़बर्ग फैलो
कुलपति

Prof. Shiban Kishan Kak
Ph.D. (Electronics Engg.)
Salzburg Fellow
Vice-Chancellor

Ref. No. : SVC/17/२136
Dated : 25-01-2010

FOREWORD

E-resources are perceived as offering great potential for learner support. The experience of various libraries shows that, with the right combination of content and access technologies, e-resources can be very helpful to the users in availing information and knowledge services, while librarians can create more dynamic, relevant and flexible collections not possible in print. E-resources have firmly established themselves as essential resources for libraries and their users in current context. The facility to have resources search for any text from among all subscribed titles at once brings more resources into play, enabling fuller exploitation of the e-resources.

The present book explores the concept of e-resources and makes efforts to encompass each facet of e-resources in a nut-shell. Major aspects have been covered with a touch of analytical method and a pragmatic approach. The chapters presented are Introduction to E-Resources, Managing E-Resources With Tools And Technologies, E-Resource Management Systems, Library Web Content Management, Networking Technologies For E-Resources, E-Archive And Digital Preservation, Retrieval Of Information From E-Resources, Cataloguing Of E-Resources, CrossRef And Resource Identification In Electronic Environment, E-

Resources And Licensing, Open Access and E-resources, and Digital Information, The Public Domain And Digital Copyright.

The book is targeted for library professional as also laymen and focuses on a systematic coverage of e-resource and their use in Libraries and Information Centers in the age of exploring knowledge and information overload in an ever changing knowledge scenario. This book will provide a comprehensive idea of e-resources within the framework of information systems and services and fulfill a genuine need of a text on the subject.

I congratulate Dr. (Ms) Shiva Sukula for bringing out such an excellent work in the form of this book.

Prof. S.K. Kak
Vice Chancellor

Acknowledgements for Glossary

Many sources were consulted for the creation of this glossary:

1) AACR2 - Anglo-American cataloguing rules. - 2nd edition, 2002 revision. - Ottawa: Canadian Library Association; London: Chartered Institute of Library and Information Professionals; Chicago: American Library Association, 2002

2) Baca, Murtha, ed. Introduction to metadata: glossary. Version 2.0 http://www.getty.edu/research/institute/standards/intrometadata/index.htm

3) BIBLINK: Objectives, Scope and Glossary

4) Caplan, Priscilla. Metadata Fundamentals for all Librarians. Chicago: American Library Association, 2003.

5) Clement, Gail and Peter Winn. A user guide for simple Dublin Core: glossary

6) DCMI Agents Working Group - Dublin Core Metadata Initiative, Agents Working Group. http://dublincore.org/groups/agents/

7) FRAD - Functional requirements for authority data: a conceptual mode

8) FRBR - Functional requirements for bibliographic records: Final report. - Munich : Saur, 1998. (IFLA UBCIM publications new series; v. 19)

9) GARR - Guidelines for authority records and references. 2nd ed., rev. - Munich : Saur, 2001. (IFLA UBCIM publications new series; v. 23)

10) IME ICC - IFLA Meeting of Experts on an International Cataloguing Code recommendations from the participants, 2001-2008.

11) ISBD - International standard bibliographic description : consolidated edition. - Munich : Saur, 2007. (IFLA Series on Bibliographic Control, v. 31)

12) Lanzi, Elisa. Introduction to vocabularies: enhancing access to cultural heritage information. Los Angeles: Getty Information Institute, 1998. Updated by Patricia Harpring. http://www.getty.edu/research/institute/vocabulary/introvocabs/

13) Moen, William. An Overview of Z39.50, Supplemented by a Case Study of Implementing the Zebra Server Under the Linux Operating System. http://www.unt.edu/wmoen/Z3950/GIZMO/appendix_d.htm

14) RDA: Resource description and access. Glossary draft. 5JSC/Chair/11/Rev (Jan. 2008, Table Available online at: http://www.collectionscanada.gc.ca/jsc/rda.html#drafts

15) Schemas glossary http://www.schemas-forum.org/related/glossary.html

16) Smith, Allison. Terms commonly used in authority control and thesaurus construction. Word document provided to DC-general listserv.

17) Webster's 3rd: Webster's third new international

dictionary of the English Language -Unabridged. - Springfield, Mass. : Merriam-Webster, 2000.

18) The e-Framewrok Glossary. Available at: http://www.e-framework.org/Resources/Glossary/tabid/642/Default.aspx

1

INTRODUCTION TO E-RESOURCES

BACKGROUND

It was during late 1990s that existing library and information services (LIS) could not handle the functions necessary for an effective electronic-resource management system. After a decade some developments took place. It was in early 2000s, that content providers initiative emerged in the form of A-Z lists. Sooner around 2002, Digital Library Federation Electronic Resource Management Initiative (DLF ERMI) developed common specifications and tools for managing the license agreements, related administrative information, and internal processes associated with collections of licensed electronic resources. The libraries have defined the need and the specification, standards, opportunity for library automation and content providers. During this time the vendors started development and various products in the market were made available such as software systems used by libraries to keep track of important information about electronic information resources. It was the result of various advances and practices that e-resources are expanding more than 60% and growing till date. The web found a world wide platform in the form of Google and "Google-ization" took place. Now the high demand for

"24x7" access has been pervasive without any discrimination. Due to various factors, the e-resource budget shares continue to grow and organizations do not hesitate in expanding and spending on the same. This is very common phenomena that the budget issues help drive shift to e-only journal access keeping in view the fact that e-resources are complex in the means of describing, funding and support.

DEFINITION OF ELECTRONIC RESOURCE

According to AACR2, 2005 Update, an electronic resource is: "Material (data and/or program(s)) encoded for manipulation by a computerized device. This material may require the use of a peripheral directly connected to a computerized device (e.g., CD-ROM drive) or a connection to a computer network (e.g., the Internet)." This definition does **not** include electronic resources that do not **require** the use of a computer, for example, music compact discs and videodiscs. An e-resource is an electronic information resource that can be accessed on the web, on or off campus. User can get the information what he or she want, when it is needed. Explaining in broader context, an e-resource is a collection of digital content delivered to the user via the internet. The types of content included in e-resources are full text, images, primary research material and data, sound and film. It is important to say that e-resources also encompass abstract and indexing databases.

VARIOUS TYPES OF E-RESOURCES

1. Databases (reference works & indexes)

The databases include products such as periodical indexes & abstracts, directories, encyclopedias, dictionaries, other reference works. In general the databases provide search facilities to users by subject, type and title or keyword (s) with the Boolean logic feature.

2. E-Journals

Electronic journals encompass information products as electronic journals, and links to e-journal collections like gateways as well as publishers such as JSTOR, Project Muse, and ScienceDirect. The users can search e-journal by title. They can browse e-journal titles alphabetically as well as by subject category. Sometimes a hierarchical outline of subject categories or A to Z Index of subjects is also available. Currently most of the modern libraries facilitate e-journal collections and databases.

3. E-Books

A good number of libraries and information centers provide links to collections of full-text books like Books24x7, Early English Books Online, NetLibrary. Libraries provide access to full-text electronic books with a focus on information technologies. For example there can be a collection of thousands of online full-text books and other materials across a variety of subject areas and a collection of online scholarly books in the field of specific single subject. In various S & T Libraries aggregated engineering and applied science handbooks, databases, and data can be accessed full text and also by utilizing specific proprietary tabular analysis tools.

4. E-News

Electronic news has already made its place in the form of news resources like LexisNexis and Factiva, and links to local, national, and international newspapers.

5. E-Images

Due to advent of electronic image facility, image databases are used specifically in subjects such as history, geography, medical sciences etc. The libraries develop in-house digital image collections and also provide access to selected external databases to their clientele.

6. E-Music and Sound Collections

Electronic music and sound collections are creating their niche which in multimedia libraries. Digital sound recording collections are facilitated by libraries.

7. Data/GIS

Numeric and geo-spatial data suitable for those interested in using either statistical or GIS software is provided.

8. Academic Commons

The intellectual output of a particular organization is also considered. Online access to university dissertations, working papers, proceedings, etc. is facilitated to the academic community. The access to such e- resources can be restricted to the organizational users only, depending on policies.

9. E-Reference

Electronic reference sources are the significant facet of e-resources. E-reference sources can be comprised of following types of resources:

i. Dictionaries
ii. Translators
iii. Encyclopedia
iv. Directories
v. Glossaries
vi. Virtual Newspapers
    a. International Newspapers
    b. Local Newspapers

10. Subject Guides

As the name suggests, the subject-focused guides to digital and print resources. These types of resource help in day today faculty needs and cater to wide variety of user demands in the academic set-up.

11. Web Search Tools

Internet search tools like search engines, Ask, Yahoo, Live Search, google including various feature such as Google Book Search, Google Earth, Google Images, Google Maps, Google Scholar and Google Co-op; are inevitable as well as significant components of library. Meta search engines such as Mamma Metasearch InfoMine, Dogpile, Grokker, and MetaGlossary do make impressive aspect. Directories/ reference sources such as Wikipedia, Bubl Link, PubMed , WWW Virtual Library, audio-visual tools such as YouTube, Radio-Locator, Singingfish blogs and web 2.0 tools such as Technorati, Flickr and guides/reviews such as search engine showdown as well as search engine watch are available.

12. The Web

The web is a useful source of online information but it is also an uncontrolled environment; anyone can post information to it for any purpose and at any time.

13. Subject or Information Gateways

Subject and information gateways are the free information and resources available on the web which have been carefully chosen and quality checked by experts in their field. The subject Gateways provide access to reliable and up-to-date web resources for all subjects, some examples are as following:

i. **Intute :** Intute is the best and most relevant resources covering all subjects, in one place. It provides trusted information, which has been evaluated by specialists for its quality and relevance.

ii. **Google Scholar :** User can search across many disciplines and sources for scholarly literature and relevant research. Resources include papers, theses, books, preprints, abstracts and technical reports.

iii. **BUBL Information Service - Internet Resources for all Subjects :** BUBL links the selected Internet resources covering all academic subject areas. BUBL uses the Dewey Decimal Classification system as the primary organization structure for its catalogue of Internet resources. The arrangement is given as following:

- **000 Generalities :** It includes: computing, Internet, libraries, information science
- **100 Philosophy and psychology** It includes: ethics, paranormal phenomena
- **200 Religion :** It includes: bibles, religions of the world
- **300 Social sciences :** It includes: sociology, politics, economics, law, education
- **400 Language :** It includes: linguistics, language learning, specific languages
- **500 Science and mathematics :** It includes: physics, chemistry, earth sciences, biology, zoology
- **600 Technology :** It includes: medicine, engineering, agriculture, management
- **700 The arts :** It includes: art, planning, architecture, music, sport
- **800 Literature and rhetoric :** It includes: literature of specific languages
- **900 Geography and history :** It includes: travel, genealogy, archaeology

iv. **Pinakes :** It is one of the vital subject launch pad linking to the major subject gateways. In ancient times, the Library of Alexandria was seen as a universal store of human knowledge. As the Library grew in size, however, it became increasingly difficult to locate relevant material. The poet Callimachus solved the problem by compiling a catalogue called *The Pinakes*. On a far smaller scale, these Web pages hope to provide a similar function for Internet resources, by linking to the major subject gateways.

It has following subject gateways:

- **AccessToLaw:** law
- **AERADE :** aerospace and defence studies
- **AHDS :** arts and humanities
- **Biz/ed :** business and economics
- **BUBL :** library and information science
- **ChemDex :** chemistry
- **ELDIS :** development & the environment
- **FMO (Forced Migration Online) :** forced migration, refugees, displaced peoples
- **GEM (Gateway to Educational Materials) :** educational resources
- **Go-Geo! :** geo-spatial data & resources
- **History :** historical studies
- **iLoveLanguages :** language-learning & linguistics
- **InfoLaw :** law
- **Internet Directory for Botany :** botany
- **Intute: Arts & HumanitiesIntute: Health & Life Sciences**
- **Intute: Science & TechnologyIntute: Social Sciences**
- **LAWLINKS :** law
- **Links for Chemists:** chemistry
- **The Math Forum Internet Mathematics Library:** mathematics
- **MCS :** media and communication studies

- **Moving Images Gateway :** Moving images & sound in Higher & Further Education
- **Music (BUBL Link) :** music
- **NBS :** architecture, engineering, construction
- **PADI :** Preserving Access to Digital Information
- **Philosophy Around The Web :** philosophy studies
- **PhysicsWeb Resources :** physics
- **Portal to Legal Resources in the UK and Ireland :** law
- **Psych Web :** psychology
- **Reproductive Health Gateway :** reproductive health
- **RUDI :** urban design
- **Sapling :** architecture, planning and landscape
- **SciCentral :** science
- **TechXtra :** engineering, maths & computing articles, books, news, jobs, reports, eprints, etc.
- **World Wide Arts Resources :** the arts

v. **Multi-Subject Gateways**

- **About.com Education :** all subjects
- **Academic Info :** all subjects
- **BUBL Link :** all subjects
- **DMOZ: The Open Directory Project :** all subjects
- **INFOMINE :** all subjects
- **Intute :** all subjects
- **Librarians' Internet Index :** all subjects
- **Scout Report Archives :** all subjects
- **WWW Virtual Library :** all subjects

UNDERSTANDING THE IMPORTANCE OF E- RESOURCES

Factors responsible for emergence and better

management of e-resources are as following :

i. Many authors and Corporate bodies resorting to publishing their own scholarly publications

ii. Researchers are interested to access full-text publications and reference linking

iii. Many (most of the) scientific journals are available online

iv. Electronic information has recorded growth market in the World

v. Web searches encouraged users in browsing content pages of journals- by Author and Keywords.

vi. Paid subscribers are allowed browse full-text articles with downloadable facility

vii. E-journals are available online through Internet and Web.

viii. Organizations are initiating e-publications and also providing On-line services to users

ix. Researchers are acquiring varieties of skills in using Internet for research. It has made it possible to explore issues that couldn't otherwise be explored in the means as:

- It has broadened research
- Kept updated on the latest information

E-RESOURCES IN LIBRARIES

E-resources in the libraries are doing great in context of connectivity, comprehensiveness and compactness. The e-resources facilitate fast information services on one hand and links to variety of sources on the other. Major aspects in context of the application and popularity of e-resources are given as following:

i. Exchange of information from Internet to Video Conferencing

ii. Simplified technology to create and distribute information with the help of library professionals

iii. Library as a center for learning resources

iv. Why libraries are intended towards e-resources can be understood keeping in view their characteristic. The e-characteristics of e-resources can't be ignored such as:

   - Potentially huge
   - Comprehensive of everything
   - Do not require physical space
   - Feasibility in full content searchability
   - Constraints that are in physical libraries are barred in e-Resources
   - Time, space and cost constraints are not a problem in search strategies
   - Hyperlinks lead the users quickly to the required information sources
   - Easy in archiving the content

Some factors must be kept in mind that e-resources are complex (and different from print) :

i. To describe

ii. To fund and acquire

iii. To support and manage

INTEGRATING THE E-LEARNING WITH E-RESOURCES

It is clearly visible through the use and popularity of e-resources that e-resources are indispensable part and process of e-learning. Various factors are given as following:

i. E-Learning depends on e-Resources

ii. Involving the experiences of students, teachers' strategies and planning schedule and teaching, learning content, it requires:

   - Staff development

- Technological delivery strategy
- Teachers' conception of preparation of teaching strategies;
- Student's learning interest

THE EXPLOSION OF E-RESOURCES

E-resource explosion has raised new access and management challenges for libraries:

i. Handling process -
   - Acquisition
   - Licensing
   - Evaluation
   - Content
   - Technical data

ii. Delivery -
   - Awareness
   - Access
   - Linking
   - Search

ADVANTAGES OF E- RESOURCES

In terms of technological aspects, the advantages are as following :

- Space
- Updating
- Security, theft, automatic returns (no fines)
- Remote and Concurrent and 24x7 access to textual aspects:
  - Added value features
  - Portability (hand-held readers for e-books)
  - Integration into Virtual learning environment (VLE) (e-learning ethos)

  - Tailoring texts (e-books)

Advantages for e-books:

- Portability
- Instant Access
- Search ability
- Annotation
- Linking
- Multimedia
- Long term preservation of the material
- Multiple titles in single book
- Online Dictionary
- Link to other sites
- Old titles cannot go out-of print
- Readers can add several chapters from several books
- Update text books minimal cost
- Low publishing cost
- Low distribution cost
- Paper saving
- Physical Space saving

Advantages for e-journals:

- Print Journal subscription has become outdated
- E-Publishing produced e-journals
- Available through CD-ROMs and on Internet
- Subscriptions can be paid
  - Individually;
  - Institutions through consortia
- Consortia subscriptions are comparatively less
- Access Journals from one's Desktops
- Accelerating growth of e-journals

- Subscribed e-journals, are available on Internet
- User can access through a Password or IP address

ADDED VALUE FEATURES TO E- RESOURCES

- Search (within) and Searching across collections
- Hyperlinks (internal /external)
- Multimedia
- Interactivity/Exercises leading to Participation
- Book marking and Information delivery
- Annotating and Highlighting
- Reference tools
- Archives
- Copying/pasting/e-mailing and Chat with editors/ authors
- Capitalizes on pupil's enthusiasm for new media
- Reduces the amount of photocopying for handouts
- Borrow e-book versions of reference books
- Technical processing costs are less
- De-selection more easily facilitated

DISADVANTAGES OF E-RESOURCES:

- Funding / budgets for hardware and resources
- Awareness & commitment, technophobia (library and IT staff / teachers)
- Authentication / password management
- Hardware / software / infrastructure
- Printing and copying
- Physical screen use / accessibility
- Interface problems / navigation
- Information Literacy / ethical issues

FRAMEWORK FOR BUILDING EFFECTIVE E-RESOURCES

The Institute of Museum and Library Services (IMLS) convened a forum to develop a framework for considering and promoting standards and good practices to guide the development of good e-resources. NISO has also issued certain guidelines in order to build e-resources and steps towards managing e-resource. The Framework of Guidance by NISO has three purposes:

1. To provide an overview of some of the major components and activities involved in creating good digital collections.
2. To identify existing resources that support the development of sound local practices for creating and managing good digital collections.
3. To encourage community participation in the ongoing development of best practices for digital collection building.

As the digital environment matured, the focus of electronic resources-building efforts has been shifted toward the creation of useful and relevant collections that served the needs of one or more communities of users. The bar of "goodness" had been raised to include levels of usability, accessibility, and fitness for use appropriate to the anticipated user group(s). Now the issues of cost/value, sustainability, and trust have emerged as critical success criteria for good electronic resources. Objects, metadata, and collections are viewed not only within the context of the projects that created them, but also as building blocks that others can reuse, repackage, repurpose, and build services upon. "Goodness" now demands interoperability, reusability, persistence, verification, documentation, and support for intellectual property rights.

The Framework of Guidance provides criteria for goodness organized around four core types of entities:

- Collections (organized groups of objects)
- Objects (digital materials)
- Metadata (information about objects and collections)
- Initiatives (programs or projects to create and manage collections)

E-resources building programs have become a core part of many organizations' missions, but this may not be reflected in the organizational structure and funding. A key component of the digital program is ensuring that the core nature of e-resources' building is explicit at every level of the organization. Building an e-resource collection often involves assembling a team of individuals from various disciplines, departments, and/or institutions.

Acquisitions Process can be explained as following while concentrating upon the some basic but inevitable differences between print and electronic resources:

- Print
    - Linear
    - Performed by a single individual at each step
    - Many tasks can be done by clerical staff
    - Not time-intensive
- Electronic
    - Iterative, multiple steps performed simultaneously
    - Team-based
    - Requires higher level of professional involvement
    - Time-intensive

1. Substantial design and planning : An e-resources initiative has a substantial design and planning component. Planning is crucial to the completion and success of any program or project. It encompasses all aspects of the initiative, from processing workflow to the ultimate look and feel of the collection interface. Early on, planners should specify the targeted audience for the e-resources and perform a needs assessment to ascertain the functional requirements of these users.

Growing focus on this need

According to a February 2004 ARL survey, the three most cited challenges were:

- workload (ensuring sufficient staffing levels to cope with increasing numbers of electronic resources)
- the need for an electronic resources management module to assist in managing and tracking electronic resources
- the accessing and cataloging of electronic resources

2. Staffing : An e-resource initiative needs an appropriate level of staffing with necessary expertise to achieve its objectives. There are many staff roles, each requiring different skills and abilities. These must work together to build a successful e-resources collection. At some point in time every e-resource initiative requires some expertise in management and project management, budget and finance, programming and systems administration, content selection, metadata creation and more. While some roles may be filled by the same person, other roles may require multiple people. In some cases, building or enhancing an organization's capacity to create e-resource collections can be an explicit goal of an initiative.

- Wide staff involvement in selection and support
- Tracking and presenting licensing terms
- Provision of user support information
- Integration of instructional information
- 24 x 7 access
- Planned/cyclic product reviews prior to renewal
- Systematic reporting of usage to staff

3. Best Practices Management : An e-resource initiative should follow best practices for project management. There are many different methodologies for effective project management, to the extent that project management has become a discipline in its own right, but most project management methodologies share a small number of key common components:

4. Evaluation : An initiative has an evaluation component. Whether the initiative is short-term or long-term, librarians should use an evaluation plan to identify and refine goals, assess progress toward goals, determine the quality, measure the impact of the project, show accountability, and demonstrate the value of the initiative to funding agencies. While output measures such as the number of items digitized can be useful, recent emphasis is on outcome assessment, which is concerned with how people, collections, organizations, and systems have been affected by the initiative.

Output measures for the electronic resource initiative may focus on the size, quality, and usage. The functionality and usability of the collection's website, and users' experience with the collection and the service, are also output measures. The impact of an e-collection is the best indicator of an initiative's value. It is most challenging to measure because it often involves many factors that are hard to quantify.

5. Creating Niche : An e-resource initiative markets itself. It broadly disseminates information about the process and outcomes. An effective e-resource initiative communicates its activities. It also broadcasts the availability of its deliverables as widely as possible. Good collection description and good interoperability features like support for the Open Archives Initiative Protocol for Metadata Harvesting can help users find collections, but good marketing and communications are essential.

6. Importance of life cycle : An e-resource initiative considers the entire lifecycle of the e-resource collection and associated services. The staff, equipment, software, and level of effort required to plan and develop an e-resource pool do vary from that required for the collection's long-term management and sustainability. Objects, regardless of storage medium, should be periodically checked for accessibility and usability.

An e-resource initiative should result in collections and services that become important and trusted parts of the organization's information repertoire. It must be maintained to the same standards that the organization has set for its other collections and services. Essentially, e-resources are continued by programs, which are ideally part of the routinely funded business of the organization.

PRINCIPLES OF GOOD E-RESOURCE COLLECTION

An e-resource collection consists of objects that are selected and organized to facilitate their discovery, access, and use. Objects, metadata, and the user interface together create the user experience of a collection.

1. Building of e-resources and explicit collection development policy

E-resource collection is created according to an explicit collection development policy. E-resource development is closely tied to an organization's goals and constituencies. The decision makers should be able to refer to the mission statement of their organization and articulate how a proposed collection furthers or supports that mission. The institution should be able to identify the target audience(s) for the collection but also think about unexpected uses and users. If the institution collects print, artifacts or other non-electric materials, the choice of e-resource should fit in with the organization's overall collection policy.

There are a few cases where a selection policy may not be required: digitization on demand, when an organization is creating e-resource content based on end-user requests, and mass digitization programs, which are often indiscriminate. Even these efforts require planning and should follow principles for building good collections as appropriate. Disciplinary or institutional repositories that encourage users to deposit their own intellectual property present an interesting case. These still benefit from a published collection policy, but it may have to be fairly flexible in acknowledgement that the users may be the best judges of relevance.

Describing collection in the context of user

Collections should be described so that a user can discover characteristics of the collection, including scope, format, restrictions on access, ownership, and any information significant for determining the collection's authenticity, integrity, and interpretation. Collection description is a form of metadata. Such description serves two purposes: it helps people discover the existence of a collection, and it helps users of the collection understand what they are viewing. Describing collections in established catalogs and registries is also a way of establishing the authority of the content.

Collection descriptions should help users understand the nature and scope of the collection and any restrictions that apply to the use of materials within it. Many project planners find a description of the methodologies, software applications, record formats, and metadata schemes used in building other collections helpful.

Curated Collection

A good collection is curated, which is to say, its resources are actively managed during their entire lifecycle. E-resource curation is concerned with the lifecycle management of a resource from the time it is created or obtained until it is purposely disposed of. Curation encompasses a set of activities that include active data management, archiving, and digital preservation. Active data management is required to ensure that objects in a collection can be used and reused over time. It can include creating, correcting, and enhancing metadata; correcting or enhancing the data itself; and adding annotations, linkages to other materials, or other enriching information. It can involve working with the creators of the digital objects to ensure they are appropriately transferred to the custody of the curator, and appropriately described and documented.

2. Broad availability of Electronic Collection

A good collection is broadly available and avoids unnecessary impediments to use. This principle encompasses three attributes: availability, usability, and accessibility.

Availability means that the collection is accessible and usable upon demand by an authorized person. This implies that collections should be accessible through the web, using technologies that are well known among the target user community. Availability does not require that use of all materials be free and unrestricted. Charging for use and limiting access may be appropriate and even necessary in some circumstances. Library must attempt to make the materials as widely available as possible within any required constraints.

Usability refers to ease of use. There is often a tradeoff between functionality and general usability. In the context the timing of the adoption of new features should be considered in light of how many potential users will be capable of using the technology as well as how many will find it a barrier. Bandwidth requirements are also a consideration. It must be kept in mind that some file formats or interfaces may not be usable by individuals on low bandwidth connections.

For general access collections, items such as the web pages and search forms providing access to the collection, as well as the metadata and digital object displays, should be tested. There items should be tested against various browsers and browser versions. It should also be kept in mind that different operating systems support different commands for manipulating screen information, such as selecting multiple items in a drop down menu on a search screen. This testing should include Windows, Mac, and Linux operating systems.

3. Dealing with intellectual property rights

The collection development policy should incorporate copyright policy. Intellectual Property Rights must be considered from several points of view:

- what rights the owners of the original source materials retain in their materials;
- what rights or permissions the collection developers have to digitize content and/or make it available; and
- what rights or permissions the users of the electronic collection are given, to make subsequent use of the materials.

For rights management, librarians should maintain a consistent record of rights holders and permissions granted for all applicable materials. Rights management is complicated by the fact that a work may include contributions from many creators. The underlying rights of complex multimedia works can be challenging to untangle. Many useful collections lack a deed of gift that clearly permits the electronic distribution of resources. In the environment of uncertain provenance, current best practices suggest:

- Actively solicit information about the creator—from the donors or their heirs or from the audience that utilizes the electronic collection; and

- Develop a risk management strategy that balances the educational value of the collections against principles of fair use, the potential commercial exploitation of the collection, and the organization's ability to identify and solicit permissions from copyright holders.

4. Risk Assessment

A risk assessment will enable the library to make practical, defensible choices among collections of uncertain provenance—a critical concern for electronic collection building. Apolicy statement can articulate the organization's reasons for making works of uncertain provenance available in electronic form to a wide audience. It should be posted prominently on the web portal to the collection,

5. Mechanism to Supply Required Data

A good collection has mechanisms to supply usage data and other data that allows standardized measures of usefulness to be recorded. Electronic collections should be evaluated periodically to monitor usage, assess service effectiveness, demonstrate return on investment, inform collection development, inform strategic planning, and support funding requests. The criteria, methods, and metrics for evaluating collections will vary by the objectives of the collections and the purposes of the evaluation. Effective collection management employs a variety of research methods to assess collection usefulness. Observation, surveys, focus groups, interviews, experiments, case studies, and transaction log analyses have been used by electronic libraries to assess usage and usability. Each method has its strengths and limitations. To obtain a clear picture of the value of a electronic collection is to answer the question: "Who is using what, how, and why?" It is often necessary for collection evaluators to use a combination of methods and measures to answer this question effectively.

The use of the electronic collection is closely related

to the collection's content, functionality, usability, and accessibility. Establishing benchmarks for use, collecting usage data over time, and following international standards for measuring use of electronic content will enable collection managers to conduct longitudinal collection assessment and compare collection services with those provided by peers. Evaluation is an iterative process. Results of evaluation should inform the design and improvement of a electronic collection.

6. Interoperable Collection

A good collection is interoperable. Collection developers should design their services to support interoperability, particularly the ability to share their metadata with external search engines. At an early stage in the collection design process, collection developers should scan the landscape for related efforts. Collection developers should be aware of and in contact with related efforts, follow widely accepted benchmarks for quality of content and of metadata, and provide adequate collection description for users to place one collection in the context of others. This is a way to expand the use and usefulness of electronic collections and may help gain sustainable support for them.

7. Collection Integrating Users' Workflow

A good collection integrates into the users own workflow. When electronic collection building represents a significant new service for an organization, it presents an opportunity to review existing workflows, and possibly reallocate resources, responsibilities and tasks. In order to successfully add electronic collections to an organization's service suite, it is important to integrate electronic resources building into staff workflows. When electronic resource building is an established activity, it is useful to periodically review staff workflows for improvement. The operational staff performing these activities will generally be the best advisors as to how to make them more intuitive and less time consuming.

End users find information most useful when it integrates smoothly with their own patterns of work. A faculty member looking for research articles and a recreational genealogist building an electronic family tree will work in different places, at different times, and using different tools. However, each will use a more comfortably if they can access it from the environment with which they are familiar.

In the emerging digital landscape, electronic resource building is increasingly a collaboration with the end user. Some sites allow users to add keywords to the metadata ("social tagging"). Some allow them to contribute digital resources, such as personal stories or family photographs to a local history web portal or preprints or postprints to an academic institutional repository. Integrating with the user's workflow enables the user to contribute without significant additional effort.

8. Sustainability

A good collection is sustainable over time. Electronic resources containing resources of long-term value should be sustained and archived permanently to ensure access. Sustainability needs to be addressed from an organizational, financial, and technical perspective. Organizational commitment requires buy-in from administrators. There must be a clear understanding of the long-term obligations necessary to ensure sustained electronic resources.

Sustaining the collection may take different sets of skills and different commitments of resources than the original collection building. Aspects of ongoing maintenance include maintaining the currency of locations, ensuring that access applications remain usable, data entry and data cleaning, logging and accumulating statistics, and providing some level of end- user support. They also include the system administration functions of upgrading server hardware and operating system software as required over time, maintaining server security, and ensuring that restoration of applications and data from backups is always possible.

In particular, electronic resources built with special funding should have a plan for their continued availability, maintenance and support beyond the funded period. Optimally, regardless of how it was initiated, the electronic resources will be integrated into the institutional collections management workflow. However, managers of collections containing materials of long-term importance should take steps to ensure not only that the objects within them will be preserved in usable form over time, but also that collection-level access to the content is maintained.

COMPONENTS OF E-RESOURCE SYSTEM

Knowledge Base - The Core Element

- One integrated platform for all Link products -> Access-Manage-Search-Find
- Content - journals , e-books , conference proceedings , working papers ,etc.
- e-TOC Metadata - title, author, volume, issue, page, date, links ,etc.
- Dynamic - real time updating

Updating Metadata

- Journal Table of Contents - Unique
- New / Existing items - Title name, ISSNs, coverage, links, etc.
- Availability via publisher/vendor collections
- Journal & article level links and structure
- Classification systems - Dewey, LC, customized

- Holding reports - catalog update files, Changenote files, CONSER MARC records, ONIX etc.

Update Process

- Gather information driven from Publisher/Vendor and Customers :
- Direct relationship with providers
  - Push/Pull - FTP server /e-mail
  - information specialists input
- Info auto re-structuring to TDNet KB format
- QA - links checked by software
- System update - online/weekly

E-RESOURCE POLICIES

The availability of electronic resources opens new vistas for teaching, research, and patient care. Although acquiring materials in digital form and organizing them for use is both costly and challenging, electronic resources will be a critical element of the libraries of the future. Cooperative acquisitions and cost-sharing with organization libraries and consortia are pursued when feasible to provide access for some of library users. The library can meet the demand for broader subject access and cross-campus access with e-resources.

Resources may be accessed in a variety of ways but internet/worldwide web is preferred. The decision to select specific products depends on projected use, licensing requirements, support services either local or remote, and other access issues. Materials must be available on campus and remotely. Reserves and various learning programs are also included. Resources can be accessed via the online catalog and/or the library web site. Resources available via the Internet are proliferating. The libraries recognize that careful selection of electronic resources, and availability of these through the Libraries' catalog will accomplish several objectives:

1) increase awareness and maximize use of significant sites;
2) provide value-added access to Internet resources often absent when using various search engines to locate resources;
3) enhance and expand the libraries' collection of traditional formats. Selection responsibility of these resources rests with individual Subject Bibliographers and the Head of Collection Development as these materials fall into their regular selecting responsibilities.

Electronic resources considered for acquisition should usually:

- Follow current collection parameters already in place as represented by the currently approved collection development policy statements, individual department policies and other related documents;
- Be available in formats currently accessible by appropriate hardware/software already in the library or available on campus. If the necessary hardware/ software is not currently available on campus, purchasing these should be considered along with the resource. Care should be taken when choosing formats to consider the usability (due to format) of the data in the long term;
- Be an enhancement and enrichment of current collections;
- Be substituted for printed information with caution because of the volatility of the information industry;
- Be evaluated in light of other potential acquisitions, and weighed against other possible acquisitions from the materials budget;

- Be evaluated for stability and integrity;
- Allow for the number of simultaneous users appropriate to the resource;
- Allow printing, sharing, downloading within copyright regulations

ELECTRONIC RESOURCES SUBSCRIPTION PRINCIPLES

The library should maintain a large collection of electronic databases, electronic journals and E books and other electronic resources in support of the teaching and research needs of staff and students of the Organization. The library should also be keen to work with its client groups to ensure that its collections meet the needs of all users and those purchases are cost effective. To assist in this process the certain principles can be developed to guide the decision making process. The library's preference when purchasing electronic resources is can be as follows:

1. The library purchases electronic resources to support the teaching and research programs of the Organization.
2. Content should be relevant to more than just a few users.
3. Overlap with existing subscriptions should be kept to a minimum. Where there is substantial overlap with other electronic resources the continuation of subscriptions for overlapping electronic resources needs to be justified.
4. There should be minimal requirement for special set up or software installation on specific PC's.
5. Electronic resources should be accessible through the library
6. Wherever a database is non-web based it should be network-able on library computers (not standalone).

7. Electronic resources should be web based products. Non-web based electronic resources should be avoided.
8. The electronic resources can be readily supported by subject librarians and reference staff, without the need for a high level of subject knowledge.
9. The electronic resources should be continuously updated (rather than one-off purchases of data), except for archival material.
10. A preference is given to multi-campus off and on campus access, using authenticate to manage access rather than being limited to particular campuses, specific groups of users or individual PC's.
11. Notwithstanding the above the cost benefit of restricting access to a particular site needs to be considered. Highly specialized electronic resources with limited audiences may not justify the additional cost of wide access.
12. The library expects the vendor to supply designated standard usage statistics to establish the value of electronic resources under consideration for renewal.
13. The library may purchase electronic resources at its own initiative where their value is readily apparent to Library Selectors.
14. Availability of funding will limit the purchase of electronic resources, with particular consideration needed when purchasing ongoing subscriptions.

Additional Purchase Principles for Highly Specialized and Restricted Electronic Resources

1. Electronic resources that have a very restricted audience (e.g. one or two staff or research students) should be purchased by the Faculty/Department rather than the library.

2. Electronic resources that require advanced subject knowledge should be located within and supported by the Faculty/Department.
3. Electronic resources that are not accessible in the library are normally to be purchased by the Faculty/Department. A small group consisting of the Faculty Team Leader, Subject Librarian, Digital Resources Librarian and Faculty representative to make the decision on what falls into this category.
4. In circumstances where potential users are limited to a small user group within a Faculty/Department the library may consider contributing to the cost, in accordance with the stated priorities of the relevant faculty and the ability of the library to contribute funds.
5. Requests by research students for electronic resources should be referred to the Department and their Supervisor for consideration prior to library involvement.
6. Requests for library staff to investigate the possible purchase of such specialized electronic resources and organize demonstrations or trials should come from a designated coordinator in the Faculty/Department.
7. The library may request the Faculty/Department to organize the demonstration of specialized electronic resources that they have proposed for purchase by the library.
8. In the case of specialized electronic resources requested by a particular Faculty/Department where ongoing IT support is necessary the Faculty/Department will be responsible for initial and ongoing installation of updates in their offices.
9. Electronic resources purchased on a shared basis should be contracted for 12 months at a time or an

agreement for continued funding for the duration of extended contracts should be made with the Faculty/ Department.

10. After a decision for a joint purchase between the library and Faculty/Department has been made the library will be involved in the negotiations to purchase (contract and price) with the vendor.
11. To help inform the library's decision making process Faculties/Departments should assign priorities to their research activities.
12. Where there are conflicting priorities greater weight will be given to more cost effective subscriptions or purchases.
13. At the end of the contract period a review process takes place between the library and Faculty/Dept to determine whether the subscription should be continued and the arrangement for continuation if the subscription is to be continued.

Policies for Commercially Available Electronic Resources

Commercially available resources must be affordable for libraries to be able to build and sustain significant collections of them. That comment served as the rationale for exploring two strategies for controlling costs—consortial purchasing and scholarly communication initiatives. Because of that, and because it is difficult to assess their current impact or to predict how either might help control prices for electronic resources over the long term, neither is being put forward here as an "effective practice." Affordability remains a necessary precondition for sustainability, however.

It is important for libraries to articulate what they wish to achieve through the acquisition of commercial electronic resources and to identify the values that should inform their decision making. Creating strategic plans for e-resource collection development seems to be another worthwhile activity. For large libraries, the purchase and presentation of electronic resources is a complex process involving large numbers of staff. Coordination of decision making and other activities is a significant problem. Quite often coordination is achieved partly through one or more e-resource committees, for which there are many interesting organizational models. An important emerging role that appears to be common to many institutions is that of e-resource coordinator. Finally, as resources grow and diversify, it seems inevitable that support responsibility for electronic resources must be distributed across the organization. As a result, a number of institutions have defined a separate but complementary stewardship role that different staff will take on for specific resources or platforms.

The acquisition of electronic resources can be operationally complex, and efforts to make the local process more coherent are important. Steps such as systematizing and documenting workflows, organizing and providing standardized information for vendors, and adopting appropriate forms all hold potential for expedited order handling. Managing the licensing of electronic resources is also one of the bigger challenges that libraries now face. Operationally, effective local licensing practice requires the adoption of clear policies and responsibilities as well as the creation and communication of smooth processes for dealing with them.

Table 1 : Idealized Model of Effective Selection and Presentation Practices

	Topic Area	Suggested Practices
1.	Selection Polices and Strategic Plans	• Create well-developed selection guidelines and policies • Articulate goals and strategic approach for developing e-resources
2.	Institutional Finance and	• Create broad-based oversight/

	Topic Area	Suggested Practices
	Organization	coordination committee structures • Appoint e-resource coordinators • Distribute responsibilities for resource stewardship
3.	Internal Procedures for Initial Evaluation and Purchase	• Create systematic, understandable workflows; use appropriate forms to expedite handling • Make it easy to determine the order status of a given e-resource • Make standardized information about the library (FTEs, IP ranges, site definition, licensing policies) available to vendors • Establish a clear system of conducting trials that includes communication of availability and process to staff (and users, if appropriate)
4.	Licensing Issues and Practices	• Establish process for smooth handling of licenses with clearly stated policies and responsibilities • Systematically inform staff and users about general and specific licenses
5.	Web Presentation Strategies	• Make aggregator database periodical holdings visible to users • Link abstracting & indexing database citations to e-journal holdings • Present resources and services in a way that meets users needs and that they can personalize ("My Gateway")
6.	User Support	• Make general support information readily available to users

	Topic Area	Suggested Practices
		• Create comprehensible problem escalation/triage paths for staff
7.	Ongoing Evaluation and Usage Information	• Conduct planned/cyclic reviews prior to renewal • Systematically report usage to staff
8.	Preservation and Archiving	• Support joint efforts to establish preservation techniques and standards • Realistically assess the preservation and access risks of relying on electronic formats, and develop an archive strategy on the basis of local circumstances and risk tolerance
9.	Toward Integrated Systems for Managing Electronic Resources	• Put in place plan e-resource support systems ,

Ideas about how best to present licensed resources to users continue to emerge rapidly. Recent initiatives aimed at making the contents of aggregator databases more visible to staff and users and at linking indexing databases to licensed e-journal collections enable libraries to derive more benefit from those resources. Establishing open standards for both seems important, for to do otherwise may mean supporting multiple vendor-specific systems. Efforts to better identify and meet the needs and interests of particular user groups, as well as to enable users to personalize their own views of relevant resources based on their own interests and usage patterns, also stand out.

Extensive reliance on vendors for access to e-resources, and the attendant proliferation of interfaces and possible sources of problems, is likely to necessitate a creative look at how the support function can best be organized. Establishing clear problem-triage paths is an important step. Reliance on vendor performance has also been problematic for libraries that rely on vendors exclusively for usage information. Ongoing efforts to establish standards for such data and to urge vendor compliance are quite important, and individual libraries should support those efforts in their contacts with vendors. The systematic, ongoing presentation of such data to staff and its review under organized, ongoing programs when resources are up for renewal also seem to qualify as effective practice.

Although clear solutions are not yet on the horizon, it is extremely encouraging that a number of organizations and libraries are taking a keen interest in archiving and preserving electronic resources. Finally, it is clear from the time and effort invested by many libraries creating local systems for managing electronic resources that existing library management systems and software lack important features and functionality. Although developing local systems probably contributes to effective local practice, coordinated efforts to define needs and establish standards may prove to be of broad benefit.

LIFE CYCLE OF E-RESOURCES

One of the main goals of the electronic resource management system is to support electronic collection development. Currently, for each resource that librarians want to acquire, they must learn which of many diverse sources will enable them to acquire the resource - and, needless to say, a librarian cannot always be aware of all the available options. ERMS facilitates this process by providing a global picture of the e-resource world: a comprehensive description of what is available, including the information about the packages, the interfaces, and the various providers. This description is the point at which the resource's life-cycle in the library begins.

The typical stages for resources not freely available would include the following:

- **Discovery :** The awareness of a new e-resource originates from a faculty member's request, a recommendation from a subject librarian, an advertisement, a message in a forum, or another source. The librarian then locates information about the e-resource in the ERM system's global knowledge base; information that might include, for example, the bibliographic details of an e-journal, the coverage period available, the packages that include it, and the interface or interfaces through which such packages are offered.
- **Trial :** In many cases, the librarian will want to try out an e-resource before reaching a decision about whether to purchase it. A trial enables the librarian to offer the e-resource to some or all users - who may include patrons and librarians alike - and then base a decision on their feedback. In the trial process, the librarian activates the e-resource in the desired areas of the library environment, notifies the relevant audience, and obtains feedback.
- **Selection :** Once the trial is over, the librarian decides whether to acquire the e-resource. A decision not to purchase the e-resource results in its deactivation in the library environment (if it had been activated as part of the trial process).
- **Acquisition :** If the librarian decides to go forward and subscribe to the resource, then the acquisition process somewhat resembles the process used for print resources; however, an additional level of detail is required, such as license information and information about the availability of the resource to various

populations of users.

- **Access :** Access is a major issue when you are dealing with e-resources, unlike print holdings. Once a library has acquired an e-resource, the librarians want to ensure that it is well used. First, they need to make certain that users can access it easily - for example, from an A-Z list; from the OPAC, if relevant; from a metasearch tool; or via a link server. Issues such as access by remote users (for instance, proxy setup) also need to be solved. After the initial configuration of access, which might have been taken care of, at least partially, at the trial stage, librarians must deal with maintenance - including routine maintenance, problems such as the temporary unavailability of the resource, and changes in the provider's address or the manner of access.
- **Decision to renew or cancel :** An e-resource subscription is typically valid for a defined time period. When the period ends, the librarian needs to decide whether to renew the subscription or cancel it. Unlike the initial decision at the selection phase, this decision is based on the information accumulated in the system, such as the actual usage of the resource while it was available, the reliability of the interface, and the responsiveness of the provider. Whatever the outcome of the decision - renewal or cancellation - the system needs to support it. Furthermore, even after a subscription has been cancelled, the library might have perpetual access or archiving rights to the data, another area that librarians must deal with on an ongoing basis. The description provided here is admittedly a simplified version of the stages involved. Many e-resources today are purchased through consortia, which wield considerable purchasing power. In a consortial environment, the procedures involved

in acquisition, access and decision-making are much more complex.

ELECTRONIC RESOURCES: WORKFLOWS & PROCEDURES			
1. New Product Announcement	5. Licensing	9. Invoicing/Payments	13. Product Assessment
2. Product Consideration	6. Ordering' Resource Record Creation	10. Cataloging/Holdings	14. Renewals/Updates
3. Trial Activation	7. Installation/Access on Library OPAC	11. Usage Statistics and Assessment	15. Cancellations/Closure
4. Product Assessment	8. Activation/Publicising	12. Maintenance	16. Archival Rights Enforcement

Chart: 1 life cycle of e-resources

Source: http://librarytrends.net/wkflow-procedures.htm

WHAT CAN LIBRARIANS DO WITH AN E-RESOURCE MANAGEMENT SYSTEM

The first challenge is to define what is meant exactly by *e-resource*. An individual electronic journal is an e-resource, as is an electronic book or an abstracting and indexing database such as MEDLINE. An e-resource can also be a package of e-journals or a database of abstracts and indexes that includes the full text of some or all articles referenced by the indexes. Furthermore, we cannot consider an e- resource without the interface through which it is offered; these elements are intricately linked, although they can be licensed separately.

The factors that are specific to e-resources and do not

apply to the traditional print world include authentication, access, administration, usage, etc. These two types of resources differ in the manner in which they are acquired, accessed and licensed. An ERM system needs to support these differences by providing the infrastructure for both the data and the workflows that are characteristic of e-resources and are missing from systems dealing with print resources. The system should provide the tools to manage e-resources throughout their life-cycle while supplying the data that administrators need to make decisions about acquisitions, renewals and cancellations of e-resource subscriptions. Moreover, the system needs to be extremely flexible and open, capable of supporting rapidly-changing business models.

Functional Requirements

- Support the 'Life Cycle' of electronic resources
- Selection and acquisition
- Access provision
- Resource administration
- User support and troubleshooting (staff and end-users)
- Renewal and retention decisions
- Store and display data not presently accommodated in current systems
- For End Users
- Auxiliary descriptive data
- License permissions and restrictions
- Availability
- Technical and platform-specific issues
- For Staff
- License information (more detailed)
- Administrative IDs and passwords
- Usage statistics and training information

- Problem-solving activities
- Troubleshooting
- Breach investigation
- Vendor communications
- Business functions
- Pricing model information
- Cost-sharing arrangements
- Renewal and termination actions and decisions
- Consortial relationships

E-Resource Management Evolution

- Late 1990s -
  - Existing ILS could not handle the functions necessary for an effective electronic-resource management system
- Early 2000s - content providers initiative - A-Z lists
- 2002 - DLF ERMI developed "common specifications and tools for managing the license agreements, related administrative information, and internal processes associated with collections of licensed electronic resources. "
  - Libraries have defined the need and the specification
  - Standards
  - Opportunity for library automation and content providers
  - Vendors started development
  - Products in the market - software systems used by libraries to keep track of important information about electronic information resources

BUSINESS MODELS FOR ERMS

Early times witnessed mainly 2 models for e-resource

management solutions. Though various models were developed, yet only few of them could find place in big number of libraries. The e-resource management solutions were developed basically for library management (routine practices) and user and services oriented. In short these e-resource management solutions can be called as:

- ERM for library management
- ERAMS for user access and library management

The e-resource management solutions were deeply governed by the content providers. Some of the industry standards were partially implemented by content providers. The major challenge is to integrate the dis-integrated environment of e-resources. It is chiefly associated with these two potential models. These models are General one and the OpenERM. The general model includes the re-indexing library modules and integrated and personalized visual layer. The second model i.e. the OpenERM includes using vendor knowledgebase facilities for e-resource management as well as integrated and personalized visual layer. Two main business models evolved:

- ILS vendors:
  - ERM module
- PAMS (Publications Access Management Services):
  - e-Resource Access & Management Services (ERAMS)

1. ILS Vendors Model

- Repository for all library e-resources metadata:
  - Administrative
- vendor information
- subscriptions
- licenses
- statistics

- Technical
- URLs
- IP addresses,
- authentication
  - Content
- collections
- packages
- individual titles
- Library has to populate the system with most of the data
- Maintenance of a local knowledgebase
- Standalone software product - Integrated with other ILS modules or standalone
- Focus on library
- Infrastructure for back room
- Accommodate library needs for:
  - Selection
  - Order
  - Implementation
  - Maintenance
  - Evaluation

2. Publications Access Management Services Vendors' Model

ERAMS

- Initiated in 2005
- Annual subscription model
- Array of modules to make e-resources accessible for patrons and manageable for librarians
  - Federated search
  - A-Z lists

  - Link resolvers
  - Electronic resource management
  - Reporting and management tools
- Comprehensive knowledgebase - Built in and routinely maintained:
  - e-Journal / e-Book / e-databases content
- Focus on e-resources
  - Individual titles
  - Collections - publishers, aggregators, consortia, customer
  - Open access
- Vendor knowledgebase
  - Comprehensive
  - Routine update
  - Institution personalizable
  - Data feed - ONIX; SOH, SRN
- Web 2.0 approach
  - Customer contribution
  - Publisher contribution
  - Aggregator contribution

Problems Concerned with ERM

- Standards - not fully implemented by the industry
  - Standardized / downloadable content data
  - Serials Online Holdings (SOH)
  - Serials Release Notification (SRN)
  - Serials Products and Subscriptions (SPS)
  - Standardized / downloadable pricing data
  - Counter & SUSHI compliance
  - Unique identifiers for e-collections & databases
  - License expression

  - XML gateway search
  - API
  - Access compliance - Shibboleth, Athens
- Disintegrated environment -
  - Library still maintains ILS, ERM, Resolver etc.
  - Users' different needs accommodated by different systems

Functional Requirements for establishing ERM: setting policies

To establish e-resources management system, the following functional requirements may usually be identified and set upon:

- provide a full workflow and approvals process to support the selection, procurement, and implementation of e-resources;
- enable dynamic generation of e-resource information for public display;
- provide automatic notification to appropriate staff of changes of status and scope in e-resource ordering and licensing (including such items as when to renew and action required after a certain number of days);
- provide for link management for e-resources, including the automatic updating of URLs in the backend database, on the campus proxy server, on library Web sites, and so on;
- provide staff with a unified, Web-based means for viewing, updating, reporting, and administering e-resources, including custom report generation;
- document and maintain information about e-resources;
- be accessible to all staff and patrons in collaborating libraries with appropriate restrictions for use of

administrative modules; and

- be interoperable with existing and future systems, including the integrated library system, the campus proxy server, and Web sites of the various campus libraries.

SPECIAL CONSIDERATIONS

In some organizations library is a centralized system and in some other the library is a decentralized organization, and the libraries of the organizations may be administratively independent. Each library may negotiate and manage its own e-resource licenses, and while the libraries negotiate some licenses on behalf of the entire organizational community, others can apply only to specific groups of organizational affiliates. In some cases, costs for e-resources are paid for by a single library, and in other cases, costs may be shared by participating libraries. In this way, an organization need for e-resource management resembles the needs of a consortium.

When library invests significant time and resources in providing catalog records for e-resources within the library catalog, data elements, required for ERM include bibliographic data already included in the library catalog, as well as many other data elements not captured in a traditional integrated library system. To avoid duplication of data entry, ERM must automatically capture appropriate data from the library catalog. In order to accommodate the goal of interoperability with existing and future systems, an XML document type definition (DTD) needed to be formulated to serve as ERM's bibliographic data import format. The future catalog system or any other data source with bibliographic metadata about electronic resources may be used to populate ERM, as long as extracts can be manipulated into the appropriate XML format. ERM may also be used as a stand-alone system; it allows for manual data entry of all elements if a load from another data source is not available or not feasible.

While it was obviously important for the ERM system to accommodate the workflow and management needs of the organizational libraries, the developer also sought to make the system useful for other libraries with different approaches to e-resource management. The system should be designed to accommodate a variety of approaches to use. With minimal modification of the application code, new workflow steps can be inserted or other similar changes made. Even without code modification, customization for local needs can be accommodated through the specific functional roles available for assignment to users of the system. These functional roles represent individual tasks and responsibilities, such as selection, acquisition, and cataloging. In general most staff of the library can have only one or two roles within ERM, while at a library with a smaller staff or a more centralized e-resource management workflow; a single staff person might be assigned more roles and granted greater rights and responsibilities.

Challenges: Localization

1. Selection and acquisitions workflow
2. Approaches to resource discovery
   a. Subjects and resource types
3. Access management
   a. Proxy servers
   b. Persistent URLs

Challenges: Integration

1. OPACS
2. Federated search portals
3. A-Z ejournal lists
4. Link resolution services

5. Course management systems

Challenges: Interoperability and Data Exchange

1. Authentication and authorization
   a. Proxy servers, Naming Systems...
2. Resource discovery
   a. Catalogs, portals...
3. Vendor data
   a. NISO/Editeur JWP: PAMS, Subscription Agents...
4. External metadata schemas
   a. ONIX for serials, DRM...

ADMINISTRATIVE MODULES OF ERMS

In order to accommodate each step of the e-resource acquisition and management workflow identified in the planning stages, following modular applications can be developed:

(i) Authentication : This module provides authentication of administrative users against a central lightweight directory access protocol (LDAP) authentication store. This module merely refers to an externally administered, ERM-independent LDAP directory to determine whether or not an administrative user truly is who he or she claims to be. If the user is successfully authenticated, this module begins a session based upon the authenticated username. Such information as username/ password generation and password resetting are all handled by the outside LDAP service and need not be administered separately by the ERM application. This reliance on an external LDAP directory obviously requires the LDAP directory available for authentication of staff users.

(ii) Authorization : This module checks an authenticated username against an internal authorization table to ensure that the user is authorized for access to the administrative modules of the application. The contents of this internal authorization table provide detailed information with respect to the functions and modules the authenticated user has authorization to access.

(iii) Selection : This module allows selectors to initiate and track the selection process. At any time selectors have the ability to view the status of their open items within the overall ERM workflow—that is, they can quickly determine what stage an item is in with respect to procurement. This offers obvious advantages over a selection process based on paper forms.

(iv) Acquisitions : This module governs the acquisitions process for ordering, receiving, renewing, and decommissioning of e-resources. It is the module where license management occurs. Within this module, license terms are defined as actionable elements to allow the system to appropriately allow or deny access to specific user groups. Furthermore, the actual legal license documents may be scanned and uploaded for easy and secure storage and retrieval.

(v) Catalog Interface : This module is perhaps the most complex and sophisticated module in the ERM application. Since libraries continue to invest effort in traditional cataloging of e-resources, the catalog interface was developed to accommodate automated interaction with the library management system (or any other source with information about e-resource subscriptions). Data in ERM can be synchronized with data from another resource such that, when a data field in a record in the external resource changes, so too will its value in the corresponding record in the ERM database. In this way, such things as titles or imprints can be maintained within the external resource, with changes flowing through on a scheduled basis to ERM. Each ERM field may be configured to accept changes coming through the catalog interface or to retain existing ERM data;

this allows ERM to serve as the authoritative source for some data elements, while the external resource serves as the authoritative source for other fields.

Technically, this process is accomplished through use of XML technologies. An XML **DTD** should be created reflecting the structure of the records held in the ERM database tables. Data need only be extracted from the external resource and formatted in accordance with this DTD. The resulting XML packet is then placed somewhere on the Web in a location accessible in programmatic fashion by the ERM application. On a scheduled basis, ERM should grab this XML-formatted extract via HTTP and pull it into the ERM database, making required updates to existing records along the way. Thus, select data in ERM can be synchronized with the contents of the local library catalog or external resource.

(vi) Catalog : This module controls the final catalog entries of e-resources. It also provides an authorized staff member the ability to manage the thesaurus of subject terms used to index records in the backend database. Subject-indexing of e-resources is ultimately performed within this module.

(vii) Library Computing Services : This module allows the administration of a lookup table of IP addresses mapped to a standard list of access locations, and a workflow process for implementing e-resources that require special attention from library computing staff (for example, networked CD-ROMs).

(viii) Public Display : This module controls the logic and display of what public clients actually see over the Web. Provision for search and retrieval of data about electronic resources is made here. Specifically, the client has the ability both to browse and search the portion of the collection of e-resources flagged as appropriate for public display from within this module. This module allows participating libraries to dynamically pass in header and footer files resulting in output to the client, resembling, as closely as possible, the look and feel of the local library Web site.

(ix) Administrative Search : This module enables authorized administrators to search the entire ERM database for records matching select criteria.

(x) Report : This module provides reports and statistics for view by authorized staff.

(xi) Scheduled Notifications : This module runs on a scheduled basis and automatically notifies the appropriate staff via e-mail of relevant changes in such items as content status and licensing.

(xii) Automated Subject Indexing : One of the interesting features of the catalog interface is its ability to automatically subject index records based on their assigned standard subject heading lists i.e. Library of Congress (LC) or MESH subject headings. Catalogers in the ERM application have the facility to map incoming LC and MESH headings to counterparts in the ERME subject schema. Once a given LC or MESH mapping has thus been created, any future records entering the ERM system via the catalog interface will automatically be mapped to the corresponding subject heading, thereby ensuring that the record is accurately subject-indexed and easily retrievable via the public display interface.

(xiii) Application Roles and Administrative Groups: During the design phase of the ERM, several administrative roles can be identified that would be required for the secure administration of the application. The following are the roles and groups that can be identified:

- **The Public :** This group—consisting of faculty, students, researchers, organization staff, and the general public—can search, retrieve, and display datasets from the backend database via the publicly accessible search interface.

- **Super-Users** : Super-Users function as system administrators of the application. This role has access to all functions, and may add administrative users, assign roles, modify several backend lookup tables, and monitor application errors.
- **Selectors** : This role allows an authorized individual to initiate the resource procurement process on behalf of a participating library and track the item's workflow progress. Each selector is assigned one or more budget codes that he or she may suggest for use in purchasing selected electronic resources.
- **Super-Selector** : The super-selector flags selected items for approval or disapproval, and thus for passage to the next phase of the procurement process, and decides what will actually be purchased from among the pool of selected items. The super-selector assigns budget codes to selectors. There must be at least one super-selector per participating library, and the super-selector has control over the selections proposed for that particular library.
- **Acquisitions Administrators** : Acquisitions administrators are responsible for procuring items and for tracking them throughout the procurement process. This role also administers and maintains license data, including scanning and upload of digital copies of the licenses themselves. Finally, acquisitions administrators maintain the table of budget codes that super-selectors may assign to selectors.
- **Catalog Administrators** : This role is responsible for properly cataloging items in ERM, including assignment of subject headings. If bibliographic data for e-resources is imported from another source such as the library's catalog, catalog administrators are responsible for completing records with ERM-specific

data and for administering the automatic subject-indexing module.

- **Library Computing Services Administrators :** This role is responsible for approving the purchase of electronic resources with special computing requirements—for example, CD-ROMs and other standalone databases.
- **Public Display Administrators :** This role is responsible for deciding, out of the domain of purchased and cataloged items, which ones appear on the publicly accessible search interface. This role can alter the bibliographic record of an item at any point, ensuring that the record for the item is sufficiently complete and fit for public viewing.
- **Administrative Query :** Certain members of the library staff who might not otherwise fit into any of the other administrative roles can log on to ERM and query the database for licensing information. Staff assigned this role include members of interlibrary loan and reserves departments. This role can only query and view records in the database—it has no insert, update, or deletes privileges on any of the data.

ADMINISTRATION AND MANAGEMENT OF VARIOUS TYPES OF E-RESOURCES

A. Administration and Management of e- Journals

1. One integrated platform for all institutional journals
2. Fully customized for library content - highly customized for interface & functionality
3. Browsing, searching, and accessing journal resources - publisher, journal, article, author etc.
4. TOC & Alerts service
5. Document delivery management
6. Online admin - Real time holdings update

7. Journal usage statistics
8. Subset of knowledgebase
   a. Group View
   b. A-Z List
9. TOC
   a. Search
10. Search
11. Results
12. Article Level
13. Link
14. TOC e-mail
15. Alert
16. Additions
17. Impact Factor
18. RSS Feeds

B. Administration and Management of e-Books

1. Manage access to institutional e-book collection
2. Optional setup - separated/integrated with Journal search
3. Updating core e-book collections
   a. records & links

C. Administration and Resolving of URLs

1. Link from a reference to most appropriate copy/ FT
2. Locate item availability within institutional resources
3. Suggest additional actions- when FT not available
4. Document delivery management
5. Use of reference Bibliographic Metadata -
   a. Save citation details
   b. Export to external software

c. Save direct links to FT

TRENDS AND DEVELOPMENTS IN ERMS

As a result of ERMI rapid progress in developing systems to manage electronic resources, the leading library system providers all have e-resource management products either currently available or in the works. First out of the gate was Innovative Interfaces. Their product, ERM, was been in commercial release for over a year. They have sold over 100 modules, many of these to libraries whose library management system is not an Innovative product. Innovative capitalized on early recognition of the e-resource needs of libraries, choosing a handful of libraries, including the University of Washington and Ohio State University, to help develop their product, which can integrate with an existing Innovative system or be used as a standalone module. Ex Libris is working with MIT and Harvard to develop their e - resource management system, Verde. Verde is designed to accommodate the DLF ERMI functional specifications, and will interact with the SFX Knowledge Base. Verde is being built as a standalone system, useful for libraries regardless of their library management system. VTLS is working with the Tri-College Consortium (Bryn Mawr, Haverford, and Swarthmore Colleges) to develop their product, Verify. Verify is framed around the DLF ERMI functional specifications, and seeks to provide an application extensible for use by both individual and groups of libraries. Like ERM and Verde, Verify is being designed as a standalone system. Endeavor Information Systems is at work on its e -resource management product, Meridian. Meridian is being developed with input from the international community. The system can operate in tandem with Endeavor's Voyageur library management system or as a standalone application.

Dynix is planning to build an e-resource system that will complement existing Horizon systems. In addition to these commercial products, a number of feature-rich library-developed systems exist. These systems include Penn State's ERLIC Johns Hopkins University's HERMIS, and Boston College's ERMdb. Some libraries, including MIT, Harvard, Ohio State, and the Tri-College Consortium, will need to address the challenge of data migration from their homegrown e-resource management systems to new commercial systems. It will be interesting to see how well these commercial systems are able to map local data elements into the DLF construct.

REFERENCES

1. Duranceau, Ellen Finnie. 2003. Using a Standard License for Individual Electronic Managing e-resources with tools and technologies. Journal Purchases: Results of a Pilot Study in the MIT Libraries. *Serials Review* 29 (4): 302-304.
2. Lugg, Rick, and Ruth Fischer. 2003. Agents in Place: Intermediaries in E-Journal Management. Available at http://www.harrassowitz.de/top_resources/docs/AgentsInPlace20031024.pdf.
3. Medeiros, Norm. 2006. House of Horrors: Exorcising Electronic Resources. In *Managing Electronic Resources: Contemporary Problems and Emerging Issues*, edited by Pamela Bluh and Cindy Hepfer. Chicago: American Library Association.
4. Grogg, Jill E. "Investing in digital: as electronic spending rises, ERAMS, ERM, and URM systems step in to help with acquisitions and reporting.(INFOTECH FEATURE) (electronic resource access and management services, electronic resource management system, unified resource management)." Library Journal 132.9 (May 15, 2007): 30(4).
5. Owens, Dodie. "Findability enable: the rise of the knowledgebase puts the ERMS on a new stage. " Library Journal. 131.13 (August 1, 2006): 30(3).
6. Electronic Resource Management: Report of the DLF ERM Initiative. http://www.diglib.org/pubs/dlf102/

dlfermi0408.pdf

7. http://www.iii.com/mill/digital.shtml#erm
8. http://www.exlibrisgroup.com/verde.html
9. http://www.vtls.com/Products/verify.shtml
10. http://www.endinfosys.com/prods/meridian.htm
11. S. Puglia and E. Rhodes, 'Digital Imaging - How Far Have We Come and What Still Needs to be Done?' in: *RLG Diginews* 15 April 2007, vol. 11, issue 1, URL: <http://www.rlg.org/en/page.php?Page_ID=21033#article2>.
12. IFLA newspaper section, URL: <http://www.ifla.org/VII/s39/>.
13. Project website at URL: <http://www.kb.nl/projectnews papers>.
14. Original Request for Information at URL: <http://www.kb.nl/hrd/digi/ddd/Request for Information.pdf>.
15. ALTO (Analyzed Layout and Text Object) homepage, see URL: <http://www.ccs-gmbh.com/alto/general.html>.
16. Chronicling America, see URL: <http://www.loc.gov/chroniclingamerica/>.
17. Australian Newspapers Digitization project, see URL: <http://www.nla.gov.au/ndp/.>
18. News Markup Language, a mark-up language for global news exchange, see URL: <http://www.newsml.org/pages/index.php>.
19. Pilot project 'Historische Kranten in Beeld', see URL: <http://kranten.kb.nl/> (in Dutch).
20. California Newspaper project, see URL: <http://www.cbsr.ucr.edu/cnp/>.
21. http://atalasoft.com/ajaxviewer/
22. http://www.dynix.com/products/erm/
23. http://www.libraries.psu.edu/iasweb/fiscal_data/ERLIC_SHARE/Publish/index.htm
24. http://hermes.mse.jhu.edu:8008/hermesdocs/
25. http://www.bc.edu/bc_org/avp/ulib/staff/erm/erm-db/
26. http://www.diglib.org/standards/imlsframe.htm

27. http://framework.niso.org/node/7

28. M. Agosti, L. Candela, D. Castelli, N. Ferro, Y. Ioannidis, G. Koutrika, C. Meghini, P. Pagano, S. Ross, H.-J. Schek, H. Schuldt. *A Reference Model for DLMSs* Interim Report. DELOS Deliverable n. 1.4.2, September 2006.

29. Borgman C.L. What are digital libraries? Competing visions. *Information Processing and Management*, 35(3):227-243, 1999.

30. BRICKS Integrated Project: Building Resources for Integrated Cultural Knowledge Services, <http://www.brickscommunity.org>.

31. DELOS Network of Excellence on Digital Libraries, <http://www.delos.info>.

32. Del Bimbo, A.; Gradmann, S.; Ioannidis, Y. (Eds.) *Future Research Directions*. 3rd DELOS Brainstorming Workshop Report, Corvara, Italy, July, 2004.

33. DILIGENT Integrated Project: Digital Library Infrastructure on Grid Enabled Technology, <http://www.diligentproject.org>.

34. Fox, E.A.; Akscyn, R.M.; Furuta, R.; Leggett, J.J. Digital Libraries. *Communications of the ACM*, 38(4):23- 28, April 1995.

35. Fox, E.A.; Marchionini, G. Toward a Worldwide Digital Library. *Communications of the ACM*, 41(4):29-32, April 1998.

36. Gonçalves, M.A.; Fox, E. 5SL - A Language for Declarative Specification and Generation of Digital Libraries. In *Proceedings of the 2nd ACM/IEEE-CS Joint Conference on Digital Libraries (JCDL'02)*, Portland, Oregon, USA, 2002.

37. Ioannidis Y. (Ed.) *Digital Libraries: Future Directions for a European Research Programme*. DELOS Brainstorming Report, San Cassiano, Italy, June 2001.

38. Ioannidis Y. Digital libraries at a crossroads. *International Journal of Digital Libraries*, 5(4):255-265, August 2005.

39. Loannidis, Y.; Maier, D.; Abiteboul, S.; Buneman, P.; Davidson, S.; Fox, E.; Halevy, A.; Knoblock, C.; Rabitti, F.;

Schek, H.; Weikum, G. Digital library information-technology infrastructures. *International Journal of Digital Libraries*, 5(4):266-274, August 2005.

40. MacKenzie, M.; Laskey, K.; McCabe, F.; Brown, P.; Metz, R. *Reference Model for Service Oriented Architecture*. OASIS Committee Draft 1.0, February 2006.
41. Schek, H.-J.; Schuldt, H. DelosDLMS - Infrastructure for the Next Generation of Digital Library Management Systems. *ERCIM News*, No. 66, July 2006.
42. Snowdon, D.N.; Churchill, E. F.; Frecon, E. (Eds.) *Inhabited Information Spaces - Living with your Data*. Springer, London 2004.
43. Soergel, D. A Framework for Digital Library Research. *D-Lib Magazine*, 8(12), December 2002, <http://www.dlib.org/dlib/december02/soergel/12soergel.html>.
44. The Digital Library Reference Model website, <http://www.delos.info/ReferenceModel>.
45. *Managing Electronic Resources* (August 2004), ARL Spec Kit #282, pp.13-14
46. http://framework.niso.org/node/32
47. http://framework.niso.org/node/34
48. Snowhill, L. "E-books and their future in academic libraries: an overview". *D-Lib Magazine*, 7 (7/8), July/August 2001. <doi:10.1045/july2001-snowhill>
49. Dublin City University, National University of Ireland, Galway, National University of Ireland, Maynooth, Trinity College Dublin, University College Cork, University College Dublin and University of Limerick.
50. *Safari*® Books Online, <http://www.safaribooksonline.com/>
51. Power, C. "Online publishing is king in geek's book" *The Irish Times*, 2 April 2004. <http://www.ireland.com/newspaper/finance/2004/0402/2011169420 BWWIRED02.html>
52. Abbott, W and Kelly, K. "Sooner of later! — Have e-books turned the page?". VALA 2004: Breaking Boundaries: Integration and Interoperability. 12th Biennial Conference

and Exhibition, 3-5 February 2004, Melbourne Convention Centre. <http://www.vala.org. au/vala2004/2004pdfs/46AbbKel.PDF>.

53. http://framework.niso.org/node/9

54. Connaway, L.S. and Lawrence, S.R. "A comparison of the functions and processes associated with identifying, selecting, acquiring and organizing paper books and electronic books". ACRL 11th National Conference: Learning to make a difference, Charlotte, North Carolina, 10-13 April 2003. <http://www.ala.org/ala/acrl/acrlevents/connaway.PDF>

55. Dillon, D. "E-books: the University of Texas experience, part 2". *Library Hi Tech*, 19(4), 2001, pp.350-362. <http://konstanza.emeraldinsight.com/vl=8912548/cl=79/nw=1/fm=docpdf/rpsv/cw/mcb/07378831/v19n4/s5/p350>

56. *Safari*® Bookshelf, <http://safari.oreilly.com/>

57. Survey: Irish Universities Safari Electronic Books User Survey, <http://140.203.12.136/survey/ebooksall/>

58. Irish Universities Safari Electronic Books User Survey, <http://www.library.nuigalway.ie/survey/ebooks.htm>

59. Golderman, G and Connolly, B. "Bundles of Books" *Library Journal*, 15 October 2003. <http://www.library journal.com/article/CA323335>

60. Golderman, G and Connolly, B. "Bundles of Books, part 2" *Library Journal*, 15 January 2004. <http://www.library journal.com/article/CA371209>

61. Hane, P.J. "Getting into deep content". *NewsLink*, 55, May 2004. <http://www.infotoday.com/newslink/newslink0405.htm#SpotLight>

62. A9.com home page, <http://www.a9.com/>

63. http://www.arnoldit.com/articles/elib_Feb2004_final.doc).

64. Michael K. Bergman (on behalf of the BrightPlanet Corporation) "The deep web: Surfacing hidden value". In: *The Journal of Electronic Publishing*. Michigan University

Press. July 2001 (http://www.press.umich.edu/jep/07-01/bergman.html).

65. Bergman uses the term "surface" web.
66. http://www.scirus.com
67. http://www.scirus.com/srsapp/aboutus/#range
68. http://www.vascoda.de
69. http://www.arl.org/access/scholarsportal/
70. http://www.rdn.ac.uk/
71. http://www.renardus.org
72. http://scout.wisc.edu/
73. Three initiatives were present at the DLF Spring Forum 2004 by the University of Michigan Libraries (http://www.diglib.org/forums/Spring2004/hagedorn0404.htm), the University of Illinois, Urbana-Champaign (http://www.diglib.org/forums/Spring2004/spring04bios.htm#habing) and OCLC (http://www.diglib.org/forums/Spring2004/young0404.htm).
74. The Fast software, for example, also includes a file traverser and some generic database connectors to load data from heterogeneous content sources.
75. 625 undergraduates and graduates returned the questionnaire within a week. See <http://www.ub.uni-bielefeld.de/portal/english/Metasuche>.
76. Bonita Wilson. "Using the Internet for Searching," *D-Lib Magazine*, March 2004, Volume 10 Number 3, <doi:10.1045/march2004-editorial>.
77. Stephen Arnold provided a figure of "$24 million per year to index one billion content sources". In: "The future of search", *Proceedings of the 26th Online Information conference 2002*. p 51.
78. http://www.fastsearch.com
79. Customers come from multinational enterprises, e-Government, e-Health etc. February 2002 to August 2002, Convera, Google, Mnogo, Lucene (2003). See <http://www.nutch.org>.

80. http://jakarta.apache.org/lucene/docs/index.html>

81. <http://isiwebofknowledge.com/technology.html>.

82. <http://www.diglib.org/forums/Spring2004/summann0404.htm>.

83. <http://base.ub.uni-bielefeld.de/>.

84. Coyle, K. "E-books: it's about evolution, not revolution". *Library Journal*, 15 October 2003. <http://www.libraryjournal.com/article/CA323334>

85. *netLibrary* home page, <http://www.netlibrary.com/>

86. *ebrary*® home page, <http://www.ebrary.com/

87. http://framework.niso.org/node/10

88. http://framework.niso.org/node/11

89. Adams, P. E., & Krockover, G. H. (1997). Concerns and perceptions of beginning secondary science and mathematics teachers. *Science Education, 81*, 29-50.

90. Darling-Hammond, L. (2001). *The Research and Rhetoric on Teacher Certification: A Response to "Teacher Certification Reconsidered"*. Washington, D.C.: National Commission on Teaching and America's Future. National Commission on Teaching and America's Future. Available at <http://www.nctaf.org/documents/abell_response. pdf>.

91. Darling-Hammond, L. (2002). *Solving the dilemmas of teacher supply, demand, and standards: How we can ensure a competent, caring, and qualified teacher for every child*. New York: National Commission on Teaching and America's Future. Available at <http://www.nctaf.org/documents/supply-demand-standards.pdf>.

92. Forlin, C. (2001). Inclusion: Identifying potential stressors for regular class teachers. *Educational Researcher, 43*(3), 235-245.

93. *Oxford Reference Online*, <http://www.oxfordreference.com/pub/views/home.html>

94. *xreferplus* home page, <http://www.xreferplus.com/>

95. *English Books Online*, <http://eebo.chadwyck.com/home>

96. *Gale Eighteenth Century Collections Online*, <http://

www.gale.com/EighteenthCentury/>

97. http://en.wikipedia.org/wiki/New_jersey_digital_highway

98. http://framework.niso.org/node/14

99. Hodson, D. (1993). Philosophic stance of secondary school science teachers, curriculum experiences, and children's understanding of science: Some preliminary findings. *Interchange*, *24*(1&2), 41-52.

100. Mardis, M. A. (2007). Unpacking the baggage of collaboration: Some factors to consider. *Media Spectrum*, *33*(3), 10-11.

101. Mardis, M. A., & Perrault, A. M. (2007, April 10-12). *Examining the information behaviors of educators to inform a model of professional exchange between science teachers and library media specialists*. Paper presented at the American Educational Research Association, Chicago.

102. Perrault, A. M. (2005). *Online information seeking practices of biology teachers and the perceived influences on instructional planning*. Unpublished Unpublished doctoral dissertation, University of Rochester, Rochester, NY.

103. Recker, M. (2006). Perspectives on teachers as digital library users: Consumers, contributors, and designers [Electronic Version]. *D-Lib Magazine*, 12. <doi:10.1045/september2006-recker>.

104. Smerdon, B., Cronen, S., Lanahan, L., Anderson, J., Iannotti, N., & Angeles, J. (2000). *Teachers' tools for the 21st century: A report on teachers' use of technology*. Washington, DC: National Center for Educational Statistics, U.S. Department of Education, NCES 2000-102. Available at <http://nces.ed.gov/pubs2000/2000102. pdf>.

105. Veenman, S. (1984). Perceived problems of beginning teachers. *Review of Educational Research*, *54*(2), 143-178.

106. Williams, T., Grimble, B., & Irwin, M. (2004). Teachers' link to electronic resources in the library media center: A local study of awareness, knowledge, and influence. *School Library Media Research*, *7*.

107. Borgman, C. L. (1996). Social aspects of digital libraries.

<http://is.gseis.ucla.edu/research/dl/UCLA_DL_Report.html>.

108. Lagoze, C., Krafft, D., & Payette, S. (2005). What is a digital library anyway? Beyond search and access in the nsdl [Electronic Version]. *D-Lib Magazine*, 11. <doi:10.1045/november2005-lagoze>.

109. Plymouth state university library [Electronic (2007). Version]. *Plymouth State Univeristy*. <http://www.plymouth.edu/library/>.

110. Polar bear expedition digital collections [Electronic (2007). Version]. *Bentley Historical Library*. <http://polarbears.si.umich.edu/>.

111. Renda, M. E., & Straccia, U. (2005). A personalized collaborative digital library environment: A model and an application. *Information Processing & Management*, 41(1), 5.

112. http://framework.niso.org/node/13

113. ScienceDirect Info, <http://www.info.sciencedirect. com/sd_updates/press/archive2004/new_product_ line.shtml>

114. Gale Virtual Reference Library(sm) home page, <http://www.gale.com/gvrl/>

115. *Oxford Scholarship Online*, <http://www.oxford scholarship.com/oso/public/>

116. *Knovel®* <http://www.knovel.com/>

117. *ebrary®* News and Events, <http://www.ebrary.com/news/040623.jsp>

118. yttle, J.M. "Library without books". *The Guardian*, 22 April 2004.

119. http://framework.niso.org/node/15

120. http://framework.niso.org/node/16

121. http://framework.niso.org/node/17

122. <http://www.guardian.co.uk/online/story/0,3605,1197495,00.html>

123. Cavendish Publishing FAQ, <http://www.cavendishpublishing.com/html/eCompilefaqs.asp>

124. Project *Xanedu®* <http: / /www.xanedu.com />

125. *Safari®U* <http: / /academic.oreilly.com/safariu-more.csp>

126. *Safari®X*, <http: / /www.safarix.com />

127. Ebooks Corporation Launches Library Platform: EBL offers a pioneering approach to ebook lending, Press release: June 26th, 2004, <http: / /www.ebl.ebooks.com/ news_events.asp?news=7>

2

MANAGING E-RESOURCES WITH TOOLS AND TECHNOLOGIES

INDUSTRY STANDARDS

A. OpenURL

The emergence of electronic publication of academic literature has rapidly produced an appreciation, as well as consequent expectation, among searchers about the availability of articles at their desktop. This kind of improvement of access to scholarly literature initiated further schemes and requirements for further enhancement. Researchers would have been benefited more if they could instantly move to articles referenced by the article they were reading. There could have been seamless access to the full text of an article from service. This kind of situation led to the first implementations of linking to articles developed by resource providers in a static way. Links from references to cited articles were 'hard coded', initially within a corpus of material such as an electronic publishing system, for example within a particular publisher's content, or within an aggregated electronic journals service. Consecutively linking services were provided between content owned by different resource providers. This situation needed particular agreements between them and in some cases; it needed an additional subscription agreement with the library. The implementation of these links generally used a proprietary syntax. Thus this specific service was supposed to implement a different set of source links for each publisher in order to link from a discovered article's citation details to the actual article.

Depending upon the requirements and developed scenario, several linking syntaxes were devised. These syntaxes utilized standard methods of identification or attributes (metadata) of the discovered object, thus making the required URL predictable. In this way, a link to a journal can be made using its ISSN, and to an article additionally using its volume, issue and page details. It is a solution that is used for example within a SICI code. Links into a content owner's electronic publications site would be via a web link that included metadata within the address, the URL being effectively parameterised or predicated. This is typically processed via a CGI program. The CGI program extracts the metadata in a URL querystring i.e., following a question mark '?' within an HTTP address. This method allows access to multiple articles via the same gateway. These links still used proprietary formats that differed between resource providers. All these exercises lead to advent of OpenURL.

The original version of OpenURL, which is now designated OpenURL version 0.1, provided both a common linking syntax and a solution to the appropriate copy problem. The OpenURL concept was developed as part of a research project (called SFX, "special effects") by Herbert Van de Sompel and Patrick Hochstenbach at Ghent University in Belgium (1998-2000). It was then acquired by Ex Libris who currently sells the SFX OpenURL resolver. It was an initial product in the OpenURL resolver market. Now it includes products from several vendors. The OpenURL version 0.1

specifications has always been public and open, its rapid take-up within the scholarly information community making it effectively a 'de facto' standard.

BACKGROUND

The OpenURL Framework for Context-Sensitive Services was endorsed as an ANSI/NISO standard (Z39.88-2004) in April 2005. This standard broadened the scope of OpenURL implementation beyond the scholarly information community. It allowed the registration of new formats and profiles for new domains, and providing an XML format with its additional potential. It is comprised of several entities that were previously being used within proprietary, private data sections in the original OpenURL specification. ANSI/NISO Z39.88-2004 enables details of a link's context, such as the user and the source of the link, to be described in a systematic way. This system opened up new possibilities for services appropriate to the user. The OpenURL Framework has separated the actionable link that was historically called the OpenURL into its payload and the means of transporting it across the network. The payload is known as the ContextObject. It details the reference and its context,. This separation of interests enables the use of the ContextObject within other applications which is beyond the immediate delivery of object information through a simple URL templating structure.

HOW OpenURL WORKS

The OpenURL linking solves the 'appropriate copy' problem as well as providing a standard, and thus universally accessible, syntax. A source application, such as an electronic journals service that includes links from references in article bibliographies, or an abstracting and indexing service that provides links potentially to the full text of the article, no longer needs to send the request to a particular target journal's site, but can instead redirect it to an OpenURL resolver at the user's institution.

OpenURL RESOLVER

An OpenURL resolver comprised of a 'knowledge base' that captures an organisation's subscriptions to electronic journals and other resources, along with details of how to encode links to a large number of target electronic resources. The e-resources include traditionally published and open access resources. The library maintains subscription details within the knowledge base and selects appropriate target services to be shown to their users. At this juncture the vendor will maintain target-linking details.

WORKING OF OpenURL RESOLVER

When a resolver receives an OpenURL from a reader who has clicked on a reference link, it can provide that reader with a link to a referenced work if the reader has a right of access. Generally, a resolver provides to a user a set of links to relevant services, including the full text of the article where appropriate. This menu contains other links to related items of possible interest, such as an abstract of the article, a search for other works by the same author, or the library catalogue.

Resolver Location

There is an additional problem to solve, namely how a source service knows the address of a user's OpenURL resolver to which to send a request. Some services maintain private registries of OpenURL resolvers, expecting organisations to provide them with details. This arrangement and process include an image and preferred text to allow customisation of the link shown to the end user. It enables a common appearance of OpenURL links across a library's resources. This strategy works well for services that authenticate access and thus know a user's location.

For freely available services, a different approach is

needed. It is inappropriate to ascertain a user's location. The most commonly used method is to record the resolver address in a cookie in a user's web browser and ask the user for their location details. Other methods are available for individual user personalization. An alternative method is for a source service to send all OpenURL requests to a public OpenURL resolver registry, which will then route requests to a user's resolver determined by their IP address. For example, OCLC has released a prototype registry, currently publicly available, with mainly US coverage. Determining the appropriate resolver for a user is an area where there is still work to be done to encourage wider uptake of the OpenURL standard.

Default Resolvers

A further problem for a source service is also faced. It asks about the provision to make for users who do not have an OpenURL resolver available. Public resolver registries show a default web page to these users to provide some assistance in finding articles, as do services that maintain private registries. For example, Zetoc provides a link to LinkFinderPlus as a default resolver. LinkFinderPlus knows where many science-based articles are available but has some limitations. For example, it has no knowledge of a user's subscriptions so is unable to provide a link to an 'appropriate copy'. On the other hand, many institutions have access to major resources. Zetoc also provides links to the publicly available, science-based search engine Scirus, and to COPAC, the union catalogue of the UK national and major research libraries.

OpenURL has created its own niche. It is not a competitor with DOI-based linking initiatives such as CrossRef, but is indeed a complementary technology. It enables localised linking to a resource so identified. If a resolver receives a DOI for an article, it can make use of it to retrieve bibliographic details about the reference before continuing its usual link provision. A CrossRef Z39.88-2004-compliant resolver, a gateway to some 19 million items, is now publicly available. Though, it was intended for personal rather than commercial or harvesting use. It has the potential to be used as a default resolver where request of an article from its publisher is desired. It has an option to supply multiple hits.

Target Services

The primary purpose of the OpenURL Framework is to support context-sensitive linking from source citations to relevant services including the full text. Details of how to link into target services are captured within a resolver's knowledge base. The target linking service required to publish its linking syntax and facilitate deep linking to the article level. The interoperability is promoted as well as the target details in the knowledge base simplified. It is requisite if linking into a target by OpenURL syntax is enabled. A service that supports OpenURL syntax for incoming target links is known as a 'Link-To' resolver.

OpenURL STAKEHOLDERS

OpenURL technology has become an indispensble part of electronic publishing services provided by both libraries and publishers to academic readers. There are several stakeholders within the scholarly information community where OpenURL technology is in use. Publishers may potentially have a dual role, both as an OpenURL 'source', or starting point, *sending* links, and as an OpenURL 'target', or network endpoint, *receiving* links into their content.

Readers

There are clear benefits for end users from the provision of seamless delivery of the full text of a discovered article directly to them. OpenURL linking is well used and appreciated, particularly by readers in institutions that have a resolver. Zetoc's logging of OpenURL linking shows considerable use.

The user experience is enhanced, particularly for novices, given an institution is able to provide a consistent interface into their OpenURL resolver's menu from all sources.

Users now expect the provision of easy connection between resources. The multiple steps required to navigate to articles through the wide variety of electronic journal sites discovered via a catalogue could deter many potential readers. An information retrieval system will tend not to be used whenever it is more painful and troublesome for a customer to have information than for him to not have it. People undertake their everyday tasks by using tools and techniques so familiar to them that they do not have to think.

Libraries

Libraries are typically the organisations within academic institutions or commercial organizations that provide OpenURL resolution services to their members. These organizations are responsible for purchasing a resolution system, incorporating into the resolver details of their subscriptions to electronic resources. They maintain the software and knowledge base with regular vendor updates, and designing the readers' view of the interface. Librarians are generally very enthusiastic about the technology because of the added value it provides to their readers.

Libraries that install an OpenURL resolver hope that the use of the resources to which they provide access will increase, thus justifying their investment in their electronic holdings. Reducing user frustration by showing consistent links from all resources means that they will make the best use of library resources rather than turning to popular search engines. Librarians appreciate the ability to customize their resolver's user interface. They prefer to show the institution's branding, to reinforce to their readers that the seamless retrieval of full text articles is in fact available because the library has purchased these resources. An OpenURL resolver is also availabile for backroom processes. The resolver's knowledge base can be harnessed to assist in central resource management, dealing with recording holdings and acquisitions details, and collection development.

Due to fast developments, OpenURL resolver has become a 'must have' for major research universities that partake in the international research community. OpenURL and federated searching are important new services in information field. They represent extensions of the library that further enable people to find their own information, which will be critical to the library of the future. Some free resolvers, are also available. Their use may be confusing to readers who do not understand why they cannot access resources that are apparently available. One initiative that partly addresses this problem is ScholarSFX (from Google Scholar and SFX). This free service enables OpenURL links to their readers within Google Scholar search results.

Publishers

Publishers are potential sources and targets of OpenURLs. They are suppliers of primary content, publishing journal articles or books, secondary publishers of resources such as abstract and indexing or citation based discovery services, or intermediaries such as content aggregators. There are benefits to publishers from implementing OpenURL both within the industry as a whole, and for themselves 'in house'.

PUBLISHERS AS OpenURL SOURCES

A publisher should become an OpenURL source is a market requirement as publisher meets customer expectations, OpenURL technology now being considered critical functionality. Increasingly libraries and funding bodies require OpenURL source links from resources to which they subscribe. Libraries worldwide regard OpenURL as a basic, standard service for accessing electronic journal content. Users expect OpenURL from their library services, although may not be aware of the technology, quoting from another librarian. Publishers need to implement OpenURL to maintain a competitive edge as a selling point.

OpenURL support should be seen as a partnership, with a need to work with all stakeholders including one's competitors. This is a change that has already been acknowledged by CrossRef participants. Publishers will reap more benefit from OpenURL linking by keeping their lists of available content up to date with the major resolver vendors.

There are also benefits to publishers from providing OpenURL source links by taking away from them the responsibility to provide what users need to librarians and resolvers. User requirements were becoming increasingly onerous before the introduction of OpenURL technology. Standard format and interoperable links are easier to maintain than the earlier bilateral agreements between different organisations. By using standards for interoperability, administration of the linking infrastructure for both publishers and librarians is easily possible. It will lead to decreasing support resource needs and hence lowering costs, increasing the quality of services, and supporting future innovation.

The OpenURL-enabling of references from journal articles and other bibliographic resources is highly wished. Major publishers who are members of CrossRef probably already support DOI-based links that can be routed to an institutional link server if the institution has chosen to register that intent with CrossRef. Additionally offering OpenURL source links enables the provision of links from citations that do not have DOIs. It introduces future possibilities of adding value beyond that offered by the centralized CrossRef service.

Many secondary publishing resources, such as abstracting and indexing databases are popular. These are already enabled as OpenURL sources. They have a clear selling point, because students and researchers increasingly are looking for journal articles in full text rather than just citations. OpenURL enabling a discovery service, such as Zetoc, adds significant value because it appears to become a source of full text articles to which the user's institution has a subscription. Thus there is no need for knowledge by the user of the relevant full text service.

Since the formal endorsement of the Z39.88-2004 standard, it is preferred if source links generated by publishers are hybrid, containing keys from both the new standard version 1.0 OpenURL, as well as the original OpenURL version 0.1. The major resolver vendors have now upgraded their software to support Z39.88-2004, but each individual resolver has to be upgraded by its owning organization. Although upgrading source links from the apparently simpler OpenURL version 0.1 is perceived as being a barrier.

USES

1. Additional OpenURL Sources

Since the development of the OpenURL Framework standard, further uses have begun to appear within the scholarly information environment. For example, Google Scholar now provides OpenURL source links for users from institutions that have registered their holdings and resolvers with Google. These links appear beside search results that are journal articles identified by a DOI or described with a PubMed record. For instance, the free service, social bookmarking tool, Connotea, includes hybrid, dual-version OpenURL source links.

1.1 Standard Bibliographic Citation Description

The standardisation of the OpenURL Framework means that journal and book metadata formats of the OpenURL ContextObject are now endorsed as a standard way to capture bibliographic citation details. The Dublin Core Metadata Initiative (DCMI) recommends using a ContextObject for capturing bibliographic citation information within a Dublin Core metadata description

2. Latent OpenURLs

A recently developed concept is that of 'embedded' or 'latent' OpenURLs. If a ContextObject were to be embedded in a web page, invisible to a human reader who might regard it as too cryptic, other applications such as web browser extensions could 'magically' provide extra functionality such as 'article autodiscovery. For example, the COinS specification embeds a ContextObject within an HTML 'span' element. COinS has a low implementation overhead, but provides powerful opportunities for additional services. It enables an application to generate an active OpenURL simply by prefixing a resolver address. An extension to the Firefox web browser, allows a user to personalize their OpenURL linking via their chosen OpenURL resolver. Further developments are appearing such as 'WAG the DOG' generates COinS using screen scraping. It is refined by holdings or ISBN lookups, in various applications. It provides an OpenURL-enabled 'more like this' service based on journal categories. Several services are COinS-enabled such as CiteULike, a free service that helps academics to share, store and organize the academic papers they are reading, and Citebase, a search and citation analysis tool for free, online research literature.

OpenURL: THE FUTURE

OpenURL was developed from a wish by readers of scholarly literature for easier 'joined up' location and delivery of resources of context. Linking technology developed quite rapidly from the original *static* and *proprietary* solutions, through those which were *predictable*, to be *parameterized*, to *persistent* but *publisher-controlled*, to the *prototype* OpenURL, to the eventual *standard*, interoperable, flexible OpenURL Framework for Context-Sensitive Services. Of course, previous stages on the way have been subsumed into OpenURL linking. In particular, incorporating a DOI within an OpenURL, where available, will take advantage of the exact resolution capabilities of DOI. Developments still continue with 'latent' OpenURLs that enable capable users to choose their own resolver, and possibilities of adding ContextObjects to screens 'on the fly'. Applications should work for the user rather than forcing us to conform to the paths laid out, and that Web 2.0 "opens up the Long Tail" servicing the interests of individuals. The major user related attributes are experience, trust and emergent: user behavior not predetermined.

OpenURL has become a ready success because it satisfied several key factors:

i. there was a clear need from end users for this kind of functionality;

ii. there are benefits to all the major stakeholders ;

iii. there is a low barrier to implementation, especially of the initial version; and, maybe most importantly,

iv. there has been a willingness to compromise by the stakeholders.

OpenURL is generally perceived as being a link to a full text article. But even the original OpenURL was intended to provide access to a range of services relevant to a referenced work, and it now has many more possibilities for use. Future opportunities based on the OpenURL Framework may include:

i. applications outside the scholarly information domain;
ii. services appropriate to the context, such as those based on a requester's role, or RSS feeds for the referring journal;
iii. collaborations and communications between resolvers sharing knowledge base content or checking use rights.

B. Digital Library Federation (DLF) Electronic Resources Management (DLFERM) initiative

The Digital Library Federation (DLF) is a consortium of thirty-three members and five allied organizations that are pioneering the use of electronic information technologies to extend library collections and services. The Electronic Resources Management Initiative (ERMI) of DLF is one such collaboration. It is a timely and wide-reaching endeavor. It finds a ready audience in libraries, systems vendors, and standards organizations.

This initiative addresses problems such as when libraries acquire licensed electronic resources, they must comprehend, transmit, and inform others about the many financial, legal, and access aspects of these arrangements. The acquisitions and licensing processes are complex. Publishers transmit this information to libraries in a variety of formats, and this correspondence to big number of licensed electronic products.

DLF ERMI has created a coordinated solution by developing the common specifications for the management of license agreements, related administrative information, and the internal processes associated with licensed electronic resources.

DLF Operations

The DLF is a program of the Council on Library and Information Resources. The DLF brings together experts needed for each DLF initiative. Funding comes from members and grants.

DLF Services

To help member libraries and allied institutions advance the work, the DLF provides -

- **leadership and support** for new research, standards development, and project start-ups
- **twice-a-year forums** for guiding the DLF, reporting developments, and sharing experiences of members in developing and managing electronic resources
- **an e-mail listserv** for exchanging information, announcing initiatives, identifying resources, and stimulating discussion
- **web site** for providing public access to information about activities, resources, developments, and the DLF itself
- **DLF publications** including printed publications, working papers, reports, forum proceedings, and other digital library information resources

DLF Initiatives

DLF initiatives do change constantly the change in needs. The DLF has promoted work on the following:

- Digital library structures, standards, preservation, and use
- Archives for electronic journals
- Online collections for use in teaching
- Internet services that expand access to resources of use to scholars
- Assessments of the future roles of libraries.

DLF Strategic Members

1. Bibliotheca Alexandrina
2. British Library
3. California Digital Library
4. Carnegie Mellon University
5. Columbia University
6. Cornell University
7. Council on Library and Information Resources
8. Dartmouth College
9. Emory University
10. Harvard University
11. Indiana University
12. Johns Hopkins University
13. Library of Congress
14. Massachusetts Institute of Technology
15. New York Public Library
16. New York University
17. North Carolina State University
18. Oxford University
19. Pennsylvania State University
20. Princeton University
21. Rice University
22. Stanford University
23. United States National Archives & Records Administration
24. University of California, Berkeley
25. University of Chicago
26. University of California, Los Angeles
27. University of Illinois at Urbana- Champaign
28. University of Michigan

29. University of Minnesota
30. United States National Library of Medicine
31. University of Pennsylvania
32. University of Southern California
33. University of Tennessee
34. University of Texas at Austin
35. University of Virginia
36. University of Washington
37. Yale University

DLF Allied Members

1. Coalition for Networked Information
2. Inter-university Consortium for Political and Social Research
3. The Joint Information Systems Committee
4. Los Alamos National Laboratory Research Library
5. Online Computer Library Center

DIGITAL COLLECTIONS

As known and in practice in the digital library, collections are transformed through the integration of new formats, licensed content and third-party information. Collection strategies and practices are not yet fully developed to take account of these changing circumstances. The same is concerned with their legal, organizational, and business implications fully understood. Fulfilling the basic aim, DLF promotes strategies for developing sustainable, scaleable, digital collection. It encourages the development of new collections and services.

ENCOURAGING NEW ONLINE COLLECTIONS AND COLLECTION SERVICES

1. DLF Aquifer

The digital library environment is evolving rapidly. Libraries provide digital collections and services in various manners. To develop the best possible systems for finding, identifying and using digital resources that are distributed on the network, the DLF promotes the development of DLF Aquifer. This initiative is developing schemas, protocols and communities of practice to enable effective use of digital library material.

DLF Aquifer puts into operation the founding idea of DLF, as expressed in the first item in the 1995 Charter: *The implementation of a distributed, open digital library conforming to the overall theme [of America's heritage and cultures] and accessible across the global Internet. This library shall consist of collections – expanding over time in number and scope – to be created from the conversion to digital form of documents contained in our and other libraries and archives, and from the incorporation of holdings already in electronic form.*

2. Registry of Digital Masters

The Registry of Digital Masters is an OCLC/DLF joint project. It is designed to record books and journals that exist in a page-image format, created in accordance with the DLF's Benchmarks for Digital Reproductions. A registry record leads one to a use-copy, where applicable. The existence of a record gives idea of existence of preservation master but it does not guarantee that the master files are generally accessible. They use MARC 21 Format for Bibliographic Data elements and OCLC current cataloging system functionality. DLF has a growing interest in helping to define and facilitate the development of key "infrastrutural services" that are required by digital libraries but beyond the capacity of any one of them to develop.

3. Production workflow good practices

Most of the libraries are aware of the design of a good digital production workflow, but there are too few places to which one can turn to learn about other people's workflow designs, file-naming choices, lessons learned, management software used or developed, etc. This DLF Initiative has assembled a team of workflow designers and managers to articulate good practices, drawing on the collective expertise.

4. Guidelines for the Cataloging of Cultural Objects

DLF joined the Getty Grant Program in sponsoring the Visual Resources Association (VRA) to review and evaluate existing data content standards and current practice that can be used to describe, document, and catalog cultural objects and their visual surrogates.

Related earlier work was research into a shared cataloguing utility for visual resources. A planning process was undertaken to assess the significance. It also stepped into developing a functional specification for a web-accessible cataloguing tool that supported in minimizing redundant effort involved in creating high-quality descriptions for works of art. The effort prepared a high-level rationale and functional specification for the tool.

5. Archivists' Toolkit

Modeled in part on work to define the functional requirement of a shared cataloging tool for visual resources, this initiative seeks to design and potentially develop of a suite of tools to support archival processing work. The work, initially co-sponsored by DLF and the California Digital Library (CDL), has evolved into a major, funded, consortial effort involving NYU, the five colleges, and UCSD.

6. The Academic Image Cooperative (AIC)

A planning process initiated to develop a scaleable database of curriculum-based digital images to be used for teaching survey courses in the history of art. It resulted in a prototype database and image collection. It also developed technical, organizational, and policy frameworks with the potential for sustaining an online service; capable of identifying, developing, and disseminating curriculum-based and scholarly image collections. It is envisaged that these collections, including the one developed by the AIC, will be incorporated into ArtSTOR. ArtSTOR is an independent not-for-profit organization that will develop, "store," and distribute electronically digital images and related scholarly materials for the study of art, architecture, and other fields in the humanities.

7. Scholarly Internet Gateways

DLF is supporting the development of a small number of Internet gateways through which users will access members' distributed digital library holdings as if they were part of a single uniform collection. The gateways will be built using a technique known as metadata harvesting. As such, the harvesting services developed by DLF will contribute to a practical evaluation of the harvesting technique and its application within libraries.

COLLECTION STRATEGIES AND PRACTICES

1. Strategies for Developing Sustainable, Scaleable Digital Collections

A publication series aims to assemble, review, and document practices adopted by libraries in developing their digital collections. Titles in the series recommend strategies for developing collections from commercially supplied electronic content, digitally reformatted content, and links to third-party public domain Internet content. Some studies provide important decision tools for those developing digital collections.

2. Licensing digital materials. The LIBLICENSE web site

The LIBLICENSE web site was funded in phases by CLIR and DLF. It offers a primer on licensing electronic information resources for libraries. It includes vocabulary, definitions, bibliographies, links to other relevant sites, a discussion list and much more. The site also includes the LIBLICENSE software. This freely available software systematically queries librarians or producers concerning the details of the information to be licensed. Based on that input, it produces a draft license agreement. The draft license agreement can then be sent to information publishers (or customers) to serve as the basis for further negotiations for license agreements with acceptable terms.

Initiatives for Developing Digital Library Architectures DLF seeks to:

- define, clarify, and develop prototypes for digital library systems and system components;
- scan the larger technical environment for and encourage the development of potentially important trends and practices;
- encourage technology transfer and information sharing between and among DLF members, and between DLF and appropriate commercial sectors; and
- communicate technical directions and accomplishments of the DLF to a wider audience.

Standards

- The Open Archives Initiative: An international initiative that is developing a technical framework for facilitating the efficient dissemination of content via the network.
- Assessing Shibboleth: With CNI, DLF hosted a meeting

of publishers and resource providers to assess Shibboleth. It is a technology to support inter-institutional authentication and authorization for access to Web pages, as proposed by Internet2.

- Z39.50 Implementers Group (ZIG): Z39.50 is an international standard search and retrieval protocol that has been widely adopted by libraries as a means of integrating access to information maintained in distributed databases.
- Digital Certificates: Digital certificates introduce work to prototype and develop a promising authentication protocol.

Practices

- DLF Service Framework for Digital Libraries: DLF established the DLF Abstract Service Framework Working Group to develop a shared understanding of how the research library and its services were organized in an increasingly networked environment.
- DLF/Crossef Institution Registry: DLF and CrossRef have examined the notion of developing an institution registry for the efficient exchange of information between libraries and library service providers.
- OCKHAM: OCKHAM was conceived of as a series of discussions about key architectural and technical issues confronting digital library developers.
- Courseware/Library System Interactions: Integration of digital library content into the courseware systems is a general need across the DLF and beyond. *A Study of the Interoperation of Learning Management and Library Information Systems* (2004) examined the interaction of digital libraries and learning management (courseware) systems. Learning management systems are increasingly ubiquitous in higher education.There is an explosion of internet-

accessible collections of digital resources relevant to the teachers and students. A natural context for such resources is course web sites. The IMS Digital Repositories Specification provides a good beginning for the understanding of the functions of discovery (search) and object access for learning management systems. To make the most effective use of digital content in teaching, learning applications need to be able to easily interoperate with digital repositories so that teachers and students can discover, access, view, quote, adapt, and evaluate appropriate learning material.

- Working with FEDORA: DLF is supporting an initiative that is implementing the FEDORA architecture as a digital object repository management system and testing the implementation through a collaborative deployment involving selected digital libraries.
- Assessment of open source software for libraries: DLF considered important to identify steps to move OSS activity into the mainstream of digital library development in a manner that might appeal to all sectors of the library community. There continues to be an abiding interest in open source software in digital libraries.
- Tools for Academic Publishing: DLF also initiated for sharing tools and technologies and for encouraging collaborative development amongst the various new electronic publishing initiatives that are beginning to emerge on university campuses and within university libraries.
- Reference linking: DLF, along with NISO and others, hosted a series of workshops to discuss options for linking between citations of digital works and the works themselves.

INITIATIVES TO ENCOURAGE STANDARDS AND PRACTICES

The DLF identifies documents, endorses, and promotes adoption of standards and best practices that support the effective acquisition, interchange, persistence, and assessment of digital library collections and services.

Standards:

- DLF Electronic Resource Management Initiative, Phase 2: This project capitalizes on and extends the visibility and success of ERMI Phase 1, with a particular focus on data standards, issues related to license expression, and usage data.
- DLF Electronic Resource Management Initiative, Phase 1: This project successfully developed common specifications and tools for managing the license agreements, related administrative information, and internal processes associated with collections of licensed electronic resources.
- Guide to Good Practice: Cataloging Standards for Describing Cultural Objects and Images: The review and evaluation of existing data content standards and current practice in order to compile a manual that may be used to describe, document, and catalog cultural objects and their visual surrogates.
- Metadata Encoding and Transmission Standard (METS). Refined and extended work on mechanisms for describing technical, structural, and administrative characteristics of digital objects.
- The Open Archives Initiative: An international initiative that is developing a technical framework for facilitating the efficient dissemination of content via the network.
- Z39.50: Z39.50 is an international standard search and retrieval protocol that has been widely adopted by libraries as a means of integrating access to

information maintained in distributed databases.

Practices

- The Exchange of Serials Subscription Information.
- Framework of Guidance for Building Good Digital Collections: The Institute of Museum and Library Services (IMLS) convened a forum to develop a framework for considering and promoting standards and good practices to guide the development of good digital collections.
- The Liblicense Model Licensing Agreement: The license attempts to reach consensus on the basic terms of contracts to license digital information between university libraries and academic publishers.
- TEI Text Encoding in Libraries : Recommendations pertaining to the application of the TEI Guidelines and particularly "best practices" for the encoding of electronic texts developed for different purposes.
- Methods to Evaluate the Quality of Images and Imaging System: Evaluate methods for evaluating the quality of images and image systems in order to determine whether common evaluation criteria might be developed to guide assessment in any domain.
- Guides to Quality in Visual Resource Imaging: These guides are designed to serve the growing community of museums, archives, and research libraries that are turning to digital conversion to provide greater access to their visual resources as well as to help preserve the original materials.

DLF ELECTRONIC RESOURCE MANAGEMENT INITIATIVE

Librarians and publishers are coming together under DLF sponsorship to create and test standards for electronic resource management. This includes an XML schema for recording the details of a license agreement. It also made efforts for managing related descriptive metadata and administrative information associated with collections of licensed electronic resources. A common XML format makes it easier to share information and thus minimize duplication of effort. It will lead to a standardized format to deliver license information to customers and information management systems.

Outcomes

The outcomes are listed here:

1. **Problem Definition/Road Map** : The ad hoc, grassroots effort has assembled an extensive collection of documents relevant to the management of electronic resources. This document gathers the most valuable data and conclusions into one document, including an overview of existing or proposed standards and XML schemas, and their relationships to the work being undertaken.

2. **Working Documents** : The specifications, standards, and best practices have been used in drafting system specifications, as well as directing vendors' development efforts. These are:

- Workflow Diagram
- Functional requirements
- Entity Relationship Diagram
- Electronic Resources Management System Data Structure
- Data Element Dictionary
- XML investigation

C. LOCKSS

Though the transition from print to online journals has had many benefits, there is at least one harmful consequence. It is pervasive that libraries do not have an easy, affordable way to build local collections of independently produced, non-commercial e-only journals and magazines. These are functioning, virtually indispensable sites for both scholarly and creative publication. LOCKSS (Lots of Copies Keep Stuff Safe) has shown promise for helping both librarians and publishers to overcome some of these obstacles. The goal of the LOCKSS program is to provide an institution's readers with transparent access to preserved material. The reader's browser fetches the URL at which the material was originally published; if the material is no longer available at the original URL, the preserved material is supplied instead. LOCKSS creates low-cost, persistent digital "caches" of authoritative versions of http-delivered content. All file formats delivered through HTTP are included (html, jpg, gif, wav, pdf, etc.). The LOCKSS software enables to build local collections; to locally collect, store, preserve, and archive authorized content, thus safeguarding their community's access to that content. LOCKSS caches collect the content as it is published. Once a library activates an e-journal title's preservation in the LOCKSS system, that title's newly published content is continuously collected and preserved. The process is halted only when a library turns off content collection or if a publisher turns off permission.

Accuracy and completeness of LOCKSS caches are assured through a peer-to-peer polling and reputation system, which is both robust and secure. LOCKSS is designed to run on inexpensive hardware and to require almost no technical administration. The software has been under development since 1999 and is distributed as open source.

LOCKSS PROGRAM

LOCKSS (Lots of Copies Keep Stuff Safe), based at Stanford University Libraries, is an international community initiative that provides libraries with digital preservation tools and support so that they can easily and inexpensively collect and preserve their own copies of authorized e-content. LOCKSS, in its eleventh year, provides libraries with the open-source software.

The ACM award-winning LOCKSS technology is an open source, peer-to-peer, decentralized digital preservation infrastructure. It preserves all formats and genres of web-published content. The intellectual content includes the historical context (the look and feel), is preserved. LOCKSS is OAIS-compliant; the software migrates content forward in time; and the bits and bytes are continually audited and repaired. LOCKSS enables libraries to collect and locally store, preserve, and archive authorized content by creating low-cost, persistent digital caches of authoritative versions of web-based content. Through LOCKSS, librarians have the opportunity to retain local control of electronic content while preserving its original functionality. LOCKSS is a thriving international community-based initiative with libraries and publishers working together with the shared goal to preserve e-content for the long-term.

PERMISSIONS

1. Librarian Permission

Finding that the LOCKSS System is functional and operative, Licensee is authorized to store and grant access, through the LOCKSS System, in order to preserve the Licensee's use of and access to such material, subject to the conditions set forth in the License. This permission is granted with the subject, Licensee installs and maintains, at its own expense, any software or other mechanism and authorizations needed to participate in the LOCKSS System.

2. Software Permission

The permission is granted to the LOCKSS software through a web page called a LOCKSS publisher manifest. A publisher manifest permits the software to crawl, collect, and preserve the content; it also lists the top level URLs so the crawler knows where to start the collection process. A publisher manifest is needed for each "archival unit" to be preserved through the LOCKSS system.

BENEFITS TO LIBRARIES

LOCKSS helps libraries stay relevant by building collection as most of the content is born digitally and published on the web. LOCKSS replicates the traditional model of libraries by keeping physical copies of books, journals, etc. in their collections. It makes possible for libraries to house copies of digital materials long-term. Hundreds of publishers and libraries around the world are working together to ensure benefits for the libraries. Content preserved by libraries through LOCKSS becomes a part of their collection, and they have perpetual access to 100% of the titles preserved in their LOCKSS Box.

Functioning of LOCKSS

A library uses LOCKSS software to turn a low-cost PC into a digital preservation equipment called a LOCKSS Box. This LOCKSS box performs the following functions:

- It collects content from the target web sites using a web crawler.
- It continually compares the content it has collected with the same content collected by other LOCKSS Boxes, and repairs any differences.
- It acts as a web proxy or cache. It provides browsers in the library's community with access to the publisher's content or the preserved content as appropriate.
- It can also serve content by Metadata (Open URLs) via resolvers.
- It provides a web-based administrative interface to target new journals for preservation.

- It monitors the state of the journals being preserved, and control access to the preserved journals.

a. Collecting

To preserve e-content, the following requisites are must:

- The publisher has to collect and preserve the journal. It is possible by adding a page to the journal's web site containing a permission statement, and links to the issues of the journal as they are published.
- The LOCKSS Box should know where to find this page, and how far to follow the chains of web links. This is accomplished using a LOCKSS Plugin, which is a list of parameters specific to each publishing platform. These Plugins are supplied by the Stanford University LOCKSS team. The Plugin is distributed automatically to the authorized LOCKSS Boxes.

b. Preserving and Auditing

At the outset, LOCKSS Boxes collect content directly from the publisher's web site. Then LOCKSS software compares the copies stored in libraries' LOCKSS boxes to the content available on the publisher's website to establish the content's authoritative version. This version is useful in order to repair lost or corrupted copies. After comparison, the LOCKSS Boxes communicate over the Internet to continually audit the content they are preserving. If the content in one LOCKSS Box is damaged or incomplete, LOCKSS Box will receive repair from the content based on other LOCKSS Boxes. This cooperation between the LOCKSS Boxes avoids the need to back them up individually. It also provides unambiguous reassurance that the system is performing its function and that the correct content will be available to readers.

c. Providing Access

Authorized readers can access LOCKSS content when a publisher is not available for any reason such as subscription canceled, network traffic, publisher server down. It is made sure that library readers have perpetual, seamless access to content for as long as the LOCKSS Box is maintained. There are no changes in the appearance of content. Content served from a LOCKSS Box looks same as the content served from the publisher with one important exception. If the publisher's site is unavailable, content instead be constant.

There are two methods for readers to access content from an institution's LOCKSS box when the original web site is unavailable:

Method One : LOCKSS Boxes provide transparent access to the content they preserve. It is common that organizations often run web proxies. This system allows off-campus users to access their journal subscriptions, and web caches, to reduce the bandwidth cost of providing Web access to their community. The organizations integrate LOCKSS box into these systems, thus intercepting requests from the browsers to the journals being preserved. When a request for a page from a preserved journal arrives, it is first forwarded to the publisher. If the publisher returns content, that is what the browser displays. Otherwise the browser displays the preserved copy.

Method Two : The LOCKSS team is implementing infrastructure so libraries can deliver content to users by making that content a target for journal-level SFX resolution.

Administering

Library administers the LOCKSS Box via a Web user interface. The interface enables new content preservation. It monitors the preservation of existing content. It controls access to the appliance, and a wide variety of other functions.

Format Migration

LOCKSS network preserves the content in its original format. Based on requirement, the content is dynamically migrated to a newer format (when a reader requests the preserved content). This approach is known as Migration on Access. It offers significant advantages, given as following:

1. LOCKSS preserves the content in its original format and it satisfies archival requirements. It also allows the LOCKSS system to be frugal with storage space. These is no preservation system that discards the original bits after migrating them to a new format. It is evident that migrating and keeping both the original and the migrated copy multiplies the storage requirements for a preservation system by the number of migrations.
2. It allows the preserved content to migrated into the most recent technology available at the time the reader requests access.
3. Preserved content is rarely accessed so performing migration takes place when it is needed. It also supports the reduction in the resource cost.
4. Content can be migrated directly from the original to the current format thus minimizing the effects of format conversion artifacts.
5. The format converters, after developing once, can themselves be preserved to document the original format.

Every piece of Web content is in a specific format (pdf, flash, html, etc.). Eventually, browsers might no longer be able to display content in a particular format. When a reader requests content that is preserved in a LOCKSS box, and the reader's Web browser cannot display the content, LOCKSS migrates the content 'on the fly' and delivers the content to the reader.

When a LOCKSS box receives a request for some preserved content but the browser indicates in a manner that it cannot display the preserved content in its original format, the LOCKSS box selects a converter that can convert the original format to one of the formats that the browser has indicated it can display. The LOCKSS box uses the converter to create a temporary access copy, which it delivers to the browser.

OAIS

LOCKSS software is based on Association of Computing Machinery (ACM) award-winning technology. It provides an OAIS-compliant, OAIS Formal Statement of Compliance open source, peer-to-peer, decentralized digital preservation infrastructure. It is format-agnostic, preserving all formats and genres of web-published content. Content must have an authoritative version. The intellectual content, includes the historical context (the look and feel), is preserved. Content preserved by libraries in their LOCKSS Box becomes a part of their collection, and they have perpetual access to all of it.

Auditing

Audit processes have the potential to reveal how well a system is meeting its stated goals. The LOCKSS system is evaluated by:

1. Librarians who are using the LOCKSS system to preserve content;
2. the Council of Library Resources; and
3. the Library of Congress.

Librarians audit their LOCKSS box via a web page interface. On that page, the preservation status of the content in that local LOCKSS box is displayed. The Library of Congress and the LOCKSS Program staff are working together to complete the Certification and Accreditation process under the Federal Information Processing Standard for categorizing security risks of federal information and systems (FIPS 199).

Installing LOCKSS

Bringing up a LOCKSS box is easy and does not require special technical expertise. The LOCKSS software turns a PC into a digital preservation appliance. The key to making the LOCKSS appliance easy to use is that it boots and runs from a CD and stores all its configuration information on media such as a floppy disk that is write-locked while the system is running. There is no software of any kind, even an operating system, on the PC's disk. The disk is used only to store preserved content.

The hardest things for a system administrator to do correctly are to install, configure and upgrade software so that there are no vulnerabilities an attacker can exploit, and especially to recover a system that an attacker has penetrated. The LOCKSS CD includes not just the LOCKSS daemon but also a pre-configured, highly secure operating system. The system includes an automatic software update system that is protected by digital signatures, so it is upgraded automatically and securely. About every six months the LOCKSS team releases a new, updated CD. All the operator has to do is to burn the new CD image, swap CDs and reboot.

Computer Specifications

A machine to run LOCKSS requires:

- Atleast 1 GHz via CPUs and 2.4 GHz celeron.
- A CD drive and optionally either:
  - a floppy disk drive
  - or a USB flash memory drive with a hardware write-protect switch.

250GB disk is sufficient to get started. The current CD supports both parallel ATA (PATA) drives and serial ATA (SATA) in native mode. Some adjustment of BIOS settings may be needed to handle SATA drives.

D. CLOCKSS: A Trusted Community-Managed Archive

CLOCKSS (*Controlled* LOCKSS) is a joint venture between the world's leading scholarly publishers and research libraries whose mission is to build a sustainable, geographically distributed dark archive with which to ensure the long-term survival of Web-based scholarly publications for the benefit of the greater global research community. CLOCKSS, or Controlled LOCKSS (for Lots of Copies Keep Stuff Safe), runs on LOCKSS technology, but unlike LOCKSS (an open network), CLOCKSS is a closed system. Libraries are joining CLOCKSS to ensure the world's e-content is protected for future generations of researchers. Publishers are joining CLOCKSS to preserve their titles in a secure dark archive without the cost-prohibitive expense of building their own preservation and storage system. The CLOCKSS Board deemed that when a publisher's content is triggered, CLOCKSS should not charge libraries for access; instead, the triggered content is made available for free at CLOCKSS' host sites.

CLOCKSS has been considered the most cost-effective archiving solution. CLOCKSS Archive Nodes are housed at institutions that have existed since long time. CLOCKSS supports the library's role in society as a "custodian of culture." These institutions are located in geographically, politically, and geologically disparate locations in North America, Europe, and Asia-Pacific. CLOCKSS runs on proven digital preservation technology. LOCKSS technology has been safely and securely preserving web-published content for over 10 years and has evolved with web advances to preserve new content types.

From Prototype to Production

Two years ago, scholarly publishers and research libraries have joined forces to build a prototype for a global dark archive to face the challenges raised due to the responsibility to preserve the digital assets of the community,. Their unique collaboration focused on creating a cooperative archive with publishers and libraries running the archive together. The prototype has been successfully built and tested.

Reasons to Support CLOCKSS

There are some basic reasons to support CLOSKSS, given as following:

- The archive is managed by, and for, its stakeholders, not a third-party.
- Publishers and librarians have equal say in deciding procedures, priorities, and when to trigger content.
- CLOCKSS is decentralized. The geographically disparate preservation model ensures the survival of digital assets. Additionally, it satisfies the demand for locally situated archives with 15 archive nodes planned worldwide by 2010.
- Low operating costs make it possible for institutions of all sizes and budgets to participate in CLOCKSS.
- CLOCKSS participants have the opportunity to be deeply involved in all aspects of our industry and help to keep the community's best interests at the forefront. CLOCKSS has already made an impact on industry policies and practices.

Functioning of CLOCKSS

CLOCKSS is a joint venture started by libraries and publishers committed to ensuring long-term access to scholarly publications in digital format. As libraries migrate to less costly online-only subscriptions, they expect assurances from publishers that their shared investments are protected and preserved for generations to come. The CLOCKSS archive provides this assurance via its secure, closed network of web-published content that can be accessed only when a trigger event is deemed to have occurred. CLOCKSS is unique because it makes all content triggered from the archive freely available to the world.

The following is a step-by-step overview of how CLOCKSS works.

Step One : The publisher provides the CLOCKSS system access to either presentation or source files of the content. Presentation files are the HTML pages that are normally displayed to the readers of the content. Source files are minimally formatted content used internally by the publisher.

i. To allow CLOCKSS crawlers to access the publisher's presentation files, the publisher needs to add to its website a CLOCKSS-provided permission statement that will tell the crawlers what content is available for collection.

ii. To allow CLOCKSS access to the publisher's source files, the publisher needs to place them on a designated FTP site.

Step Two : Special CLOCKSS boxes located at Rice, Indiana, and Stanford Universities ingest the content the publisher made available.

Step Three : The content in each CLOCKSS box must go through a verification process to confirm that their versions of the content are identical to each other. This establishes the authoritative version of the content.

Step Four : The majority of the CLOCKSS boxes are preservation machines with the objective of performing the main storage and audit functions. When the quality of the content on the ingest machines is validated, it is collected from them by the preservation CLOCKSS boxes.

Step Five : The content is preserved through the system of audit and repair. When the content in one CLOCKSS box is damaged or incomplete, that CLOCKSS box receives repairs of the content based on other CLOCKSS boxes' holdings and/or by referring to the publisher's original presentation files. This cooperation between the CLOCKSS boxes avoids the need to back them up individually. It also provides unambiguous reassurance that the system is performing its function and that the correct content is always available.

Step Six : When a trigger event occurs and the CLOCKSS Board decides to release the content from the archive, two things happen:

i. Content is automatically migrated to the newest format.

ii. Content is copied from the CLOCKSS boxes to a publicly available web server at a CLOCKSS host organization (currently the EDINA Data Center, University of Edinburgh, and Stanford University).

Step Seven : The released content is now freely available from Stanford University and EDINA at the University of Edinburgh. It is also directly available via Open URL's through CrossRef or local library link-resolvers.

CLOCKSS: trigger event

Everyone gets access to content impacted by a trigger. The materials are moved to a hosting platform and made available to everyone *for free*. Trigger events include situations of non-availability of archived content in which:

i. **Publisher No Longer in Business :** The publisher is no longer in business or publishing content or providing access to previously published content. There are no successor interests or reversions or transfers of rights.

ii. **Titles No Longer Offered :** The publisher has stopped publishing and is no longer providing access to the content. There are no successor interests or reversion or transfer of rights.

iii. **Back Issues No Longer Available :** The publisher has stopped offering or providing access to some or all of the back issues of the content. There are no successor interests or reversion or transfer of rights.

iv. **Catastrophic Failure :** While still publishing content, the publisher is not able to provide access to the content electronically due to technical or similar catastrophic and permanent failure.

Managing e-resources with various software applications/ products

The exponential growth of e-resources requires the library to implement new solutions for managing e-materials as well as providing access to them. New paradigms allow users to maximize the advantages of electronic media while providing staff with the tools to effectively manage these resources. Some library software vendors provide a complete solution for managing the full spectrum of library materials and processes. These vendors offer a family of e-resource products that can be used on a stand-alone basis or as part of an integrated system. For example, the Ex Libris e-product family helps libraries to capitalize their e-collections by elevating the user experience, increasing staff efficiency, and establishing management processes and control.

THE EX LIBRIS E-PRODUCT FAMILY

Features

i. The MetaLib gateway and metasearch system: It allows users to simultaneously search multiple databases and receive combined results in a uniform format.

ii. The SFX OpenURL link resolver: It interconnects

library-controlled resources and services. It keeps on providing users with context-sensitive links to these services based on the library's e-collections and policies.

iii. The Verde electronic resource management system: It enables library staff to centrally manage all essential aspects of the electronic product life cycle.

iv. The Primo unified discovery and delivery solution—leverages SFX and MetaLib to provide users with a one-stop access point to all types of resources—electronic, digital, and print.

Maximizing the User Experience : It provides various means for users to maximize the experience that

i. Users can enjoy the most up-to-date collection of journals and e-books available from their institution.

ii. Users can be facilitated to search via a single, intuitive interface for e-resources from a wide range of information providers.

iii. Users find immediate view of full text, citations, and other retrieval options and services provided by their institutions.

Empowering Libraries with Customization and Interoperability

i. Libraries may provide tailored user interfaces and services to the unique needs of users.

ii. Libraries are empowered to offer a single user interface for searching all material types such as electronic, digital, and print.

iii. Libraries are free to embed access points to e-resources in commonly used environments such as institutional Web sites and course management systems.

Increasing Efficiency and Control

i. It provides a centralized solution for managing e-resources and their metadata that enables the library to define consistent, enforceable workflows throughout the e-resource life cycle.

ii. It enhances the extensive usage and cost statistics to help the library effectively optimize collection development decisions as well as supporting the library to balance user needs and budget considerations.

iii. It equips the library with in-depth reports provide management with visibility into the full range of library e-resource information—including budget, usage statistics, and licensing permissions—via a single interface.

Facilitating Integration and Collaboration

i. It supports for consortial needs extensively and encourages collaboration and sharing of e-resources among consortium members.

ii. It facilitates built-in integration with Ex Libris integrated library systems with streamlines sharing of information across resource types.

ALEPH INTEGRATED LIBRARY SYSTEM

Most of the libraries are facing the challenges posed by a diverse and expanding information universe. The increased user expectations for relevant information go hand in hand with institutional demands for increased operational efficiency.

The Aleph® integrated library system facilitates academic, research, and national libraries with the efficient, user-friendly tools and workflow support. The libraries need such support to meet the increasing requirements of the industry today and in the future. Aleph has been the integrated library system of choice for libraries and library consortia worldwide that require the ultimate in configuration flexibility. Aleph system configuration is tailored to meet virtually any library policy or procedure, enabling the creation of unique policies and workflows.

Key benefits of Aleph system

Flexible : The customizable components of the system are tailored to accommodate the requirements of libraries of various types, regardless of size, from single-branch libraries to the largest of consortia and national libraries.

Easy to use : Its user-friendly workflows and intuitive graphical interfaces tend to increase the staff efficiency and supply to user experience.

Scalable : The growth and expansion features of this system enable libraries and different types of consortia to continually re-envision and recreate their unique working environments.

Open : Since Aleph is built on an Oracle® database, it runs on a range of operating systems. Employing system-wide XML technology. It offers third-party integration through an XML gateway.

Multilingual and multiscript : Full Unicode support provides multidirectional and multiscript text capabilities. This feature is much celebrated. Users can interface with the system in their preferred language, and libraries can create new language interfaces.

Future proof : The inherent multi-tier client/server structure and conformance with the latest industry standards guarantees that Aleph will meet needs today and in the future. The software design continually evolves to include products and components aimed at enhancing the system and ensuring that it continues to meet the changing needs of the library.

SFX

SFX is the original, award-winning context-sensitive link server from Ex Libris™. SFX allows context-sensitive linking between Web resources in the scholarly information environment. It is an OpenURL-compliant. SFX accepts an OpenURL as input from an information resource, which is referred to as an SFX source.

An SFX server facilitates the management of a library's interlinked electronic collection by providing libraries with an independent means of seamlessly interconnecting their ever-increasing collections of heterogeneous resources. Because SFX allows libraries to define the links between information resources, the resources become fully integrated in the overall library service no matter who hosts them- the library itself or external information providers.

The SFX solution offers libraries flexibility and choice for reference librarians, who, can choose appropriate content from a range of information vendors, interconnect this content as desired, and then provide links to "appropriate" services for their end users. Reference librarians need not depend solely on the linking services defined by the information providers, on a specific set of identifiers (such as ISSN, SICI, or DOI), or on particular communication protocols (such as Z39.50 or HTTP).

The key benefits of SFX:

1. Linking services are independent of an information resource, so the institutional librarian can define the relevant links.
2. The librarian configures links only once, and they are available to many information services.
3. Extended linking beyond just links to full text can be offered to library patrons.
4. A consistent linking approach across a range of information resources makes it easier for the patron to

navigate heterogeneous resources.

5. Vendor-independent measures of use are available.

SFX sources : An SFX source is a Web-based resource in which a library patron searches and from which the patron can link out to additional resources and services by clicking an SFX button. The SFX button activates an OpenURL that sends metadata to the SFX server. A resource can be an SFX source only if the resource provides an OpenURL.

SFX targets : An SFX target is, the target of a link from an SFX source. SFX relies on "link-to" or search syntaxes for a target information service. Much syntax exist today and vary quite widely from one information service provider to another- be they publishers or OPAC vendors. The "deeper" an SFX link can go, the more effective the SFX link will be. In most cases, the syntax available from the publishers allows direct linking to the journal article level.

Usages of SFX : SFX is setting the standard for OpenURL link servers. Used by more than 1000 libraries, SFX is the most widely used link server in libraries worldwide.

Development of SFX : The SFX server technology was developed during the research work undertaken by Dr. Van de Sompel and was acquired by Ex Libris in February 2000. After a successful beta test with five U.S. institutions during 2000, SFX was released to the market in February 2001. SFX supports Shibboleth. During December 2003, Ex Libris and key SFX customers were participating in feasibility tests for Shibboleth. The purpose of this important new initiative from the Internet2/MACE group is to address the problems inherent in cross-domain authentication and authorization.

The relationship between SFX, CrossRef, and the DOI

CrossRef is a consortium of primary publishers. CrossRef members use a digital object identifier (DOI) to link between their resources- for example, to link from a reference in an article published by one CrossRef member to the full text of the article itself, published by another CrossRef member. Although it offers a persistent linking solution, DOI-based CrossRef linking does not take into account a user's affiliation and therefore does not provide for context-sensitive linking services. However, when used within the SFX framework, a DOI can deliver such context-sensitive linking services. The OpenURL framework with SFX and the CrossRef framework with DOI are compatible and complementary, and libraries that join CrossRef as affiliates can take full advantage of this synergy. CrossRef library affiliate membership is free of charge.

Implementing and maintenance of SFX server : The main work involved in implementing SFX is the localization of the preconfigured SFX resources (sources and targets) in the SFX global knowledge base, which is delivered with the SFX server. A smooth, rapid SFX implementation depends on the availability of detailed data about SFX targets, particularly the ISSNs, date ranges, and service providers for e-journal subscriptions. Users can broaden the range of SFX sources from which links may be presented and increase the range of service options. For preconfigured SFX sources-those already defined in the KnowledgeBase- this stage might simply involve a call to the information service provider to add SFX server address to institution's profile; or it may involve some localization. If a local data repository needs to be incorporated as an SFX source, library might have to implement the OpenURL first. With SFX, some ongoing maintenance of the KnowledgeBase is required to ensure that the links are current. SFX can save libraries time and resources, particularly if a library is currently configuring links in multiple systems. With SFX, all links are configured in one place, the SFX KnowledgeBase, and are then available to all systems.

It must be kept in mind that the SFX link for a document-delivery service can be a mediated service such

Verde: role in e-resources life cycle:

Verde Helps To Manage the Electronic Resource Life Cycle

Task	Library Challenges	How Verde Helps
Discovery	Staff is often required to access multiple individual publisher websites and compile a list in Word, Excel, or some other application each time they look for up-to-date information.	From a single point of access, the Verde KnowledgeBase assists staff in easily finding up-to-date information about titles, where they are available, and how they are packaged.
Trial	With no centralized place to manage trials, information is often scattered in multiple files and locations. • Communication with users and feedback collection is handled by e-mail, which is difficult to track and consolidate.	The library centrally sets up and tracks any number of trials, defining trial dates, inviting user participation, and collecting their feedback.
Acquisition	Libraries find it difficult to track e-product acquisitions information in the organization's integrated library system. The use of Excel worksheets and other manual data tracking tools often results in inaccuracies and requires constant updating.	The integrated library system can create a direct feed, or batch-load acquisition information to Verde. Library staff can drill-down to track acquisitions on any level—interface, package, or a single journal or e-book. Staff can use workflows to manage and track the acquisition process. Management can centrally control the budget and

Task	Library Challenges	How Verde Helps
		track departmental chargebacks. Libraries can quickly analyze actual expenditure vs. budget.
Licensing	Libraries can not track, compare, and proactively manage licensing terms from one central point, as this information remains in the agreements signed with each content provider. Library users are not informed what their permissions and use restrictions are.	The library can centrally store all license information and terms such as number of users and permission to make copies, printouts, and interlibrary loans. Licensing workflows can be defined to enforce uniformity and compliance. License data is made available to other applications through Web services.
Admini-stration	Libraries struggle to make informed collection enhancement decisions as they do not have access to information. This is either not collected or is scattered across multiple locations.	As information about the properties of each resource, downtime incidents and contract breaches during renewal, and decisions and contract negotiation are maintained in one central location, libraries can easily find and use it.
Access	Libraries typically rely on technical personnel to keep track of access information, which may not be readily available when needed.	Library staff can readily retrieve information about authentication methods, supported protocols, failover sites, and proxy server setup, as well as about how each resource is accessed.
Usage	Disparately held usage information is downloaded	Staff can easily derive cost-per-use metrics as

Task	Library Challenges	How Verde Helps
	from each vendor separately and manually consolidated into Excel or other in-house systems.	vendor usage data is automatically retrieved and uploaded into the system using the industry-standard SUSHI protocol.
Review/ Renew	Data supporting the review process has to be collected from multiple sources. Renewal decisions rely on manual ad-hoc processes.	Library staff canReceive system alerts to proactively manage renewals in a timely manner. Use workflows to define and manage the review and renewal process. Easily analyze cost, usage, and licensing information in making renewal decisions.

as that provided by the institution's ILL department. SFX can be hosted locally on a Solaris or Linux system. SFX is also available on an ASP basis. SFX has been available from the outset, through the SFX subscription service hosted by Ex Libris, and many SFX customers use this service today. Sites benefit from the full power of the SFX server, including integration in the local environment, without having to host and manage this server locally.

Through the SFX subscription service:

- Library users benefit from all the SFX services, including advanced link server features such as dynamically generated services, complex logic-display options, full statistical and reporting options, and local customization
- Libraries can take advantage of the full range of consortium models
- Libraries can automatically generate alphabetical e-journal lists with optional MARC record generation for loading into a local catalog
- No KnowledgeBase maintenance tasks (Ex Libris carries out all updates)

While concentrating on the working of SFX with any integrated library system (ILS), it is interesting to know that SFX operates independently of the ILS. Another feature is that SFX works in a consortium setting. Factors that determine the best model for a consortium include:

- The nature and size of the consortium- academic, public, corporate, special, or mixed
- The desired proportion of centralized control and local autonomy
- The desired branding- consortial or institutional
- The consortium's concept of the information landscape- shared core collections or institutional collections.

Manage "dead" links by SFX : A "dead" link can result from a number of situations, including server downtime, but typically occurs when an information provider has moved a Web resource to a new address or has changed protocols for linking to their service. A message that says "HTTP 404- File not found" is usually evidence of a dead link. In a dynamic linking environment such as SFX, links are created on the fly when requested by a user, and powerful algorithms determine the probability of the link resource's availability. In such an environment, links are not preprocessed or verified. For each service provider participating in the SFX framework, a single global template is modified in SFX to reflect changes at an information provider's site.

SFX Hosting Services : Many customers use the SFX subscription service hosted by Ex Libris. These sites benefit from the full power of the SFX server, including integration into the local environment, without having to host and manage this server locally:

i. Users benefit from all the SFX services, including advanced link server features such as dynamically generated services, complex logic-display options, full statistical and reporting options, and local customization

ii. Libraries can take advantage of the full range of consortial models.

iii. Libraries can generate alphabetical and searchable e-journal lists automatically. MARC record generation for loading into a local catalog is optional.

iv. Additional managed-services options for setup and ongoing configuration of services are available

SFX is the original and most widely-used OpenURL link server, providing libraries with a standards-based method for linking diverse electronic resources.

Extensive Customization Options

i. It allows libraries to provide a solution that best fits local user requirements.

ii. It enables librarians to easily add SFX links, including local targets such as catalogs, databases, library Web pages, and even blogs and tagging services.

iii. The targets added to the SFX database are available for immediate access by users.

iv. A-Z List and Citation Linker can be customized by the library to become an integral part of the library Website or any other place the user may have a need for them.

Automated Administrative Tools

i. Automated tools for uploading local resources simplify administrative tasks such as localization of data.

ii. Plug-in integration with the library catalog optimizes the use of local resources with no need to sync or reload print holdings.

iii. MARCit! - an optional MARC enhancement service - provides libraries with complete MARC records for their e-journal collection and reduces librarian workload.

MANAGING DIGITAL ASSETS

Digital content has rapidly become a significant component of academic library collections. As a result, many libraries face the daunting task of organizing and managing myriad digital assets—including images, audio/video materials, and digitized texts—and efficiently sharing these assets with patrons.

DigiTool : To meet the challenges of the digital era, Ex Libris offers the cutting-edge DigiTool solution for digital asset management. Developed in partnership with top-tier university libraries responsible for large, heterogeneous digital collections, DigiTool is the product of choice for libraries that focus on managing, maintaining, and sharing special collections, as well as for libraries serving as institutional repositories. DigiTool provides libraries with the technology and workflows required for managing all aspects of a digital collection. Objects and associated metadata are deposited and ingested into the DigiTool repository, where they are enhanced, categorized, stored, and managed. DigiTool empowers end users to search for these assets in a variety of formats, to locate them, and to have them delivered in the most efficient fashion.

DigiTool supports multiple administrative units, providing a single repository for institutions consisting of numerous branches or departments. Library patrons of all types—students, faculty, and guests—search for assets via a single interface. This interface can also be customized to correspond with the workflow requirements and look and feel of each member unit.

Orchestrating Institutional Repositories : By nature, an academic institution manages and disseminates a wide variety of digital materials created by the institution itself, by affiliated organizational entities, and by user communities. Libraries, the traditional holders and distributors of institutional knowledge, often have difficulty managing the vast quantity of diverse institutional assets that have come under their custodianship. Using the DigiTool solution, libraries can create and manage institutional repositories with ease. The open-access platform also facilitates the sharing of scholarly information in a library's user community.

Illuminating Special Collections : Academic institutions that manage and maintain special collections must be able to upload materials quickly and easily and deliver these materials to staff and patrons in a user-friendly manner. JPEG 2000 compression and built-in object-enrichment processes such as the addition of item-descriptive thumbnails help library staff maximize the use of an institution's special collections. The display of icons representing the types of materials contributes to an intuitive discovery experience for DigiTool end users.

Flexible metadata schema : DigiTool also features flexible metadata schema, such as MARC, Dublin Core, Metadata Object Description Schema (MODS), and Metadata Encoding and Transmission Standard (METS), which support the cataloging of various collection types. With the DigiTool configuration tools and open APIs, institutions can easily customize a collection's look and feel.

Key Features

A standards-based system, DigiTool provides across-the-board interoperability with Ex Libris products and other institutional systems.

- Open architecture facilitates interactivity with third-party systems.
- A flexible structure ensures support for a range of file formats and a variety of collections.
- Industry best practices guarantee that the system will meet current and future IT needs.
- Collaborative development with leading academic institutions ensures that DigiTool will continue to address the requirements of the market
- Digital collections managed by the library for the benefit of the general public
- The digital experience to its fullest:
  - i. DigiTool brings digital assets to life by providing high quality presentation and easy access to digital collections and institutional repositories.
  - ii. By enriching the user experience, DigiTool encourages the use of the library's digital

collections.

iii. Digital collections are accessible through a variety of interfaces, including the native DigiTool interface, the Primo® discovery and delivery application, institutional portals, e-learning systems, and custom interfaces built by the institution.

iv. DigiTool allows the user to enjoy the richness of digital resources—whether by zooming into a high quality image or viewing a complex index structure of a digital object.

v. The highly customizable user interface enables the library to showcase the unique characteristics of specific collections.

- Effectively manage and control the institution's digital collections:

Using DigiTool, libraries are able to consolidate disparate collections in one system that supports best practices for digital asset management and maintenance, replacing ad-hoc solutions and protecting against loss and misuse. DigiTool streamlines digital asset management processes from ingestion to metadata editing, collection organization, and access right management, enabling libraries to administer the growing volume of digital collections while minimizing the use of resources.

Faculty and non-library staff has direct access to the system. It allows them to share material either via deposit or discovery. This local and global collaboration serves to reduce library overhead and encourage the use of library-sanctioned digital repositories instead of localized ad-hoc solutions.

MetaLib : Reach Out and Discover Remote Resources : MetaLib provides a consolidated search environment for remote information resources. It helps users find the information they need quickly and effectively. MetaLib streamlines the discovery process by presenting users with content from multiple information providers in one clear, familiar user interface. By eliminating the need to learn different search methods and interfaces, MetaLib transforms the user experience from tiring to inspiring.

MetaLib: Bringing Remote Information Closer to the User : MetaLib provides users with a coherent and friendly environment for metasearching - simultaneously searching heterogeneous remote resources from a single search interface. Users view the retrieved results in a manageable, unified format, enabling them to:

i. See retrieved results in a merged, de-duplicated list
ii. Compare diverse result lists
iii. Preserve the records they find; and Locate the actual material.

X-Server: Embedding Remote Search into the User's Environment : MetaLib's X-Server enables the library to embed metasearch functionality into other applications such as:

i. Course management systems
ii. Library Web pages
iii. Institutional or Web portals

Easy to Manage :

i. MetaLib provides libraries with a set of tools to ease the management of the vast universe of remote resources, including:
ii. A comprehensive knowledge base with preconfigured access to commonly-used resources
iii. KnowledgeBase configuration tools to enable access to institution-specific resources
iv. Integration with the Ex Libris SFX® link server

v. A range of options for user authentication and authorization

vi. Flexible consortia models that support a range of consortia workflows which enable sharing while maintaining autonomy

Preserving information : Designed in collaboration with the National Library of New Zealand and reviewed by an international peer group of recognized leaders and innovators, the Ex Libris Digital Preservation System enables institutions to preserve and provide access to the collections in their care, now and in the future.

i. **Scalable :** Built on a distributed architecture that can support multiple, flexible server configurations, the system can scale up to manage digital collections of any size. By separating the permanent and working repositories, the system offers the security and redundancy required to keep collections safe.

ii. **Expandable :** The Ex Libris Digital Preservation System supports the functional needs of institutions that receive vast numbers of digital items on an ongoing basis. Batch loads, staging areas, and multiple deposit hierarchies enable users to manage the ingestion of new material efficiently and effectively.

iii. **Flexible :** Easy setup options allow institutions to configure the system to support their unique requirements and adhere to governing bodies' guidelines.

iv. **Standards-based :** Based on the Open Archival Information System (OAIS) model and conforming to trusted digital repository (TDR) requirements, the system provides institutions with the infrastructure and technology needed to preserve and facilitate access to the digital collections under their guardianship.

v. **Accessible :** Preserved digital entities are delivered via viewers that are compatible with the constantly evolving format types and are supplied as part of the system and third-party applications. With built-in integration capabilities, the system can accept delivery requests from discovery and delivery applications such as the Ex Libris Primo® solution while ensuring that item-level access rights are enforced.

REFERENCES

1. Apps, A. and MacIntyre, R. (1999). The SuperJournal Project: Data Handling Using SGML. In *Proceedings of the Third ICCC/IFIP Conference on Electronic Publishing (Electronic Publishing '99), Ronneby, Sweden, 10-12 May 1999.* (ICCC Press) pp 215-224, ISBN 1-891365-04-5. <http://epub.mimas.ac.uk/papers/ep99apps.html>.
2. Berners-Lee, T. (1994). Uniform Resource Locators (URL): A Syntax for the Expression of Access Information of Objects on the Web. <http://www.w3.org/Addressing/URL/url-spec.txt>.
3. The Digital Object Identifier System. <http://www.doi.org/>.
4. CrossRef. <http://www.crossref.org/>.
5. Beit-Arie, O., Blake, M., Caplan, P., Flecker, D., Ingoldsby, T., Lannom, L.W., Mischo, W.H., Pentz, E., Rogers, S. and Van de Sompel, H. (2001). Linking to the Appropriate Copy. *D-Lib Magazine*, 7(9). <doi:10.1045/september2001-caplan>.
6. http://www.diglib.org/
7. http://www.bibalex.org/
8. http://www.bl.uk/
9. Van de Sompel, H. and Beit-Arie, O. (2001). Open Linking in the Scholarly Information Environment Using the OpenURL Framework. *D-Lib Magazine*, 7(3). <doi:10.1045/march2001-vandesompel>.
10. Ex Libris. SFX Context Sensitive Linking. <http://www.exlibrisgroup.com/sfx.htm>.

11. HENSON, V. An Analysis of Compare-by-Hash. In *Proceedings from the HotOS IX Workshop* (May 2003). <http://www.usenix.org/events/hotos03/tech/full_papers/henson/henson_html/>.

12. HESLOP, H., DAVIS, S., AND WILSON, A. National Archives Green Paper: An Approach to the Preservation of Digital Records. <http://www.naa.gov.au/record keeping/er/digital_preservation/Green_Paper% 25.pdf>, 2002.

13. INTERNET ARCHIVE. About Internet Archive. <http://www.archive.org/about/about.php>.

14. http://www.cdlib.org/

15. http://www.library.cmu.edu/

16. http://www.columbia.edu/cu/libraries/digital

17. http://campusgw.library.cornell.edu/

18. http://www.clir.org/

19. ISO. Reference model for an open archival information system: Iso iso 14721:2003. <http://ssdoo.gsfc.nasa.gov/nost/isoas/ref_model.html>, 2003.

20. JEROEN BEKAERT AND HERBERT VAN DE SOMPEL. A standards-based solution for the accurate transfer of digital assets. *D-Lib Magazine* 6, 11 (June 2005). <doi:10.1045/june2005-bekaert>.

21. OpenURL Products and Vendors. <http://www.loc.gov/catdir/lcpaig/openurl.html>.

22. NISO. (2005). Z39.88-2004, The OpenURL Framework for Context-Sensitive Services. <http://www.niso.org/standards/standard_detail.cfm?std_id=783>.

23. Van de Sompel, H. and Beit-Arie, O. (2001). Generalizing the OpenURL Framework beyond References to Scholarly Works: the Bison-Futé model. D-Lib Magazine, 7(7/8). <doi:10.1045/july2001-vandesompel>.

24. Hodgson, C. (2005). Understanding the OpenURL Framework. *NISO Information Standards Quarterly*, 17(3), 1-4.

25. http://purl.oclc.org/DLF/collections/reg/OCLCservice

26. DLF Services Framework home page. Available at: <*http://www.diglib.org/architectures/serviceframe/*>.

27. Dempsey, L. and Lavoie, B., "DLF service framework for digital libraries: a progress report for the DLF Steering Committee." May 2005. Available at: <*http://www.diglib.org/architectures/serviceframe/dlfserviceframe1.pdf*>.

28. Consultative Committee for Space Data Systems, *Reference Model for an Open Archival Information System (OAIS)*. CCSDS 650.0-B-1, Blue Book, National Aeronautics and Space Administration, Washington, D.C. January 2002. Available at: <*http://public.ccsds.org/publications/archive/650x0b1.pdf*>.

29. e-Framework for Education and Research home page, Available at: <*http://www.e-framework.org/*>.

30. Acquifer project, <*http://www.diglib.org/aquifer/*>. For an update on current progress, see: Kott, K., Dunn, J., Halbert, M., Johnston, L., Milewica, L., and Shreeves, S., "Digital Library Federation (DLF) Aquifer Project." *D-Lib Magazine*, v.12, no.5, May 2006. Available at: <*doi:10.1045/may2006-kott*>.

31. http://shibboleth.internet2.edu/.)

32. http://www.oclc.org/research/memberscouncil/2004-02/cobb-dlfregistry.ppt

33. NISO AX and Apps, A. (2004). Z39.88-2004: The Key/Encoded-Value (KEV) Format Implementation Guidelines. <http://www.openurl.info/registry/docs/implementation_guidelines/>.

34. Zetoc, Electronic Table of Contents from the British Library. <http://zetoc.mimas.ac.uk/>.

35. Web of Knowledge. <http://wok.mimas.ac.uk/>.

36. http://middleware.internet2.edu/shibboleth/

37. Firefox. <http://www.mozilla.org/products/firefox/>.

38. SFX Targets. <http://www.exlibrisgroup.com/sfx_targets.htm>.

39. Rothenberg, J., Ensuring the Longevity of Digital Documents. *Scientific American* 272, 1 (1995).

40. Ockerbloom, J., *Mediating Among Diverse Data Formats*. Tech. Rep. CMU-CS-98-102, Carnegie-Mellon University, 1998. <http://tom.library.upenn.edu/pubs/thesis/>.

41. Fielding, R., Gettys, J., Mogul, J., Frystyk, H., Masinter, L., Leach, P., and Berners-Lee, T. *Hypertext Transfer Protocol-HTTP/1.1*. <http://www.w3.org/Protocols/rfc2616/rfc2616.html>, 1999.

42. van Wijngaarden, H., and Oltmans, E. Digital Preservation and Permanent Access: The UVC for Images. In *IS&T Archiving Conference* (San Antionio, TX, USA, 2004), pp. 254-258. <http://www.imaging.org/store/epub.cfm?abstrid=30329>.

43. http://www.imsglobal.org/digitalrepositories/index.cfm

44. The OpenURL Router. <http://openurl.ac.uk/doc/>.

45. OCLC OpenURL Resolver Registry. <http://www.oclc.org/productworks/urlresolver.htm>.

46. Endeavor Information Systems, LinkFinderPlus. <http://www.endinfosys.com/prods/linkfinderplus.htm>.

47. Scirus. <http://www.scirus.com/>.

48. The COPAC research library online union catalogue service. <http://copac.ac.uk/>.

49. OpenURL & CrossRef. <http://www.crossref.org/02publishers/16openurl.html>.

50. CrossRef's OpenURL Resolver. <http://www.crossref.org/02publishers/openurl_info.html>.

51. http://fedora.comm.nsdlib.org/

52. Eason, K., Harker, S., Apps, A. and MacIntyre, R. (2004). Towards an Integrated Digital Library: xploration of User Responses to a 'Joined-Up' Service. *Lecture Notes in Computer Science*, 3232, 452-463. <http://epub.mimas.ac.uk/papers/eham-ecdl2004.html>.

53. Mooer, Calvin. (1960). Mooer's Law. *American Documentation*, 11(3), p.ii.

54. http://www.lockss.org/lockss/How_It_Works

55. http://www.eecs.harvard.edu/~mema/publications/SOSP2003.pdf

56. Heidegger, M. (1977) The question concerning technology. Harper & Row, New York.

57. Zipf, G.K. (1949). *Human Behaviour and the Principle of Least-Effort*. Addison-Wesley, Cambridge MA.

58. http://www.dlib.org/dlib/january05/rosenthal/01rosenthal.html

59. http://www.crl.edu/content.asp?l1=13&l2=58&l3=142&l4=71

60. http://csrc.nist.gov/publications/fips/fips199/FIPS-PUB-199-final.pdf

61. http://www.clockss.org/clockss/Home

62. Eason, K. and Harker, S. (2003). The Impact of OpenURLs on End Users. <http://metadata.mimas.ac.uk/ITAM/evaluation.html>.

63. Cervone, F. (2005). What We've Learned from Doing Usability Testing on OpenURL Resolvers and Federated Search Engines. *Computers In Libraries*, 25(9), 10-14.

64. ScholarSFX. <http://www.exlibrisgroup.com/scholar_sfx.htm>.

65. JISC. <http://www.jisc.ac.uk/>.

66. http://www.vraweb.org/CCOweb/index.html

67. http://www.loc.gov/standards/mets/

68. http://www.openarchives.org/

69. Powell, A. (2002). 5 step guide to becoming a content provider in the JISC Information Environment. Ariadne, 33. <http://www.ariadne.ac.uk/issue33/info-environment/>.

70. Apps, A. and MacIntyre, R. (2003). Using the OpenURL Framework to Locate Bibliographic Resources. In *Proceedings of the 2003 Dublin Core Conference (DC2003 - Supporting Communities of Discourse and Practice - Metadata Research and Application), Seattle, Washington, USA, 28 September - 2 October 2003*, pp 143-152, ISBN 0-9745303-0-1. <http://epub.mimas.ac.uk/papers/appsmacdc2003.html>.

71. Openly Informatic JournalSeek Coverage for e-Journals.

<http://www.openly.com/journalseek/publishers.html>.

72. SFX Sources (OpenURL Enabled Resources). <http://www.exlibrisgroup.com/sfx_sources.htm>.
73. http://www.internet2.edu/
74. http://www.diglib.org/architectures/
75. CAPRICORN TECHNOLOGIES. Web site. <http://www.capricorn-tech.com/>, 2005.
76. CELESTE, E. Preservation via LOCKSS? <http://blog.lib.umn.edu/archives/efc/mystery/000278.html>, Apr. 2004.
77. CREATIVE COMMONS. Web site. <http://creativecommons.org/>.
78. DONALD J. WATERS. Managing Digital Assets: An Overview of Strategic Issues. <http://www.clir.org/activities/registration/feb05_spkrnotes/waters.htm>, Feb. 2005.
79. ELSEVIER. Elsevier and Koninklijke Bibliotheek finalise major archiving agreement. <http://www.elsevier.com/wps/find/authored_newsitem.librarians/companyne%ws05_00020>, Aug. 2003.
80. Heslop, H., Davis, S., and Wilson, A., *National Archives Green Paper: An Approach to the Preservation of Digital Records.* <http://www.naa.gov.au/recordkeeping/er/digital_preservation/Green_Paper.pdf>, 2002.
81. Walker, F., and Thoma, G., A Web-Based Paradigm for File Migration. In *IS&T Archiving Conference* (San Antionio, TX, USA, 2004), pp. 93-97. <http://www.imaging.org/store/epub.cfm?abstrid=30297>.
82. DAITSS Overview. <http://www.fcla.edu/digitalArchive/pdfs/DAITSS.pdf>, 2004.
83. Graphics Interchange Format version 89a. <http://www.w3.org/Graphics/GIF/spec-gif89a.txt>, 1990.
84. MOCKAPETRIS, P. V. RFC 1034: Domain names - concepts and facilities, Nov. 1987. <http://www.faqs.org/rfcs/rfc1034.html>.
85. MOORE, D., PAXSON, V., SAVAGE, S., SHANNON, C., STANIFORD, S., AND WEAVER, N. The Spread of the Sapphire/

Slammer Worm. <http://www.caida.org/outreach/papers/2003/sapphire/>.

86. NASA. Aviation Safety Reporting System. <http://asrs.arc.nasa.gov/>.

87. NATIONAL LIBRARY OF AUSTRALIA. Preservation Metadata for Digital Collections. <http://www.nla.gov.au/preserve/pmeta.html>.

88. NIST. Overview of the AES development effort. <http://csrc.nist.gov/CryptoToolkit/aes/>, Feb. 2001.

89. OCLC. Persistent uniform resource locator. <http://purl.oclc.org/>.

90. PATTERSON, D. A., GIBSON, G., AND KATZ, R. H. A Case for Redundant Arrays of Inexpensive Disks (RAID). In *Proceedings of the ACM SIGMOD International Conference on Management of Data* (Chicago, IL, USA, June 1988), pp. 109-116.

91. BAKER, M., KEETON, K., AND MARTIN, S. Why Traditional Storage Systems Don't Help Us Save Stuff Forever. In *Proc. 1st IEEE Workshop on Hot Topics in System Dependability* (2005). <http://www.hpl.hp.com/techreports/2005/HPL-2005-120.pdf>.

92. HARVARD UNIVERSITY LIBRARY. Format-Specific Digital Object Validation. http://hul.harvard.edu/jhove/>,1999.

93. JPEG COMMITTEE. JPEG2000: Our New Standard. <http://www.jpeg.org/jpeg2000/>.

94. JSTOR. About JSTOR. <http://www.jstor.org/about/>, Mar. 2005.

95. JUNQUEIRA, F., BHAGWAN, R., HEVIA, A., MARZULLO, K., AND VOELKER, G. M. Surviving Internet Catastrophes. In *Proceedings of the Usenix Annual Technical Conference* (Apr. 2005).

96. KEENEY, M., KOWALSKI, E., CAPPELLI, D., MOORE, A., SHIMEALL, T., AND ROGERS, S. Insider threat study: Computer system sabotage in critical infrastructure sectors. <http://www.secretservice.gov/ntac/its_report_050516.pdf>, May 2005.

97. KLIMA, V. Finding md5 collisions - a toy for a notebook. Cryptology ePrint Archive, Report 2005/075, 2005. <http://eprint.iacr.org/2005/075>.

98. LETTICE, J. Building disaster into the network: how UK.gov does IT. <http://www.theregister.co.uk/2004/11/30/dwp_crash_analysis/>.

99. LIBRARY OF CONGRESS. Digital Repository Development: Core Metadata Elements. <http://www.loc.gov/standards/metadata.html>. [32] LIBRARY OF CONGRESS. Metadata Encoding and Transmission Standard. <http://www.loc.gov/standards/mets/>, Jan. 2005.

100. LOCKSS PROJECT. LOCKSS: Related Projects and Resources. <http://www.lockss.org/related/related.htm>.

101. LORIE, R. Preserving Digital Documents for the Long-Term. In *IS&T Archiving Conf.* (San Antonio, TX, USA, 2004), pp. 88-92.

102. MANIATIS, P., AND BAKER, M. Secure History Preservation Through Timeline Entanglement. In *Proceedings of the 11th USENIX Security Symposium* (San Francisco, CA, USA, Aug. 2002), pp. 297-312. <http://mosquitonet.stanford.edu/publications/Sec2002.pdf>.

103. MANIATIS, P., ROUSSOPOULOS, M., GIULI, T. J., ROSENTHAL, D. S. H., AND BAKER, M. The LOCKSS peer-to-peer digital preservation system. *ACM Trans. Comput. Syst. 23*, 1 (2005), 2-50.

104. MARGARET BRANSCHOFSKY. Building an institutional repository. <http://cites.boisestate.edu/v5i3f.htm>.

105. MENAFEE, S. Drivesavers cuts price for lost data recovery. <http://www.findarticles.com/cf_dls/m0NEW/n39/20324409/p1/article.jhtml>, Feb. 1998.

106. RLG. An Audit Checklist for the Certification of Trusted Digital Repositories: Draft for Public Comment. <http://www.rlg.org/en/pdfs/rlgnara-repositorieschecklist.pdf>, Aug. 2005.

107. RONALD JANTZ AND MICHAEL J. GIARLO. Digital preservation: Architecture and technology for trusted digital repositories. *D-Lib Magazine 11*, 6 (June 2005).

<doi:10.1045/june2005-jantz>.

108. ROSENTHAL, D. S. H. A Digital Preservation Network Appliance Based on OpenBSD. In *Proceedings of BSDcon* 2003 (San Mateo, CA, USA, Sept. 2003). <http://lockss.stanford.edu/david1.htm>.

109. http://www.library.yale.edu/~llicense/index.shtml

110. http://www.diglib.org/standards/tei.htm

111. ROSENTHAL, D. S. H., LIPKIS, T., ROBERTSON, T. S., AND MORABITO, S. Transparent format migration of preserved web content. *D-Lib Magazine 11*, 1 (Jan. 2005). <doi:10.1045/january2005-rosenthal>.

112. ROTHENBERG, J. Ensuring the Longevity of Digital Documents. *Scientific American 272*, 1 (1995). <http://www.clir.org/pubs/archives/ensuring.pdf>.

113. http://www.niso.org/standards/resources/SerialsWP.html

114. ALTZER, J. H. Fault-tolerance in Very Large Archival Systems. In *Proceedings of the Fourth SIGOPS European Workshop* (Bologna, Italy, Sept. 1990). <http://web.mit.edu/Saltzer/www/publications/fault-tol/fault-tolerance.html>.

115. SAN DIEGO SUPERCOMPUTER CENTER. Storage Resource Broker. <http://www.sdsc.edu/srb/>.

116. SEAGATE. ST3200822A Configuration and Specifications. <http://www.seagate.com/support/disc/specs/ata/st3200822a.html>, Sept. 2003.

117. SHIRLEY HYATT AND JEFFREY A. YOUNG. OCLC research publications repository. *D-Lib Magazine 11*, 3 (Mar. 2005). <doi:10.1045/march2005-hyatt>.

118. SMITH, M. Practical preservation activities. In *Workshop on Long-Term Curation Within Digital Repositories* (July 2005), Digital Curation Centre.

119. SMITH, M., RODGERS, R., WALKER, J., AND TANSLEY, R. Dspace: A year in the life of an open source digital repository system. *Lecture Notes in Computer Science 3232* (Jan. 2004), 38-44.

120. http://www.diglib.org/forums/Spring2004/Guenther0404_files/frame.htm

121. http://www.vraweb.org/ccoweb/

122. STANIFORD, S., PAXSON, V., AND WEAVER, N. How to Own the Internet in Your Spare Time. In *Proceedings of the 11th USENIX Security Symposium* (San Francisco, CA, USA, Aug. 2002), pp. 149-167. <http://www.icir.org/vern/papers/cdc-usenix-sec02/cdc.web.pdf>.

123. Connotea. <http://www.connotea.org/>.

124. Chudnov, D., Cameron, R., Frumkin, J., Singer, R. and Yee, R. (2005). Opening up OpenURLs with Autodiscovery. *Ariadne*, 43. <http://www.ariadne.ac.uk/issue43/chudnov/>.

125. Hellman, E. (2005). OpenURL COinS: A Convention to Embed Bibliographic Metadata in HTML. <http://ocoins.info/>.

126. OpenURL Referrer from Openly Informatics. <http://www.openly.com/openurlref/>.

127. WAG the Dog. <http://www.library.gatech.edu/research_help/WAG_faq.html>.

128. CiteULike. <http://www.citeulike.org/>.

129. Citebase. <http://www.citebase.org/>.

130. Apps, A. (2004). zetoc SOAP: a Web Services Interface for a Digital Library Resource. *Lecture Notes in Computer Science* 3232, pp 198-208. <http://epub.mimas.ac.uk/papers/appsecdl2004.html>.

131. The OpenURL Registry. <http://www.openurl.info/registry/>.

132. Bekaert, J., Balakireva, L., Hochstenbach, P. and Van de Sompel, H. (2004). Using MPEG-21 DIP and NISO OpenURL for the Dynamic Dissemination of Complex Digital Objects in the Los Alamos National Laboratory Digital Library. *D-Lib Magazine*, 10(2). <doi:10.1045/february2004-bekaert>.

133. Apps, A. (2005). A Middleware Registry for the Discovery of Collections and Services. In *NCeSS2005: Proceedings of the First International Conference on e-Social Science, Manchester, UK, 22-24 June 2005*. <http://epub.mimas.ac.uk/papers/ncess2005/apps-ncess2005. html>.

134. Chudnov, D. and Frumkin, J. (2005) Library Dialtone:

Bootstrapping with Autodiscovery and Service Registries. In *Access 2005, Edmonton, Canada, 17-19 October 2005.* <http://curtis.med.yale.edu/dchud/talks/20051019-access-dialtone/dialtone.pdf>.

135. STONE, J., AND PARTRIDGE, C. When the CRC and TCP checksum disagree. In *SIGCOMM* (2000), pp. 309-319.
136. http://www.rlg.org/visguides/
137. http://www.umdl.umich.edu/moa4/
138. http://www.clir.org/pubs/abstract/pub99abst.html
139. http://www.library.cornell.edu/cts/elicensestudy/nisodlf/home.htm
140. http://www.library.cornell.edu/cts/elicensestudy/dlfdeliverables/home.htm
141. THEO VAN VEEN. Renewing the information infrastructure of the Koninklijke Bibliotheek. *D-Lib Magazine 11*, 3 (Mar. 2005). <doi:10.1045/march2005-vanveen>.
142. VAN DE SOMPEL, H., NELSON, M. L., LAGOZE, C., AND WARNER, S. Resource harvesting within the OAI-PMH framework. *D-Lib Magazine 10,* 12 (Dec. 2004). <doi:10.1045/december2004-vandesompel>.
143. VAN WIJNGAARDEN, H., AND OLTMANS, E. Digital Preservation and Permanent Access: The UVC for Images. In *IS&T Archiving Conf.* (San Antionio, TX, USA, 2004), pp. 254-258.
144. WARD, J., LLONA, E., AND LALLY, A. Barriers to Adoption of an Institutional Repository. <http://hdl.handle.net/1773/2019>.
145. WILLIAMSON, M. Throttling Viruses: Restricting Propagation to Defeat Malicious Mobile Code. In *Proceedings of the 18th Annual Computer Security Applications Conference* (Las Vegas, Nevada, USA, Dec. 2002). <http://www.acsac.org/2002/papers/97.pdf>.
146. SMUG (SFX / MetaLib Users Group) 4 EU. <http://www.igelu.org/sfxmetalib/newsletter>.
147. Apps, A. and MacIntyre, R. (2005). Emerging Uses for the OpenURL Framework. In *Proceedings of the Ninth ICCC*

International Conference on Electronic Publishing (ELPUB2005 - From Author to Reader), Katholieke Universiteit Leuven, Belgium, 8-10 June 2005 (Peeters Publishing Leuven), pp 283-289, ISBN 90-429-1645-1. <http://epub.mimas.ac.uk/papers/elpub2005/appsmac-elpub2005.html>.

148. Google Scholar. <http://scholar.google.com/>.

149. Brunning, D. (2003). Interview with Herbert Van de Sompel, Creator of OpenURL/SFX. *The Charleston Advisor*, 4(4). <http://charlestonco.com/features.cfm?id=124&type=np>.

3

E-Resource Management Systems

BACKGROUND

Looking back over the evolution of digital library technologies reflects on how the developments got where today are. It is important to consider the contributions of technically supported developments and also to note the provenance of other emerging information technologies. The pragmatic support for digital library research was formulated in a series of community-based planning workshops sponsored by the National Science Foundation (NSF) in 1993-1994. The first significant federal investment in digital library research came in 1994 with the funding of six projects under the auspices of the Digital Libraries Initiative (now called DLI-1) program. These DLI-1 research and development projects were jointly funded by a federation comprised of the National Science Foundation (NSF), the National Aeronautics and Space Administration (NASA), and the Defense Advanced Research Projects Agency (DARPA).

During late nineties, at the cessation of the DLI-1 program, federal funding for the DLI-2 program was instituted with support from NSF, NASA, DARPA, the National Library of Medicine (NLM), the Library of Congress (LC), the Federal Bureau of Investigation (FBI), and the National Endowment for the Humanities (NEH). Also, in 1998, the Corporation for National Research Initiatives (CNRI), under DARPA support, funded the three-year *D-Lib Test Suite* program which provided continuing funding for several of the digital library Testbeds created under DLI-1. In aggregate, between 1994 and 1999, a total of $68 million in federal research grants were awarded under DLI-1 and DLI-2. DLI-1 funded six university-led projects to develop and implement computing and networking technologies that could make large-scale electronic test collections accessible and interoperable. The six funded institutions with their primary focus were:

- The University of Michigan for research on agent technology and mechanisms for improving secondary education;
- Stanford University for the investigation of interoperability among heterogeneous digital libraries and the exploration of distributed object technology;
- The University of California-Berkeley for imaging technologies, government environmental information resources, and database technologies;
- The University of California-Santa Barbara for the Alexandria Project to develop GIS (Geographical Information Systems) and earth modeling distributed libraries;
- Carnegie Mellon University for the study of integrated speech, image, video, and language understanding software under its Informedia system; and
- The University of Illinois at Urbana-Champaign for the development of document representation, processing, indexing, search and discovery, and delivery and

rendering protocols for full-text physics, computer science, and engineering journals.

In the Illinois project, the overarching focus of the Testbed component was on the deployment and evaluation of journals in a marked-up format within an Internet environment. Probably the most significant contribution of the Illinois project was the transfer of technology to the publishing partners and other publishers. Many of these publishers supported feature sets that closely follow those that were originally developed within the Illinois Testbed project. These include: full-text display using HTML and Cascading Style Sheets (CSS), internal linking between citations and footnotes, forward and backward links to cited articles using DOIs and OpenURLs, and, less commonly, the display of complex mathematics and special Unicode characters directly in the HTML or XML full text.

When DLI-1 began, the World Wide Web was in a very nascent stage. At that time, the University of Illinois' National Center for Supercomputing Applications (NCSA) Mosaic 2.0 beta was the Web browser of choice, the HTML 2.0 standard was still under development, Netscape had yet to release its first Web browser and Microsoft Windows 3.1 was the standard personal computer operating system. Another interesting effect of the increased federal funding for research was that senior scholars from other computing disciplines were brought into the field. Computer and networking technology has changed dramatically over the last 15 years and nowhere is this more evident than in the rapidly evolving world of digital library implementation and practice. A large number of significant digital library standards and technologies have been developed by entities outside of the federally funded projects. Asampling of these includes:

- Publishers (professional societies such as AIP and commercial publishers such as Elsevier),

- Publisher consortiums (CrossRef),
- Bibliographic utilities (OCLC's work with the Dublin Core and Resource Description Framework (RDF) standards),
- W3C (XML, XSLT),
- ISO (SGML)
- Academic consortia such as the Digital Library Federation and the Association for Research Libraries (OAI, the ARL Portal),
- NISO (OpenURL and Metasearch Initiative)
- Library of Congress (Zing, SRU/SRW, METS),
- Library integrated system vendors (Ex Libris with SFX, Endeavor Link Finder Plus),
- Metasearch vendors (WebFeat, Muse Global, Ex Libris MetaLib, Endeavor EnCompass),
- Web search engines (Google Scholar and Google Print, Yahoo),
- Computer companies (HP and D-Space, Oracle and Microsoft SQL utilizing XML),
- The open source community (DSpace, Greenstone, Fedora, Sakai).

INITIATIVES

1. For Developing Digital Library Architectures

Libraries face a range of technical and administrative challenges when they move their collections and services online, attempt to make them scalable, and plan for their sustainability. In context with developing e-resource based architecture, it is needed to:

- define, clarify, and develop prototypes for e-resource and such systems and their components;
- scan the larger technical environment for and

encourage the development of potentially important trends and practices;

- encourage technology transfer and information sharing;
- communicate technical directions and accomplishments of the e-resources to a wider audience

2. E-resources Management Systems

Following are the names of universities which have taken Initiatives for e- resource management:

- California Digital Library
- Colorado Alliance (Gold Rush)
- Columbia
- Griffith University (Australia)
- Harvard
- Johns Hopkins (HERMES)
- MIT (VERA)
- Michigan
- Minnesota
- Notre Dame
- Penn State (ERLIC)
- Stanford Texas (License Tracker)
- Tri-College Consortium (Haverford, Bryn Mawr, Swarthmore)
- UCLA
- University of Georgia
- University of Washington (w/III)
- Virginia
- Willamette University
- Yale

3. E-resource building

Libraries began collecting and building its digital collection since long before commercial digital asset management system was available. To manage its growing collections, libraries devoted internal resources to the development of a homegrown application for managing, searching, and presenting these materials. As digital asset management technology advanced and commercial applications became more readily available, libraries began exploring the possibility of migration of its digital objects to a system that would foster collection growth without overtaxing university resources.

THE SEARCH FOR A ONE-STOP SOLUTION

There was no software that libraries could purchase at the time to provide access to digital collections. The solution created by libraries served the organization well for over ten years, a period marked by impressive growth in digital collections. However, the amalgam of homegrown and commercial systems became difficult to maintain. With several applications playing a role in the solution, the inconsistency of the metadata associated with the digital objects was of major concern to libraries. Libraries have a lot of fragmentation. The goal was to have a one-stop solution that would ensure consistent metadata for the entire collection. Most of the libraries ultimately decide to acquire its own instance of the software thinking it would be an exciting opportunity for libraries to have the creative freedom of an independent digital asset management solution while retaining the ability to contribute and share content.

Several factors have rendered the job of such librarians extremely challenging. The amazing growth of electronic collections and the increasingly central role they are playing in libraries. The large budgets are involved in acquiring these collections. The endless variation in the packages is offered by the many publishers. Interface providers and subscription agencies are deluded in the market. The frequent changes in business models and the lack of automated tools to deal with the complexity of e-resource management are among the challenges. In addition to the initial effort of setting up information in multiple places and the potential lack of consistency between systems, there might also be considerable duplication of effort.

When e-resources are part of collection, there is a lot of extra information that must be tracked such as:

- Who will keep up with the contents of both standard and customized e-journal packages?
- Who will keep up with journal access models?
- Who will be able to provide comprehensive, quality data on information resources across publishers and formats?
- Who will have the data to feed ERM systems?

PRAGMATIC PROBLEMS AND ISSUES

- vendors may provide "modules" in time, but libraries need short-term fixes
- Previous/ongoing investments in systems
- Major changes to longstanding record-keeping practices probably undesirable
- Multiple data streams need to be brought together

GUIDING PRINCIPLES

Some guiding for principles are given as following :

- Integrated, non-duplicating management and access environment.
- Global updating, flexible addition of fields, ability to hide fields and records.

- Single point of maintenance for each data element.
- Interoperation and/or dynamic sharing data with existing OPACs, web portals, library management systems, and link resolution services.

GENERAL REQUIREMENTS

The basic requirements are listed below:

- Identify bibliographic entities covered or provided through a license
- Associate license terms or characteristics with all the biographic entities
- Offer security features to control views

Functional Aspects

The ERMS demands some functional aspects such as:

- Store license rights and terms for reference, reporting, and control of services
- For services including but not limited to ILL, reserves, distance education, course web sites, and course packs
- Identify whether a given title may be used for the service and under what conditions
- Generate reports of all materials that may or may not be used for the service with notes about conditions

MANAGING ELECTRONIC INFORMATION AND COLLECTIONS

The digital library, deals with collections which are output of the integration of new formats, licensed content and third-party information. Collection management strategies and practices are yet to be fully developed due to these changing circumstances. The larger the library, the bigger the e-resource management problem do exist. Most academic libraries struggle with it, and larger public libraries also do — to some degree. For the academics, the problem is clearly getting bigger very quickly as they rely more heavily on databases and electronic journals. Managing such things effectively requires sophisticated tools. It is evident that users can discover the library's thousands of e-resources not only through the online catalog but also through the gateway services. These services provide access to research-quality online indexes, abstracting services, full text resources and e-journals. Most of these services are not available on the Internet to the general public. The technical services staff of libraries provides, maintain, manage, and troubleshoot access to the e-resources. The number of locally-developed e-resource tools is amazing, and new systems are being developed all the time. The libraries begin developing databases to help manage administrative metadata. It is not sure who should get the credit for creating the first e-resource management system or database, since many libraries have been using different tools to track related information for some time, and at some point a few of those libraries began experimenting with database software. The entire digital lifecycle includes planning and processing to management, archiving and discovery of primary source materials. Some library solutions serve the needs just starting to explore digital possibilities as well as those that are committed to ongoing digitization and preservation efforts. Various organizations offer a digital collection management system that libraries can integrate with their software and programs, to surface the digital collections, not only to the library's own users, but to people all over the globe.

Libraries approached the web application developer and related the need for an easier way to manage the hundreds of links to both licensed and unlicensed electronic resources on the library's web site. The creation of a simple database-enabled e-resource application would allow creating a bibliographic record for a particular e-resource and to subject-index the record using multiple subject headings. The public display for the application would pull data directly from the database and would dynamically generate subject-specific lists of e-resources, along with their corresponding URLs. Since the URL would be stored in a single place, any updates to that URL would automatically appear within each of the individual subject lists on the site. In this way, the need for locating and updating multiple instances of the same URL whenever a change to that URL occurred would be eliminated. E-resource management (ERM) can be initiated by hiring person to perform data entry to populate the backend database work could be begun. Just when this process is reaches to complete, developing specifications for an e-resource license tracking database can be initiated. The facts that most integrated library systems do not adequately provide for the workflow and approval processes surrounding e-resource licensing prompt the need for in-house development of such a system. Committees and subcommittees can be formed for developing specifications for individual modules of the application. These subcommittees can be devoted to, among other things, the development of a public display interface, and compilation of a list of appropriate subject headings, identification of data elements that should be captured by the backend database, and discussion and preparation of the necessary technical infrastructure. Advances in scholarship depend on access to what has come before. Technologies of the past two centuries have enabled the creation and capture of information in many forms. Keeping the products of these technologies fit for use, however, has become more challenging with time.

Up-to-date kind of search interface is long overdue in library catalogues. Library Management System (LMS) suppliers ought to have provided such functionality as standard as their OPACs (Online Public Access Catalogues) have developed. To do this well, it is worth investing in a new and flexible search layer that can include resources and databases beyond the library catalogue and which is free from the constraints of the backroom aspects of the ERM. Since the vast majority of users are now using sites like Google and Facebook, there is little point trying to develop own local interfaces to resources. Libraries should concentrate their efforts on making their resources visible within the wider network of search engines and open repositories. A suitable strategy would be to examine what makes them successful and apply some of their features to more local interfaces. Libraries are likely to encourage people to use the library's interfaces and obtain the highest-quality resources. Libraries have the upper hand in providing high quality content. This is where ERM steps in providing attractive interface. The system is about finding, not just searching, and delivering resources no matter where they originate. In this respect, system is more than just a glorified replacement for the library catalogue. The benefit of such system is that it represents a one-stop shop for access to institutional repository and remote databases. The relevancy ranking algorithm can be sophisticated, leading to results by relevance not just year of publication; it can work more like the search engines the users are familiar with on the Web.

ELECTRONIC RESOURCE MANAGEMENT: FEW REQUISITES

The goal envisioned in these requirements is a system that supports management of the information and workflows necessary to efficiently select, evaluate, acquire, maintain, and provide access to e-resources in accordance with their business and license terms. Such a system should support the service requirements of e-resources while building on existing investments in library technology, through seamless interaction and efficient sharing of data with traditional MARC-based online catalogs, Web portals, federated searching tools, local resolution services, local authentication and access-management systems, and traditional library-management functions. Whether implemented as a standalone system or as part of an existing library-management system, the ERM functions should complement, rather than duplicate, the capabilities of other systems deployed by the library. The ERM system should offer an integrated environment that supports both management and access. The system should offer a capacity for global updating and flexible addition of fields with the ability to hide fields and records from public view and have a single point of maintenance for each data element. It should support interoperation and dynamic data sharing with existing OPACs, Web portals, library-management systems, and link resolution services.

1. Functional Requirements

The ability to support complex, multiple-to-multiple relationships that accurately map how resources, business terms, licenses, and other components interrelate is an essential building block for supporting the functionality. For all areas of functionality, it must be possible to:

- Identify what bibliographic entities are covered by or provided through a given license, set of business terms, package, or online interface platform (hereinafter "interface");
- Associate the characteristics of a given license, set of business terms, package, or interface with all the bibliographic entities (electronic and print) to which they apply;
- Offer security features to control staff views and maintenance rights and hide confidential information from certain staff as well as restrict the ability to add, update, or delete certain data to designated staff;
- It should provide the ability to construct simplified data views by hiding unused fields; and perform ad hoc

queries and generate reports across a broad range of fields and table values.

2. Resource-Discovery Requirements

While adequate facilities for searching and browsing for e-resources already exist in OPACs and portals at many libraries, facilities to cull e-resources for resource-discovery purposes are lacking at other institutions. The ERM system should provide a user interface for libraries that require one as well as a means of integrating appropriate license data into the results of searches. The system should provide Web developers' database table- or view-level access and present data to the user in any number of custom-configurable ways. An ERMS implementation should include a dedicated user interface that is able to capture appropriate data in other systems or to share its information with elements in other supported systems to create unified user displays. It should be possible to:

- Make resources available through or pass on information about resources to OPACs and Web-presentation services using traditional resource discovery methods, including the ability to search and browse by author, title, alternate titles, cross-references, subject, and keywords, facilitate the generation of dynamic, database- driven Web pages that constitute pathfinders, course- or discipline-specific pages, or lists of selected e-resources in a given subject area and of a given type while supporting fully customizable presentation templates that are not limited to the branding and look and feel of the native interface;
- Offer contextual presentation of relevant license information to the user at the point of access, regardless of the access path taken through any supported tool and make apparent to users whether or

not they are authorized for access under the license;

- Display relevant permitted uses, use restrictions, and special requirements such as: permission to use in course packs, course Web sites, unusual prohibitions, such as record download limits and time of day restrictions;
- While looking into citation requirements; it should support site-defined and auxiliary descriptive data. Such data might include: locally defined fields for descriptive needs not covered in existing MARC records, locally defined lists and descriptors;
- Make available information about and provide access to other versions of the resource being viewed, including links to catalog holdings information for physical manifestations and direct links to all accessible electronic versions;
- Offer advisory notices of planned downtime and other time-sensitive information.

3. Bibliographic Management Requirements

In many libraries, both traditional and auxiliary bibliographic data may be distributed among a variety of systems, including the library-management system, a federated searching portal, and a link resolution service. Nevertheless, to the extent possible, each unique data element should have to be maintained only once. Updates in one system should be automatically reflected in corresponding systems, either through the dynamic sharing of data or, where redundant storage cannot be eliminated, by propagation to other systems. Loading of data from external systems should also be supported. Specifically, it should be possible to:

- Provide a single point of maintenance for bibliographic and auxiliary descriptive data that can be exchanged or shared between the OPAC, portal lists, federated search tools, local resolution services, and other bibliographic systems and services; and

- Import subscription-management data from external providers using standard software and developing protocols, lists of titles, ISSNs, and uniform resource identifiers (URIs) delivered in Excel or delimited format, holdings updates supplied by a publisher or subscription agent to facilitate electronic check-in.

4. Access-Management Requirements

All libraries rely on authentication and access-management systems that are external to the systems and tools. These external systems may be as straightforward as reliance on the remote-authorization mechanism of an online provider or as complex as a locally developed access-management service that assigns persistent identifiers to resources, passes connection requests to a system that validates users according to a local authentication scheme, and routes valid users through a proxy server. Institutions with complex local environments can be expected to have customized systems and tools with which to perform these functions, and the ERM system must interoperate with them. The ERMS should accommodate both simple and complex environments with a disparate range of needs. To accomplish this, the following generalized requirements are necessary:

- Management of basic access-related information, such as URIs, user IDs and passwords, and lists of institutional IP addresses;
- A set of export functions by which an ERMS can communicate its information to a local system or service. Specifically, it should be possible to store and maintain access URIs and make these actionable for end users, according to local requirements;
- Store vendor-supplied primary and secondary URIs (e.g., for mirror sites) used for access to the resource

and support the creation, storage, and updating of persistent URIs and/or integration with external systems for managing persistent identifiers;

- For a given resource or online provider, indicate whether IP addresses are/were registered online and record the registration URI and send automated e-mail notifications to vendors and providers when IP addresses are updated and record the date on which notifications are sent. Include the ability to record an acknowledgment date. This implies the ability to designate a vendor or provider contact address for IP address-notification purposes;
- Store one or more user IDs and passwords and provide the ability to generate secure screen displays of this information for authorized users and staff, with associated text or for JavaScript auto-submission and implement access restrictions, record authorized user categories and authorized sites.

5. Staff Requirements

i. Staff Interface: An ERM system requires a staff interface that enables to efficiently carry out the work. The interface should be organized into views that are optimized for particular areas of staff activity or interest, such as resource acquisition, troubleshooting, license administration, or administration and statistics. Through this interface, staff should be able to:

- Search, browse, and retrieve records by attributes unique to e-resources, such as license, vendor, interface, record status, licensed site, consortium, and library selector or other local contact individual;
- View the full range of information appropriate to the staff member's security profile and functional role to the extent possible, link to other relevant information stored in library management systems, portals, or

related systems and view records that are hidden from the public.

ii. Selection and Evaluation Process: During the selection and evaluation process, it is typically necessary for a decentralized group of individuals to coordinate a complex and iterative series of steps. The ERM system should provide support for recording actions at each of these steps and be capable of performing specified actions upon completion of a given task and of sending alerts when anticipated actions do not occur. A typical selection and evaluation process might involve the following steps and require the following reminders and notifications, all built from stored action dates and locally definable status fields:

- Build request record for trial
- Flag resource as trial
- Notify interested parties that trial is live and provide the access instructions and expiration date
- Allow staff (and, optionally, users) to access the trial via stored URL
- Send reminder to those notified of a trial that expiration date is near
- Record opinions of key players and final purchase decision, allowing for both central and local input of opinions and funding commitments into notes fields in request record
- Prompt licensing/acquisitions contact to report purchase decision. The most common options are "Approve," "Reject," or "Put on Hold"
- For resources that are approved for purchase, additional statuses and actions would be required, including notify licensing contact to obtain and negotiate license, and remind the contact if license is not completed by a given deadline notify access

contact if status has not changed to "live" by deadline

- Notify cataloging and selector/product sponsor, as well as other interested parties, when access is available

To support these processes, it should be possible to:

- Create provisional records for resources that may or may not be permanently acquired and track the selection and evaluation process through acquisition or rejection
- Assign locally definable status fields to request records and associate particular actions with those statuses. Examples of such fields include "New Request," "On Trial," "Trial Expired/Decision Pending," "Approved," "Rejected," and "On Hold"
- Assign locally definable fields to request records for license routing and status and associate particular actions with those fields. Site should be able, for example, to define a list of individuals from whom sign-off is required, send reminders to license reviewers, and record approval or rejection status, with notes
- Store trial URIs and passwords and make these available, securely if necessary and record a trial expiration date and, optionally, send an alert to designated recipients in days prior to trial expiration
- Record a decision due date and, optionally, send an alert to designated recipients days prior to decision date

6. Resource Administration and Management Functions

Some of the data and functions pertain to the license itself, while others pertain to the management of individual resources. The system should be able to record data at the most efficient level required to avoid redundancy, relying on the relationships among entities to make the information available at other applicable levels. It should be possible to:

- Store license rights and terms for reference, reporting, and control of services for services including, but not limited to, interlibrary loans, reserves, distance education, course Web sites, and course packs, identify whether a given title may be used for the service and under what conditions;
- Generate reports of all materials that may or may not be used for the service with notes about under what conditions, and include a mechanism for adding new services, allowing staff to specify the name of the service and associated actions such as public displays, reports, and alerts;
- Record the categories of users and sites that are authorized for access to a given resource and generate displays for end users and staff on the basis of this information;
- Support breach investigation and cure activities and other activities that may be required to fulfill license obligations;
- Record additional license terms and metadata for contract management and auditing purposes, such as license commencement date, duration of agreement, confidentiality provisions, and other site-definable key terms;
- Manage the library's archival rights in electronic content, and record whether permanent rights to the year level exist in a given resource and, if so, their source, dates of coverage, manner of execution, and the applicable license thr,ough which rights are provided. It should be possible to associate multiple archival field clusters with a given resource to track successive rights with multiple providers;
- Support the administration of e-resources, and store administrative URIs, IDs and passwords, and associated

notes and make them available to authorized staff;

- Provide the capabilities for configuration options, including but not limited to features such as institutional branding, hooks to holdings, Z39.50 and OpenURL support;
- Record the number of licensed concurrent users for a given resource, interface, or pooled user group and record cataloging-related data such as, the availability and quality of MARC records for package items that include individual entities, including the status of loading or prioritization and additional notes the person or unit responsible for cataloging, if applicable related specifications, such as specific entries or other data to be included in cataloging records;
- Support management of and access to usage statistics, indicate whether usage statistics are provided, and record associated data such as frequency, delivery method, and available format(s) and record URIs and IDs and passwords for access to online statistics while storing information about and/or links to locally stored data
- Support the troubleshooting of access and performance-related problems.
- Integrate a support incident log into the system to record and track problems, including date and source of initial report, category and description of problem, open/closed status, resolution date, and a record of actions taken.

7. Workflow Concerns

Electronic resource management systems are just one step in helping libraries manage e -resources. Effective e - resource management requires changes to the ways libraries do their work. The libraries would soon be hiring an "e- resources person" to assist with the burgeoning array of tasks affiliated with the access, administration, and control of e-resources. According to a study, a trend was clear: staffing for e-resource activities is being vastly outpaced by the growth of e -resource collections in libraries. Libraries have responded about their ability to manage electronic resources. It's the combination of e-resource systems, sufficient and proper allocation of staff, adoption and standardization of the ERM functional specifications, and an unreferenced but critical issue, agreeable model licensing, that will help libraries overcome the challenge presented by today' digital information environment.

Electronic publications epitomize the problems of the long term preservation and access to digital objects. They are easily lost, can become corrupted, inadvertently deleted, become inaccessible through changes in technology and even deliberately updated or moved. Electronic publications utilize multi-media and may even provide an interactive environment for the reader. To develop a solution to address the problems of ERM and access is one of the major challenges of the time. Another facet of electronic publications is the role of the creator, the editor, the publisher and distributor. With the Internet, these roles can very easily be taken on by an individual working outside of normal publishing circles. For this reason, the role of preservation and access has to be recognized as the initial responsibility of the creator of an electronic publication. This is a fundamental issue for cultural, collecting institutions as they will have limited opportunities to influence the products and standards selected to create digital objects and to influence the initial strategies for their management and access. It is the nature of digital objects that they can become inaccessible or lost in a very short time after their creation.

CHALLENGES IN ERM

In a digital library, how collections are developed and presented online affects whether, to what extent, and how it can be used. Challenges in ERM looks for initiatives that will help libraries:

- Build better, more useful, and more useable online collections and services.
- Gather and analyze information that reveal how and why library use is changing.
- Build user support services that are effective and appropriate in evolving online library environments.
- The ERMS need to consider licensing, rights management standards as well as administrative support.
- Licensing; Rights management standards.
- Administration, Access, and Support.

TYPES OF ERMS

Defining and understanding e-resource is a challenge in itself. An electronic book or an abstracting and indexing database; all are e-resources. An e-resource can also be a package of e-journals or a database of abstracts and indexes. It can include the full text of some or all articles referenced by the indexes. Some factors are specific to e-resources such as authentication, access, administration, usage, etc. The e-resources differ in the manner in which they are acquired, accessed and licensed. An ERM system needs to support the features associated with e-resources. It should provide the infrastructure for both the data and the workflows. The data and workflow are characteristic of e-resources. The system should provide the tools to manage e-resources throughout their life-cycle. At the same time, it should supply the data needed to make decisions about acquisitions, renewals and cancellations of e-resource subscriptions. Moreover, the ERM system must be extremely flexible and capable of supporting rapidly-changing business models.

1. Unified Resource Management (Type 1): General

- Integration of library managed repositories + external indexes into one new index
- Integration of user's environment
- One stop solution for e-resource management & delivery
  - User - search & access
  - Back room services and applications
- Acquisition model + annual maintenance

2. Unified Resource Management (Type 2) OpenERM

- Transforming library modules into institutional area within vendor's knowledgebase
- Integration of user's environment
- OpenERM -
  - Neutral
  - Any e-resource
  - Compliant with library local systems
  - Scalable solution
- Facilitate integration of the dis-integrated environment
- Low cost solution - technology & knowledgebase hosted and maintained by the vendor
- Subscription model
- Licensing model

FEATURES AND BENEFITS OF ERMS

The steps required for managing e-resources are more complex than those for print resources. Aprocess is consisted of selecting, ordering, cataloging and binding. It includes selecting, evaluating, approving, licensing, billing and registering access and is accompanied by a series of technical aspects, such as usability, performance, access technologies, public interfaces, troubleshooting and usage statistics. E-resource management is a time-intensive and iterative process, often requiring more staff with a greater skill set at each stage. As demand for e-resources grew, storing and managing administrative information in spreadsheets, paper files or email folders became increasingly cumbersome, and a more integrated solution was called for.

1. Title List Management

- An easy-to-use Title Wizard allows to take advantage of the extensive knowledge base to select titles by vendor or package, and also individual titles can be chosen to add to list
- Administrators can add or change titles in the list, decide what data is seen by end users (title names and links, or full details), without worrying about managing the underlying knowledge base themselves.
- Titles can be maintained from hundreds of different sources, including all major database vendors and e-journal providers, publisher e-journal and e-book packages, stand-alone e-journals and free online journals
- List can also include other titles submitted by the library, such as print journals.
- Downloading collection and select specific features to edit, tailoring list to almost any need
- Adding custom titles—including titles in a variety of language character sets

2. Full-featured platform for administration

- Administrators have secure access to a full-featured, easy-to use Admin site to control all their list's features.

- Adding custom logos, custom headers and footers, changing the display template (e.g., font, size and color of text) and more.
- Selecting the fields users want to display (ISSN, subject choose a default subject classification Congress or Medical).
- Setting a default language.
- Local notes and icons can be added. These can be controlled down to the resource-location level
- Customized notes and control where the notes display can also be added.
- Icons and symbols that can be used to convey information can be added to enhance the display. Text can be added to show when the user places the mouse over the icon, or make the icon clickable so the user is taken to a library-specified URL, or so that a pop-up window displays with a library-provided note.
- Valuable usage data, including overall usage (sessions, searches, link-outs) and use of each journal (link-outs by target), are captured for downloadable statistical reports.
- Provided as an alphabetical list on simple Web pages
- Keeps resources from being overlooked.

3. Proxy Support

- Open proxy servers may not be used to provide access to licensed e-resources by unauthorized users. Publishers and service providers who discover that open proxy servers are being used in this way may take action to block access, either to the individual IP address or the whole institutional domain.
- Multiple proxy servers can be designated. Such proxy servers can be assigned globally, to specific vendors or

to all packages from a vendor.

- Individual packages or publishers or to a specific e-journal only can be assigned.
- The system can be configured to use a backup proxy server if the main proxy server is not available, allowing the primary proxy server to be offline with minimal effect on end users.
- Easy setup when libraries purchase resources through a consortium and must have some resources use the consortium's proxy server and others use the institution's proxy server.

4. Browsing and Advanced Searching

- Find titles easily by browsing the alphabetical list or a list by subject
- Users can search by title, publisher, ISSN or all fields simultaneously, and control the search type.
- Provides a list of and links to database providers and journal hosting sites used by the library.
- Through partnership, federated search engine functionality may also be added.

Much of a librarian's ability to carry out necessary tasks is dependent upon personal experience. Moreover, the knowledge and experience gained from dealing with e-resources is often vested in too few people, a situation that leaves libraries exposed. Furthermore, providing meaningful metrics, such as detailed cost analyses and statistics on past performance and usage, remains problematic. Without such metrics, managers cannot make fully- informed decisions. With spending on e-collections increasing rapidly, a better solution is needed. For this purpose, required solutions are as following:

- Searcher Analyzer
- Journal Manager

- E-Book Manager
- Holdings Manager
- Knowledgebase

CONSOLIDATED USAGE STATISTICS MANAGEMENT SERVICE

The usage statistics supports future decision-making process. The consolidated Usage Statistics Management Service (USMS) includes facets such as accessed, total use by platform, average use by platform, most-and least-used journals and more. Usage data for e-journal and database products is included within scholarly statistics. Due to orderly scholarly statistics following benefits can be identified:

- Measuring the cost effectiveness of online content purchases
- Exploring usage at organization
- Understanding and analyzing trends in user behavior
- Identifying training issues
- Making budgeting decisions based upon real usage
- Demonstrating the value that online access provides to patrons.

NEED FOR ERMS

Various software and programs are now enabling libraries to manage a diverse collection of digital materials in one integrated system. The collection consists of open-access journals, electronic theses and dissertations, audio files and transcripts, maps, newspapers, photographs, manuscripts and rare books, and historical materials. These objects are a vital resource for members of the academic community. These tools have enabled libraries to build a strong digital collection using minimal staff resources. They allow doing extraordinary things with an extremely small staff. For example, the academic institution can upload students' theses and dissertations independently, streamlining the library staff's workload. Even more exciting are the opportunities that such solutions have opened up for collaboration with other institutions around the globe.

Researchers at distant place can deposit material directly into the system. Global relationships are one of the most important strategic initiatives for any university. Such systems give a real opportunity to develop and foster these relationships in the area of e-resources. Many libraries see potential for even greater use of such systems. Certain librarians might have the capability to write software in components that are external to existing systems but that work within the environment. The e-resources of libraries will grow in a number of ways, including increased publishing of open access journals and special collections that include medieval manuscripts. The commitment to ERM system is based on the significance that libraries place on digital collections.

IMPLEMENTING ERMS

There are many sources of information. Information sources are more varied than ever. It is very difficult for users to start from a suitable point. For a librarian, the single task does not lie in locating the right platform to initiate and help users in navigating the resources. The selection/ordering/ acquiring process is far more complex for electronic resources than for print sources. The methods for managing often include buying packages of titles or services, many with value-added features. Reviewing and negotiating proper terms for resources' licenses is a major aspect of the complexity. Additionally, new variables must be considered e.g., graphics, linking options, comparability with the corresponding print publication, web interface functionality, and other value-added features. This has met with limited success so far, but does have the advantage of educating publishers about the needs. The various requirements are as following:

1. Operational aspects : The functional requirements were developed from the definition of necessary functions of an ERM system. The result displays the information and workflows that an ERM system should integrate in the key areas of selection and acquisition, access provision, resource administration, user support and troubleshooting, renewal and retention. The result contained data elements new to ERM systems at that time, relevant to both users (e.g., license permissions and restrictions, resource availability) and staff (e.g., detailed license information, administrative IDs and passwords, usage statistics, training information). It also addresses problem-solving activities e.g., troubleshooting, vendor communications and business functions e.g., pricing models, renewal and termination information.

2. Visual representation : The entity-relationship diagram (ERD) is a visual representation of the major entities needed for managing electronic resources and the relationships between them. It is the basis for the database structure of an ERM system. At the heart of the ERD is the relationship of e-resources to licenses. The electronic product, which is an e-journal package or an article database, is a set of hierarchical relationships between the interface, the resources that use the interface and the child resources that are part of the product. License and access data relate to any level of that hierarchy. For example, the access information may relate to the entire interface or to an individual resource, while the license information may also relate to the entire interface as well as to each constituent product. The terms, governed by the license or acquisitions entity, define the number of simultaneous users, the various participating sites and the license permissions. They may have to be combined into prevailing terms to correspond to specific situations. While the ERD presents the relationships between the entities, the data element dictionary defines the system's data elements. The data structure document in turn links each data element with the entities and relationships represented in the ERD.

3. System Technology : Vendors like Innovative Interfaces and VTLS built their system as an integral part of their ILS platform. In the traditional integrated systems model, the ERM component is integrated directly with the ILS system. In other cases, application protocol interfaces mediate the integration with relevant ILS modules. User interfaces can be built for the Windows or browser environment, and the Web services technology allows integration across computer platforms. Non-integrated systems built by Ex Libris and Endeavour need to work in conjunction with their ILS systems or stand-alone products developed by different solution providers. ERM system comprised of a knowledge base, containing bibliographic, URL and holdings information.

4. Interpretability, Ambiguity, Adaptability : Usually it is found that licensing values are often kept open to a number of varying interpretations. ERMI has developed a value schema to take into account the entire range of permissions, explicit or not: Permitted (explicit), Prohibited (explicit), Permitted (interpreted), Prohibited (interpreted), Silent (uninterpreted), Not Applicable. It is noticeable that rights expression languages (RELs) only support two values which are Permitted (explicit) and Prohibited (interpreted). It is also believed that any new licensing language would have to accommodate a certain level of ambiguity. This system would require a novel encoding system. ERMI planned to develop an ERM language. This language is open enough to accept new trends and address the needs of all relevant communities. In participation with the joint National Information Standards Organization (NISO)/DLF/EDItEUR License Expression Working Group (LEWG), it seeks to develop a single standard to support internal library management. It will facilitate exchanges between publishers, libraries and various cultural communities. EDItEUR is the international group coordinating the development of electronic commerce in the books and serials sector. EDItEUR has become involved in the license expression work initiated by ERMI and is working on a license transmission standard that will be part of the ONIX (Online Information eXchange) for Serials format.

5. ERM System Interoperability : A long-term goal for e-resource management is ensuring interoperability between systems. Imported data could originate from several sources. This is concerned with acquisitions data from the library's serial vendor, XML-formatted license terms from publishers, and aggregator packages from e-journal management services, serial subscription and holdings data in the ONIX for Serials format from publishers. ERM system data describes downtimes or use restrictions. The same could be exported to the library's online public access catalog (OPAC), link-resolver menu or Web-based news blog.

ERM system developers look into integrating public interfaces providing information relevant to users. It should also concentrate to raise an open structure that can enable library staff to build their own interfaces, with the existing backend interfaces designed for staff use. It is not necessary that the MARC format is found incompatible with ER data. At other hand, XML-based standards represent the current trend in streamlining data exchange between ERM systems and OPACs. The library community is becoming familiar with the new format, and XML-based standards. There new formats and standards including like ONIX for Serials for presenting licensing rights and package level data, may prevail. Besides online resources, like e-journals, databases and e-books, ERM systems may also include print journals. Multiple instances of the same journal may not be managed efficiently by an OPAC especially in a consortial environment but in an ERM system. An ERM system can provide a single entry for all instances, because the knowledge base can integrate both the title level and package level data. Although library systems can provide reports of broken record links .The various companies like TDNet or SerialsSolutions update links as part of their journal management service. There solutions are best suited for facilitating URL verification. The staffing issues in the online age must cause a rift and shift in responsibilities. It should not result in loss of work, as e-resource management, in general, and ERM system implementation, is work-intensive processes.

Vendors plan to include overlap analysis and cost-per-use analysis into their ERM systems. This will also help the collection development. Integration with content modules, such as e resource registration processes, incident report mechanisms and license descriptions. Standardizing usage data collection is a major objective of the ERM industry. This practice has been represented by the Standardized Usage Statistics Harvesting Initiative (SUSHI), with the objective is to develop a standard for downloading COUNTER-compliant (Counting Online Usage of Networked Electronic Resources) usage statistics from vendor sites into ERM systems.

WHAT ERM SYSTEMS ADDRESS

Librarians have learned a great deal from the process. There is interest throughout the library sector in the potential benefits of separating or decoupling the search and retrieval interface layer from the database layer when presenting library resources. The problem ERM system looks to solve is the overwhelming evidence that users prefer other search, retrieval and delivery services over the library catalogue and subscribed institutional resources. The reasons for preferring search engines like Google include ease and speed of use, relevance-ranked results, few authentication challenges, and what can be described as the overall aesthetic experience.

Many people argue that a more up-to-date kind of system management is long overdue in Library catalogues and that Library Management System (LMS) suppliers ought to have provided such functionality as standard as their OPACs (Online Public Access Catalogues) have developed. The counter-argument contends that merely updating the interface is investing a great deal of effort in old technology. To do this well, it is worth investing in a new and flexible ERMS that can include resources and databases beyond the LMS. It addresses following aspects:

1. Relationships
   a. Packages and their constituent parts
   b. Knowing which resources share the same interface, license terms, business terms...
2. Information
   a. License permissions and constraints
   b. User IDs, passwords, administrative info
   c. Contacts for support and troubleshooting
   d. Cancellation restrictions, price caps, etc.
3. Workflows
   a. Mounting Trials
   b. Routing Licenses
   c. Placing Orders
   d. Implementing access
   e. Notifying relevant staff

Library ought to concentrate the efforts on making the resources visible within the wider network of search engines, union catalogues and open repositories. The idea is to concentrate on making the library's e-resources more visible in the wider network and then to funnel users back to the e-resources. As they attempt to maintain some control over their e-collections, librarians find themselves lost in a morass of spreadsheets and e-mail messages, and dealing with a variety of independent systems and data containers that are not integrated with each other. Too often librarians rely on their memory alone to co-ordinate systems such as the acquisition module of their integrated library system, their alphabetic lists of electronic journals and databases, a metasearch tool, and their local link server. The librarian's ability to carry out necessary tasks is dependent upon personal experience. The knowledge and experience gained from dealing with e-resources is often vested in too few people. It is a situation that leaves libraries exposed. It provides meaningful metrics, such as detailed cost analyses and statistics on past performance and usage, remains problematic. Without such metrics, managers cannot make fully- informed decisions. With spending on e-resources increasing rapidly, a better solution is needed.

REFERENCES

1. Grogg, Jill E. "Investing in digital: as electronic spending rises, ERAMS, ERM, and URM systems step in to help with acquisitions and reporting. (INFOTECH FEATURE) (electronic resource access and management services, electronic resource management system, unified resource management)." *Library Journal* 132.9 (May 15, 2007): 30(4).
2. Owens, Dodie. "Findability enable: the rise of the knowledgebase puts the ERMS on a new stage. " *Library Journal.* 131.13 (August 1, 2006): 30(3).
3. Electronic Resource Management: Report of the DLF ERM Initiative. *http://www.diglib.org/pubs/dlf102/dlfermi0408.pdf*
4. *Bulletin*, August/September 2006 Recent Developments in Electronic Resource Management in Libraries by Rafal Kasprowski. Available at *http://www.asis.org/bulletin.html*

5. Duranceau, E.F. & Hepfer, C. (2002). "Staffing for Electronic Resource Management: The Results of a Survey," *Serials Review*, vol. 28, no. 4: 316-320.

6. Duranceau, E.F. (2004). "Electronic Resource Management Systems From ILS Vendors,"*Against the Grain*, vol. 16, no. 4: 91-94.

7. Grahame, V. & McAdam, T. (2004). *Managing Electronic Resources*. Washington, DC: Association of Research Libraries

8. Medeiros, N. (2003). "A Pioneering Spirit: Using Administrative Metadata to Manage Electronic Resources," *OCLC Systems and Services*, vol. 19, no. 3: 86-88.

9. White, G. W. and Crawford, G. A. "Cost-Benefit Analysis of Electronic Information: A Case Study." *College and Research Libraries*, 59:6 (November 1998): 503-10.

10. Hawbaker, A. C. and Wagner, C. K. "Periodical Ownership Versus Full-text Online Access: A Cost-Benefit Analysis." *Journal of Academic Librarianship*, 22:2 (March 1996): 105-9.

11. eLib: The Electronic Libraries Programme. <*http://www.ukoln.ac.uk/services/elib/*>.

12. Evaluation of the Electronic Libraries Programme: Guidelines for eLib Project Evaluation. <*http://www.ukoln.ac.uk/services/elib/papers/tavistock/evaluation-guide/intro.html*>

13. JSTOR: The Need. <*http://www.jstor.org/about/need.html*>.

14. Odlyzko, A. M. "Competition and Cooperation: Libraries and Publishers in the Transition to Competition Electronic Scholarly Journals." *Journal of Electronic Publishing*, 4(4) (June 1999): 163-85.

15. (ARL) Association of Research Libraries, Statistics and Measurement Program. 10<*http://www.arl.org/stats/index.html*>.

16. Tenopir, C. and King, D. W. "Towards Electronic Journals: Realities for Scientists, Librarians, and Publishers."

Washington, DC : Special Libraries Association, 2000, p. 216.

17. Fox, B. L. "Library Buildings 1999: Structural Ergonomics." *Library Journal*, 124:20 (December 1999) 57-67.

18. Montgomery, C and Sparks, J. "Framework for Assessing the Impact of an Electronic Journal Collection on Library Costs and Staffing Patterns." *<http://www.si.umich.edu/PEAK-2000/montgomery.pdf>*

19. Blieler, R. and Plum, T. *Networked Information Resources*. SPEC Kit 253. Washington, DC. Association of Research Libraries. December, 1999.

20. Mercer, L. S. "Measuring the Use and Value of Electronic Journals and Books. *Issues in Science and Technology Librarianship*, Winter 2000. *<http://www.library. ucsb.edu/istl/00-winter/article1.html>*.

21. Shemberg, M. and Grossman, C. "Electronic Journals in Academic Libraries." A comparison of ARL and Non-ARL Libraries. *Library Hi Tech*, 17 (November 1, 1999): 26-45.

22. Abels, E. G., Kantor, P. B., and Saracevic, T. "Studying the Costs and Value of Library and Information Services: Applying Functional Cost Analysis to the Library In Transition." *Journal of the American Society for Information Science*, 47 (March 1996):217-27.

4

Library Web Content Management

CONTENT MANAGEMENT

Content management (CM) can be defined as a process of collecting, organizing, categorizing, and structuring the informational resources of any type and format so that they can be saved, retrieved, published, updated, and repurposed or reused in any way desirable. Today's content management solution is either a sophisticated software-based system or a database-driven application. A full-featured content management system "takes content from inception to publication and does so in a way that provides for maximum content accessibility and reuse and easy, timely, accurate maintenance of the content base". Theoretically, content management encompasses a broad spectrum of areas such as document management (DM), knowledge management (KM), records management (RM), and electronic content management (ECM), financial content management (FCM), and Web content management (WCM). Web content management is one of the branches of content management. Content management gained importance during the explosion of Web sites in the mid-1990s. The value of published material goes beyond its finished physical form, and the true added value of content becomes evident "if it can be re-purposed continually and profitably".

CONTENT MANAGEMENT SYSTEM

A **content management system** (CMS) also known as document management system (DMS) is a computer application used to manage work flow needed to collaboratively create, edit, review, index, search, publish and archive various kinds of digital media and electronic text. CMS are frequently used for storing, controlling, versioning, and publishing industry-specific documentation such as news articles, operators' manuals, technical manuals, sales guides, and marketing brochures. The content may include computer files, image media, audio files, video files, electronic documents, and Web content. These concepts represent integrated and interdependent layers. There are various nomenclatures known in this area such as Web Content Management, Digital Asset Management, Digital Records Management, and Electronic Content Management and so on.

DESCRIPTION OF A CMS

While describing, it can be said that a Content Management System (CMS) makes it easy for non-technical contributors to maintain and expand their website. A CMS uses software and a database to manage and organize website content. Once a visitor makes a request to the website, the CMS selects the correct content and displays it in a custom interface template. This system enables to manage large amounts of content from multiple authors. Further describing in a layman's terms, it can be said that Content Management Systems come in all shapes and sizes. Organizations observed that this could be useful within their environment. For example if a particular department needs to get a piece of information up on the Web site, often it has to follow numerous steps:

1. Write the piece of information and get it approved
2. Send the piece of information out on the wire
3. Send the piece of information to the Web group
4. The Web group then converts the document to HTML and puts it on the Web site
5. Most larger companies have some sort of staging server where Web documents sit until they are pushed live
6. If a piece of information has sensitive information, it can't be released to the Web group until it has been sent to the wire, but often upper management wants it on the Web site immediately

This situation causes a lot of stress for both the Web group and the staff. It would be a lot easier if the staff could post the release to the Web at the same time that they post it to the wire services. *But*, often staff does not know HTML or don't have access to the Web site. This is where a content management system comes into play.

KEY PROCESSES IN CMS

Meaning of Content Management depends on whom the organization is referring to. The key elements and processes in web content management are given as following:

Content Management divides logically into three areas:

- Content creation and contribution
- Content management and administration
- Content publishing and serving

The meaning of the terms is reasonably self-evident. Each of them encompasses a number of processes; typically they include the items shown below. The actual processes provided by a solution vary from system to system.

Creation and Contribution	*Management and Administration*	*Publishing and Serving*
• Page creation and editing	• Template creation	• Text entry
• Image creation	• Style sheet creation & editing	• Submission for approval
• Content properties & attributes	• Meta data	• Live date and expiry
• Personalisation attributes	• Product attributes	• Marketing attributes
• End user access permissions	• Content approval	• Properties approval
• Content workflow	• Security, roles assignment, editing permissions	• Versioning, archiving and backup
• Content output to final media		
• Publishing to production server		
• Search capability		
• Personalisation		
• Replication		
• Syndication		
• Load balancing		
• Caching and acceleration		

The boundaries between these areas are not always rigidly fixed. These may be further modified and edited by someone in an administrative or approval role. In response to the need for content management solutions, there has been tremendous in growth,in number of products in the industry. Some of these are based on existing document management products while others have grown out of web editing tools. Most of these have come from a code management and software version control background.

Only few of these products cover every aspect of content management as defined above. For example, quite a number have limited authoring capability, making use instead of third party creation tools such as Macromedia Dreamweaver®, or Microsoft Office® programmes for content design and creation. Load balancing and cache acceleration are also outside of the scope of most content management products. All of them, to varying extents, offer the management and administration functions, which are essential to ensuring accuracy of information and site coherence. The CMS toolset consists of a number of interlocking components, which together provide the foundation blocks for building a web site from the ground up. These components are as following:

- **Editor** - the primary tool for content contribution and editing
- **Manager** - the suite of management and administration functions
- **Server** - a set of components including client and server side applications that provide specific site functionality.

Between them these components cover all aspects of the content life cycle. They are defined as: ***design; create; manage; and deploy.***

FEATURES OF CMS

A CMS may support the following features:

- Identification of all key users and their content management roles.
- The ability to assign roles and responsibilities to different content categories or types.
- Definition of workflow tasks for collaborative creation, often coupled with event messaging so that content managers are alerted to changes in content.

- The ability to track and manage multiple versions of a single instance of content.
- The ability to capture content (e.g., scanning).
- The ability to publish the content to a repository to support access to the content. (Increasingly, the repository is an inherent part of the system, and incorporates enterprise search and retrieval.)

Given below is the tabular presentation of interrelated aspects of CMS:

Design	
Template management	Allows the creation and re-use of html templates.
Navigation Management	Dynamic navigation generation.
Publishing	
Content publication page	A function for displaying information with the option of formatting text, images, links, etc.
Multi language pages	A function for working with several languages on the web site, where the information is stored in the same location, regardless of the language.
News	
News listings	A function for listing information from organization's own website or another website by transferring RSS data.
RSS source	A function for publishing information in RSS format.
Forms	
Forms	A function in which one can easily create various types of forms using a form editor. Visitors fill in the form and information is sent by e-mail to a specified address. This is for form design and email of data only. To create analyzable databases we have to build custom module.
Feedback	Visitors fill in the form and information is sent by e-mail to a specified address. The data is held in a database.

Request management / Phone me	A form that sends data to specified email addresses; data is also held in an analyzable database.
Survey/Poll	A function in which visitors can vote for the answer to a question on the site and then view a summary of how others have voted.
Search	
Site Search	A function for visitors to search the content of the website. Searches can also be made in documents using advanced search options. Records and enumerates searches made on site
Personalization	
Registration	A function in which it is possible to store information about individuals and allow access to restricted areas. Registrants can update their own information. Profiles may be searched. A login routine may be added and lost password retrieval
Communications	
Newsgroups / Discussion forum	A function in which visitors can discuss different topics in various newsgroups with or without a threaded discussion.
File upload and download	A function by which system administrator can upload documents, list them, and allow visitors to download them. It can also be used as picture gallery or a press centre.
General	
Calendar	A function that shows the events of one or more days in a calendar.
Document list	A back office function that displays all new and updated pages.
Alphabetical contents	A function that displays the content of the website in alphabetical order.
Flash viewer	A function that allows uploading of flash files.
Sitemap	A function that displays the content of a

website in the form of a map with links to all pages. Automated XML maps fed to Google.

ELEMENTS OF CMS

There are two fundamental elements to content management:

1. Storing stuff in a *content repository*, and
2. Supporting the workflow of a group of people engaged in putting stuff into that repository.

NEED OF CMS

A Content Management System is a Web application that makes content authoring and delivery easy. It enables users to quickly and efficiently build, deploy, and maintain content-rich web sites by streamlining the web publishing process. Content Management Systems can reduce the need for costly site maintenance and thus empowering users to manage their own content.

- **Do-it-yourself :** For clients those prefer to update and maintain their site themselves, a web content management system is the ideal solution.
- **No knowledge of web design needed :** Having a content management system ensures that the design of organization's website remains unchanged and the content can be updated without the need for programming or HTML knowledge. A Content Management System facilitates everyone with little or no experience in web design to update and maintain their own site. This is achieved through any computer connected to the Internet and without the need for additional client software.
- **Centralized location :** By using a Content Management System the organization can provide employees with a central location to provide and access up-to-date,

accurate information and applications. This surely results in increased employee productivity which is critical to achieving the most streamlined business processes.

CMS understands that organization wants control over organization's website. CMS provide with the administrative tools needed to maintain organization's own content. Using these content management system/administrative tools, updating content items such as press releases, news, copy changes and price changes may be made easy and cost free.

With the above do-it-yourself option, organization can manage the contents of organization's website on organization's own. Content Management System can then act as web design & development organisation to take care of bigger changes such as linking or re-setup the navigation, aesthetic changes or application enhancement

TYPES OF CMS

There are four main categories of CMS, with their respective domains of use:

- Enterprise CMS (ECMS)
- Web CMS (WCMS)
- Document management system (DMS)
- Mobile CMS

1. Enterprise content management systems

An enterprise content management (ECM) system is concerned with content, documents, details and records related to the processes of an enterprise. The purpose is to manage the organization's unstructured information content, with all its diversity of format and location.

2. Web content management systems

A **'web content management'** (WCM) system is a CMS designed to simplify the publication of Web content to Web sites, in particular allowing content creators to submit content without requiring technical knowledge of HTML or the uploading of files.

SCOPE OF WEB CONTENT MANAGEMENT

The scope of WCM includes combinations of WCM systems and WCM tools or applications. A fully featured WCM system includes the process from content inception to publication, in a system that allows Web administrators to streamline workflows and to enable all content contributors to easily edit, update, and publish Web content without in-depth knowledge of HTML. Many libraries have utilized WCM applications to create or maintain portions of their Web content, such as subject guides or bibliographies, online electronic resource lists, and library personnel rosters.

Boiko (2001) categorizes Web content management systems, into four levels:

i. **Nominal WCM systems** are those tools like Microsoft's Notepad, FrontPage, and Macromedia Dreamweaver. These tools provide basic web management mechanisms such as page templates to all authors to create standard page layouts across a Web site, site outlines and link managers to verify that all links are working properly, and a publication manager that allows Web managers to upload newly created or modified pages to Web servers. These tools are suited for creating and managing small and single Web sites.

ii. Database-driven or dynamic Web sites, in a strict technical sense, are not WCM systems, but are rather Web-based applications. A dynamic Web site is a "system for producing Web pages 'on the fly' as users request them". Usually, the application contains a data source stored on a Web server. The data source can be built using a relational database, or XML structure, or a structure constructed by other scripting languages, such as JavaScript. There is a template page that connects the data source and the user, and there are HTML codes and programming scripts or objects in the template page that can interpret the user's request, activate the data source, and send appropriate content to the user's Web browser as an HTML page. Dynamic Web sites and WCM systems both have databases to process content.

iii. Full WCM systems function throughout the process from content collection to publication, and manage content contributors and workflow. A full WCM system contains a relational database serving as a repository of all types of content, from text, HTML files, and graphics, to style sheets; a live data source generated by the WCM system for the dynamic parts of a Web site; and many HTML files managed by the WCM system for the static parts of a site.

iv. Enterprise CM systems encompass the entire content creation and management for the organization, not just the Web site. A full picture of a Web content management system contains a complex mix of technologies, repositories, processes, and quality control, all of which need to work together. Technically, integration across these areas is a key for a successful implementation of Web content management. Many WCM systems offer advanced content management features such as version control, editorial sign-offs, and live date or time control. A WCM system can also set up controls to determine who approves certain pages before they are published live. Successful Web content management should contribute to a user-centered Web site for the user and streamlined workflow for internal Web developers.

Content Management Software

- Joomla Customization
- Drupal
- Mambo

- Custom CMS Development

Need of Content Management

Exploiting the Web is an essential element of any strategy for extending organization's business, growing market and gaining competitive advantage. The Web brings organization closer to organization's markets, but creates transparency that quickly reveals poor service. Users are demanding more access to information and they expect it now. Traditional Web technologies inhibit this intimacy. They create distance for service providers from web site content because their use depends upon some technical expertise. They sometime, generate web sites with limited capabilities that are costly to deploy and maintain. CMS gives control of content to the experts. It ensures fast, consistent, accurate and efficient publication of organization's intellectual assets and business processes on the Web. It delivers benefits that generate substantial cost savings.

Advantages of CMS

1. Separation of design, structure, and content : The division of these three layers allows many advantages throughout the life cycle of the website. Each area of the site can be recreated and adjusted independent of the other areas. The design layer can be completely reworked for a new user interface without the need for any adjustments to structure or content. The structure can be adjusted for additional functionality with no changes required to design and content. Content can be changed with no need to adjust the front-end design or functional structure. The separation of these three areas creates the flexible strength of a content management system.

2. Content production without programming or design experience : A Content Management System allows the editor to interact with the site in several ways. It provides a graphical user interface that allows the editor to create content, add images and multimedia files, create content schedules, and much more.

Other Common advantages of a CMS:

- Decentralized maintenance. It is based on a common web browser. Editing anywhere, anytime removes bottlenecks.
- Designed with non-technical content authors in mind. People with average knowledge of word processing can create the content directly. No HTML knowledge needed.
- Configurable access restrictions. Users are assigned roles and permissions that prevent them from editing content which they are not authorized to change.
- Consistency of design is preserved. Because content is stored separate from design, the content from all authors is presented with the same, consistent design.
- Navigation is automatically generated and adjusted. Menus are typically generated automatically based on the database content and links will not point to non-existing pages.
- Content is stored in a database. Central storage means that content can be reused in many places on the website and formatted for any device (web browser, mobile phone/WAP, PDA, print).
- Dynamic content. Extensions like forums, polls; shopping applications, searching, and news management are typically modules.
- Cooperation. It encourages faster updates, generates accountability for authored content (logs) and cooperation between authors.
- Content scheduling. Content publication can often be time-controlled, hidden for later use or require user login with password.

WEB PUBLISHING CMS

A **Web Publishing System** (CMS for Web publishing) is a combination of large database, file system, and other related software modules which are used to store and later retrieve huge amounts of data. These web publishing systems are different from the databases in the sense that these can index text, audio clips, video clips, or images in a database. Users of the web publishing system can find relevant content from within a database by searching for keywords, authors, date of creation, etc. Web Content Management Systems can be used to create information portals serving as the backbone of data management. The software modules also allow anyone to contribute information to a website via a graphical user interface (GUI). They are usually based on a pre-written template that acts as a platform for each page in the site as those pages are created.

At the organization level, CMS store and manage an organization's electronic document and web content so that the employee of the company can reuse the information across different applications. The web published content can also be distributed to users and partners outside the organization. The core application of the CMS is to manage content during its entire lifecycle i.e. from creation through publishing. Web publishing system enables organization to establish a consistent look and feel throughout organization's site, and gives organization's non-technical content authors the power to publish and update the own content using simple, yet powerful, browser-based tools. Some of the CMS systems integrate with content delivery applications to deliver the content via a web site.

There are three basic participants in the web publishing CMS system:

- Content Editors (Decide what content to publish and where)

- Content Publishers (Publish the content on the web)
- Content Authors (Create the content for the web)

A Web Publishing CMS allows non-technical authors and editors to easily and quickly publish their content which is otherwise done by technical programmers. It establishes defined publishing processes and specific publishing rights to various individuals. By using these facilities, the organization can save the time for training, while facilitating more people to publish. It also reduces the daily stream of calls to the IT department for changes to the website. It time-to-publish, allowing organization to get content published faster.

This can be characterized as:

- Simple pages for normal presentation
- Complex pages, with specific layout and presentation
- Dynamic information sourced from databases and will change on regular time intervals
- Training material
- Online manual
- Thousands of pages in total for different categories of users
- Extensive linking between pages

CONTENT MANAGEMENT SYSTEM BENEFITS

If someone is planning to build a site that contains hundreds of pages, needs constant updating without needing to upload web pages to organization's web host, he should consider using a content management system or CMS. If not having HTML or other relevant language skills in the organization, one should consider deploying a content management system. With a content management system, organization does not require the skill of a skilled programmer to write organization's contents. Using the content management functionalities of the content management system, organization can easily manage creation, modification, and removal of contents from a Web site, without any knowledge of HTML language, while the content delivery application of the management system would compile the information and update it to organization's website. The features of a content management system varies, but generally includes, Web-based publishing, format management, revision control, indexing, search, and retrieval.

A content management system does wonders to organization's work and performance, by helping organization to easily manage organization's website information. The information in organization's website is its asset and needs to be managed. Keeping the contents updated is the only way organization can put its services at the forefront of organization's competitors. These contents need inevitable changes, and the CMS allows to manage these contents with perfect ease. Without a CMS and with none of the relevant skills available in organization, the website would surely but steadily erode the business prospects.

A content management system provides effective media for managing the informative content, results in the management of the information content, which in turn generates generous return. The use of a content management system lowers the operating costs, there-by increasing the profits. The key benefits, achieved through the deployment of a suitable content management system, and weighed against organization's investments, may be considered as follows:

1. **Easier and rapid magnet :** The content management system renders easier and rapid management of organization's website information.
2. It allows organization to create, edit, and publish the

contents on a website, without any technical programming skill what-so-ever.

3. It has a direct positive implication on cost saving in organization's operation.
4. It allows organization to set up a discipline amongst the individuals, responsible for each management activity of the system, and the departments responsible for disseminating the necessary information required for management of the contents.
5. The process automates the management of website, with proper check-points, and expedites the delivery of the newly created or edited content information to organization's website, intranet, and extranet.
6. It makes the management of such sites more effective and efficient, changing the way organization interacts externally with organization's users.
7. It is necessary that organization maintain the accountability of the system that organizations are managing. It allows organization to track the changes that organization are making and maintain a log of work history.
8. This enables organization to identify which specific content has been changed, and review the history at times to look at the specific concerned pages that have been changed.
9. **Managing work flow :** Organization can manage organization's work-flow through the inherent intelligent feature of such a management system. The process of internal messaging and tracking ensures a smooth work-flow process, which provides constant review and control of the management system in place.

BRANDING

Organization will need to manage consistency through out the design of website and controlling the branding. A CMS allows organization to maintain such a consistency through out Webpage, maintaining it to a desired level. This can be done regardless as to who is responsible for the management of the actual content. Organization's website gets a more professional outlook thus, provideing confidence to the clients.

CREATING AND RE-USING THE CONTENT

A content management system allows organization to create a content once, which can be re-used many times. This facility provides the opportunity to deliver the same content to multiple locations in various presentation formats and multiple languages.

1. Update information

It is very important to know whether the organizations are being able to keep pace with competition. CMS makes it easy to keep website updated through effective management of contents, enabling the partners, customers, and employees to find the correct information at any point of time. The search engines require the website to maintain consistency, in order to find relevant contents in organization's website rapidly and effectively. A CMS manages the required consistency all through organization's website pages, making it search-engine friendly and providing a better visibility. It is entirely undesirable to have an ad hoc development of any website, having a manual editing feature, as associated with traditional static websites. This results in confused appearance of the site, in its appearance and navigation. Such designs inevitably lead to dilution of corporate image and branding, and require extreme supervision and control.

2. Consistent design philosophy and uniformity

A content management system provides a way to establish consistent design philosophy and maintains uniformity in maintaining corporate branding and its identity. As one of the most important features, a content management system allows templates to be designed once, to be re-used through out. This maintains the consistency of the webpages. This make it far easier to implement and cost effective, allowing the information to be presented in a suitable manner.

Here are the benefits of a content management system:

1. **A CMS web site is database driven :** This allows organization to create and store hundreds or thousands of pages in the database without the need to update each one of them.

2. **Separate design and content :** The design of the site template is separate from the content. This allows organization to change the design any time without affecting the content stored on the site.

3. **Cascading style sheet (CSS) to control site appearance :** Altering one CSS file will allow organization to change the design and/or color of organization's CMS site. The consistency of the design can be preserved.

4. **Multiple authors :** If organization has different authors that wish to contribute to organization's CMS web site organization can set up multiple user access in the administration panel. They can just login and begin adding their content.

5. **Access from anywhere :** Authors and editors can access the site from any computer with an internet connection. This means users can update the site at the same time from any location in the world.

6. **Web site management panel :** The backend

administration panel not only provides the ability to add content but also to add modules such as polls, banners, forums, shopping applications, news management and menus. Authors can be given limited permissions to prevent them from editing content which they are not authorized to change.

7. Schedule content updates : Publishing content can be controlled by creating a draft first then publishing it later. This is handy if organization needs to coordinate content from multiple authors.

8. HTML knowledge not required : A CMS site allows non-technical people to add content. They just need to login with a user name and password then use the web editor that's built into the CMS to add their content.

9. Saves time : If organization was using a static site to add content from multiple authors, each author would have to download the pages from the server to their computer first, update them, and then upload them back to the server. This would be very time consuming and could generate a lot of errors.

10. Create search engine friendly pages : The separation of content from design allows organization to easily include keywords in the URL of each page.

Some CMS sites automatically generate the correct meta tags for each web page which would help them to spidered by the search engines.

11. Attracts visitors : A CMS site attracts visitors because it can be constantly and rapidly updated. It not only generates pages that are search engine friendly but can produce lots of links from the new content that is added and syndicated.

12. Create automatic RSS Feeds : RSS or really simple syndication is integrated automatically into many CMS sites. Every time organization creates a post or makes a comment it creates a feed for it. This allows visitors with RSS Feeders to read the post at their own leisure. Thus we can say that a content management system is a powerful tool for organisations that want to present lots of content from multiple authors and gain lots of visitors.

Some important facets of CMS:

A. **CD Presentation Copywriting :** Today, most businesses and professional across the globe have identified and opted for advanced and interactive CD presentations as the absolute medium to market their products and ideas.

Tagline Creation : Admittedly, taglines are still considered to be the shining star that guides and influences the behavior, company allegiance and product preference of organization's consumers.

B. **Mailer And Flyer Copywriting :** Mailers and flyers have been an integral part of direct mailing advertising campaigns since the ancient times.

C. **Copy Editing :** The job of a copy editor is no easy task. Not only are web copy editors responsible for delivering cleverly knit and grammatically correct web manuscripts, but are also accountable for providing professional articles that are devoid of syntax errors or typos.

D. **Ad Copywriting for Pay Per Click Advertisers:** In order to be able to acquire maximum return on investments from organization's expensive pay per click (PPC) campaigns, it is essential that organization's advertisements are able to get a high number of clicks than organization wish to target!

E. **The significance of brief website content that is artistically and attractively knit :** Writing web content for an Online audience is very different from writing for a traditional print publication like a newspaper or a magazine.

F. **Writing Web site content that lures visitors :** The phrase "Content is the king," is true though when organization take a look at some of the web content, there is little to justify the quality.

G. **Printer Friendly Web Pages :** With most web users preferring to take prints of the pages they read, the importance of creating printer friendly web pages is being recognized.

MANAGING WEBSITE WITH THE HELP OF A CONTENT MANAGEMENT SOFTWARE

The websites created in the initial years of Internet were static in nature. This means the websites once created & uploaded on the Internet could not be changed. With time Internet grew to become an essential requirement for business development, information, advertising & entertainment. This generated the need for websites to be constantly updated to provide the latest information on business schemes, news, reviews etc. Also static websites composed of simple web pages provided limited information. The entire website had to be browsed in case of searching for something specific. People wanted websites to be more concise and informative at the same time.

Problem with Upgrading Websites

- Either the website required special software to be upgraded or the platform on which it was built was obsolete. Due to this the site owners either had to launch a new website or spend big amounts of money on software and technical expertise. This was a slow and tedious process.
- Launching a new website meant more pages to be added and more research work and structuring of the

website was a time consuming job.

- The site owners also had to rely upon the availability of software and software engineers.

Content Management Software or the ***CMS solution*** provides the optimum solution to this problem. This web based CMS is used for creating, changing, editing or even updating websites with ease. Websites designed nowadays comprise of different types of content. This content can be defined as graphics, text or audio visual elements. A CMS solution is an effective ***Content Management Tool*** that arranges content in particularly organized manner automatically. This is an easy to understand application which can be operated by anyone with just a little understanding of computers.

This ***Web Based CMS*** gives the control of the websites back into the hands of their owners. Because of its easy operational features :

- Website owners can themselves update their websites at their own leisure with the help of a CMS solution.
- Websites designed on any given software can be edited, changed or updated through CM Software.
- Websites can store large amounts of data with the help of a Web based CMS.
- A Content Management Software provides quicker and more accurate access to the websites.
- A Content Management Tool saves valuable time and money on maintenance and upgrading.

These are just a few of the beneficial features that a Content Management Software provides. By using CMS there are a whole lot of other benefits that come into picture.

For maintaining websites, CMS is the most robust, effective and economical choice. A CMS solution provides features and benefits that have changed the face of the modern day websites. From being simple webpages containing only text, to dynamic websites that can display graphics, store data, hide specific content, update menus automatically, add additional pages and a lot more. Quick editing or upgrading of websites increases the scope of opportunities in various different fields.

REASONS FOR CHOOSING CONTENT MANAGEMENT SOFTWARE

Content Management Software is a revolutionary breakthrough in the field of web designing. With CMS, content management on a website has become far more convenient. This system enables the web owners to make changes on their websites faster and more often compared to other options of website editing.

How CMS scores over its counterparts

With CMS, Content on a website is no longer of static nature. Though, there are a number of alternatives available that can modify or change a websites outlook, but a CMS proves to be the best in its class.

Benefits of Content Management Software:

A Convenient Application : A Content Management Software is easy to use as it does not require its user to be a technical expert. This allows the website owners to edit their websites without the help of a web designer.

Faster Upgrading : With the constraint of relying upon technical assistance removed, web owners can upgrade or modify their websites at will. The best part of a Content Management Software is that the websites can even be upgraded online. With the help of a CMS, without disabling the site, the upgraded content can be displayed in a matter of minutes.

Dynamic Websites : A Content Management Software changes the basic structure of a website. Unlike static webpages, websites can now store large amounts of data, interact with other websites and update accordingly, display all sort of animated, audio or video content.

Enhances Accessibility : *CMS* can store all content of a website in text form. This proves beneficial as any text typed on a search engine can quickly relate to the website's content. Thereby, it increases the accessibility to the website.

Restricted Editing : On a CMS based website anyone can modify the content. In a professional website, CMS can restrict access for editing.

Auto Upgrading : A CMS content based website can be used as a forum. Here data can be added in specific fields which automatically adds a new page to the website and even updates the menu on the home page.

Timing Feature : With CMS, websites can be programmed to store and hide content to be displayed later. This hidden content is automatically displayed on the website on a pre-specified time & date.

Customized Content Display : With CMS professional websites can be programmed with a 'login' feature. Upon login the website identifies the user and accordingly displays the content relevant to the user.

Internal Site Search : Content Management Software provides an internal search mechanism. This mechanism pulls out any specific information on the website without having to browse it completely.

Website Creation : CMS is used for creating websites. Because of its user friendly features dynamic websites can be created by using standard office applications.

These are only a few basic features of a standard **Content Management Software.** Various other advanced and beneficial features of a CMS make it economically viable and the most effective solution to almost all web related problems.

ORGANIZATIONAL CULTURE AND ACCEPTANCE

Many issues are associated with the move to WCM solutions. These include acceptance of changes, decisions on the allocation of personnel, equipment, assignments and tasks. Boiko (2002) suggests asking the following questions when making strategic changes to the Web using a WCM solution:

- Does the staff accept the idea of very organized and constrained processes with known tasks and times?
- How can organization maintain people's sense of independence and creativity within these defined cycles?
- How does organization recognize that someone doesn't accept the basic premise of workflow?

In library, librarians created different names for the same categories of materials, and it was a tremendous effort to get librarians to negotiate on the terms used for metadata. The way the old HTML subject guides were organized and presented, to some extent, reflected the library's organizational culture-people acted along this situation and indicates that these technical solutions demand a fair amount of compromise in terms of creativity. In many libraries where individuals, not teams, drive the content development process and creativities are most highly rewarded, these technical solutions do not seem feasible. Library staff buy-in and administrative support are key elements in project success. Either database-driven applications or a WCM system can consume significant staff resources, may require a substantial financial investment in the short run, and involve ongoing support in the long run. Westman suggests a number of questions about implementing a WCM solution:

- What will be the benefit of the project? Answers can include saving time, providing better access to information, or allowing for more efficient workflow.
- What will be costs in terms of money and staff time?
- Can it be done with the existing infrastructure, hardware, and software?
- What is the timeframe for its implementation?
- How much time and effort will it take to maintain this application?
- How much data inputting and updating will be involved?

Answers to these questions should help raise staff awareness and obtain the understanding and support.

DYNAMIC WEBSITES

If organizations are still living in the boring genre of static websites, then it is about time that organization should opt for dynamic websites. Dynamic websites are the word of the day.

Benefits Using Dynamic Websites

- If organizations wish to show the added or updated data feed of organization's products with the latest range that organization offer, then a dynamic website design would support all organization's requirements.
- Dynamic website development also allows organization to change the layout of web pages on a frequent basis.
- A dynamic flash website would also give authority to create webpage automatically.
- A dynamic web site can be the best solution for organization in case organization wishes to manipulate the data stored in the database.
- The CSS layout of dynamic web pages can also equip organization to make changes only once and the order

would follow sequentially in all the other web pages corresponding to that specific CSS.

- The dynamic webpage structure is extremely user friendly, enabling organization to customize organization's website at the own directions whenever organization want.
- Dynamically created websites would help to save on invaluable time and effort in building and maintaining a website.
- Dynamic web design provides the power to change the design and content anytime organization so desire.
- Dynamic websites provide increased user interactivity.
- A dynamic flash website provides the user with a better experience and enjoyable stay, making them enjoy every moment they stay on the web page.
- The availability of various search criteria makes dynamic websites a better choice.
- A dynamic site accompanies a control panel that would aid organization in keeping track of the visitor traffic for analysis of organization's web pages, edit/delete/ add content, images, products, tabs or any other feature that organization wish to add to organization's website

USER CENTERED DESIGNS

User centered designs (U C D) refers to an approach of design where the processing of information is focused on the users who will use the said product. Through phases comprising planning, design and development, a product is finally produced because of adopting the user centered design approach.

Designing User Centered Designs with the User Centered Design approach

Asking Questions : This is one of the most vital

elements of user centered web design. By using this approach, one needs to ask questions about the users, their tasks and goals, and conclude as to how these findings can be used to drive development with design. The following basic questions are integral to user centered design. Some basic questions relating to user centered web design are as follows:

- Who are the users?
- What are the tasks and goals of the users?
- How have the users' experience levels been with this product?
- What functions do the users expect or require from this product?
- What kind of information would the users find useful?
- How can the user centered design propel the development of the users' cognitive processes?

Useful and Usable : All user centered design must essentially be useful and usable. Usefulness implies that the user must be able to relate to the relevance, carry forward with the functions and utilize this information. Usability, on the other hand, refers to the ease of use for a user.

Reducing Memory Load : User centered design techniques should reduce the user memory load. To make users recognize rather than memorize or remember, it is important for screen elements to be meaningful and consistent.

Information Accessibility : User centered design techniques should help the users find information quickly and easily by providing information in small nuggets rather than in loads. Another good option is to provide clues so that users can find information by scanning instead of reading.

Easy Navigation : User centered designs should provide easy navigation experience. The links should be descriptive in a way that lets users understand what to expect when they click the link. The pages should also have visible elements to let a user know what page they are visiting, how it is related to the concept they want to know more about and how to get to other related pages.

Text Legibility : The text should be easy to read. Ornamental fonts may be strictly avoided. Italics are also a strain to read, so it is best to avoid the use of italics.

Language : Last but not least, to ensure clarity, it is best to use short sentences, active voice and active verbs along with simple, easy to understand sentence structures.

PHP IN WEB DEVELOPMENT

Originally designed by Rasmus Lerdorf, Personal Home Pages or **PHP** is a parsing language that runs on Linux and Unix servers, making it a popular choice for web developers. PHP is in fact, one of the most popularly used languages for web development as well as web application development. Here's why:

Perfect Database Interaction : PHP is an excellent language choice when it comes to building dynamic websites that interact with databases, as it can exchange all sorts of information with ease.

Cost : Another reason why PHP website development and web development is admired by developers is that PHP programs run on Linux, which is free. Also, the database connectivity is less expensive as compared to that of other programs such as ASP which is based on MSSQL, a Microsoft product that needs to be purchased. However, web development with PHP through MySQL is free to use.

Incredible Speed : PHP has an upper hand when it comes to speed. This is mainly because; the PHP code runs faster as it runs in its own memory space.

How is PHP used in Web Development?

PHP is used in following manner:

- For starters, the server side scripting programming language of PHP can be used for creating dynamic pages with dynamic content, that are full of flash and animation, enabling organization to develop customized web pages that can attract more visitors.
- Apart from server side scripting, PHP web development tools can also be used from stand alone client side or command line scripting GUI applications.
- As PHP website development software is freely available, thus it can easily be embedded into HTML.
- PHP takes just the code as an input and in return provides organization with appropriate web pages as an output.
- The PHP MYSQL programming enables PHP web developers and programmers to perform script installation, script repair as well as manage every front and back end activity, hassle free.
- PHP website development programming can be used to make a slew of off-the-shelf applications through software packages like SugarCRM, Typo3, Joomla, osCommerce, C, Simple Machine Forum, phpBB, Eventum, phpAdsNew, vBulletin etc.

Based on C++, PHP is considered to be the best programming language for both website development and web development. Both programmers and designers love this language alike, due to the manifolds of advantages it provides. PHP is considered to be an all round better choice for web development than other programming languages.

Free Content Management Systems (CMS) PHP Scripts

The content management systems scripts listed here, allow organization to install a PHP script onto their web account that makes this possible. Depending on the script organization install, content management scripts may allow users to easily change content on their site, define their site appearance site-wide by modifying a template, provide a search engine, site map, web statistics, online file manager, online content editor, etc.

List of Free Content Management Systems (CMS) PHP Scripts

1. ocPortal Content Management : This CMS is a web content management system that features galleries, news, file downloads, community forums and chats, *wiki*, content commenting and rating, a built-in search engine (site search), newsletters and mass mailing facilities, support ticket system, featured content (eg, image of the day, random quotes), paid membership sections with support for payment gateways like PayPal, banner support, etc.

2. Expression Engine Core : The Core version of this software is free for personal sites. It is a fully featured content management system and blogging software that has one of the easiest to understand and modify template system (for organization's site design and theme). It is versatile, has a sophisticated user/user-group system (for managing organization's users), easy to setup and get started, highly configurable, etc. It uses MySQL for its database.

3. Drupal : Drupal is an open source content management system (CMS) or platform that uses PHP and MySQL. It allows an individual user or even a community of users to publish, manage and maintain organization's website. Organization can use it to create blogs, forums, and picture galleries, file upload and download sites, forums, collaborative authoring environments, podcasting, peer-to-peer networking sites, etc. The system is modular and highly customizable. It is licensed under the GNU General Public License.

4. TextPattern Content Management System : TextPattern is an open source CMS that attempts to make it easier for the average user to modify its templates. Its templates use a simple syntax known as Textile that allow organization to use a few simple markers to indicate things like images, hyperlinks, etc. The software allows multiple contributors, supports plugins, etc. TextPattern uses PHP and MySQL.

5. eZ Publish : Like most content management systems eZ Publish allows organization to publish the content of organization's site from within organization's web browser, using an online rich text editor. It supports content versioning, multimedia publishing, extensions, user management and access controls, workflows, the ability to publish from Microsoft Word, and so on. The CMS uses a MySQL database. It is licensed under the GNU General Public License (GPL).

6. Contentteller : This is an open source content management system that purports to be search engine friendly, in that it has a site map (using the site map protocol?) generator and automatically creates search engine friendly URLs. It allows organization to manage multiple websites from a single installation, has built-in caching to reduce the number of database queries (otherwise organization may exceed organization's web host's resource limit), has a template and style sheet system so that organization can customise the site, and is able to share its user database with 3rd party applications like certain forum software so that organization's users only need to register once for organization's site. The software is released under the GNU General Public License.

7. Drake CMS : Drake CMS is a PHP-based open source content management system that does not need any database system to be installed, although it supports a number of them (including MySQL, PostgreSQL, SQLite,

Sybase, Frontbase, MaxDB, MS SQL, etc) if organization have them. It can be used to create community-based portals, magazines and newspapers, simple personal or family websites, company or organisation websites, etc. It has a hierarchy of users, starting with the Admistrator down to the simple website visitor, with the facility to control the access rights of each of these user levels. Organization can create subsites with this CMS without replicating the CMS files.

8. Joomla! Content Management : Joomla! is an open source content management system that can be used to power organization's website and allow organization to easily manage it from an online interface. It includes an integrated WYSIWYG editor, support for multiple users/editors, a simple poll engine, several templates, etc. Organization can augment the features provided by the basic CMS installation by adding their extensions. Extensions available include blogging software, calendars, directory services, email newsletters, e-commerce and shopping cart engines, image and multimedia galleries, forums and chat software, banner advertising systems, business and organizational directories, dynamic form builders, etc. Joomla! requires that organization's web server be running Apache and has PHP and MySQL installed.

9. OpenCMS : OpenCMS is an open source website content management system that uses Java, JSP, XML, MySQL on Tomcat (a Java Servlet container and web server). It comes with an integrated WYSIWYG editor and a simple text editor for Internet Explorer and Mozilla-based browsers like Firefox. The CMS software allows organization to view organization's workspace in an Explorer-like window, edit files by changing specific elements within the page or directly editing them using the built-in WYSIWYG editor, etc. This program is licensed under the GNU General Public License.

10. PHP-Fusion : PHP-Fusion uses a MySQL database to store the contents of organization's website. It requires PHP 4 running on an Apache server. The program is released under the GNU General Public License.

11. CMSimple Content Management : CMSimple Content Management is designed for webmasters with relatively small sites (less than 2 Mb in text content). It does not need organization's site to have a database - the content of organization's site is stored in a single HTML file. It has an online JavaScript-based WYSIWYG editor that works in Mozilla and IE 5.5 and above (doesn't work in other browsers). The program is free, but requires organization to preserve the link to their site.

12. phpwcms - Web Content Management System : phpwcms uses PHP and MySQL. It includes multiple WYSIWYG editors, a frontend CSS editor, image resizing capabilities, file manager, support for meta tags, template editor, W3C conforming frontend rendering, etc. It can be installed on Windows 2000/XP, Mac OSX and Linux. The package is released under the GNU General Public License.

13. TYPO3 Open Source Content Management System : TYPO3 is an open source content management system that is multilingual and allows WYSIWYG editing using a rich text editor (this feature is only for IE Windows's users). It has wizards for making tables, bullet lists, mail forms, etc; allows multiple page editing. It also allows offline editing, preview of content online, scheduled publishing; has an indexed search engine, a direct mail or newsletter system, etc. Administrators have access control (the ability to control access to various parts of the system), statistics, logging, version control with unlimited undos, raw database access, etc. Organization can use HTML templates, PHP scripts, create protected areas, and so on. The entire system is released under the GNU General Public License.

14. BIGACE Web CMS: Content Management with Smarty Templates : The BIGACE CMS supports multiple websites on a single installation, template support, autogenerated menus, content hierarchy with unlimited depth and size, a category system, workflows, online WYSYIWYG editor, full-text search (including the name, description, catchwords as well as the content), integrated statistics, search engine friendly URLs, etc.

15. ezContents Content Management System : ezContents is an open source website content management system that uses PHP and MySQL. Organization can add authors that write content, manage permissions, workflow, create a layout, etc. It supports both sites with frames and those without.

16. phpCMS - PHP Content Management System : This PHP content management script includes a file manager, full text search engine, online editor, statistics, dynamic menus, etc. Unlike many of the other content management systems this one works with flat files.

PICTURE LIBRARY AND CONTENT MANAGEMENT

All pictures and graphics (and files) are added to the content management system's library so that they are available for any page organization want to build. Also, following features supports the picture management in CMS:

- **Update a graphic** – and it will update itself all over the site wherever it is used.
- **Click on *List images* :** (in the Image Library) to see all pictures and graphics currently in the library. Organization can preview any image by clicking on the *view image* link.
- Fill in the Title, keyword and caption fields to help identify organization's image, then use the *Browse* button to navigate to the image organization want to upload, on organization's local machine.

- There should be a JPEG (.jpg), GIF (.gif) or PNG (.png) file to ensure that organization's image will show in all modern browsers.

The CMS requires that the image is round about the actual size organization want to use it. Organization can resize the picture on any page in the wysiwyg editor, but the actual file size remains unchanged.

By clicking the *Submit* button and the image will be uploaded by the content management system from the machine to the site library. Once the upload has finished, organization can add the picture to any of organization's pages. If organization has other images and wants to add to pages, it can use the content management system to upload them to the library at the same time.

INTEGRATING LIBRARY CONTENT INTO COURSE MANAGEMENT / LEARNING MANAGEMENT SYSTEMS

Because libraries can't rely on students coming to the library's webpage, integrating library content into course management systems is really important. This means integrating the information literacy information and tutorials. It also means integrating the content of "research guides" or "course pages" into course management systems as well.

One of the biggest challenges that librarians face in doing this is gaining access to the course management system. For the maximum effect, librarians need to be able to add materials to each course just as the teacher would be able to. Asking a teacher to add library materials themselves only adds to the teacher's burden. However, many teachers don't want to give librarians administrative rights over their courses in the CMS. Thus far it is yet to experience a CMS / LMS where librarians could have permissions to add content to a specific page but not view/edit any other portion of the course. This is too bad because it makes collaborating with teachers on course guides in course management systems. While libraries could create such pages on their own library website and IT staff to automatically create a dynamic link to this content for every course in the CMS, usability would suggest that it would be more useful for the content to be part of the CMS.

Regardless of the existing technical issues, libraries need to work harder to get library content in the CMS/LMS. The Google Scholar OpenURL project, persistent linking to databases, WAG the Dog, and Open WorldCat, are all part of these efforts. However, libraries need to continue to find other ways of reaching potential users wherever they may be physically or electronically.

It is found that blackboard has the same limitation that WebCT apparently has, in the lack of adequate flexibility in levels of administrative rights. Until and unless that problem is fixed, librarians can only help the academic/faculty members add library content if they let librarians in, or teach them to do it themselves. Most librarians won't take the time to learn to do it themselves- as faculty members are busy. If the faculty members want the content, they need to trust librarians. Librarians do understand the privacy concerns. But librarians want partnerships to be a two-way street. Many librarians go out of their way to work with faculty members to get good library materials in the course sites-the faculty members side of the partnership needs to be helping librarians understand enough about the course content and objectives to select the right library material to include, and enough trust to let librarians in to do it.

Website Content Vs Website Design

The battle of debate relating to Content vs. Design is an ongoing one. The truth is that both are complementary to securing the best business advantages. One cannot trigger success without the other.

1. Relevance of Good Website Content : There is no place for lifeless, dull and insipid content on web. Good content is considered so invaluable.

2. Living Sites : Many websites change or go through updating almost every week. Some websites change their content every day. There are still some exceptional websites that change every few minutes during a day. Every revision in web content implies new writing using new words. Such frequent change is appreciable as it would generate high traffic and revenues at one go. These sites are sometimes terms as 'living sites. Organizations have to visualize a different verbal treatment of any given subject. When organizations have a living website, the content has informative and accurate.

To make sure that the writing stays dynamic and interesting, here are some simple aspects:

I. *Reason for a website* : Without understanding, the purpose of content organization won't be able to reflect conviction and clarity in organization's writing.

II. *Output and product of organization* : If organization's web site showcases a service or product, it must love it in order to represent it to others. The organization must develop its own way to show case in innovative manner.

III. *Interweave topics* : Knowing the facts in well mannered way, organization can interweave other topics to garner interest. Organization must not overshadow the importance of the website, organization are representing.

IV. *Website Design* : None can ignore the growing relevance of website designing. Organization's website should not have lots of content without design. One would give it a second look.

Website designing is the 'zing' factor that gives visual

treatment to content. Visual attractiveness, easy navigation features and good graphics can bring more web visitors to a site than expected.

Here are some useful tips to preserve visual attractiveness to impress web visitors:

- **Balanced layout :** A balanced layout is significant to bring in balance.
- **Titles :** The titles of navigation links must be short as well as descriptive.
- **Provide liquid design :** This refers to the latest trend by which a website adapts to the available space on its own.

NEEDS AND BENEFITS OF IMPLEMENTING WCM SOLUTIONS

Libraries are seeking to manage their Web content for a number of reasons, some of which reflect standard business practices and some of which are unique. WCM is used to get a handle on the increasing local content, the number of sources of information, and the variety of documents produced. The sheer volume and complexity of information provided by library staff is increasing. As a result, more staff is included as contributors, many with non-technical backgrounds. Administrators also have expectations that more library services be web enabled, resulting in more access and information services going online. Some of these services are handled by library automation software, but increasingly web sites are designed to integrate these services into a one-stop portal-like environment. Library users are becoming more demanding in their information needs and demanding higher levels of personalization based on their experiences with commercial sites such as those hosted by online booksellers. Expectations are that all library services should be represented on the website. Content often requires re-purposing for different audiences or different uses such as handhelds. Additionally, libraries are beginning to focus on content that is unique to the online environment including online news, digital collections, live interaction, and tutorial delivery. Processes and tools must therefore be developed to publish library events, policies, and other activities to the library Web site.

A website grows in size and complexity. Web administrators find it often growing beyond the ability to manage it as a collection of static HTML pages. Other aspects surrounding web development also come into play. More functionality is required to serve web users and internal web developers, and standards need to be implemented for a more consistent look and feel. Some of the pressing needs that are consistently emerging are as follows:

- The ability to personalize or customize content for different user groups
- The ability to streamline internal workflow and reduce workload stemming from tedious and repetitive tasks
- The ability to achieve quality control
- The ability to reduce cost of managing the organization's web
- The ability to re-purpose, or reuse, content in multiple information sets, to deliver the content to both library Internet and intranet, and for other publications

Hackos (2002) indicates that "content management is no longer an option, given the complexity of information access and retrieval." To meet the above stated needs, content must be organized in a content management system or application to ensure that it is managed effectively, retrieved easily, and delivered in different formats.

CONTENT NETWORKING

The content networking doesn't refer to a single product or product line or even to a particular task. It refers to being able to get content to the user as fast as possible with a minimal amount of fuss. There are some content devices that are separate boxes and others that can be routers running extra services. It all depends on what organization wants to do.

Process

A content networking device, called a Distributed Director can reroute the request to a Web server much closer to where the user is, reducing latency and bandwidth usage. There are a couple of different ways to do this. First, through the use of recursive requests, the initial DNS request for a given domain will be forwarded to a device that figures out where the connection should be rerouted to based on Director Response Protocol (DRP) metrics. The second method is for the content device. It knows what servers can serve pages for a particular website and based on the DRP metrics configured, it does an HTTP redirect.

In this context it is essential to understand that DRP is a protocol that figures out how far a given location is based on routing information. In external mode, it uses BGP autonomous system (AS) numbers to figure out distance on a hop-by-hop basis. One AS equals one hop. Server mode uses the metric used by an (IGP) to determine which is closest. Random mode just randomly selects servers in a pseudo-load balancing fashion. Other modes exist, but those are the major ones. In the event that outside distribution and load balancing isn't needed, there are lower costs devices that can do roughly the same thing without taking BGP into account. The Local Director is used to reroute traffic for load balancing and optimization purposes but is used inside a single autonomous system. This means organization can use a Local Director to reroute requests for intranet access to the server closest to the user, rather than using slow WAN links for all requests to go to the headquarters.

Content devices vary in what they can do. Some of the

devices speed up content; others, like IP/TV devices, actually serve content. If organizations are involved in supporting a high-traffic Web site using SSL or are considering multiple hosting providers, then it is recommended that organizations do more research into these devices. Organizations will make the customers much happier.

CONTENT DELIVERY NETWORK (CDN)

1. **Competitive organizations need a high quality content delivery network :** Having a superior content delivery network is a definitive competitive advantage in a industrial world dominated by information. This network of content delivery should provide quick and easy access to the best content available throughout the world. An exceptional content delivery network will leverage both external and internal content and integrate it into daily workflow, where employees can use it to accelerate decision-making.

2. **A content delivery network that's driven by world-class content :** The content network system helps organizations integrate information into their daily workflow.

CONTENT NETWORKING TECHNIQUES

The Internet was designed according to the end-to-end principle. This principle keeps the core network relatively simple and moves the intelligence as much as possible to the network end-points: the hosts and clients. As a result the core network is specialized, simplified, and optimized to only forward data packets.

Content Delivery Networks augment the end-to-end transport network by distributing on it a variety of intelligent applications employing techniques designed to optimize content delivery. The resulting tightly integrated overlay uses web caching, server-load balancing, request routing, and content services. These techniques are briefly described below:

1. Because closer is better, web caches store popular content closer to the user. These shared network appliances reduce bandwidth requirements, reduce server load, and improve the client response times for content stored in the cache.
2. Server-load balancing uses one or more layer 4-7 switches, also known as a web switch, content switch, or multilayer switch. It shares traffic among a number of servers or web caches. The switch is assigned a single virtual IP address. Traffic arriving at the switch is then directed to one of the real web servers attached to the switch. This has the advantages of balancing load, increasing total capacity, improving scalability, and providing increased reliability by redistributing the load of a failed web server and providing server health checks.
3. A content cluster or service node can be formed using a layer 4-7 switch to balance load across a number of servers or a number of web caches within the network.
4. Request routing directs client requests to the content source best able to serve the request. This may involve directing a client request to the service node that is closest to the client, or to the one with the most capacity. A variety of algorithms are used to route the request. These include Global Server Load Balancing, DNS-based request routing, Dynamic metafile generation, HTML rewriting, and anycasting. Proximity—choosing the closest service node—is estimated using a variety of techniques including reactive probing, proactive probing, and connection monitoring.
5. Simple CDNs require manual asset copying. Earlier CDNs used active web caches and global hardware load balancers. Modern CDNs use cheap and simple edge

servers and intelligent central CDN management technologies that distribute assets dynamically.

CONTENT SERVICE PROTOCOLS

Several protocols suites have been designed to provide access to content services that are scattered throughout a content network. The Internet Content Adaptation Protocol (ICAP) was developed in the late 1990 to provide an open standard for connecting application servers. A more recently defined and robust solution is provided by the Open Pluggable Edge Services (OPES) protocol. This architecture defines OPES service applications that can reside on the OPES processor itself or be executed remotely on a Callout Server. Edge Side Includes is a small markup language for edge level dynamic web content assembly. It is fairly common for websites to have generated content. It could be because of changing content like catalogs or forums, or because of personalization.

P2P CDNS

Although peer-to-peer (P2P) is not traditional CDN technology, it is increasingly used to deliver content to end users. P2P claims low cost and efficient distribution. Even though P2P actually generates more traffic than traditional client-server CDNs as it's welcomed by parties running content delivery/distribution services. The real strength of P2P shows when one has to distribute highly attractive data, in short period of time. Ironically, the more people who download the (same) data, the more efficient P2P is, thus slashing the cost of the peering fees that a CDN provider has to pay due to inter-peer delivery (in comparison to the same amount of data distributed using traditional techniques).

On the other hand, the "long tail" type material does not benefit much from P2P delivery schema, since, to gain advantage over traditional distribution models, a P2P-enabled CDN must force storing (caching) data on peers—something that is usually not desired by users and which is rarely enabled.

Contrary to popular belief, P2P is not limited to low-bandwidth audio-video signal distribution. There is no technical boundary, built-in inefficiency, or flaw-by-design in peer-to-peer technology to prevent distribution of full HD audio+video signal at, for example, 8 Mbit/s. It's just environmental factors, like low (upload) bandwidth or inadequate computing power in consumer electronics devices, that prevent HD material being publicly available in P2P CDNs. Low bandwidth problems also apply to traditional CDN, though.

PEERING CDN

Service providers often geographically distribute their Web servers' facilities to improve performance, reliability, and scalability. Content Delivery Networks, which first evolved in 1998, replicate content over several mirrored Web servers, strategically placed at various locations to deal with flash crowds and to enhance response time. A CDN improves network performance by maximizing bandwidth, improving accessibility, and maintaining correctness through content replication.

Unfortunately, although many commercial CDN providers exist, they don't cooperate in delivering content to end users in a scalable manner. In addition, content providers typically subscribe to one CDN provider and thus can't use multiple CDNs at the same time. Such a closed, non-cooperative model results in "islands" of CDNs.

HOW IT IS DONE: PEERING CDN

A CDN combines a content-delivery infrastructure, a request-routing infrastructure, a distribution infrastructure, and an accounting infrastructure. In such a CDN environment, the original server fetches the Web content based on user requests and then serves the content to the user from the nearby replicated server.

However, because CDNs are proprietary, they comprise their own closed delivery networks, which are expensive to set up and maintain. CDN, have limited scalability. Running a global CDN is even more costly, requiring an enormous amount of capital and labor. Furthermore, commercial CDNs make specific commitments to their end users by signing a Service Level Agreement, which outlines specific penalties if they fail to meet those commitments. To cut expenses, and to avoid adverse business impact through SLA violations, CDN providers should partner together.

The CDN provider can accomplish this by establishing peering with other CDN providers that have caching servers located near its client. That way, CDN providers can share each others resources to serve their clients' requests effectively and meet their quality-of-service (QoS) requirements. To ensure sustained resource sharing between CDN providers, peering arrangements must ensure sufficient incentives exist.

To make content services an Internet infrastructure service, vendors have implemented content service networks (CSNs), which act as another network infrastructure layer built upon CDNs and provide next-generation CDN services. So, a CSN is another variation of the conventional CDN. This logical separation between content and services under the "content delivery and distribution" and "content services" domains is undesirable considering the ongoing trend in content networking. A unified content network that supports the coordinated composition and delivery of content and services would be much better.

WEB SERVER

The Web server is a CSDN's most important element.

Servers are responsible for storing content and value-added services as infrastructure services and delivering them in a reliable and cooperative manner. Servers within each CSDN can deliver content and services to meet end-user QoS requirements.

A server's structure can be divided into two layers: an *overlay layer* and the *core*. In the overlay layer, a server comprises a Web-service host (for example, Apache or Tomcat), an SLA-negotiation service module, and an SLA-based allocator. The negotiation module, with the help of a coordinated VO scheduler, is responsible for cooperating and coordinating with other servers (located in a local or global CSDN) through SLA-based negotiation. The SLA-based allocator delivers content and services based on the negotiated SLAs with other local or global CSDNs' servers.

The Web server's core consists of high performance computing systems such as symmetric multiprocessors, cluster systems, or other enterprise systems (such as desktop grids). The server's underlying devices and tools must store the content and services and assist in responding quickly and reliably to client requests to meet the negotiated QoS requirements. For content and service location and routing, the Web servers' underlying technologies perform on-demand cooperative caching through coordination with other servers. Efficiently balancing the load across different Web servers is critical to produce the required QoS. Hence, servers are adopted with appropriate load- and resource-distribution strategies.

SERVICE REGISTRY

A service registry enables CDN providers to register and publish their resources and service details. An SLA-negotiator service and allocator module uses this service registry to discover CDN providers and negotiate QoS parameters and resource allocation to maximize cooperative CSDNs' potential.

POLICY REPOSITORY

A policy repository stores the policies that the administrators generate. These policies are a set of rules to administer, manage, and control access to VO resources. They provide a way to consistently manage the components deploying complex technologies.

CHALLENGES IN WEB CONTENT MANAGEMENT

As library Web sites continue evolving into a gateway for nearly all library resources and services, the underlying technical structure of most library Web sites also needs to grow in parallel. Many library Web managers are struggling to control their sites using only the primitive tool of HTML which generates obstacles to delivering information. As discussed above, the need for Web content management solutions arise and is identified when Web managers can no longer maintain Web sites with continuously growing content and user demands. The current lack of turn-key library WCM packages presents a great challenge for libraries in selecting a viable one. At the same time, many libraries lack the needed technical expertise to attempt to build in-house WCM systems or applications. Funding constraints also prevent many libraries from purchasing commercially available Web content management systems. Recent developments like meta-searching or federated searching for library databases also impact how libraries manage their electronic content. Organizational and cultural obstacles add another layer of challenges to the implementation of WCM solutions. From the management perspective, challenges are being faced during the entire process of WCM implementation-from the initial strategic planning, when to use a WCMS, through the selection of applications or tools, the implementation of workflow management, quality control, and finally to ongoing updates, site modifications, and technology upgrades.

A fully functional WCM system with rich and specialized features geared toward library functions and services has yet to come. To move in that direction, librarians must stop thinking of their Web sites as collections of HTML pages. Librarians should view the content of the Web site as dynamic resources for information and services that patrons will use in highly individualized ways. The trend is that content production and presentation will be increasingly separated aspects of the library Web site. Tools that libraries can afford and use quickly to create useful content management applications are now available, but the tools are only part of the picture. The hardest part of transforming Web sites into dynamic systems is the conceptualization of the library Web site strategically. Doing it right is becoming much more crucial than just doing it.

REFERENCES AND NOTES

1. Holly Yu (2001). Library Web Content Management: Needs and Challenges. Search for web reference.
2. Warren, R. (2001). Information architects and their central role in content management. *Bulletin of the American Society for Information Scienceand Technology, 28*(1).
3. Kartchner, C. (2001). Fulfilling the promise of content management. *Bulletin of the American Society for Information Science and Technology, 28*(1).
4. *http://contentmanagementsoftwares.net/cd_presentation_copywriting_tips.htm*
5. http://contentmanagementsoftwares.net/tagline_creation_tips.htm
6. http://contentmanagementsoftwares.net/mailer_flyer_copywriting_tips.htm
7. *http://contentmanagementsoftwares.net/copy_editing_tips.htm*
8. *http://contentmanagementsoftwares.net/ad_copywriting_tips.htm*

9. http://contentmanagementsoftwares.net/printer_friendly_web_pages.htm
10. ttp://www.bigace.de/index.htm
11. http://www.broadbandtvnews.com/?p=13148
12. Boiko, B. (2001). Understanding content management. *Bulletin of the American*
13. *Society for Information Science and Technology, 28*(1).
14. Boiko, B. (2002). *Content management bible.* New York: Hungry Minds.
15. *http://www.drostdesigns.com/content-management-system-benefits/*
16. *http://contentmanagementsoftwares.net/content-writing-whitepapers.htm*
17. Clay III, E. (2003). Content management and library Web site. *Public Libraries, 42*(5).
18. Guenther, K. (2001a). What is a Web content management solution? *Online, 25*(4).
19. *http://contentmanagementsoftwares.net/writing_web_content.htm*
20. *http://contentmanagementsoftwares.net/web_site_content.htm*
21. *http://contentmanagementsoftwares.net/website_content_vs_website_design.htm*
22. Guenther, K. (2001b). Choosing Web content management solution. *Online, 25*(5).
23. Hackos, J.T. (2002). *Content management for dynamic Web delivery.* New York: Wiley Computer Publishing.
24. *http://www.immediacy.net/resource_centre/cms_faqs.aspx*
25. http://www.immediacy.net/resource_centre/cms_faqs/what_is_content_management.aspx
26. *http://contentmanagementsoftwares.net/web-design-whitepaper.htm*
27. *http://www.boldendeavours.com/publication/content/433.htm*

28. *http://www.cpdservices.com/53.0.htmll*
29. http://clk.about.com/? webdesign.about.com/library/weekly/aa031300c.htm
30. Mach, M. (2004). Web site maintenance workflow at a medium-sized university library. In H. Yu (Ed.), *Content and workflow management for library Web sites: Case studies.* Hershey, PA: Idea Group Publishing.
31. Westman, S. (2002). Building database-backed Web applications: Process and issues. *Information Technology and Libraries, 21*(2).
32. Whang, M. (2004). PHP and PostgreSQL Web content management system at Western Michigan university libraries. In H. Yu (Ed.), *Content and workflow management for library Web sites: Case studies.* Hershey, PA: Idea Group Publishing.
33. http%3A//webdesign.about.com/library/weekly/aa031300a.htm
34. *http://contentmanagementsoftwares.net/php_development.htm*
35. *http://contentmanagementsoftwares.net/php_development.htm*
36. Sen, P. (2007, March 1). *Key Benefits Of Content Management.* Retrieved June 9, 2009, from *http://ezinearticles.com/?Key-Benefits-Of-Content-Management&id=47242*
37. *http://contentmanagementsoftwares.net/managing_your_website_with_the_help_of_a_CMS.htm*
38. *http://www.dpbolvw.net/tl68mu2-u1HKQKLJRHJIMRQNIO*
39. http://ocportal.com/
40. http://www.expressionengine.com/index.php?affiliate=nstsw
41. http://drupal.org/
42. http://www.textpattern.com/
43. http://ez.no/
44. http://code.google.com/p/contentteller/ http://drakecms.sourceforge.net/

45. http://www.joomla.org/
46. http://www.opencms.org/opencms/en/
47. http://www.php-fusion.co.uk/
48. http://www.phpwcms.de/
49. http://typo3.com/
50. http://www.bigace.de/index.html
51. http://www.ezcontents.org/ezContents2x/
52. http://www.phpcms.de/index.en.html
53. http://www.back-end.org/
54. http://www.thefreecountry.com/php/contentmanagement.shtml
55. ttp://www.accent-on-business.co.uk/add_a_picture_to_the_library.html
56. *http://contentmanagementsoftwares.net/dynamic_website_privileges.htm*
57. *http://contentmanagementsoftwares.net/user_centered_designs.htm*
58. *http://erptoday.knowledgehills.com/CMS/Content-Management-Tutorial.aspx*
59. *http://contentmanagementsoftwares.net/website_content_vs_website_design.htm*
60. *http://www.seofleet.com/content-networking.html*
61. *http://www.factiva.com/information-services.html*
62. http://www.broadbandtvnews.com/?p=13148
63. Rajkumar Buyya, Al-Mukaddim Khan Pathan, James Broberg, and Zahir Tari, "A Case for Peering of Content Delivery Networks," *IEEE Distributed Systems Online*, vol. 7, no. 10, 2006, art. no. 0610-o10003.
64. G. Peng, *CDN: Content Distribution Network*, tech. report TR-125, Experimental Computer Systems Lab, Dept. of Computer Science, State Univ. of New York, 2003; *http://citeseer.ist.psu.edu/peng03cdn.html*.
65. M. Arlitt and T. Jin, "A Workload Characterization Study of 1998 World Cup Web Site," *IEEE Network*, May/June 2000, pp. 30-37.

66. G. Pallis and A. Vakali, "Insight and Perspectives for Content Delivery Networks," *Comm. ACM*, vol. 49, no. 1, ACM Press, 2006, pp. 101-106.

67. W.Y. Ma, B. Shen, and J.T. Brassil, "Content Services Network: Architecture and Protocols," *Proc. 6th Int'l Workshop on Web Caching and Content Distribution* (IWCW 01), Boston Univ., 2001, pp. 89-107.

68. R. Buyya, D. Abramson, and S. Venugopal, "The Grid Economy," *Proc. IEEE*, vol. 93, no. 3, 2005, pp. 698-714; *http://www.gridbus.org/~raj/papers/ieee-grideconomy.pdf* (pdf).

69. Antelman, K. (Ed.). (2002). *Database-driven Web sites*. New York: Haworth Information Press.

70. Antelman, K. (1999). Getting out of the HTML business: The database-driven Web site solution. *Information Technology and Libraries, 18*(4).

5

NETWORKING TECHNOLOGIES FOR E-RESOURCES

Electronic information sources offer today's students different opportunities from their predecessors. The information needed can be delivered from the most appropriate source to the user; the user can re-specify his or her needs dynamically; the information is obtained when it is wanted, so becomes "just in time" rather than "just in case"; the user selects only the information needed to answer the specific question and, finally, the information is only stored should the user wish. Electronic information can therefore provide a number of advantages over traditional print based sources. These advantages include the fact that electronic information sources are often faster than consulting print indexes, especially when searching retrospectively, and they are straighter forward when wishing to use combinations of keywords. They open up the possibility of searching multiple files at one time, a feat accomplished more easily than when using printed equivalents. Electronic resources can be printed and searches saved to be repeated at a later date; they are updated more often than printed tools. One main advantage, especially to distance learners or those with limited time to access the library, is their availability from outside the library by dial-up access.

STORAGE AREA NETWORKS (SAN)

In *computing*, a **storage area network** (**SAN**) is an architecture to attach remote computer storage devices such as *disk arrays*, *tape libraries* and *optical jukeboxes* to *servers* in such a way that, to the *operating system*, the devices appear as *locally attached*. By contrast to a SAN, *Network Attached Storage* (NAS) uses file-based protocols such as *NFS* or *SMB/CIFS* where it is clear that the storage is remote, and computers request a portion of an abstract file rather than a disk block.

A SAN is a network specifically dedicated to the task of transporting data for storage and retrieval. Technically speaking, SAN architectures are alternatives to storing data on disks directly attached to servers or storing data on *NAS* devices which are connected through general purpose networks.

Definition: A **storage area network** (SAN) is a type of *local area network (LAN)* designed to handle large data transfers. A SAN typically supports data storage, retrieval and replication on business networks using high-end servers, multiple disk arrays and *Fiber Channel* interconnection technology.

SAN technology is similar but distinct from *network attached storage (NAS)* technology. While SANs traditionally employ low-level network protocols for transferring disk blocks, a NAS device typically works over *TCP/IP* and can be integrated fairly easily into computer networks. The term *SAN* can sometimes refer to *system area networks* instead of a storage area network. System Area Networks are *clusters* of high performance computers used for distributed processing applications requiring fast local network performance. Storage area networks are designed specifically for data management.

A SAN is a dedicated network that is separate from LANs and WANs. It is generally used to connect all the storage resources connected to various servers. It consists of a collection of SAN Hardware and SAN software; The hardware typically has high inter-connection rates between the various storage devices and the software manages, monitors and configures the SAN.

- From webopedia: Storage Area Network (SAN) is a high-speed subnetwork of shared storage devices. A storage device is a machine that contains nothing but a disk or disks for storing data.

A SAN's architecture works in a way that makes all storage devices available to all servers on a LAN or WAN. When more storage devices are added to a SAN, they too will be accessible from any server in the larger network. The server merely acts as a pathway between the end user and the stored data

- From Enterprise Storage Forum: A SAN is a network of storage devices that are connected to each other and to a server...in some configurations a SAN is also connected to the network. ...

Thus it can be said that SANs originated to overcome the problems with network attached storage (NAS) devices, which are difficult to manage and difficult to expand the capacity on like ordinary servers. NAS devices also add to the traffic on the network and suffer from the delays introduced by the operating systems' network stacks. A SAN is made up of a number of fabric switches connected in a network. The most common form of SAN uses the Fibre Channel fabric protocol with Fibre Channel switches. Connected to the SAN will be one or more Disk array controllers and one or more servers. The SAN allows the storage space on the hard disks in the Disk array controllers to be shared amongst the servers.

OBJECTIVES OF SAN

The main objective of a SAN is to facilitate the exchange of data between operating systems and storage elements. Components of a SAN infrastructure include communication infrastructure, storage elements, computer systems, and a management layer. The connecting elements of a SAN are routers, gateways, hubs, switches and directors. The flexible networking of a SAN eliminates the need for physical proximity between the server and the storage devices. Benefits of a SAN include faster transfer of data to the intended destination with minimum utilization of server capacities, access for multiple hosts to several storage devices, independent storage speeds up applications and offers better availability. The management of stored data is easier and centralized and devices are more amenable to scalability.

HOW DATA TRANSFER OCCURS

The high-speed transfer of data via a SAN can occur in the following ways:

1. Connecting server/s to storage devices: This is the most commonly used method and allows for the access of a storage device by servers either serially or simultaneously.
2. Connection between servers: SAN enables high-volume transfer of data between servers.
3. Connection between storage devices: Useful for moving data between storage devices.

THE NEED FOR SAN

The I/O bandwidth of the networks that were earlier used to connect the data storage devices and the processors was not commensurate with the capacities of the disk arrays and computers that utilized the data stored in them. The access to data is further complicated by the different database software run on different platforms. The traditionally distributed storage has been a huge drain on management resources and inefficient as well in terms of capacity utilization of hardware resources. Scalability can not be ignored when disk capacity is tied down to a single server or client. Sharing of data often requires creating duplicate copies, moving these copies slows down the LAN/ WAN and often co-ordination between applications that are spread over the entire organization becomes very difficult.

SAN INFRASTRUCTURE

SAN topologies were developed using fiber channels. Fiber channel is an open technical standard developed for networking. It is especially useful for handling storage communications as it offers flexible connectivity and fast access to data. Optical fibers are used for long-distance networking. Fiber channels can support different protocols and a large number of devices, a quality very desirable in any networking solution.

The American National Standards Institute (ANSI) has laid down the standards on which fiber channel networks are based. These standards define the manner in which data is to be moved across networks. The standards are exhaustive and cover physical interfaces, data encoding practices and protocols, data delivery methodologies, and common services. Fiber channels offer the advantage of a high level of hardware processing to ensure high performance. The serial data transport scheme used in a fiber channel can be implemented using simple cables and connectors. The information can be routed easily through switched networks. Since fiber channel transport layers are protocol independent, they enable the transmission of multiple protocols. Apart from being extremely flexible in its application, fiber channel delivers data at the rate at which the receiving application is able to handle; besides there is no loss of data.

STORAGE

Storage devices commonly connected through SAN include disk systems and tape systems. Disk systems offer simple integration as the I/O control is centralized. Disk systems are classified as Just A Bunch Of Disks (JBOD) and Redundant Array of Independent Disks (RAID). Disks in a JBOD are treated as individual storage devices by the applications to which they are connected to. RAIDs are treated as a single device that has a higher fault tolerance. An array of disks can be made to behave as a JBOD or RAID depending upon the performance requirements of a SAN. Disk systems are preferred for online data storage because of their high performance.

Tape systems make use of tapes arranged serially. In tape system parallel arrangements are not possible. Tape system consists of drives, autoloaders and libraries. Tape drives connect the tapes to the devices and enable the reading/writing from and to the tapes. Tape autoloaders are tape drives that perform the function of auto backup; Tape autoloaders are used for devices that generate a lot of data constantly. Tape libraries are autonomous sets of tape drives and autoloaders. Tape systems are used for offline storage due to higher storage capacity requires tap libraries cost efficiency.

SAN PROTOCOLS

SAN are traditionally connected over Fibre Channel networks. There have also been built using *SCSI (Small Computer System Interface)* technology. An *Ethernet* network which is dedicated solely to storage purposes would also quality as a SAN. Internet Small Computer Systems Interface (iSCSI) is a SCSI variant which encapsulates SCSI data in *TCP* packets and transits them over IP networks. Fibre Channel over TCP/IP (FCIP) tunnels Fibre Channel over IP-based networks. A SAN is a high-speed special-purpose *network* (or subnetwork) that interconnects different kinds of data storage devices. These data with storage devices are associated data *servers* on behalf of a larger network of users. Typically, SAN is part of the overall network of computing resources for an *enterprise*.

SAN is usually clustered in close proximity to other computing resources such as IBM *z990 mainframes* It may also extend to remote locations for *backup* and archival storage, using wide area network carrier technologies such as *ATM* or *SONET* (Synchronous Optical Networking). Astorage area network can use existing communication technology such as IBM's *optical fiber ESCON* or it may use the newer *Fibre Channel* technology. Some SAN system integrators liken it to the common storage *bus* (flow of data) in a personal computer that is shared by different kinds of storage devices such as a hard disk or a CD-ROM player. SANs support disk mirroring, backup and restore, archival and retrieval of archived data, data migration from one storage device to another, and the sharing of data among different servers in a network. SANs can incorporate subnetworks with (*NAS*) systems. The Internet Fibre Channel Protocol (iFCP) transports Fibre Channel Layer 4 FCP on IP networks.

BASIC NETWORK

Most storage networks use the *SCSI* protocol for communication between servers and disk drive devices. However, they do not use SCSI low-level physical interface (e.g. cables), as its *bus topology* is unsuitable for networking. To form a network, a mapping layer is used to other low-level protocols:

- "*iFCP*" or "SANoIP" mapping SCSI over *Fibre Channel Protocol* (FCP) over IP.
- *iSCSI*, mapping SCSI over *TCP/IP*.
- *ISCSI Extensions for RDMA* (iSER), mapping *iSCSI* over *InfiniBand* (IB).

- *HyperSCSI*, mapping SCSI over *Ethernet*.
- *FICON* mapping over Fibre Channel (used by *mainframe computers*).
- *ATA over Ethernet*, mapping *ATA* over Ethernet.
- Fibre Channel over Ethernet

STORAGE SHARING

Previously data centers created "islands" of *SCSI disk arrays*. Each island was *dedicated* to an application, and visible as a number of virtual hard drives Essentially, a SAN connects storage islands together using a high-speed network, It allows all applications to access all disks. Operating systems still view a SAN as a collection of LUNs, and usually maintain their own *file systems* on them. These *local* file systems, which cannot be shared among multiple operating systems/hosts, are the most reliable and most widely used. Sharing data between computers through a SAN requires advanced solutions, such as *SAN file systems* or *clustered computing*.

It is found that SANs help to increase storage capacity utilization, since multiple servers share the storage space on the disk arrays. The common application of a SAN is for the use of transactionally accessed data that require high-speed block-level access to the hard drives such as email servers, databases, and high usage file servers. In contrast, NAS allows many computers to access the same file system over the network and synchronizes their accesses. Lately, the introduction of *NAS heads* allowed easy conversion of SAN storage to NAS.

SAN-NAS (NETWORK-ATTACHED STORAGE) HYBRID

Despite the differences between NAS and SAN, it is possible to create solutions that include both technologies. Hybrid uses *DAS*, NAS and SAN technologies.

BENEFITS OF SAN

One of the chief benefits of SAN is that it simplifies the network infrastructure and makes it easier to manage. This is done by means of consolidation, virtualization, automation, and integration. Consolidation aims at centralizing the storage to improve scalability, reducing infrastructure complexity, and increasing efficiency. Virtualization helps improve availability and reduces costs as it offers a holistic view of storage components. Automation of routine tasks allows the administrators to focus on critical tasks. Integration helps organization furnish users with the desired information in a more systematic manner.

1. Easing the information life cycle management : A SAN makes information lifecycle management easier because of the integrated view of the data that it offers. The biggest benefit of a SAN is that it complements expensive business applications that demand instant and real-time information. ERP and CRM systems can fulfill their business promise only if the right type of data is made available at the right time to the right person. Sharing storage usually simplifies storage administration and adds flexibility. Other benefits include the ability to allow servers to boot from the SAN itself. This allows for a quick and easy replacement of faulty servers since the SAN can be reconfigured so that a replacement server can use the LUN of the faulty server..

2. Effective disaster recovery management : SANs also tend to enable more effective *disaster recovery* processes. A SAN could span a distant location containing a secondary storage array. It enables *storage replication* either implemented by *disk array controllers,* by server software, or by specialized SAN devices. Since IP *WANs* are often the least costly method of long-distance transport, the *Fibre Channel over IP* (FCIP) and iSCSI protocols have been developed to allow SAN extension over IP networks. Consolidation of disk arrays economically accelerated advancement of some of their advanced features. Such as I/O caching, *snapshotting* and volume cloning (*Business Continuance Volumes* or BCVs).

3. SAN infrastructure : SANs often utilize a Fibre Channel *fabric* topology - an infrastructure specially designed to handle storage communications. It provides faster and more reliable access than higher-level protocols used in *NAS*. A typical Fibre Channel SAN fabric is made up of a number of *Fibre Channel switches*. Today, all major SAN equipment vendors also offer some form of Fibre Channel routing solution, bringing substantial scalability benefits to the SAN architecture. These offerings use proprietary protocol elements, and the top-level architectures being promoted are radically different. They often enable mapping Fibre Channel traffic over IP or over *SONET/SDH*.

4. Compatibility : One of the early problems with Fibre Channel SANs was that the switches and other hardware from different manufacturers were not entirely compatible. Except the basic storage protocols FCP were always quite standard, the higher-level functions did not interoperate well. Similarly, many host operating systems would react badly to other operating systems sharing the same fabric.

5. SANs in the Media and Entertainment : Video editing workgroups require very high data transfer rates. Outside of the enterprise market, this is one area that greatly benefits from SANs. Per-node bandwidth usage control, sometimes referred to as quality-of-service (*QoS*), is especially important in video workgroups as it lets organization ensure fair and prioritized bandwidth usage across the network if there is insufficent open bandwidth available.

6. Storage virtualization and SANs : *Storage virtualization* refers to the process of completely abstracting logical storage from physical storage. The physical storage resources are aggregated into storage pools, from which the logical storage is created. It presents to the user a logical space for data storage and *transparently* handles the process of mapping it to the actual physical location. This is currently implemented inside each modern disk array. However, the goal is to virtualize multiple disk arrays, scattered over the network, into a single monolithic storage device, to be manage uniformly.

NETWORK-ATTACHED STORAGE (NAS)

Background

Far early *floppy drives* have been widely used to share data files, but today the storage needs of the average person far exceed the capacity of floppies. Businesses now maintain an increasingly large number of electronic documents and presentation sets including video clips.

What Is NAS?

NAS challenges the traditional file server approach by creating systems designed specifically for data storage.

Like traditional file servers, NAS follows a client/server design. A single hardware device, often called the NAS *box* or NAS *head*, acts as the interface between the NAS and network clients. These NAS devices require no monitor, keyboard or mouse. They generally run an *embedded* operating system rather than a full-featured Networking operating system. One or more disk and possibly tape drives can be attached to many NAS systems to increase total capacity. Clients always connect to the NAS head, rather than to the individual storage devices. Clients generally access a NAS over an Ethernet connection.

A NAS can store any data that appears in the form of files, such as email boxes, Web content, remote system backups, and so on. NAS systems strive for reliable operation and easy administration. They often include built-in features such as disk space quotas, secure authentication, or the automatic sending of email alerts should an error be detected.

Definition of NAS

Network-attached storage (NAS) is hard disk storage that is set up with its own network address rather than being attached to the department computer that is serving applications to a network's workstation users. By removing storage access and its management from the department server, both application programming and files can be served faster because they are not competing for the same processor resources. The network-attached storage device is attached to a local area network (typically, an Ethernet network) and assigned an IP address. File requests are mapped by the main server to the NAS file server.

Webopedia defines; a network-attached storage (NAS) device is a server that is dedicated to nothing more than file sharing. NAS does not provide any of the activities that a server in a server-centric system typically provides, such as e-mail, authentication or file management. NAS allows more hard disk storage space to be added to a network that already utilizes servers without shutting them down for maintenance and upgrades. In this storage-centric design, the server still handles all of the processing of data but a NAS device delivers the data to the user. A NAS device does not need to be located within the server but can exist anywhere in a LAN and can be made up of multiple networked NAS devices.

In a summarizing manner, NAS is designed to separate storage resources from network and application servers, in order to simplify storage management and improve the reliability, performance and efficiency of the network. Network Attached Storage devices attach directly to the existing LAN. A file system is located and managed on the NAS device and data is transferred to clients over industry standard network protocols (TCP/IP, AppleTalk, or IPX) using industry standard file sharing protocols (SMB/CIFS, NCP, AFP, NFS or HTTP). This intelligence on the NAS device enables data sharing among heterogeneous network clients.

Building of NAS

NAS devices are built around a highly-tuned and optimised appliance with an array of hard disks, attached directly into an existing local or wide area network for "plug and play" connectivity. Users access the shared storage space using standard file based protocols like NFS and CIFS. NAS systems offer a "plug and play" storage solution because the operating system is pre-installed and no additional drivers are required to access the appliance. Many NAS appliances offer a web-based interface to configure user access rights and other options, making the deployment very straightforward. NAS is hard disk storage that is set up with its own network address rather than being attached to the department computer that is serving applications to a network's workstation users.

Working of NAS

Network-attached storage is one way around the slowdowns and service interruptions that occur in a conventional file server model. NAS effectively moves storage out from behind the server and puts it directly on the transport network. Unlike file servers that have SCSI and LAN adapters, a NAS appliance uses a network interface card to transmit LAN and storage communications. These specialized storage devices bring with them some major benefits over file server systems. Since they don't require a file server, any user with access rights, anywhere on the network, can directly access stored data. NAS devices are also optimized to process storage I/O transactions much faster than conventional parallel SCSI schemes.

NAS appliances use a common file server access

protocol, so they can process requests from systems around a network, running multiple types of operating systems. This solves cross-platform issues that arise frequently in today's heterogeneous enterprises. NAS also mitigates the physical complexity associated with file servers that use parallel SCSI buses to connect servers to storage disks.

Yet for all its advantages over a file server model, one drawback of NAS is that it shifts storage transactions from parallel SCSI connections to the production network. This means the LAN has to handle both normal end-user traffic and storage disk requests, including backup operations. Thus, NAS doesn't resolve bandwidth consumption during backups. Unlike storage-area networks, which remove back-up traffic from the LAN, NAS still uses the production network for backup and recovery.

NAS Protocols

Communication with a NAS head occurs over TCP/IP. More specifically, clients utilize any of several higher-level protocols (*application* or *layer seven* protocols in the OSI model) built on top of TCP/IP. The two application protocols most commonly associated with NAS are Sun Network File System (NFS) and Common Internet File System (CIFS). NFS was developed originally for sharing files between UNIX systems across a LAN. Support for NFS soon expanded to include non-UNIX systems; however, most NFS clients today are computers running some flavor of the UNIX operating system. The CIFS was formerly known as Server Message Block (SMB). Many NAS systems also support Hypertext Transfer Protocol (HTTP). Clients can often download files in their Web browser from a NAS that supports HTTP. NAS systems also commonly employ HTTP as an access protocol for Web-based administrative user interfaces.

Crafting a NAS Consolidation Plan

Network-attached storage consists of hard disk

storage, including multi-disk RAID systems, and software for configuring and mapping file locations to the network-attached device. Network-attached storage can be a step toward and included as part of a more sophisticated storage system known as a storage area network (SAN). NAS software can usually handle a number of network protocols, including Microsoft's Internetwork Packet Exchange and NetBEUI, Novell's Netware Internetwork Packet Exchange, and Sun Microsystems' Network File System. Configuration, including the setting of user access priorities, is usually possible using a Web browser.

BENEFITS OF NETWORK ATTACHED STORAGE

1. Streamlined Architecture : NAS Appliances have a streamlined architecture designed for one function - to serve data files to clients in heterogeneous network environments. Powered by an operating system optimized for file I/O activity, file serving performance is greater than that of a general purpose server, which is designed to perform a multitude of functions.

2. Reduced Server I/O Bottlenecks : The largest source of network and application server degradation is file service. Separating storage from the server reduces the file serving activity and I/O bottlenecks and increases server bandwidth. CPU cycles can then be dedicated to handling application requests, resulting in improved client response time.

3. Increased Reliability and Data Availability : Separating storage resources from the server decreases both the number of components and the amount of file I/O activity, reducing the probability of server downtime and increasing the reliability of the network and application servers. A more reliable and efficient network saves the organization time and money.

Most networks do experience server downtime at some

point, whether for planned maintenance or due to unexpected crashes or outages. Because NAS Servers operate independent of network servers and communicate directly with the client, files remain available in the event of network server downtime. In the case of thinserver appliances, the architecture is designed around a specific function. All components, both hardware and firmware, are tightly integrated to perform that single function. This "closed box" architecture provides for extremely high reliability.

4. Efficient Allocation and Use of Resources : NAS provides a common pool of storage that can be shared by multiple servers and clients, regardless of their file system or operating system. This enables organization to efficiently allocate storage. This alleviates the problem of one server running out of storage while another server might have more than needed. NAS enables organization to locate storage where it's needed on the network and provide clients with direct, server independent communication to storage resources. Localizing file I/O traffic facilitates a more efficient use of network resources.

A NAS appliance connects directly to the existing LAN and transfers data over standard network access protocols (TCP/IP or IPX) using standard file sharing protocols (SMB/CIFS, NCP, NFS, FTP or HTTP). No additional software or client licenses are required for clients to access storage. This enables organization to implement a storage solution and leverage the existing network investments.

5. Simplicity : The traditional methods of adding storage are too cumbersome for today's network environments. NAS enables to add storage anywhere on the network in minutes simply by plugging in a network cable, applying power and configuring a few settings. There is no server re-configuration and no network downtime.

Management of NAS Appliances can be performed from anywhere on the network or over the Internet using a standard web browser or alternative management tools.

6. Increased Productivity : NAS provides increased productivity for the whole organization. Network clients benefit from the ability to share storage resources with clients from another network environment. They also benefit from reduced data access times and improved application server response times.

7. Lower Total Cost of Ownership : Network Attached Storage, with its many benefits, features a lower total cost of ownership than other methods of adding storage to the network.

I. **Easy to deploy**- by plug and plug attachment to the existing network.

II. **Easy to manage**- managing and allocating disk space is faster on a centrally-administered, easy-to-use web-based interface.

III. **Future scalability** - NAS appliances can be expanded easily as storage requirements grow, and can be integrated in a larger, more sophisticated storage solution when the requirement arises.

Even in environments where organizations have different servers with different operating systems the storage, management and the backup of the data can be centralized.

Some of the big advantages of NAS include it's expandability. It's easy to add extra storage. NAS also brings an extra level of fault tolerance to the network as organization can include mirror RAID features. Availability of data might potentially be increased with NAS if it provides built-in RAID and clustering. The performance of NAS devices, though, depends heavily on the speed of and traffic on the network and on the amount of cache memory (RAM) on the NAS computers or devices.

It should be noted that NAS is effectively a server in

itself, with all major components of a typical PC, a CPU, motherboard, RAM, etc. and its reliability is a function of how well it is designed internally. A NAS without redundant data access paths, redundant controllers, redundant power supplies, is probably more reliable than Direct Attached Storage (DAS) connected to a server which does have redundancy for its major components.

Limitations

Due to the multiprotocol, and the reduced CPU and OS layer, the NAS has its limitations compared to the DAS/SAN systems. If the NAS is occupied with too many users, too many I/O operations, or CPU processing power that is too demanding, the NAS reaches its limitations. A server system is easily upgraded by adding one or more servers into a cluster, so CPU power can be upgraded, The NAS is limited to its own hardware, which is in most cases not upgradeable.

Certain NAS devices fail to expose well-known services that are typical of a file server, or enable them in a way that is not efficient. Examples are: ability to compute disk usage of separate directories, ability to index files rapidly (locate), ability to mirror efficiently with rsync. The key difference between DAS and NAS is that DAS is simply an extension to an existing server and is not networked while NAS sits on a network as its own entity; it is easier to share files with NAS. NAS typically has less CPU and I/O power compared to DAS.

NETWORK ATTACHED STORAGE APPLIANCES VS. GENERAL PURPOSE SERVERS

A Network Attached Storage Appliance is characterized by a streamlined architecture designed and optimized for performing one function - data delivery. This "closed box" approach results in more efficient performance, higher reliability, easier installation, management and use, and lower total cost of ownership as compared to a general-purpose server.

	NAS Appliance	General Purpose Server
Performance	Operating system and hardware platform designed and optimized to perform a specific function very efficiently	Operating system and hardware platform designed for serving applications and multiple general-purpose functions
	Low Overhead	High Overhead
Reliability & Data Availability	Streamlined , architecture with specialized	A greater number of non-embedded components and complex, general purpose software
	OS results in high reliability and data availability	OS means a higher chance of failure and downtime
Administration	Simple web-based administration of specialized operating system	High administration overhead of complex NOS system
Connectivity	Multi-protocol client support	Network operating system dependent Client must meet the server's interface and protocol requirements
Maintenance	Low	High
Costs	Streamlined costs. All hardware and software components are for specific function - Data I/O Unlimited Users - No license required	Unnecessary costs. More than the needed components for file services Client licenses
Total Cost of Ownership	Low	High

	NAS	Fibre Channel SAN	iSCSI SAN
Network	Ethernet	Fibre Channel	Ethernet
Data Transfer & Protocols	File level data transfer over industry standard network protocols (TCP/IP & IPX) via industry standard file sharing protocols (SMB, CIFS, NCP, AFP, NFS, FTP & HTTP)	Raw, block-level data requests directly to disk drive or RAID LUN using SCSI commands over Fibre Channel	Raw, block-level data requests directly to disk drive or RAID LUN using SCSI commands over IP
File System	The file system is located at the storage	The file system is located at the application server	
Data Sharing	True data sharing between heterogeneous clients because file system is at the storage side and data is transferred to client using industry standard file sharing protocols	Software required on all nodes on SAN in order to share files	
Performance	Limited by Ethernet overhead and available network bandwidth	Direct communication with disk over dedicated wire	Direct communication with disk limited by TCP/IP overhead. Can take advantage of 10Gb Ethernet

	NAS	Fibre Channel SAN	iSCSI SAN
Environment	Workgroup to Enterprise	Production Workgroup to Enterprise	
Installation	Plug and Play into existing network with no additional components	Utilizes Fibre Channel infrastructure with server/ software or appliance to link nodes	Utilizes existing network infrastructure with server/ software or appliance to link nodes
Technology	Based on mature industry standard technologies	Interoperability issues may occur	Based on mature SCSI and Ethernet technologies

NETWORK ATTACHED STORAGE (NAS) VS. STORAGE AREA NETWORKING (SAN)

Network Attached Storage (NAS)

A NAS appliance is a self-contained, intelligent storage device that attaches directly to the LAN and transfers data at the file level over network protocols (TCP/IP or IPX) using industry standard file sharing protocols (SMB, CIFS, NCP, AFP, NFS, HTTP). Network clients communicate directly with the storage server.

Storage Area Network (SAN)

A SAN is a discrete network of servers and storage devices (RAID, Tape Libraries, etc.) attached together via a high speed I/O interconnect, such as Fibre Channel or standard network infrastructure utilizing iSCSI technology. Data is transferred via serial I/O rather than network protocols, and raw data requests are made directly to disk without the need for file sharing protocols. Network Attached Storage and Storage Area Network solutions utilize different technologies and each serves a different purpose in a storage networking environment.

REFERENCES AND NOTES

1. Ankeny, M.L (1991) Evaluating End-user services: success or satisfaction. *Journal of Academic Llibrarianship*, 16 (2), 352-356
2. Bawden, D. (1990) *User-oriented evaluation of information systems and services*.Aldershot: Gower.
3. Biddiscombe, R (Ed). (1996) *The end-user revolution CD-ROM, Internet and the changing role of the information professional*. London: LA Publishing.
4. Blandy, S.G and Libutti, P.O'B (1995) As the cursor blinks: electronic scholarship and undergraduates in the library. *Library Trends*, 44(2), 279-305.
5. Brophy, P. (1993) Networking in British academic libraries. *British Journal of Academic Librarianship*, 8(1),49-60.

6. Dutton, B.G. (1990) An introduction to end-user searching. In: Bysouth, P.T. (ed) *End-user searching: the effective gateway to published information*. London: Aslib, 1-18.
7. East, H., Shappard, E. and Jeal, Y. (1995) *A quantitative and qualitative examination of the development of access to database services at British Universities, 1988-1994*. London: British Library Board. (CCIS Policy Paper No. 5. BLR and D Report 6202).
8. National Committee of Inquiry into Higher Education. (1997) *Higher Education in the Learning Society*. London: HMSO, 1997 (NCIHE Chair: Sir Ron Dearing, CB)
9. Ramsden, A. (1996) Electronic information for students - the ELINOR project. *The New Review of Academic Librarianship*, Vol. 2, 91-100.
10. *http://open-fcoe.org/*
11. www.eric.ed.gov/ERICWebPortal/recordDetail
12. *http://www.enterprisestorageforum.com/*
13. www.educause.edu/Resources/.../159422
14. *http://www.enterprisestorageforum.com/*
15. Faries, C. (1992) User reactions to CD-ROM: the Penn State experience. *College and Research Libraries*, 53(2), 139-149.
16. Follett Report. (1993) *Joint Funding Councils' Libraries Review Group: Report*. Bristol: HEFCE.
17. Goldfinch, R. (1990) The impact of end-user searching of CD-ROM on on-line use. In: Armstrong, C.J. and Hartley, R.J (eds.). *On-line information retrieval: today and tomorrow*. Oxford: Learned Information Ltd.
18. McClure, C. (1992) A user perspective on developing Internet services. *Computer in Libraries*, 12(4), 53-55.
19. technologysource.org/.../electronic_resources_in_the_freshman_seminar_classroom/
20. *http://www.b2net.co.uk/solutions/san/*
21. http://www.bestpricecomputers.co.uk/reviews/advice/network-attached-storage.htm
22. *http://www.webopedia.com/TERM/S/SAN.html*

23. www.btstream.com/resc.html
24. *http://compnetworking.about.com/lr/network_storage/169327/1/*
25. Ray, K. (1997) *Student attitudes towards electronic information*. MA Dissertation, University of Northumbria at Newcastle, Department of Information and Library Management.
26. Schultz, K. and Salomon, K. (1990) End users respond to CD-ROM. *Library Journal*, 56-57.
27. Winship, I. (1996) *The student's guide to the Internet*. London: LA Publishing.
28. *The case for network-attached storage*, Network World on Storage, 03/20/00.
29. *http://compnetworking.about.com/od/itinformationtechnology/l/bldef_nas.htm*
30. *http://www.amsstorage.com/html/dakotaraid_lp.html*
31. http://www.networkworld.com/links/Encyclopedia/S/493.html
32. http://www.bestpricecomputers.co.uk/glossary/product-lifecycle-management-software.htm
33. *http://compnetworking.about.com/od/networkstorage/f/san-vs-nas.htm*
34. *http://www.b2net.co.uk/solutions/nas*
35. Collins, K.L.K. and Takacs, S.N. (1993) Information technology and the teaching role of the College Librarian. *Reference Librarian*, No. 39, 41-48.
36. Ray, Kathryn & Day, Joan (1998) "Student attitudes towards electronic information resources." *Information Research*, 4(2) Available at: http://informationr.net/ir/4-2/paper54.html
37. Culbertson, M. (1992) Analysis of searches by end-users of science and engineering CD-ROM databases in an academic library. *CD-ROM Professional*, 5(2), 76-79.
38. Day, J., Edwards, C., Walton, G., Curry, S., Bent, M., and Jackson, M. (1996) Higher education, teaching, learning and

the electronic library: a review of the literature for the IMPEL2 project: monitoring organisational and cultural change. *New Review of Academic Librarianship*, 2, 131-204.

39. http://www.bestpricecomputers.co.uk/glossary/raid.htm
40. *http://searchstorage.techtarget.com/topics/0,295493,sid5_tax298616,00.html?asrc=SS_TAGCLOUD*
41. http://www.hardwarecentral.com/hardwarecentral/sanderscolumn/2942/1/
42. *http://www.planetit.com/techcenters/docs/enterprise_apps_systems-storage/opinion/PIT19990615S0009/3*
43. *http://www.sun.com/storage/white-papers/nas.html*
44. *http://www.win2000mag.com/Articles/Index.cfm?ArticleID=9018*
45. *http://www.bestpricecomputers.co.uk/glossary/storage-area-networks.htm*
46. http://www.bestpricecomputers.co.uk/glossary/Network-Attached-storage.htm
47. http://www.hardwarecentral.com/hardwarecentral/sanderscolumn/2942/1/
48. *http://searchstorage.techtarget.com/topics/0,295493,sid5_tax298667,00.html?asrc=S_TAGCLOUD*
49. *http://www.amsstorage.com/html/dakota_nas.htm*
50. http://searchnetworking.techtarget.com/sDefinition/0,,sid7_gci214038,00.html

6

E-Archive and Digital Preservation

Defining as e-archive may be simple yet complex task. The terms 'perpetual access', 'archiving', and 'long-term preservation' are sometimes used interchangeably. Perpetual access is most commonly associated with e-journal license clauses designed to provide assurance of continued access to subscribed material in certain circumstances, including post-cancellation. Archiving describes the process and procedures whereby e-resource content may be managed for the short or long term. Long-term preservation refers to the processes and procedures required to ensure content remains accessible well into the future, regardless of any technical or organizational changes. While attempting to describe, archives can be described:

- Special software based boxes, which preserve a local archive of a library's holdings, available to the library in the event of failure of their usual access route;
- National library archives held under legal e-deposit laws or by virtue of voluntary deposit by publishers. These may be accessible, but only to users with physical access to a reading room, as the terms of use

are based on 'walk-in' access only;

- Archives created locally for the purposes of distribution with the consent of publishers
- Publishers' own internal archives

The general features associated with archives are as follows:

1. Organization : The mission and solidity of the organization that supports the archive will affect the repository's prospects for continuity. Archives vary, from those created for the express purpose of preserving content for academia to those embedded within scientific, publishing and aggregator organizations. It is important to know the extent to which preservation is integral to the parent organization's mission, and how important the repository functions are to that organization's revenue stream.

2. Content : What content is maintained by the archive and what are its critical characteristics? The extent and scope of the journal titles, databases, and other materials archived should be listed, or easily discovered, and verifiable. What mechanisms are in place to ensure the continued deposit of the listed content, and prevent its withdrawal by the publisher?

3. Ingestion : Trustworthy archives disclose specific data on the form and functionality of the content ingested. Most archives reformat or normalize content in order to limit the cost of managing and migrating complex formats. Normalization may make the archived content look or behave differently than it does when delivered directly to users by producers or publishers. Clarity about the nature and degree of normalization can provide a sense of the scale of investment the library and/or the repository will have to make, if any, to provide an acceptable level of functionality in the future.

4. Technical Systems and Data Security : The most

obvious indicator of the reliability of an archive is the stability and robustness of the technical infrastructure that supports digital preservation. Factors here include whether the archive conforms to the Open Archives Information Systems Reference Model, to various system security requirements and standards developed in government and other domains, and whether the policies and methods for backup, redundancy, authentication, distribution of functions and services are clear and conform to accepted best practices. Also important is the scalability of the system. Is the archive likely to be able to accommodate new and complex forms of content and functionality?

5. Governance and Accountability : The governance of the organization that supports the archive determines which communities' interests will drive the activities of the archive. How accountable is the organization to the user community, and in what ways is that accountability assured? Conversely, how accountable is the organization to the producers or publishing community?

6. Cost Structure and Distribution : The costs of a repository can be structured and distributed in several ways, with differing implications for future costs to the library. The archive may assess the library or users a combination of initial capital fees and ongoing maintenance fees, or simply a subscription fee. Some costs might also be borne by the publisher of the archived content. While there are limits to how precisely a archive can project future fees in advance, libraries should be clear about the cost drivers (such as amount and complexity of content, frequency of migration, royalties to content publishers, etc.) and how the costs are distributed in the event of changes in those drivers.

7. Rights : Archives should disclose documentation of the rights they hold to deliver the content in the event of failure by the producer or publisher, the duration of the grant of those rights, and whether said rights are transferable.

Such documentation should be clear about what constitutes failure. Failure is often defined as when a publisher no longer offers the content, but drastic subscription price increases, the decision to make the content available only as part of a larger, prohibitively priced bundle, and similar events can also put content out of reach of libraries.

8. Results and Outputs : Longevity and performance are important indicators of the reliability of an archive. While digital preservation is only just emerging, organizations and systems that have demonstrated competency in effectively fulfilling preservation functions are likely to continue to support persistence identified what they believed were basic characteristics of archiving:

i. The archive commits to continuing maintenance of digital objects for identified community/communities.

ii. Demonstrates organizational fitness (including financial, staffing structure, and processes) to fulfill its commitment.

iii. Acquires and maintains requisite contractual and legal rights and fulfills responsibilities.

iv. Has an effective and efficient policy framework.

v. Acquires and ingests digital objects based upon stated criteria that correspond to its commitments and capabilities.

vi. Maintains/ensures the integrity, authenticity and usability of digital objects it holds over time.

vii. Creates and maintains requisite metadata about actions taken on digital objects during preservation as well as about the relevant production, access support, and usage process contexts before preservation.

viii. Fulfills requisite dissemination requirements.

ix. Has a strategic program for preservation planning and action.

x. Has technical infrastructure adequate to continuing maintenance and security of its digital objects.

The key premise underlying the core requirements is that for repositories of all types and sizes preservation activities must be scaled to the needs and means of the defined community or communities' registry of electronic resources in an archive

NEED IN CURRENT SCENARIO

There is a need for more information, and more easily accessible information, about where e-journals are archived. However, what has also emerged strongly is that this issue cannot be considered in isolation, either from the overall context of relationships within the scholarly communication system, nor from other initiatives being undertaken to improve information flows e.g. in relation to the transfer of titles between publishers. Another aspect is that the library community would expect a solution to the information problem which went beyond simply recording where a title was archived and tracking any changes over time. Librarians feel they need to understand and be reassured about what their access route would be to a title in the event of problems in their normal means of access.

REGISTRY

The scope of the registry system is specifically about where e-journals are archived, but discussion of the idea of a registry raised much wider concerns about the role of libraries as custodians of e-journals, and the difficulties they experience in guaranteeing uninterrupted access to them and in managing licences. In fact, it will be impossible to scope the registry without viewing its place within this system. Ultimately, what all libraries want is to deliver seamless and uninterrupted access to archival material for their users; this encompasses everything from day-to-day management of electronic resources. It includes dealing with temporary technical problems, subscription administration, title transfers, changes in access models, authentication issues and complying with licence conditions to being assured that content is preserved and accessible for the long term.

CONCERNED ISSUES

The general issue of access routes has exposed some further questions about how complete and accurate the information record is (either on the library/consortia side or the publisher side) of contractual relationships formed over the period since e-resources began to be available. There are considerable ambiguities about rights of archival access in cases where libraries received an electronic copy of a journal 'free' with a print subscription. A registry in and of itself cannot be expected to solve these problems; at the most, all it can do is record the outcome. It is very important for all users to be clear about what the registry is and is not able to achieve at various stages of its implementation. In particular it is vital that librarians are not given the impression that because a title is in the registry, they will necessarily have access to it. Librarians felt that they were most likely to consult a registry in situations where they were considering taking out or renewing a subscription; considering cancellation of a print subscription in favour of an e-only subscription; contemplating relocating or discarding print holdings.

Benefit and Drawbacks

Registry facilitates the exposure of gaps in archive provision. Librarians would want to be alerted to risks to any of their holdings. Publishers would like to see their efforts recognized and pressure placed on publishers who are not making satisfactory arrangements. Archival sections would also benefit as that effect fed through to more demand for their services. The drawbacks to a registry as a solution to the acknowledged information gap were mainly seen as ones of practicality such as keeping the information accurate and up to date, trust, especially whether a national solution is appropriate, and conversely whether an international solution is feasible and sustainability of the funding model. Apart from the desirability and feasibility of the registry, there is a separate question as to whether now is the right time for such an initiative, or if it is premature in relation to the problem of archiving. Some also suggested a pilot stage which can give some indication both of the scale of the problem in terms of titles not being archived anywhere and of the real practical difficulties.

Above all else, the question of the sustainability of a registry needs to be carefully considered. The primary purpose of a registry or registry-like service would be to direct libraries to the archives where particular journals are located and preserved; the archives themselves have to be sustainable over the long term. Concerns about archiving have increasingly come to the fore in recent years, driven by the accelerating move towards electronic-only access to journals, and the potential divergence between the electronic and print versions of journals. More features such as interactivity and links to underlying datasets are built into articles. Librarians are under increasing budgetary pressures, including the need to save physical space and cut labor costs, which is leading many to consider canceling print subscriptions, moving print collections to remote storage, or discarding print archives.

Recommendations for Academic Libraries and Organizations

1. Libraries should participate in developing a registry of archived scholarly publications that indicates which programs have preserved them. This registry can be used to identify gaps in publisher or content coverage.

Models for such registries include the Registry of Open Access Repositories (ROAR) and ROARMAP.

2. Publishers should be overt about their digital archiving efforts and enter into archiving relationships with one or more e-journal archiving programs.
3. Publishers should extend liberal archiving rights in their licensing agreements with content aggregators and consortia. Digital archiving of e-journals should be a distributed responsibility.
4. Independent, trusted e-journal archiving services are emerging. They are still at an early stage and the community needs to invest in different options in order to retain a vigorous and healthy diversity of services most likely to be able to accommodate the range of requirements.

The question of preservation is raised as a barrier to the transition to e-journals. Although the importance of preservation is widely acknowledged, license agreements do not always make it clear what responsibilities publishers are agreeing to take on. Lack of clarity within licenses concerning ongoing access rights or archiving arrangements is a problem. It is found that some libraries were pressing ahead with discarding print in the hope that solutions would be found, while others, in more research-intensive institutions which saw themselves as having a mission to maintain collections, were more cautious. There is the need to demonstrate that electronic archives can meet expectations when the need arises, and thus to "put the trust in trusted archive."

REGISTRY MODELS

There is really no single view on the constitution of a registry. Bodies describing themselves as such have been created for many different functions. Recording details of licensed drivers or practitioners, allocating domain names, recording consistent definitions of data (metadata registries) are some functions. They may be actual physical locations where an act of registration takes place, or virtual entities. A registry tends to imply a monolithic, somewhat bureaucratic, central structure, perhaps not well suited to the distributed, interlinked nature of digital information. E-journal archives are themselves distributed. It is recognized that communities feel more comfortable about something fairly local. ROAR and ROARMAP are examples of registries.

i. **ROAR** : ROAR has two functions:

- To monitor overall growth in the number of e-print archives and
- To maintain a list of GNU E-Prints sites.

ii. **ROARMAP** : ROARMAP has following functions:

- To record the open-access policies of those institutions who are putting the principle of Open Access into practice. Universities and research institutions who officially commit themselves to implementing a systematic policy of open-access provision for their own peer-reviewed research output are invited to describe their policy in ROARMAP. The ROARMAP site states about signing. Signing will:
    1. Record institution's commitment to providing open access to its own research output,
    2. Help the research community measure its progress in providing open access worldwide and
    3. Encourage further institutions to adopt open-access provision policies (so that institution's users can have access to the research output of other institutions as well).

ROAR and ROARMAP are certainly registries within the scholarly communications arena, but since their focus is on *inviting* participation and since they also have a campaigning aspect, their relevance for the purposes be small. This is because, although accuracy, timeliness and comprehensiveness are clearly desirable attributes of these registries, they are hardly critical, whereas for the proposed e-journal archive registry, these factors would be crucial. Registries such as PRONOM and the Global Data Format Registry, have obvious connections with digital preservation. PRONOM is an online registry of technical information, a resource for anyone requiring impartial and definitive information about the file formats, software products and other technical components required to support long-term access to electronic records and other digital objects of cultural, historical or business value.

It may be worth mentioning the Romeo service here, now under the auspices of Sherpa, which records publishers' policies on self-archiving. There are several reasons for considering Romeo. Firstly, it has been suggested to us that archive information could be integrated into it. Secondly, the white, yellow, blue and green classification or something similar might be a useful template for the way information is presented in the archive registry. Thirdly, there was some criticism of it for being inaccurate, used as an example of problems that could arise if this registry was unable to establish good mechanisms for updating.

Significance of Registry

The library community and the publishers are broadly in favor of registry system. Some of the archiving organisations expressed reservations. The key benefits were seen as:

- It can function as a one-stop-shop for librarians, compared with looking in licences, on publishers' websites, contacting subscription agents or aggregators, or searching individual archiving organisations' websites
- It would put pressure on publishers to make archive

provision for their titles, as the gaps would be much more visible to the community

- It would encourage transparency and the provision of detailed information by the archiving organisations about their holdings.

What information should a registry contain?

There were two main points of view about the information which library people would expect such a registry to contain. Proponents of the 'lightweight' view may argue that all the registry needs to have is t he simple information that 'x title, for y volumes and issues, is archived in z'. The user will then be pointed to z to check other information, including the conditions of access; the format in which the title is stored e.g. is the original 'look and feel' preserved, and the preservation strategies being followed. Limiting the scope of the registry will allow it to focus on what it is uniquely for, keeping the costs down and making it more likely that the information is accurate and timely.

The second view is that information on how the content can be accessed is crucial. It is not simply the absence of a central directory of where titles are archived that is problematic to many libraries. It is also that they find the information about the terms under which access is allowed confusing and obscure. Proponents of this view also argue that users don't really care if something is in an archive unless they can get at it. However, the latter is not perhaps as straightforward as it appears.

There are certain questions whether content would be made available to non-participating but subscribing libraries. The licences which publishers have made with the different archiving organisations are based on a common core with each organisation. There can be publisher-specific variations. The danger would be for the registry itself to confer a level of reassurance about access which was not accurate, and given that this would be one of the key reasons for consulting the registry, this could be a significant problem. It also demands attention to allow a library to see its **own** route to accessing a copy in terms of its actual contractual rights. There are some ambiguities. Some obvious questions are there, for example, what are the archival rights, if any, attached to an electronic copy which came 'free' with a print subscription? What is the contractual position for an institution?

Essentially, such questions have been in picture and will continue to be settled by negotiation. It may be that bodies and their negotiating agents can achieve some collective agreements on certain points rather than institutions themselves having to negotiate individually with publishers. A further point which needs to be emphasized is that it is just as important, if not more so, for a registry to be capable of being used to identify titles which are not archived anywhere, and are therefore at risk. Undermining trust can be developed due to poor quality of information and lack of timeliness. The registry would need to be governed in such a way as to secure and maintain the trust of both the library community and publishers.

DIGITAL PRESERVATION

Digital preservation is an area characterized by a high level of uncertainty. It deals with continuum of experimentation, discovery are employed in the search for preservation techniques and solutions. In order to effectively operate in such an environment, a high technological awareness is essential for the digital preservation. Librarians need to keep pace with technological change, monitor trends in thinking about digital preservation issues, and maintain an awareness of international standards. Libraries should be ready to explore new methods of application. Appropriate knowledge bases can be developed through accessing of internet resources such as subscription to discussion lists, networking, monitoring research and projects, and participation in state-of-the-art conferences. Knowledge of the technological implications and the legal and political framework is must within which digital preservation initiatives may operate.

The Importance of Preserving Digital Information

Since the advent of computers in the early part of the last Century, the society has been moving into the electronic world at an increasingly rapid pace. With this comes the transformation of the cultural materials from their traditional forms into digital forms. This change has caused some alarm given the ephemeral nature of the digital environment.

The rapidly evolving nature of the electronic medium renders technologies obsolete in a remarkably short time and the ability to access older electronic documents. The artifactual value of electronic art is much different than the artifactual value of more conventional art forms. Because of changing technologies, electronic art originals can only be accessed/viewed/played for a very short time period. Libraries in particular have struggled to address these issues given the ease of creating electronic texts driving the resultant growth of electronic scholarly publishing but these problems are rapidly catching up to museums as digitization projects take hold and creators begin to experiment with the unique properties and abilities of the digital medium.

Of particular concern are artifacts that are born digital and have no physical instance to transcend the digital limitations; that is, artifacts which are "created digitally and [have] functionality which requires use of appropriate hardware and software. To understand a born digital artifact is to rely heavily on its technological context for meaning and saving the digital bits while losing the technical context is still losing the artifact forever. Even the ability to save the digital bits is in doubt as the physical media on which they are stored may become obsolete in as little as five years. If it is difficult to save one format, consider how the difficulty is compounded when faced with the incredible array of formats that currently exist. Given the rapid increase in digital collections since last decade, it is reasonable to suggest the number of formats has also grown at a comparable pace.

The Digital Preservation Challenge

1. **Scale** : With the tremendous increase in electronically generated and digitized material over the past decade, the collections of academic and national libraries contain many millions of digital items, including digitized prints, electronic articles, audiovisuals, and Web sites.

2. **Life cycle** : The ease with which electronic resources can be updated results in shorter information life cycles. A digital preservation system must therefore support the timely ingest of new material, as well as the management of different versions of the material.

3. **Format** : As digital formats continue to change, institutions must ensure that digital content is preserved so that it can be viewed, listened to, and explored in the future, even if the original technology becomes obsolete.

Images and audio-visual materials are being stored in digital formats more than ever before. These digital files:

- may have been captured in a traditional format such as film photography, then scanned, or transferred from film or tape to a digital format
- may be created directly into digital formats with the use of digital cameras or other digital equipment.

Digitization is sometimes recommended as a preservation strategy for materials that are in fragile formats and should not be used frequently. For example, digitizing pages of delicate manuscripts preserves access to the information on the pages. However, digital objects themselves must be preserved. Rapid changes in technology require institutions to create preservation strategies to ensure longevity for digital materials. There are certain technological changes that affect digital files. These are changes in the media on which digital objects are stored and format changes in technical environments.

STRATEGIES FOR PRESERVING E-RESOURCES

The following strategies function as components of a digital preservation process:

1. Refreshing data

- addresses the decay, change, or obsolescence of physical formats - media on which files are stored
- involves periodically moving a file from one physical storage medium to another. Changes to physical storage devices require this to be an ongoing process.

2. Emulation and Migration

- **Emulation :** focuses on the application rather than the files produced. Emulation tries to recreate application environments on which the original files can run.
- **Migration :** involves moving files from one file encoding format to another. For example, upgrading a file type to the newest version of particular software product

Ideally, a combination of Refreshing with either Emulation or Migration should be adopted as a preservation strategy for digital information objects.

3. Archival Images

Any project creating digital images, even if the main purpose of the project is to create images for the Web, should create master images. These will be images captured at a high resolution, on which no manipulation or change is made. Copies of these archival files can be made and used for later projects, but the original captured files should always be maintained and preserved.

4. Preservation Metadata

Recording preservation metadata is a key component of a digital preservation strategy. This type of information is administrative or structural. It includes information about the date of capture, the capture device, change history, and other information about the files, including relationships to other files. This metadata is different from descriptive information about the content of the file, which may be used for resource discovery.

There is general recognition of the importance of metadata in an overall strategy for digital preservation. However, as there is no single standard for preservation metadata widely accepted, many organizations and projects have created their own schemes for local use. Fortunately, there are enough common factors between the local schemes that convergence should be possible with appropriate crosswalks to convert existing metadata to the emerging standards. For resource discovery metadata and structural metadata, there are emerging standards which have some degree of consensus. Most guides that identify the need for structural metadata recommend the usage of the Metadata Encoding Transmission Standard (METS) while Dublin Core is often recommended for resource discovery.

Some of the preservation initiatives are as given:

a. **CEDARS – Curl Exemplars in Digital Archives** : This United Kingdom project objectives include:

- promoting awareness of digital preservation issues
- identification of strategic frameworks for developing digital collection management policies

- developing guidelines for long-term preservation

b. **Nedlib— Networked European Deposit Library :** This collaborative effort among European national libraries aims to develop the infrastructure for a networked European deposit library, with a focus on preservation of electronic publications.

c. **Preservation Metadata for Digital Collections :** The OCLC and RLG collaboration is also focusing on the OAIS (Open Archival Information System), which is an information model for handling archiving of physical and digital information.

5. Web sites - Archiving

Web sites present a different set of problems for preservation. There are not only individual files that need to be preserved, but the relationships and linkages between them, and their structured indices, pose further preservation issues. The issues for websites are important such as:

- instability of URLs
- viruses
- the need for change documentation

In 2001, the Internet Archive introduced the *Wayback Machine*, where users can view snapshots of Web sites as they appeared at various points in the past. Although this project provide useful snapshots, it does not record

- Changes in structure of a Web site
- Databased material

Here are given Smithsonian recommendations for design and authoring of Web sites and HTML pages for long-term access Good Dublin Core metatags on pages

- HTML markup should be XML compliant
- Avoid the use of a third-party proprietary search engine not under control of the site's Webmaster

- All links within the site should be relative
- Copies of Web site should be periodically created and maintained
- Major revisions to a Web site should be fully documented

Prototype Web Archiving Projects

a. Minerva : Mapping the Internet Electronic Resources Virtual Archive project of Library of Congress

b. Pandora - Preserving and Accessing Networked Online Resources of Australia : National Library of Australia. Archive of selected Australian online publications, including Web sites developed strategy for long-term preservation.

CONCEPTUALIZATION OF DIGITAL PRESERVATION ISSUES

Almost the primary problems associated with digital preservation are media deterioration/obsolescence and technology obsolescence. In particular, the NINCH guide suggests preservation faces two types of long-term accessibility challenges: machine accessibility (bit integrity) and human accessibility (semantic integrity). Similarly, the Visual Arts Data Service guide distinguishes between physical reliability and continued usability. There is also general consensus on digital archiving or preservation as a continuous activity in the form of a series of managed activities or as a lifecycle management approach. On the other hand, the source of digital objects is an area of divergence. A number of guides focus on digitized surrogates of physical objects while others encompass both digitized and born-digital objects with the preservation recommendations biased accordingly.

The 3-M Preservation Cycle - Materials/Management/ Migration Materials

1. **Materials :** The 3-M Preservation cycle includes selecting materials appropriate to the work. The choice of

hardware and software for the development of a work greatly influence strategies for its preservation and future access. If the work is for short term consumption then the use of obscure technology is most probably not an issue unless there is an intention to encourage wide-spread access and distribution. The greatest ally for long term preservation and access is the use of materials that confirm to recognized, long lasting standards.

2. Management : The greatest threat in the preservation of multimedia works is that software components will get lost or corrupted and that necessary specialized hardware components will be removed or become incompatible. The elements that comprise work and the links between these elements need to be identified, recorded and maintained over time. Versions of hardware and software need to be tracked and decisions made when it is necessary to migrate to new versions. A good management strategy is to encourage access, and to widely distribute work. Works that are frequently accessed have a greater probability of survival.

3. Migration : Migration of works to current technology can be expensive. However if works are being created using products that have wide acceptance and conform to recognized, long lasting standards then migration should be reasonably straight forward without requiring the use of additional software or hardware. The main challenge with migration is identifying the appropriate time when to migrate. Timing is dependent on the trade-off between effort/cost against ease of migration/functionality. Migration will inevitably result in some loss of functionality or corruption of the work.

ANALYSIS OF STORAGE MEDIA AND DIGITAL FORMATS

In comparison to strategies, there is less consensus in recommending specific media or formats. This can be attributed to the need to support the significant properties of a broad range of artifacts, often requiring specific formats and media. Even with more general issues such as whether or not to use a compressed format, there is little consensus. While some are explicit about holding only non-compressed items, others only recommend the format be lossless to retain maximum fidelity. One argument for why compression of any type (including lossless) is problematic for archival files is the introduction of an additional level of complexity which only serves to increase the recovery/migration problem in the future. The use of a standard format that is non-proprietary as these kinds of formats are more likely to have a preservation path in the future. One recommendation to handle media issues is to create backups, using more than one kind of backup software to write the copies so as to safeguard against software bugs. In this scenario, at least one copy should be maintained in an offsite location and the media periodically checked as per the refreshing methodology.

DIGITAL PRESERVATION STRATEGIES

While digital technologies are enabling information to be created, manipulated, disseminated, located and stored with increasing ease, preserving access to this information poses a significant challenge. Choice of strategy will depend upon the nature of the material and what aspects are to be retained. Refreshing (copying information without changing it) offers a short-term solution for preserving access to digital material by ensuring that information is stored on newer media before the old media deteriorates beyond the point at which the information can be retrieved.

The migration of digital information from one hardware/software configuration to another or from one generation of computer technology to a later one, offers one method of dealing with technological obsolescence. While adherence to standards will assist in preserving access to digital information, it must be recognized that technological standards themselves are evolving rapidly. The importance of documentation as a tool to assist in preserving digital material is universally agreed. In addition to the metadata necessary for resource discovery, other sorts of metadata, including preservation metadata, describing the software, hardware and management requirements of the digital material, will provide essential information for preservation.

1. Emulation

Emulation refers to the process of mimicking, in software, a piece of hardware or software so that other processes think the original equipment/function is still available in its original form. Emulation is essentially a way of preserving the functionality of and access to digital information which might otherwise be lost due to technological obsolescence. Emulation may offer a viable alternative strategy to ensure access to digital information in the future. One of the benefits of the emulation strategy compared with migration is that the original data need not be altered in any way. It is the emulation of the computer environment that will change with time. This helps maintain the integrity and "look and feel" of the material. Another advantage of implementing emulation is its possible efficiency. Once the data is archived with appropriate metadata and software, no other action is required apart from media refreshing until access is desired. One emulator can also be used as a solution for several data objects requiring the same operating environment.

2. Encapsulation

Encapsulation in the context of preserving digital materials is a technique of grouping together a digital object and anything else necessary to provide access to that object. This technique aims to overcome the problems of the technological obsolescence of file formats because the details of how to interpret the digital bits in the object can be part of the encapsulated information. Encapsulation can be achieved by using physical or logical structures called "containers" or "wrappers" to provide a relationship between all information components, such as the digital object and other supporting information such as a persistent identifier, metadata, software specifications for emulation.

The types of supporting information that should be included in an encapsulation, apart from the digital object itself, are: the representation information used to interpret the bits appropriately for access; the provenance to describe the source of the object; the context to describe how the object relates to other information outside the container; reference to provide one or more identifiers to uniquely identify the object; and fixity to provide evidence that the object has not been altered. An alternative to storing the representation information to decode the bit-stream with every digital item archived is to include a pointer to a single storage area for that information. This could be stored in the same repository or another dedicated centralized repository.

3. Migration

The migration of digital information refers to the "periodic transfer of digital materials from one hardware/ software configuration to another, or from one generation of computer technology to a subsequent generation." This term is sometimes used to refer to the transfer of information to non-digital media. Migration includes refreshing, that is, copying digital information without changing it. Migration to new operating environments often means that the copy is not exactly the same as the original piece of information. Decisions need to be made about what aspects of the material to be migrated (eg functionality, presentation) need to be preserved.

Providing information about successive migrations in the form of metadata will assist in determining what changes have occurred to the digital object. The complexity of the migration process depends on the nature of the digital resource which may vary from simple text to an interactive multimedia object. At its simplest, migration may entail copying digital information to a more stable non-digital medium, such as paper or microfilm. While these media have better proven long-term reliability, frequently they provide inadequate representations of the original object and result in severe loss of the functionality and presentation of the original digital object. Transfer to a more stable digital medium (eg. from floppy disk to CD-R) offers a short- to medium-term strategy for preserving access, but still requires the CD-R to be migrated when the technology changes.

Another approach to preserving access to digital information entails initially migrating it to standard formats which are expected to be less volatile than the wide array of formats in which digital material may originally be accessible. However, it is important to realize that technical standards are in a state of rapid flux and this strategy cannot be solely relied upon to ensure that digital information remains accessible. Using software which is 'backwards compatible', that is, a later version of the software can decode files created on an earlier version, will simplify migration. Interoperability of systems will also facilitate migration by obviating the need to run a specific program in order to be able to access a digital resource which was created using it. However, at its most complexes, migration can be time-consuming and costly. Migration requires a unique solution for each new format and type of document that is to be converted and that costs are recurrent and unpredictable. While further testing and investigation will be required to facilitate this approach, nevertheless, currently migration offers the most promising approach for preserving access to digital information.

RISK MANAGEMENT IN DIGITAL PRESERVATION

Risk management involves several stages, including identifying what can go wrong, assessing the risks and categorizing them by level of risk and the implementation of strategies to minimize or negate those risks. Given the constantly evolving nature of digital preservation, risk management should be an ongoing process, to be reviewed on a continuous basis.

1. The Digital Curation Challenge

The curation of digitally encoded content has become a fundamental priority within the cultural heritage community. The researchers, curators and consumers increasingly rely on technological means for content delivery and reproduction. The most natural responses to the unerring transition towards an increasingly digital world view focus on the implicit opportunities. Broader and more interactive access to all kinds of information assets, filtering and discovery, and information analysis are natural benefits of the digital platform. Numerous influences threaten the integrity of digital data in the face of an uncertain future. Physical deterioration over time is a familiar concept from traditional analogue archiving environments. The heightened complexity implicit within most contemporary digital storage is accompanied by a commensurate increase in the likelihood of hardware and media failure. The problem is further compounded as even isolated errors occurring on digital platforms or within encoded materials can restrict access to disproportionate quantities of information or at worst render content completely inaccessible. The fundamental vulnerability of data extends beyond comparatively trivial questions of carrier integrity. Unlike in the analogue world, data require appropriate software, hardware and semantic mediators to enable their comprehension, digestion or manipulation. In the absence of appropriate contingencies, technological, social, organizational and political changes pose considerable threats to data availability, integrity, authenticity and usability. Knowledge upon which information interpretation is dependent may be lost; and diminishing organizational commitment to data management can threaten its availability.

2. Challenges

The collective understanding of information security issues has reached a considerable level of maturity, and the challenges associated with bit-level preservation are now regarded as rather trivial. Preservation is much more difficult. Certain factors such as when information exchange possibilities might result in data sharing by highly diverse and disassociated communities (including those separated by a temporal dimension) and maintaining consistent semantic interpretability and structural authenticity can never be ignored. How, when the commercial realities of information technology favor proprietary solutions and digital rights management provisions, can libraries ensure the continued usability of digital materials long after software vendors, service providers or facilitators have ceased trading or discontinued support for legacy products need to be ensure. The most well established data creators and curators are likely to be survived by the value of their data.

3. Intellectual Property Rights and Rights Management

The issue of intellectual property rights and rights management is consistently raised with the primary emphasis on ensuring that institutions have sufficient rights for digital preservation activities. Current and further changes to copyright laws may prevent preservation either by preventing copying or preventing modifying the digital object and represent a possible future barrier to preservation.

PRESERVATION THREATS

The preservation threats fall into four preservation threat categories: media failure, hardware failure, software failures, and operator errors.

1. Media Failure

Media failures are common in e-environment. In particular, problems are encountered with portable hard drives used to transfer file. However, fixity checks performed on the files as part of the transfer process readily catch these problems. Procedures required to maintain local copies of the files is their verification and backup.

2. Hardware Failure

The storage systems also encounter a number of hard drive failures. However, the storage system is composed of multiple hard drive arrays, each configured as RAID 5 with a hot spare. This helps to prevent both data loss and downtime in the case of the failure of a single hard drive in a hard drive array. An array can also face while the storage system is rebuilding the hot swap to replace a failed hard drive. This results in the loss of a small amount of data from the storage system. The file system diagnostics can be able to identify the corrupted files, and they can be restored, since some repositories do not support auditing data under its management for bit-level errors.

3. Software Failures

The software failures relevant to preservation occur usually during project development. The software failures can involve repository code as well as file system software.

4. Operator Errors

The most significant threats to preservation can occur

as a result of operator errors. The operator error involves the deletion of a large number of files from a section of a file system managed by repository. The reason that the operator can be manually deleting files from the repository managed file system to compensate for the difficulty in performing cleanup of repository when an error occurs in the midst of a lengthy ingest. Repository's lack of auditing capabilities contributes to this problem.

Relative to the long-term obligation to preserve the digitized content, the beta development phase can take place over an extremely short period of time. Nonetheless, within that period a broad range of preservation threats were experienced. However, it further proves that developing digital repository systems is an extremely difficult and complex process.

ASSESSMENT OF PRESERVATION STRATEGIES AND RECOMMENDED METHODOLOGY

There is relative uniformity identifying the two dominant strategies in digital preservation as being emulation and migration. However, some guides only identify these two strategies while others present them as two in a wider spectrum of possibilities. In most cases though, there appears to be an implicit acceptance of migration as the primary strategy, ranging from presenting migration as the only strategy to identifying a list of strategies but explicitly recommending migration. Some emphasize on the retention of the original digital object supplemented by migration upon request while some suggest migrating with every version of a format, an undertaking requiring the application of greater resources over the long-term. One reason given for why migration is favored is that emulation-based approaches are experimental; while emulation may be the best hope for complex digital objects in the future, there are few institutions with the technological expertise to create emulators in the short term.

While there is not a clear answer as to which strategy to choose, there is agreement that all digital preservation strategies require that the digital bits be available for future use. To this end, refreshing is identified as the best practice for long term machine readability. Refreshing can be implemented in a number of ways from immediately moving files onto a common media maintained for all digital objects to more traditional approaches emphasizing environmental stability and routine maintenance and migration of the media.

CHECKLIST FOR CREATING A PRESERVATION POLICY

Organizational

1. *Selection/Acquisition*

a. Importance of the object important in the context of the institution's core holdings or collection strengths

b. Fitting object into the current or planned digital preservation infrastructure of the institution

2. *Roles and Responsibilities*

a. Status of institution being the primary holder of record for the digital object

b. Responsibilities or restrictions for access to the object

3. *Retention/Deselection*

a. Are there other institutions with greater capacity or expertise in the type of the object at hand?

b. Does the object fit with the continuing mission of the institution?

Media

1. *Choosing a media type to use:*

a. Multi-vendor support for hardware readers and media manufacturing?

b. Environmental fluctuations.

2. Management of the media:

a. How long between checks for media readability and integrity? Between media replacement?

b. Is there an identified offsite location? How often will the offsite store be updated?

c. Is there an asset tracking system in place for media and how will media be labeled/identified?

Formats

1. Choosing archival formats:

a. Does the format have broad support in viewers/ editors?

b. Is the format open/non-proprietary and does it have published specifications?

c. Does the format have support for including metadata?

d. Does the format support for significant properties of the original (if a digital surrogate)?

e. Does the format support lossless compression or no compression/encryption?

2. Management of files:

a. Is the version of software that created the file recorded? Is the current version recorded?

b. How often are format emulators/migrators identified and investigated?

c. What data loss would constitute a loss of a significant property for the format?

Metadata

1. General

a. Can the digital objects use a global standard or is there a compelling reason to create a local standard?

2. Resource Discovery/Descriptive

a. Does the standard meet the discipline or domain requirements?

b. Does the standard chosen address interoperability/ general resource discovery needs?

3. Structural

a. Does the standard chosen address the types of aggregation important to the collection?

4. Administrative/Preservation

a. Is there an authenticity indicator (e.g. a checksum) that can be applied to the object?

b. Can the change history and technological context of the object be traced sufficiently to ensure human readability and authenticity?

5. Persistent Identifier

a. Has the object been assigned an identifier that ensures locally uniqueness?

b. Is it important for the institution to have a universal or global persistent identifier for its objects? If so, which mechanism (e.g. PURL, DOI)?

Intellectual Property Rights

1. Is the right's holder information tracked and stored as part of the metadata?
2. How are the rights of the rights holder protected from abuse (e.g. limited public access, attribution statement)?
3. Are the usage restrictions consistent with institution policy and mandate?
4. Does the institution have sufficient rights for a preservation regimen?
5. Will the costs of securing rights for long-term access be

sustainable over the period of enduring value?

DIGITAL PRESERVATION OF MUSEUMS

A point that is continually emphasized in the literature is that creators and publishers must take the burden of digital preservation more seriously. The implications of allocating priorities are much more severe than for paper. A digital resource which is not selected for active preservation treatment at an early stage will very likely be lost or unusable in the near future. Therefore, it makes sense that "creation is where long-term archiving and preservation must start. Creators and publishers, when selecting format and media, need to align their decisions with the support capacities of institutions which are charged with the task of their preservation.

Also consistent in the literature is the need for a distributed approach. Avirtue of decentralized preservation is broader cost sharing and redundancy necessary given the enormous scope of digital preservation. Moreover, expertise is unlikely to be concentrated in one institution but tends to reside over a broad spectrum of institutions and corporate entities. Location, selection, identification/cataloguing and retention of digital objects will be best achieved through the coordinated distribution of responsibilities. As a result, most projects have emphasized cooperative approaches to digital preservation with interoperability critical to the solution. A third area of emphasis is the necessity of preservation metadata. Effective management of all but the crudest forms of digital preservation is likely to be facilitated by the creation, maintenance, and evolution of detailed metadata in support of the preservation process.

Finally, most digital preservation efforts model their activity on the Open Archival Information System (OAIS) reference model. Initially proposed by the Consultatitve Committee for Space Data Systems for use with space datasets, the reference model has been embraced by the broader digital preservation community as a way digital archives should work. Both Cedars and NEDLIB have adopted the OAIS model to build their research prototypes. However as the OAIS model is a high-level conceptual model, implementation details are not specified and institutions wishing to comply with the OAIS model must invest heavily to develop a local implementation as off-the-shelf OAIS compliant systems are not readily available

RECOMMENDATIONS FOR MUSEUMS

Keeping into context the environment in which museums operate, two kinds of recommended actions can be provided. Actions that can be implemented at an institutional level are those that each individual museum should be doing immediately. Broader recommendations may require either collaboration or an umbrella organization to execute or is only relevant in the context of a longer-term view of activities.

Action recommendations:

- Establish a set of policy documents governing activities related to digital preservation within the institution.
- Inventory existing digital holdings and quantify their significant properties.
- Assign at least 1 staff member clear responsibilities for overseeing digital preservation activities and mainstreaming digital preservation activities into the operations of the institution.
- Consolidate and reduce the number of media types in the collection.
- Prioritize the relative importance of each format type and the resources allocated to supporting that format.
- Ensure that each digital object in the collection is assigned a persistent identifier.

- Develop a timetable for evaluating holdings including integrity checks of the bit-level data, media refreshing and retention evaluation.
- Identify a metadata standard that fits with the institution's community of practice and develop local implementation procedures or adopt an available usage guide to formalize the institutional approach to the usage of the standard.

Broader Recommendations

- Implement a technology watch protocol to ensure that no media type, file format or standard becomes obsolete.
- Establish collaborative links with other institutions to share expertise and resources.
- Identify and endorse standards and formats with broad support and sustainable potential.
- Adopt a system that automates much of the lifecycle management of the digital objects.
- Secure from copyright holders rights in perpetuity to copy and modify the object in support of preservation activities.

Given the overall fluity with which the digital landscape changes, it is doubtful that the techniques of today will be sufficient for the problems of tomorrow. However, the real solution for digital preservation may lie less in technology and more in policy. For museums, having sound policy that maintains human accessibility to the digital objects is critical.

PRESERVING ACCESS TO DIGITAL INFORMATION (PADI): INTRODUCTION

The Preserving Access to Digital Information (PADI) initiative aims to provide mechanisms that will help to ensure that information in digital form is managed with appropriate consideration for preservation and future access.

Its objectives are:

1. to facilitate the development of strategies and guidelines for the preservation of access to digital information;
2. to develop and maintain a web site for information and promotion purposes;
3. to actively identify and promote relevant activities; and
4. to provide a forum for cross-sectoral cooperation on activities promoting the preservation of access to digital information.

The Operating Model: the operative model takes following aspects into consideration:

- *Distributed Archive*
- *Extension of Legal Deposit Legislation*
- *Specialist Agencies*
- *Permanent Retention*
- *Selectivity*
- *Standard Formats for Preservation*
- *Restricted Access to Electronic Publications*
- *Public Funding*
- *Who Should be Responsible for Archiving Digital Materials?*
- *How Should this be Paid For?*

1. Distributed Archive

There are a number of issues which need clarification here. Does the model assume all digital data? It is widely acknowledged that many of the boundaries which exist for print blur in the digital environment. However in practice some distinctions remain as different strategies tend to be appropriate for, say spatial data, or for electronic records originating as part of the business records of an agency as opposed to digital publications which may be created by a much wider range of authors and in a wider range of formats.

2. Extension of Legal Deposit Legislation

Most of the librarians can agree with this. It also reflects the approach in which the national council of libraries and information centers and national library can have made submissions to the respective copyright Law committee making a strong case for the extension of legal deposit to include digital publications. The national libraries can also pursue other alternatives, pending legal deposit legislation, such as voluntary deposit. Given the apparently broad definition of digital data in the proposed model, it would be useful to clarify what digital objects are included here as there is much digital data which is not "published".

3. Specialist Agencies

There needs to be a more sophisticated model than for print and one which needs to accommodate varying levels of participation, which is what this seems to be advocating. Is it assumed that each of these specialist agencies will develop different strategies according to the medium/subject they archive? It will be the responsibility of each agency to develop own preservation paths.

4. Permanent Retention

It is important to ensure a commitment to keeping material for longer than current use alone dictates but forever is a major undertaking and may lead to a more restricted approach to selection than might otherwise occur, because of the resource implications of such a commitment. In Australia, the NLA Statement of Principles for the Preservation of and Long-Term Access to Australian Digital Objects was that *Access to digital objects should be preserved only for as long as they are judged to have continuing value and significance*. This assumes that professional judgments will need to be applied, balancing costs and benefits as well as the anticipated needs and interests of future generations. This does introduce a more complex approach than a blanket permanent retention.

5. Selectivity

It is important to establish guidelines on selection criteria and these need to be public documents. This is especially important in a digital environment where the implications of not selecting for archiving will generally be more severe than for paper.

6. Standard Formats for Preservation

The statement *As far as possible store in standard formats* does not seem to take account of the speed of change in this area. For example, even where standards do exist (such as HTML) there are varying generations, not all of which can be easily read by the same browsers. There are also an increasing number of documents which combine a number of formats (including embedded software) as well as a wide array of standards, or at least de facto standards. While appealing, the suggestion that dependence on hardware and software can be substantially reduced in this way seems to over simplify the mágnitude of the problem. It does still make sense to encourage the use of standards where they exist and also to raise awareness of the inherent difficulties (and perhaps impossibility) of maintaining access to digital objects originating in non standard formats. However it needs to be recognized that there will still be significant challenges to be overcome in maintaining the multiplicity of digital documents over time, even when they do adhere to standards at any one time.

7. Restricted Access to Electronic Publications

A standard retention time is administratively appealing but is likely to encounter significant practical problems. The reality is that commercial publications will vary markedly in the length of time they are considered to be commercially viable so in practice it tends to be negotiation with the publisher on a case by case basis - which of course adds much to the workload but it is difficult to see how this can be avoided. There are also other reasons, apart from commercial ones, why access might need to be restricted for a defined period of time. A standard retention time would be impossible in these cases as, depending on the reason, the restriction on access may vary from a few weeks to several decades.

8. Public Funding

It is not clear how the statement that users should not be required to pay at the point of access relates to the standard retention time referred to above. This is surely not advocating that depository libraries make documents deposited via legal deposit freely available immediately. For networked publications especially this would impose severe economic penalties on the publisher.

9. Who Should be Responsible for Archiving Digital Materials

This is intended to convey the complexities of a digital environment in which a whole range of responsibilities need to emerge and intersect. These responsibilities are likely to shift over time. If this question is asking only about the long term then it is unlikely that there will be more than a few agencies with the necessary infrastructure and ongoing resources to make such a commitment. Depository libraries seem the logical choice to play a role in preserving "published" digital documents. Larger academic institutions that also create digital documents should also play a role in ensuring their investment in creating those important resources is maintained for future scholars.

10. How should this be paid for: Publicly funded institutions would be preferable, provided there was acknowledgment that there would need to be additional funding provided for the purpose.

It could not reasonably be expected to be absorbed with other roles. There will continue to be an information provider role for libraries as well as an information keeping role and there will inevitably be tensions between these roles unless appropriate funding is provided.

REFERENCES AND NOTES

1. Besser, Howard. "Digital Longevity." pp 164-176 in *Handbook for Digital Projects: A Management Tool for Preservation and Access* (edited by Maxine K. Sitts). Andover: Northeast Document Conservation Center, 2000. 182 pp. URL: http://www.nedcc.org/digital/dighome.htm
2. Cedars Project. *Cedars Guide to Digital Collection Management*. Online: The Cedars Project, 2002, pp. 23. URL:http://www.leeds.ac.uk/cedars/guideto/collmanagement/
3. Betsy Kruger, Library of the University of Illinois at Urbana-Champaign, *D-Lib Magazine*, January/February 2008, Volume 14 Number 1/2: <doi:10.1045/january2008-featured.collection>.
4. Robert Buckley, William Stumbo, and Jim Reid, Xerox Research Center Webster (USA), The Use of JPEG 2000 in the Information Packages of the OAIS Reference Model, in *Archiving 2007. Final proceedings of conference held May 21-24, 2007, Arlington, Va*. Springfield, Va.: The Society for Imaging Science and Technology.
5. "The promising - but not yet generally accepted - JPEG 2000" says Edwin Klijn, The Current State-of-art in Newspaper Digitization. A Market Perspective, *D-Lib Magazine*, January/February 2008, Volume 14 Number 1/2: <doi:10.1045/january2008-klijn>.
6. Oya Y. Rieger, *Preservation in the Age of Large-Scale Digitization. A White Paper*, February, 2008 (CLIR pub 141), p. 20, http://www.clir.org/pubs/abstract/pub141abst.html;

7. Ronald Jantz, Michael J. Giarlo, Digital Preservation. Architecture and Technology for Trusted Digital Repositories, *D-Lib Magazine*, June 2005, lume 11 Number 6, <doi:10.1045/june2005-jantz>.

8. Stephen Abrams, Stephen Chapman et al., Harvard's Perspective on the Archive Ingest and Handling Test, *D-Lib Magazine*, December 2005, Volume 11 Number 12, <doi:10.1045/december2005-abrams>.

9. Heminger and Robertson, 1998] A.R. Heminger and S.B. Robertson, "Digital Rosetta Stone: a conceptual model for maintaining long-term access to digital documents." *Proceedings of HICSS'98*, Vol. 2., Hawaii, 1998, pp. 158-167 <doi:10.1109/HICSS.1998.651695>.

10. Jantz, 2005] R. Jantz, "Digital Preservation: Enabling Technologies for Trusted Digital Repositories." *D-Lib Magazine*, 11, 6 (June 2005) <doi:10.l045/june2005-jantz>.

11. Jones, 2004] W. Jones, "Finders, Keepers? The present and future perfect in support of personal information management." *First Monday*, 9, 3 (March, 2004) <http://www.firstmonday.org/issues/issue9_3/jones/index.html>.

12. Maniatis et al., 2005] P. Maniatis, M. Roussopoulos, T. Giuli, D. Rosenthal, M. Baker, and Y. Muliadi, "LOCKSS: A peer-to-peer digital preservation system." *ACM Transactions on Computer Systems*, 23(1): 2-50, Feb, 2005. <http://doi.acm.org/10.1145/1047915.1047917>.

13. Marchionini, 2006] G. Marchionini, "Exploratory search: From finding to understanding." *Communications of the ACM*, 49(4): 41-46. <http://doi.acm.org/10.1145/1121949.1121979>.

14. Marshall, 2007] C.C. Marshall, "How People Manage Personal Information over a Lifetime." In *Personal Information Management* (Jones and Teevan, eds.), University of Washington Press, Seattle, Washington, 2007, pp. 57-75. <http://www.csdl.tamu.edu/~marshall/PIM%20Chapter-Marshall.pdf>.

15. Marshall, 2008] C.C. Marshall, "From Writing and Analysis to the Repository: Taking the Scholars' Perspective on Scholarly

Archiving." To appear in *Proceedings of JCDL 2008*. (Pittsburgh, PA, June 16-20, 2008), New York: ACM Press.

16. Justin Littman, A Technical Approach and Distributed Model for Validation of Digital Objects, *D-Lib Magazine*, May 2006, Volume 12 Number 5, <doi:10.1045/may2006-littman>.
17. Cedars Project. *Cedars Guide to Digital Preservation Strategies*. Online: The Cedars Project, 2002, pp. 18. URL: http://www.leeds.ac.uk/cedars/guideto/dpstrategies/
18. Cedars Project. *Cedars Guide to Intellectual Property Rights*. Online: The Cedars Project, 2002, pp. 19. URL: http://www.leeds.ac.uk/cedars/guideto/ipr/
19. Cedars Project. *Cedars Guide to Preservation Metadata*. Online: The Cedars Project, 2002, pp. 18. URL: http://www.leeds.ac.uk/cedars/guideto/metadata/
20. <http://www.irfanview.com>.
21. <http://www.lizardtech.com>,
22. Luratech <http://www.luratech.com>
23. ErMapper <http://www.ermapper.com>.
24. <http://www.lizardtech.com/download/dl_options.php?page=third>,
25. http://www.luratech.com/download/jp2>.
26. Cedars Project. *Cedars Guide to The Distributed Digital Archiving Prototype*. Online: The Cedars Project, 2002, pp. 26. URL: http://www.leeds.ac.uk/cedars/guideto/cdap/
27. Gatenby, Pam. "Digital Archiving - Developing Policy And Best Practice Guidelines At The National Library Of Australia" in *Digital Archiving: Bringing Issues and Standards Together*. Online: ICSTI Press, 2000. URL: http://www.icsti.org/2000workshop/gatenby.html
28. Grout, Catherine, Phill Purdy and Janine Rymer. *Creating Digital Resources for the Visual Arts: Standards and Good Practice*. Online: Visual Arts Data Service, 2000. URL: http://vads.ahds.ac.uk/guides/creating_guide/contents.html
29. Hodges, Gail M. "Best Practices for Digital Archiving." *D-Lib Magazine* 6,1 (2000). URL: http://www.dlib.org/dlib/january00/01hodge.html

30. The Humanities Advanced Technology and Information Institute (HATII), University of Glasgow, and the National Initiative for a Networked Cultural Heritage (NINCH), The NINCH Guide to Good Practice in the Digital Representation and Management of Cultural Heritage Materials. Online: The National Initiative for a Networked Cultural Heritage, October 2002. URL: http://www.nyu.edu/its/humanities/ninchguide/index.html

31. Institute of Museum and Library Services. *A Framework of Guidance for Building Good Digital Collections*. Online: Institue of Museum and Library Services, November 2001. URL:http://www.niso.org/framework/Framework2.html

32. Jones, Maggie and Neil Beagrie. *Preservation Management of Digital Materials: A Handbook*. Online: Digital Preservation Coalition, 2002. URL: http://www.dpconline.org/graphics/handbook/

33. Littman, Justin. A Technical Approach and Distributed Model for Validation of Digital Objects. *D-Lib Magazine*. <doi:10.1045/may2006-littman>.

34. Beagrie, 2005] N. Beagrie, "Plenty of Room at the Bottom? Personal Digital Libraries and Collections." *D-Lib Magazine*, 11, 6 (June 2005). <doi:10.1045/june2005-beagrie>.

35. Dumais et al., 2003] S. T. Dumais, E. Cutrell, E., J. J. Cadiz, G. Jancke, R. Sarin and D. C. Robbins, "Stuff I've Seen: A system for personal information retrieval and re-use." *Proceedings of SIGIR 2003*: 72-79. <http://doi.acm.org/10.1145/860435.860451>.

36. Gemmell et al., 2006] J. Gemmell, G., Bell, R. Lueder, "MyLifeBits: a personal database for everything." *Communications of the ACM*, 49 (1): 88-95. <http://doi.acm.org/10.1145/1107458.1107460>.

37. Gladney, 2006] H.M. Gladney, "Principles for Digital Preservation." *Communications of the ACM*, 49 (2): 111-116. <http://doi.acm.org/10.1145/1113034.1113038>.

38. Kenney, Anne R. "Projects to Programs: Developing a Digital Preservation Policy." in *Moving Theory into Practice: Digital Imaging for Libraries and Archives* (edited by A. Kenney and

O. Rieger). Mountain View: Research Libraries Group, 2000, pp 189.

39. http://www.rlg.org/preserv/mtip2000.html.
40. Collecting and Preserving the Web: The Minerva Prototype (RLG Diginews, Vol 5, No 2. William Y. Arms, et al., Cornell University
41. Collecting and Preserving the Web: Developing and Testing the NEDLIB Harvester, National Library of Finland (RLG Diginews, Vol 5, No 2)
42. National Library of Canada Electronic Collections Coordinating Group. *Networked Electronic Publications Policy and Guidelines*. Online: National Library of Canada, 1998. URL: http://www.collectionscanada.ca/9/8/index-e.html
43. NINCH Working Group on Best Practices. *The NINCH Guide to Good Practice in the Digital Representation and Management of Cultural Heritage Materials*. Online: The National Initiative for a Networked Cultural Heritage, October 2002. URL: http://www.nyu.edu/its/humanities/ninchguide/index.html
44. Smith, 2005] M. Smith, "Eternal Bits: How Can We Preserve Digital Files and Save Our Collective Memory?" *IEEE Spectrum*, July 2005, 22-27. <http://spectrum.ieee.org/print/1568>.
45. Whittaker et al., 2006] S. Whittaker, V. Bellotti, and J. Gwizdka, "Email as personal information management." *Communications of the ACM*, 49 (1): 68-73. <http://doi.acm.org/10.1145/1107458.1107494>.
46. Chickering, A. W. and Ehrmann, S. C. 'Implementing the Seven Principles: Technology as Lever', *AAHE Bulletin*, October, 1996, pp. 3-6.
47. RLG/OCLC Working Group on Digital Archive Attributes. *Trusted Digital Repositories: Attributes and Responsibilities*. Mountain View: Research Libraries Group, 2002. 62 pp. URL: http://www.rlg.org/longterm/repositories.pdf

48. Museum Context Canadian Heritage Information Network. *Information Technology in Canadian Museums: A Survey by the Canadian Heritage Information Network*. Online: Canadian Heritage Information Network, 2001. URL: http://www.chin.gc.ca/English/Reference_Library/Information_Technology/index.html

49. Hedstrom, Margaret and Sheon Montgomery. *Digital Preservation Needs and Requirements in RLG Member Institutions*. Online: Research Libraries Group, 1998. URL: http://www.rlg.org/preserv/digpres.html

50. Institute of Museum and Library Services. *Status of Technology and Digitization In the Nation's Museums and Libraries 2002 Report*. Online: Institute of Museum and Library Services, 2002. URL: http://www.imls.gov/publications/TechDig02/index02.htm

51. Jones, et al., 2002] W. Jones, S. Dumais, and H. Bruce, "Once found, what then? : a study of 'keeping' behaviors in the personal use of web information." *Proceedings of ASIST 2002*, 39 (1): 391-402. <doi:10.1002/meet.1450390143>.

52. Kotla et al., 2007] R. Kotla, L. Alvisi, and M. Dahlin, "SafeStore: A Durable and Practical Storage System." *Proceedings of Usenix Annual Technical Conference (USENIX 2007)*, CA, 2007, pp. 129-142. <http://www.usenix.org/events/usenix07/tech/kotla/kotla_html/index.html>.

53. Saracevic, T. 'Digital library evaluation: toward and evolution of concepts', *Library Trends*, (2000) 49(3), pp. 350-369.

54. Furh, N., et al, 'Evaluation of Digital Libraries', *International Journal on Digital Libraries*, 8(1), November, 2007.

55. Warren, P., Boldyreff, C. and Munro, M. 'The Evolution of Web Sites', *Proceedings of the 7th International Workshop on Program Comprehension*, (1999) IEEE Computer Society, Washington DC, p. 178.

56. Storey, M.A. and Jahnke, J.H. 'Web Site Evolution - Towards a flexible integration of Data and its Representation', *First Workshop on Web Site Evolution (WSE'99)*, October 1999. p. 3.

57. Kreger, H. 'Fulfilling the Web Services Promise', *Communications of the ACM*, June 2003, 46(6). pp 29-30.

58. Kuny, 1998] T. Kuny, "A Digital Dark Ages? Challenges in the Preservation of Electronic Information." *International Preservation News*, 17 (May 1998). <http://www.ifla.org/IV/ifla63/63kuny1.pdf>.

59. Lesk, 1995] M. Lesk, "Preserving Digital Objects: Recurrent Needs and Challenges." *Proceedings of the 1995 National Preservation Office (NPO) Conference* (Brisbane, Queensland, Australia, November 27-30, 1995), National Library of Australia, Canberra, Australia, 1995. <http://www.lesk.com/mlesk/auspres/aus.html>.

60. Lorie, 2002] R. Lorie, "A Methodology and System for Preserving Digital Data." In *Proceedings of JCDL'02* (Portland, Oregon, July 14-18, 2002). ACM Press, New York, NY, 2002, pp. 312-319. <http://doi.acm.org/10.1145/544220.544296>.

61. Manes, 1998] S. Manes, "Personal Computers; ... But With Luck and Diligence, Treasure-Troves of Data Can Be Preserved." *New York Times*, April 7, 1998. <http://query.nytimes.com/gst/fullpage.html?res=9B05E4DD113AF934A35757C0A96E958260 &sec=&spon=&partner=permalink&exprod=permalink>.

62. Literature Surveys. Carroll, B. C. and G. Hodge. *Digital Electronic Archiving : the State of the Art and the State of the Practice*. Online: International Council for Scientific and Technical Information: Information Policy Committee, 1999. URL: http://www.icsti.org/Dig_Archiving_Report_1999.pdf

63. Conway, Paul. *Preservation in the Digital World*. Online: Council on Libraries and Information Resources, 1996. URL: http://www.clir.org/pubs/abstract/pub62.html

64. Council of Library and Information Resources. *The State of Digital Preservation: An International Perspective*. Online: Council on Libraries and Information Resources, 2002: URL: http://www.clir.org/pubs/abstract/pub107abst.html

65. Archival Preservation of Smithsonian Web Resoures: Strategies, Principles, and Best Practices July 20, 2001

66. METS 2006. *Metadata Encoding and Transmission Standard (METS) Official Web Site. Version 1.6.* <http://www.loc.gov/standards/mets/>.

67. PREMIS Working Group, May 2005. *Data Dictionary for Preservation Metadata: Final Report of the Premis Working Group, version 1.0.* <http://www.oclc.org/ research/projects/pmwg/premis-final.pdf>.

68. MODS 2006. *Metadata Object Description Schema. Version 3.2.* <http://www.loc.gov/standards/mods/>.

69. Bray, T. et al. eds. 2006, *Extensible Markup Language (XML) 1.0 (Fourth Edition)*. <http://www.w3.org/TR/REC-xml/>.

70. CCSDS, January 2002. *Reference Model for an Open Archival Information System (OAIS). CCSDS 650.0-B-1, Blue Book* (the full ISO standard). <http://public.ccsds.org/publications/archive/650x0b1.pdf>.

71. Fresko, M. "Digital Preservation: State of the Art November 1999 Update" in *Consolidating the European Library Space Conference Proceedings*. Online: DG Information Society, 1999. URL: http://cordis.europa.eu/libraries/events/fp4ce/speech/fresko.html#freskop

72. Gould, Sara and Marie-Therese Varlamoff. *The Preservation of Digitised Collections: An Overview of Recent Progress and Persistent Challenges Worldwide*. Online: UNESCO, 2000. URL: http://www.unesco.org/webworld/points_of_views/preservation_1.shtml

73. Lee, Kyong-Ho, Oliver Slattery, Richard Lu, Victor McCrary and Xiao Tang. "The State of the Art and Practice in Digital Preservation." *Journal of Research of the National Institute of Standards and Technology*, 107,1 (2002), pp. 93-106.

74. http://nvl.nist.gov/pub/nistpubs/jres/107/1/j71lee.pdf

75. Waters, Donald and John Garrett. *Preserving Digital Information: Final Report and Recommendations*. Online: Commission on Preservation and Access and The Research Libraries Group, 1996. URL: http://www.rlg.org/ArchTF/

76. http://www.nla.gov.au/scoap/scoap.html

77. http://www.naa.gov.au/

78. http://pandora.nla.gov.au/pan/52389/20050913-0000/www.naa.gov.au/recordkeeping/er/keeping_er/how_long.html

79. Dyson M.C. and Moran K. 'Informing the Design of Web Interfaces to Museum Collections' *Museum Management and Curatorship*, 18(4), 2000, pp. 391-406 & Sabin R. 'Museums and their Websites: An examination and assessment of how museums are coping with the challenge of the World Wide Web', *Journal of Conservation and Museum Studies*, No. 2, May 1997.

80. Avenier, P. 'Putting the Public First: The French Experience', *Museum International*, 204(4), Oct-Dec 1999, pp. 31-34.

81. Diaz, L.A.B and del Egido, A. 'Science Museums on the Internet', *Museum International*, 204(4), Oct-Dec 1999, p. 37.

82. Cuncliffe, D., Kritou E. and Tudhope D. 'Usability Evaluation for Museum Websites' *Museum Management and Curatorship*, 19(3), 2001, pp. 229-252.

83. http://pandora.nla.gov.au/pan/52389/20050913-0000/www.naa.gov.au/recordkeeping/er/keeping_er/summary.html

84. Ensuring the longevity of digital documents', Scientific American, vol. 272, no. 1, January 1995, pp. 24-29

85. http://www.nla.gov.au/preserve/digital/princ.html

86. Emulation. http://www.nla.gov.au/padi/topics/18.html

87. Encapsulation http://www.nla.gov.au/padi/topics/20.html

88. Migration http://www.nla.gov.au/padi/topics/21.htm

89. Rosenthal, David S. H., Thomas Robertson, Tom Lipkis, Vicky Reich, Seth Morabito. Requirements for Digital Preservation Systems: A Bottom-Up Approach. *D-Lib Magazine*. <doi:10.1045/november2005-rosenthal>.

90. To provide continuity with the valuable framework provided by Rosenthal et al, <http://agilemanifesto.org/>.

91. Littman, Justin. A Technical Approach and Distributed Model for Validation of Digital Objects. *D-Lib Magazine*. <doi:10.1045/may2006-littman>.

92. <http://digitalarchive.oclc.org/da/ViewObjectMain.jsp?fileid=0000070519:000006287816&reqid=24150#interview>.

93. General trends in digital imaging, Steven Puglia - Erin Rhodes, Digital Imaging - How Far Have We Come and What Still Needs to be Done?, in *RLG DigiNews* Volume 11, Number 1, April 15, 2007. <http://digitalarchive.oclc.org/da/ViewObject.jsp?objid=0000068890&reqid=26384>.

94. Tim Vitale. Digital Image File Formats - TIFF, JPEG, JPEG 2000, RAW, and DNG. July 2007, Version 20. Available at <http://aic.stanford.edu/sg/emg/library/pdf/vitale/2007-07-vitaledigital_image_file_formats.pdf>.

95. Robert Buckley, JPEG 2000 - a Practical Digital Preservation Standard? *Technology Watch Report*, Digital Preservation Coalition February 2008. Available at <http://www.dpconline.org/docs/reports/dpctw08-01.pdf>.

7

Retrieval of Information From E-Resources

ERMS preparation and implementation requires extensive planning and coordination of various sections, workflow, resources, record-keeping systems, and relationships. Appropriate data, process analysis, and unbiased evaluation help this process. Feedback plays a significant role in the organization implement change. Since library collections become electronic gradually, librarians strive all of sudden to develop lifecycle management approaches to administer them. One major issue is the anxiety over the long-term sustainability of e-resource. Digital preservation, or archiving of e-journals, is a major concern within the lifecycle perspective. However, several developing technologies, services, and strategies are available for archiving e-resources.

OPTIMIZING COLLECTIONS AND SERVICES: USER EXPECTATIONS

Advances in scholarship depend on access to what has come before. Technologies of the past two centuries have enabled the creation and capture of information in many forms. Keeping the products of these technologies fit for use, however, has become more challenging with time. New interfaces in the scholarly environment (such as Google Scholar and Scirus), and the success of popular Internet services (such as Google, Amazon.com, YouTube, Flickr, MySpace, Facebook, and del.icio.us) suggests about several patterns of user expectations and preferences. It is found that, users clearly prefer familiar and easy-to-learn discovery interfaces. The typical searcher relies on the Internet to find many types of content, not just scholarly information. This information is required to accomplish many everyday tasks. Users expect scholarly interfaces to provide an experience similar to the interfaces with which they are most familiar. Indeed, more and more information services in the scholarly environment, such as Scirus, PubMed, and JSTOR, are now providing a query interface that is similar to that of Google: one search box, where users can enter one or more terms, on which the search engine performs a keyword search; and an advanced search interface. This can be more comprehensive and at the same time this allows better control over the search.

Users expect to find results in a way that does not require precision searching. Users expect the system to overcome incorrect or alternative spellings and to handle multiple forms of a word, such as the singular and plural. Other factors that affect users' preferences are the kind of materials that a specific resource offers and the breadth and quality of the resource. People are attracted to search engines due to provision of multiple types of sources such as online books, online articles, websites, images, videos, conference presentations. Many users prefer searching in the scholarly information resources. The quality of the materials has been verified by the publisher of the materials and confirmed by the institution's selection of these resources. Users see the discovery process as a means to obtain the material. They value a system's ability to electronically deliver any type of material too. Recommendations from fellow users play a significant role in the choice of information resources and materials.

The success of web services that are based on user collaboration, community-initiated projects such as Wikipedia, and social community based features added to some sites (such as the reviews available on Amazon.com) leaves no doubt that users are willing to contribute their expertise and to trust the community when it comes to recommendations. Today's users also seem to prefer services that are always available and require little effort to access. Users have difficulty switching to the other side of the spectrum, to the interfaces of library systems and scholarly information resources due to the omnipresence of the Google toolbar and Google desktop gadgets, regardless of the Web site or application in use. The process of scholarly discovery and delivery is not yet sufficiently integrated with other user spaces to enable users to access such services when they need them. Finally, users expect an engaging and gratifying process. The various services offered on the web provide user centric, friendly, and reassuring interaction. Most library systems have yet to offer their users a similar experience.

Many of the changes have been introduced by Internet services in the last few years as a platform for user collaboration and sharing. These are described as adhering to the Web 2.0 concepts of building on the Internet. Libraries often express the way in which Web 2.0 as "Library 2.0": The heart of Library 2.0 is a model for library service. It encourages constant and purposeful change, inviting user participation in the creation of both the physical and the virtual services. It is supported by consistently evaluating services. It also attempts to serve current ones by improving customer-driven offerings. Each component by itself is a step toward better serving users. It is through the combined implementation. However, Library 2.0 remains a goal for libraries to strive toward.

ARCHITECTURE

Current systems in libraries fall short when the user experience that they provide is compared with that of popular services on the Web. Today libraries are better equipped to satisfy user needs due to quality and relevance of collections, the rich metadata for accurate searching, the tailored services and the controlled workflow and terminology. The look and feel of the application also play significant role. Libraries are likely to offer discovery and delivery services by leveraging their unique qualities and providing a better user experience.

Implementing new end-user interfaces for systems in the library is not a simple task. It cannot be successfully achieved by only making improvements to current interfaces. The librarian-centric design in terms of data structures and workflows is focused on library administration and hence severely limits the possibilities for the end-user interface. The existing library collections are fragmented as offered by multiple library systems. Each of them focuses on specific types of materials such as physical items, locally digitized materials, remote e-journal collections and many others. Libraries cannot present a unified entry point to their many types of offerings, unless an interface that overarches the multiple library collections is implemented. The stakeholders such as libraries and vendors have embarked on a path toward creating a better user experience. The library solutions deriving from this path are based on decoupled architectures. In this system the integrated library system and digital asset management system will continue to serve librarians as management tools, the user-experience layer is developed as a separate platform.

This decoupling provides the capability to create a better user experience as well as unifies the discovery processes across given heterogeneous collections.

There is a growing desire to hide boundaries between databases such as catalog, repositories, etc. in some cases especially where these boundaries are seen more to reflect the historical contingencies of library organization than the actual discovery needs of users. These new solutions can harvest and preprocess some of the collections. So optimizing the search in such collections libraries will still need to provide seamless access, to resources that are not necessarily harvestable. It can be due licensing restrictions or the library's policies or technological capabilities. It is found the North Carolina State University (NCSU) Endeca-based catalog was the first system to go live with what the NCSU library refers to as a new catalog built on decoupled architecture. Other solutions, such as the Primo system from Ex Libris and AquaBrowser® Library from Medialab Solutions (also acquired by Bowker), adhere to the same kind of architecture.

THE USER EXPERIENCE

The new-generation end-user interface involves vendors and librarians use expressions. These vary from visual faceted search that connects to any number of data sources to a product that brings together content, community, and discovery in a single search. In this context new online catalog should provide the speed and flexibility of popular online search engines. The process of searching for and locating scholarly materials is the main concern for the user experience. This discovery process is accompanied by a delivery mechanism to complete the user's quest for information. Some related services such as saving queries, set alerts, store records in various formats, set their preferences, and perform other such tasks that facilitate research are worth mentioning here. Some library systems are interactive. Users can add information for their own benefit, by tagging records to make them easily accessible at a later time, by reviewing and tagging materials to enhance the searching experience for other users. Once these tags are available in the system, they can help users search the library collection according to the popularity or timeliness of specific topics.

SEARCH PROCESS

Libraries must create an interface that is as familiar and intuitive that serves the user better. Such an interface would yield more appropriate results and would offer immediate gratification by making items readily available in a variety of ways. These can provide links to electronic materials, showing the locations where the user can pick up physical items. It can enable the user to submit requests related to items of interest. The success of a search process depends on several factors such as the research data available to the user, the search engine, the search interface, the user who initiates the process, and the order in which the results are returned.

THE RESEARCH INFORMATION

The research information available to the user needs to be as complete and relevant. Few library systems address this requirement according to the library's specifications. They harvest data from multiple resources regardless of the type of resource, its cataloging format, or its location. The data elements originate from heterogeneous repositories. The library system can normalize the harvested data makes the data conform to one set of rules. The library system converts it into a unified format that is designed to fully support the task at hand a quick, efficient, and friendly search process.

Functional Requirements for Bibliographic Records (FRBR) offers a fresh perspective on the structure and relationships of bibliographic and authority records. It also offers more precise vocabulary to help future cataloging rule makers and system designers in meeting user needs. Most information resources do not support "FRBRized" groupings as part of the bibliographic information. Some library system can build groups while constructing its indexes. Such system can provide the functionality that users expect without requiring any modification of the original resources.

These is certain gap between the technological capabilities available for handling controlled, harvestable collections and those available for providing just-in-time access to remote resources through a metasearch. Some library system includes metasearching as an integral part of the user experience. They send the user's query to remote resources through a metasearch engine and integrate the results returned from these resources with the results obtained through a search of the local system indexes.

THE SEARCH ENGINE AND INTERFACE

The requirements for a search engine include a well-built infrastructure to enable it to operate efficiently and rapidly. Addressing user expectations means that the system provides results instantaneously as well as accurate results. It needs to support queries of various types and to allow users to employ the search interface as a query authoring tool for defining their needs as precisely as possible. The search process starts with the query interface, which enables users to express their search requirements and obtain and process the search results. The simpler the query interface, the more sophisticated the system needs to be. It must enrich the query with additional information. The user is most likely seeking information that relates to all of the words, not to the query terms as one phrase. Some library system adds an implicit Boolean AND between the query words before performing the search. The search interface displays the results along with various options to help the user process the results.

USER POINT OF VIEW

Though the complexity of the interface might be faced, the success of the search depends on the way in which researchers use the search interface to articulate their research needs. An interface needs to accommodate all users with respect to research needs, expectations and search expertise. Furthermore, users tend to apply the searching methods with which they are already familiar. The searcher's behavior is not likely to invest time in mastering a new kind of search behavior.

THE DISPLAY OF RESULTS

The success of a search is measured in terms of documents that the search engine locates and by the order in which it presents them. An exploratory search for information about a topic is likely to yield a large number of results. Users will probably find difficult to manage. Relevance ranking of the result set helps users focus on those results that are likely to be the most valuable for their research. Web search engines and some recently developed search engines in the scholarly environment, such as Scirus and Scopus®, both from Elsevier, rank the results by relevance. However, a system's relevance ranking may not always be adequate; determining whether certain materials are more relevant than others is a complex issue. The developers of relevance-ranking algorithms must keep in mind the context of the search, such as who the user is and what the user's goals and areas of interests are. Because the default sorting of results by relevance is not helpful in every context, an option to re-sort the results by other criteria, particularly by date, is provided. In some research areas, the most recently published materials are often of greatest interest.

These should be some concentration on the display of a linear list of results. The utility of a search engine is affected by multiple factors. The primary factor is the soundness of the underlying retrieval model and ranking function. Organizing and presenting search results is also a very important factor that can affect the utility of a search engine significantly. A search interface can present results in such a way that will help users understand the content of the result list and focus on the aspects that are relevant.

THE DESIGN OF THE SEARCH INTERFACE

In a typical search process, users go through the following stages:

1. Defining and submitting a query
2. Examining the result list, this includes a brief description of each result
3. Refining the query. In some cases, the user refines the query by adding search terms or by selecting an option from a set of refinements offered by the system.
4. Identifying the relevant materials by either skimming the result list and examining the results in greater detail
5. Obtaining the material if it's available physically or electronically.
6. Obtaining some other services that are relevant to the specific material, such as the option to save the bibliographic record as a reference

To meet out the needs and expectations of today's users, the design of the interface should adhere to the following guidelines:

- The information displayed on the screen should be

minimal, with the goal of satisfying a user's needs in the specific context.

- The default workflow and search options are appropriate.
- Queries can be as simple or as complex as needed; complex options do not clutter the simplicity of the interface, and complexity is achieved in stages.
- No training is required for searchers.

Query Definition

The query interface is designed to offer three levels of complexity: for most users, most of the time, the query interface looks very simple; the users might notice a slight increase in complexity when they want to make a more specific query; and the query interface becomes more complex for those who want all search options to be available. The design uses two forms—one for simple searches, and other for advanced searches. Several options enable less experienced users to frame their query more accurately without being intimidated by an advanced search form. These options allow the researcher to direct the search to specific metadata fields, material, and data. Users have added to the information originating from the library, such as tags. Users can choose to limit the search to a specific domain, such as a library collection or a group of databases.

Since most of the users are accustomed to the query syntax of Web search engines, the search syntax can be designed to resemble that of the Web engines. The user can type one or more words, and the system interprets them as having an implicit AND between them. The user can employ Boolean operators and certain punctuation marks, such as quotation marks and parentheses, to create a complex query.

WORKING WITH THE RESULT LIST

A user can search for the items that he has in mind and

can identify when they are displayed, or any items that satisfy the user's research needs. When a user searches for a known item, the first page of results is likely to display the item. In most cases, the result list is short, because the user has probably entered enough information for the system to identify the results accurately. However, a result list yielded by a search for unknown items might be very long, because users of scholarly information are not necessarily experienced searchers and might enter broad terms. Relevance ranking provides only a partial solution, because the relevance of items is not always well defined.

Long result lists are not the only challenge that users face. Sometimes their queries are ambiguous, so the result list may contain items that are very different from each other. Some library system provides a "faceted" browsing feature: in which the system analyzes the search results and groups them according to predefined categories, called facets, such as topic, author, type of material, language, and date. For each facet, the system lists the most frequently occurring data. The user can narrow down the result list by clicking these refining options. Although users may not be able to articulate their initial queries in a precise manner, once they are presented with a list of available options. While scanning the initial result list, a user might realize that the query was not effective enough. The interface can help by offering suggestions for further searching. These suggestions may include features such as directing the user to tools already present on the screen or offering other resources and services, relating to the specific query and result list.

In most of the cases, the details as well as a statement of the item's availability given about an item, are sufficient for the user to decide whether the item is of interest or not. Finding these details insufficient, the user can navigate to a full-record display. Full recode display contains additional bibliographic information; various forms of community input, such as tags, ratings, and reviews; and information from resources outside the library that the library has decided to add to the bibliographic record. The user starts a new search for related items based on some of the information displayed. The search process typically ends when the user has identified the items of interest and clicks the "Get it" link to obtain the actual material.

Till recent times, the changes in the search experience on the Web were not reflected in library interfaces. Internet services were providing users with friendly interfaces. A rapid response time was being integrated with user spaces. It enabled users to interact with each other, describing information as desired, and participating in creating information. At that time libraries were still focusing on developing and maintaining content. Libraries are starting to adopt new interfaces that bring together library collections and methodologies as well as contemporary user experience elements to catch up with user expectations and regain their clientele. Several solutions are now available to bridge the gap between libraries and their users. Designed around the user's needs, such systems can serve as a feasible, robust model for the new approach.

THE ACTION TO BE TAKEN

The e-resources access point should provide a list of all sources in collection with an electronic format and detail for each title. The access point should indicate how many years of access are allowed with current subscription to the title, as well as the types of authentication allowed (including IP, username/password and Athens authentication.) If institution can only support IP authentication, the new report will allow user to quickly identify titles where username/ password authentication is the only option so library can prevent links for those titles from being added to library site.

This facility should be designed to include as much information as possible in a single location, so that users can quickly and easily activate their e-resources subscriptions, thereby taking advantage of all e-resources purchases.

When electronic sources are a part of library's collection, library need tools to manage these sources. There should be a system to handle this need and should offer extensive features that help with e-journal management tasks such as: tracking the registration status of e-resources authentication assistance to facilitate both on campus and remote access to e-content, automatic management of e-resources URLs and much more. Required enhancements can expand the functionality of such tracker. Administrators can now indicate the registration status of their e-resources on subscription, view access, authentication and registration details for these e-resources, block end user access to titles not yet registered and more. An expanded notes capability can enable the system to send out automated reminders on the dates that specific actions are to be taken. Other enhancements can help administrators log their registration activities and streamline access to titles requiring username and password authentication.

CROSS-ORGANIZATIONAL ACCESS MANAGEMENT

Cross-organizational access management for web-based resources has emerged as a topic of great interest among many information consuming institutions and information resource providers. These organizations wish, as precisely and as flexibly as possible, to enable access to particular networked resources to particular members of institutional consumer communities. Access should be simple for the user and guarantee a large measure of privacy to the user. It should not depend entirely on the user's location or network address but rather on the user's membership in appropriate communities. It should concentrate on necessary management and demographic information to institutional consumer administrators and to resource providers. A flexible and robust access management service is more than a technical architecture. It must address a number of other difficult issues, including policy and infrastructure considerations, deployment of technology in an uncertain market and broad consensus and development of standards among key players.

Two technical infrastructure components are minimally required for an institutional access management system: the ability of a user to obtain an identity on the network, known as authentication; and the ability to correlate a user's identity with rights and permissions to use various services, called authorization. Often these two services are combined in simple ways which blur their distinction, such as the UNIX implementation of file permission policy through group membership, "uids" and "gids." More robust and scalable authentication and authorization services may instead arise independently and be supported by special purpose systems rather than as side-effects of particular operating systems or other technologies.

FEDERATED SEARCHING

Federated searching can be sectioned as:

1. Query conversion
2. Connectors
3. Authentication

Federated Search Server : the functioning of federated search server can be found in general as:

1. Request
2. HTML Query
3. HTML Display
4. Document

5. Converter
6. XML
7. Cache
8. Response
9. Databases User Screen

SEARCHER ANALYZER

A federated search is an information discovery tool. A federated search tool is designed to provide a single search interface that can be used for virtually all of a user's online resources. The typical use would be a user keying in a word or phrase that describes a topic and the federated search will return matching citations from the various library resources. *To provide a full and comprehensive end-user experience, all three of these resources work together.* These should be a list is where an end user would go when they know the title of the resource they want. For literature searches, end users may choose to use the federated search as a one-stop search point, or they may choose individual databases from the various host services. Regardless, what is discovered will be a range of citation-only and full-text results? It is the link resolver that will allow these citation only results to take the user directly to the appropriate full text. Federated search engine results are often citation-only, and the federated search technology cannot connect a citation to its appropriate full text without the introduction of a link resolver.

Federated search across all types of information resources, post search processing provide :

- Description / Abstract (original)
- Document Summarization
- Key concepts extraction
- Clustering / categorization

Users may personalize the system for preferences, profiling, alerting, etc. Post Search Processing based on real time Text Analysis -

- Create semantic mapping of documents without prior training or taxonomy.
- Extracting Key concepts from document.
- Ranking Key concepts within each document and full search results set.
- Create Clustering / categorization for search results.

SEARCH RESULTS DISPLAY

1. Automatic on-the-fly clustering
2. Automatic on-the-fly summarization
3. Automatic on-the-fly keyword extraction and meta-tagging

The information age shows very interesting times. Effective search and discovery over open and hidden digital resources on the Internet remains a problematic and challenging task. The difficulties are exacerbated by today's greatly distributed scholarly information landscape. This distributed information environment is populated by silos of: full-text repositories maintained by commercial and professional society publishers; preprint servers and Open Archive Initiative (OAI) provider sites; specialized Abstracting and Indexing (A & I) services; publisher and vendor vertical portals; local, regional, and national online catalogs; Web search and metasearch engines; local e-resource registries and digital content databases; campus institutional repository systems; and learning management systems.

Components of federated search:

a. Portal
    - Authorization

- Linking mechanism between resources and other resources
- Simultaneous search
- Navigation

b. Web client

- User query

c. Linking

- Between full text using DOI, Crossref
- Between A&I and full text
- Between OPAC and full text

Information providers have focused on developing mechanisms to transform the myriad distributed digital collections into true "digital libraries" with the essential services that are required to make these digital libraries useful to and productive for users. There is a huge difference between providing access to discrete sets of digital collections and providing digital library services. To address these concerns, information providers have designed enhanced gateway and navigation services on the interface side and also introduced federation mechanisms to assist users through the distributed, heterogeneous information environment. The mantra has been: aggregate, virtually collocate, and federate. The goal of seamless federation across distributed, heterogeneous resources remains the holy grail of digital library work

Presently the prevalent web architecture relies on a more fundamental method of access policy: by Internet address ("IP source address"). This method identifies the topological location of a user on the network. Many institutions have also deployed web proxy servers, which alleviate some of the access management difficulties of the basic IP source address method. But neither of these methods enables access management based on the characteristics of the user. They provide authentication and authorization in a single, imprecise step, based primarily on network location.

As remote service providers create increasingly sophisticated services which are customized to individual users, they find they must implement independent user "registration" infrastructures: essentially building duplicate id, password, and user-profile systems for populations that are already part of well established and carefully maintained institutional id systems and directories at their "home" institutions. This is an unfortunate duplication of effort for the provider and annoyance to the user (who must login to each such service independently). Its problems are compounded by its underlying security model: still largely by IP source address or proxy web server.

VARIOUS ARCHITECTURES FOR INFORMATION RETRIEVAL

1. Initial Model

The initial architecture included a locally customized server module. In this model, both the user and the service provider are members of the same institution. A single transaction in this scenario proceeds as follows:

1. User requests a restricted service.
2. Web server asks browser for user credentials.
3. Browser prompts user for name and password, and resubmits the request with these user credentials.
4. Web server's access management module passes user's credentials to institutional validation system to check if the credentials are valid.
5. Web server's access management module collects user attributes from institutional directory system. Based on the user's attributes it determines whether the user is permitted to access the requested service.

6. Web server delivers the service.

This system allows the server to leverage the existing infrastructure of the institutional ID system and directory. It assumes that there is a secure communication channel (SSL) between the browser and the web server. The access management module maintains a cache of user credentials and attributes so that it need not contact the authentication and directory systems for every user request. Public facilities pose their traditional problems in this model. User credentials are kept in the browser until the browser is closed or until the user logs out. Therefore, if the user does not remember to log out or exit the browser, the next user who sits down at the same workstation will inherit their credentials and capabilities.

This model does not scale well. If more than one such web server exists at the institution, each must be modified to communicate with the institutional authentication and directory systems. Any change to institutional authentication or directory systems requires a change to all modified servers. This method cannot be scaled to access management between an institution and a remote service provider. Each web server providing restricted services would need to support the authentication and directory systems of all subscribers to its services; this would rapidly become unmanageable.

2. Broker Model

A more scalable architecture can be established by introducing a "broker" service to consolidate and generalize access management. This service includes a new Access Management Broker server and a new plug-in module for web servers. Here requirements for granting service are encoded, in advance, in sets of "rules." The new Access Management Broker server uses a particular rule to decide which authentication and authorization components to use and how to combine and interpret the information retrieved from them. The protocol between web server and broker server permits the web server to suggest a preferred rule.

A single transaction would thus be:

1. User requests a restricted service.
2. Web server asks browser for user credentials.
3. Browser prompts user for name and password, and resubmits the request with user credentials.
4. Web server's access management module sends to the broker: the user's credentials, the service desired by the user, and any user attributes it wishes sent back.
5. Broker determines which authentication and authorization rule to use based on the requesting host and the requested service. Broker passes user's credentials to the appropriate authentication system to check the credentials.
6. Broker uses the same rule to collect user attributes from the appropriate institutional directory system(s). It then determines, based on the user's attributes, whether the user is permitted to access the requested service.
7. Broker notifies the web server whether user is permitted to access to the service and also returns any permissible user attributes which may have been requested by the web server.
8. Web server provides access to the service.

Maintenance is much easier in this model. Web servers need only to talk to the broker through a single protocol. Changes made to institutional ID or directory systems are reflected by changes in the broker software and nowhere else. The broker maintains a cache of credentials and attributes, preserving the performance of the previous model. A web server may request that a cache entry be considered stale beyond some interval. User privacy has been given due consideration in this model. The entire directory (names, demographics, all user attributes) is no longer known to the web server by default. A web server must explicitly request any user attributes it requires for business (e.g., a fax number if the service to be performed requires fax to the user, or cost center identification). Broker server rules can therefore implement useful access management policies.

3. Cross-Organizational Access Management by Proxy

The above methods cannot be extended out of an institution because the user name and password still move through the web server unencrypted. In a cross-organizational setting, that web server would be operated by a remote or "third-party" service provider, i.e., a provider at another institution, commercial or otherwise. The interaction might work like this. The user must have previously authenticated with the proxy in order to use it. These credentials are present in every request the user sends to the proxy and are kept in the proxy's cache.

1. User requests a restricted service through proxy.
2. Proxy forwards request for restricted service to third-party server.
3. Third-party server asks proxy for user credentials.
4. Proxy checks user credentials from cache with broker, including an identifier for the third-party and the name of the restricted service as additional parameters.
5. Broker validates user credentials as before.
6. Broker does authorization check as before.
7. Broker sends result back to proxy.
8. Proxy sends an institutional credential previously agreed upon with the service provider back to the third-party server along with the user's request for service.

9. Third-party server checks the institutional credential against a local table, verifies it, and allows proxy access to the service.
10. Proxy forwards service to user.

Future requests from the user for the same service must be intercepted by the proxy so that the institutional credential can be passed along to the third-party service provider with the request. This setup is relatively easy to roll out quickly, as it requires modifications only to the institutional proxy server. But it has the usual drawbacks associated with proxies: if the proxy does not handle all requests, the user is initially directed to the proxy through another resource at the user's institution. In this case, absolute URLs in documents returned from the third-party through the proxy must be rewritten to point back to the proxy; and relative URLs must be rewritten so that the proxy recognizes them as requests to forward. If the proxy handles all traffic, it may become a bottleneck. Since many institutions are moving towards the use of proxies as gateways to third-party services, this model may be a natural first step for them.

4. Cross-Organizational Access Management via Cryptographic Module

This model was in development but appears to have the best long-term promise. Before any services are requested, the user must activate the browser module. This is currently done in Netscape by choosing the module and selecting "login." The user will be prompted for a "PIN" and responds with an id, password and an identification of the local institutional access management broker.

1. The browser module, acting over a secure channel, contacts the broker and presents the user's credentials (id and password) and the preferred processing rule for the broker.

2. The broker validates the use and then obtains or generates a temporary private key and a temporary digital certificate, which are returned back to the module. The certificate contains the address of the broker and an opaque identifier of the user, again temporary, and known only to the broker. This new certificate is then available within the browser for subsequent use with third-party services. In current browsers, the user must then explicitly select it, indicating a desire to be "known" by this identity.
3. Again, library has provided a server plug-in which handles the broker communication at remote, third-party providers. Third-party service providers use this server plug-in and use SSL (secure channel). The user's new certificate is sent to the third-party server during initialization of the SSL channel. The plug-in will use the certificate as the user's credentials rather than id and password.
4. Because the certificate contains the address of the broker, the third-party server can establish contact with that broker, send it the user's certificate, the class of service it plans to provide, and any further user attributes to be retrieved back for business purposes.
5. The broker can perform authentications as above and return authentication and any requested (and permitted) attributes back to the third-party.
6. The service is delivered to the user.

This model appears the most secure and most flexible of any. Because the certificates are temporary, library avoid several administrative problems usually associated with certificates. It does not need to establish a complex distribution system or invent special methods to accommodate people using more than one workstation. Because a single certificate is installed by the browser module for all transactions, users do not require extensive training in certificate handling (installation, update, etc.) although they do need to be educated about the use of the browser module itself. Membership in networked communities is increasingly important, and many areas of research, including legal and public policy, play as critical a role as the technology work.

REQUIRED QUALITIES IN ARCHITECTURES

Given the limitations in the existing approaches and the redundant efforts required, architectures can leverage the existing authentication and authorization databases at the local organization based on the following guidelines:

- It must be a real-world solution; that is, it must take into account the browsers and web servers currently in use, existing ID and directory systems and an average level of user expertise. Web server modifications must be as modular and as simple to maintain as possible.
- It should allow the retrieval of user information (user "attributes") when specifically needed for the business of a service, while otherwise protecting user information from illegal or inappropriate use.
- It should protect any user "secrets." In particular, a user's password may never travel across the network in the clear.
- It should restrict access to services with the desired granularity.
- It should be reasonably efficient, both in terms of Web server processing and in terms of network traffic.

RETRIEVAL PROTOCOLS

Various retrieval protocols are available and their use and application depends upon the requirement and architecture employed in library. These are as following:

- **Z39.50 :** Supports information retrieval among different information systems
- **SRU/SRW (Search and Retrieve URL/Web Service) :** Web services for search and retrieval based on Z39.50 semantics
- **CQL (Contextual Query Language) :** Formal, user-friendly query language for use between information retrieval systems

REFERENCES AND NOTES

1. OITP, American Library Association. Principles for the Development of the National Information Infrastructure. *http://www.ala.org/oitp/principles.html*
2. W. Arms. Implementing Policies for Access Management. D-Lib Magazine. *http://www.dlib.org/dlib/february98/arms/02arms.html*
3. Web Services, NC State University. Welcome 2 WRAP. *http://www.ncsu.edu/wrap/*
4. RSA Laboratories. PKCS-11: Cryptographic Token Interface Standard. *http://www.rsa.com/rsalabs/pubs/PKCS/html/pkcs-11.html*
5. Stanford University Web Authentication. *http://www.stanford.edu/group/dcg/webauth*
6. ISO/IEC 9594-1/ITU-T Recommendation X.500. "Information Techonology - Open Systems Interconnection – The Directory: Overview of Concepts, Models and Services". 1997 edition.
7. Akselbo, J.L., Arnfred, L., Barfort, S., Bay, G., Christiansen, T.B., Hansen, J.H., Jensen, H.T., Markussen, G.B., Morthorst, A.M., and Nielsen, M.P. (2006), *The Hybrid Library: From the Users' Perspective*", The National Library and Copenhagen University Library, the Aarhus School of Business Library, the State and University Library, the University Library of Southern Denmark, available in English at: http://www.statsbiblioteket.dk/publ/fieldstudies.pdf
8. Arth, J. (2007), "Primo Usability & Views: The Minnesota

Report", presentation given at the ELUNA meeting, Spearfish, South Dakota, June 2007.

9. Casey, M. and Savastinuk, L.C., (2006), "Library 2.0: Service for the next-generation library", *Library Journal*, No. 14, available at: http://www.libraryjournal.com/article/CA6365200.html
10. IFLA Study Group on the Functional Requirements for Bibliographic Records (1998), *Functional Requirements for Bibliographic Records: Final Report*, KG Saur, Munich, available at: http://www.ifla.org/VII/s13/frbr/frbr.pdf
11. Law, J. (2007), "Understanding student expectations in conducting course research", presentation given at Online Northwest Conference, February 16, 2007, available at: http://www.ous.edu/onlinenw/2007/presentations/law.ppt
12. Mele, S. (2007), "A Poll on HEP Information Systems", available at: *http://indico.cern.ch/getFile.py/access?contribId=46&resId=0&materialId* =slides&confId=11611
13. OCLC Online Computer Library Center (2005), *Perceptions of Libraries and Information Resources: A Report to the OCLC Membership*, Dublin, Ohio, available at: *http://www.oclc.org/reports/2005perceptions.htm*
14. http://cf.uba.uva.nl/uba2006/english.html
15. http://ublibsprod.ub.tu-berlin.de/F?RN=657376414& func=file&file_name=findb&local_base=TUB01
16. http://library.ucl.ac.uk/F?RN=862302169
17. http://www.wikipedia.com
18. http://orweblog.oclc.org/archives/001021.html
19. http://www.lib.ncsu.edu/catalog
20. OCLC Online Computer Library Center (2006), *College Students' Perceptions of Libraries and Information Resources: A Report to the OCLC Membership*, Dublin, Ohio, available at: http://www.oclc.org/reports/perceptionscollege.htm
21. Rosen, D. (2006), *Ex Libris PRIMO Usability Evaluations*,

University of Minnesota Usability Services, Minneapolis, Minnesota.

22. Rosen, D. (2007), *Ex Libris PRIMO Round 2 Usability Evaluations Summary Report*, University of Minnesota Usability Services, Minneapolis, Minnesota.
23. Sadeh, T. (2006), "Google Scholar versus metasearch systems", *High Energy Physics Libraries Webzine*, No. 12, available at: *http://library.cern.ch/HEPLW/12/papers/1/*
24. Sadeh, T. (2007), "Time for a change: new approaches for a new generation of library users", *New Library World*, Vol. 108 No. 7/8, pp. 307-316, available at: http://www.emeraldinsight.com/10.1108/03074800710763608
25. http://www.medialab.nl
26. http://www.bowker.com
27. http://www.iii.com
28. http://www.lib.ncsu.edu/endeca
29. http://www.exlibrisgroup.com/primo.htm
30. Schiessl, M., Duda, S., Thölke, A., and Fischer, R. (2003), "Eye tracking and its application in usability and media research", *MMI interaktiv*, Vol. 6, available at: http://useworld.net/ausgaben/3-2003/MMIInteraktiv0303_
31. SchiesslDudaThoelkeFischer.pdf Schnipke, S.K. and Todd, M.W. (2000), "Trials and tribulations of using an eyetracking system", proceedings of CHI 2000 Conference on Human Factors in Computing Systems archive, pp. 273-274.
32. Tillett, B. (2004), *What is FRBR? A Conceptual Model for the Bibliographic Universe*, Library of Congress Cataloging Distribution Service, Washington, DC, available at: http://www.loc.gov/cds/FRBR.html
33. Wang, X., Zhai, C. (2007), "Learn from Web Search Logs to Organize Search Results", Conference proceedings of the 30th SIGIR conference, July 2007, available at: http://sifaka.cs.uiuc.edu/czhai/pub/sigir07-org.pdf
34. *http://scholar.google.com*
35. *http://www.scirus.com*

36. *http://www.google.com*

37. Computing Services, Carnegie Mellon University. Project Minotaur. *http://andrew2.andrew.cmu.edu/minotaur/*

38. Columbia University - Presbyterian Hospital Committee on Data Security. Network User Authorization and Authorization Architecture. *ftp://ftp.columbia.edu/cpsec/nua.ps*

39. Student Services Office, Columbia University. "Appendix A: Policy on Access to Student Records under the Federal Family Educational Rights and Privacy Act (FERPA) of 1974." Facets – Facts About Columbia Essential to Students. *http://www.columbia.edu/cu/facets/50.html*

40. Electronic Privacy Information Center. The Cookies Page. *http://www.epic.org/privacy/internet/cookies/*

41. C. Lynch, ed. A White Paper on Authentication and Access Management Issues in Cross-organizational Use of Networked Information Resources. Coalition for Networked Information. *http://www.cni.org/projects/authentication/authentication-wp.html*

42. http://www.amazon.com

43. http://www.youtube.com

44. http://www.flickr.com

45. OCLC. (2005) *Perceptions of Libraries and Information Resources*. Retrieved from http://www.oclc.org/reports/2005perceptions.htm

46. Amazon Web Services http://www.amazon.com/gp/browse.html?node=3435361 is free but requires a prominent link back to Amazon from your site.

47. Murray, P. (2007) *Faceted Classification of Information*. Retrieved from *http://www.kmconnection.com/DOC100100.htm*

48. FRBR (Functional Requirements for Bibliographic Records) UKOLN. (2005) *Bibliographic Management Factfile: FRBR (Functional Requirements for Bibliographic Records)*. Retrieved from http://www.ukoln.ac.uk/bib-man/factfile/cataloguing-rules/frbr/

49. Danskin, A. & Chapman, A. (2003) Bibliographic records in

the computer age. *Library & Information Update*, 2(9), 42-43. Retrieved from http://www.cilip.org.uk/publications/updatemagazine/archive/archive2003/september/update0309d.htm

50. http://www.myspace.com
51. http://www.facebook.com
52. http://del.icio.us
53. http://www.ncbi.nlm.nih.gov/sites/entrez?db=pubmed
54. http://www.jstor.org/search/
55. http://libserv2.rhul.ac.uk/F?RN=599275615
56. http://www.scopus.com
57. Riva, P. (2007) Introducing the Functional Requirements for Bibliographic Records and Related IFLA Developments. *Bulletin of the American Society for Information Science and Technology*, 33(6), 7-11. Retrieved from http://www.asis.org/Bulletin/Aug-07/Riva.pdf
58. Syndetic Solutions http://www.syndetics.com
59. WorldCat http://www.oclc.org/worldcat/default.htm
60. deli.icio.us http://del.icio.us
61. AJAX (Asynchronous JavaScript and XML). Vanderbilt University http://discoverlibrary.vanderbilt.edu;
62. Royal Library of Denmark *http://primo-7.kb.dk/primo_library/libweb/action/search.do?vid=KGL*;
63. The University of Minnesota http://prime2.oit.umn.edu:1701/primo_library/libweb/action/search.do?vid=TWINCITIES;
64. The University of Iowa *http://smartsearch.uiowa.edu/primo_library/libweb/action/search.do?vid=uiowa*
65. Connotea http://www.connotea.org
66. RefWorks http://www.refworks.com
67. Encore *http://www.iii.com/encore/* Glasgow University *http://encore.lib.gla.ac.uk/iii/encore/app*
68. Breeding, M. (2007) Encore. *Library Technology Reports*, 43(4), 23-27.

69. Aquabrowser: *http://www.aquabrowser.com/*

70. Columbus Metropolitan Library: http://catalog.columbuslibrary.org

71. Breeding, M. (2007) AquaBrowser. *Library Technology Reports*, 43(4), 15-18.

8

CATALOGUING OF E-RESOURCES

Electronic resources have been a matter of great interest in recent years. They are still evolving—both in their nature and their deliver. Libraries are still striving to find ways to provide optional access to them. Librarians are still considering the fundamental issues related to electronic resources and are exchanging practical advice about bibliographic control of these resources in a constantly changing online environment. They are still seeking to answer some conceptual questions such as the nature of e-resources, providing access and discovering them. E-resources are consisted of data such as information representing numbers, text, graphics, images, maps, moving images, music, sounds, etc., programs such as instructions, etc., that process the data for use, or these can be the combinations of data and programs. E-resources often include components with characteristics found in multiple classes of materials.

For cataloguing purposes, e-resources may be treated in one of two ways depending on whether access is local (direct) or remote (networked). Direct access is understood to mean that a physical carrier can be described. Such a carrier (e.g., disc/disk, cassette, and cartridge) must be inserted into a computerized device or into a peripheral attached to a computerized device. Remote access is understood to mean that no physical carrier can be handled. Remote access can only be provided by use of an input-output device for example, a terminal, either connected to a computer system, for example, a resource in a network, or by use of resources stored in a hard disk or other storage device.

DEFINING

AACR2 is oriented toward basing cataloging treatment on carrier. Until 1997 the definition of computer file in USMARC (Leader/06 code"m") also indicated that the record would be coded for carrier. However, as a result of a change approved by MARBI in June 1997, Update No. 3 (July 1997) to the *USMARC Bibliographic Format* revised the definition of code "m" to allow for computer files to be coded for their most significant aspect. That definition now reads:

Code m indicates that the content of the record is for the following classes of electronic resources: computer software (including programs, games, fonts), numeric data, computer-oriented multimedia, online systems or services. For these classes of materials, if there is a significant aspect that causes it to fall into another Leader/06 category, code for that significant aspect (e.g. vector data that is cartographic is not coded as numeric but as cartographic). Other classes of electronic resources are coded for their most significant aspect (e.g. language material, graphic, cartographic material, sound, music, moving image). In case of doubt or if the most significant aspect cannot be determined, consider the item a computer file. In conjunction with this change, field 007 for computer files is now mandatory in any record representing an item whose carrier is a computer file.

Directly accessed electronic resources have been treated like computer files at LC. Directly accessed electronic resources have been represented in the COMPUTER FILES file, the BOOKS file (those that accompany books), and, with format integration, in the SERIALS file. With respect to cataloging remotely accessed electronic resources, LC has been most active in cataloging electronic serials/journals and electronic counterparts or subsets of tangible, original items or collections. In most cases, the latter do not receive separate catalog records; instead, they are delineated in records for the original items or collections. The special format divisions are interested in providing an integrated approach to the bibliographic records for the materials of interest to them.

In the mean time the shift has approached from carrier to content is implemented at LC. The special format divisions continue to focus on cataloging (except for Music, RBSCD) and servicing material acquired for the collections in their custody. The change in approach that emphasizes content means, electronic resources be represented throughout the files that constitute the catalog. An issue of potential significant impact relates to those computer-related electronic resources acquired by the special format divisions for their collections. The Library of Congress develops workflow and cataloging policies related to "content vs. carrier" issues and will make them available to the larger cataloging community. Remotely accessed electronic resources of a dynamic nature that are currently excluded from serial treatment are:

- Databases (including directories, A&I services, etc.) Electronic discussion groups (e.g., SERIALST)
- Electronic discussion group digests (e.g., AUTOCAT digest)
- Gopher servers (e.g., LC-MARVEL)

- Online public access catalogs (e.g., OCLC, RLIN)
- Online services (e.g., America Online)
- Web sites (e.g., the CONSER home page)

Single Manifestation

An electronic resource that exists solely in a single manifestation, e.g., a publication that exists solely online, by definition is represented by a single bibliographic record in the same manner as other non-electronic resources that exist in a single manifestation. Currently, those judged to be monographs are cataloged as computer files or as cartographic materials or, if judged to be accompanying material, by the general cataloging divisions. Both monographs and serials are cataloged according to AACR2R, LCRIs, DCM, LCSH, SCM, LCC, USMARC, and supplementary documentation appropriate to each category of material.

Multiple Manifestations

An electronic resource that is another manifestation of a work is likely to be one of the following:

a) a manifestation that is a counterpart or subset of a published resource (tangible or otherwise, usually directly accessed) or an adjunct to it;

b) a directly accessed manifestation that is :

   1. a counterpart or subset of a tangible resource (either at the collection level or item level or both);
   2. an adjunct to material described in 1) immediately above;
   3. a reproduction in electronic form done by or for the Library of Congress of a resource (including material that may have been published) held by the Library;

c) a remotely accessed manifestation that is :

1. a counterpart or subset of a tangible resource (either at the collection level or item level or both);
2. an adjunct to material described in 1) immediately above;
3. a reproduction in electronic form done by or for the Library of Congress of a resource (including material that may have been published) held by the Library.

A manifestation of conventionally published materials, including directly accessed electronic resources, usually consists of multiple copies. Unique collections usually occur in a single instance, although electronic manifestations of the original collection may be mirrored or copied and therefore exist at several storage locations. The data elements contained in the USMARC bibliographic format are predicated on data elements common to all the copies of a manifestation. Those applicable to a particular copy are generally treated as "local" or as holdings information. This concept is less appropriate to a unique tangible resource such as an archival collection, although this does not preclude the concept of "copy specific" as applied to a particular item in a collection when the manifestation of the item itself consists of multiple copies.

Multiple Presentations of the Same Electronic Resource

If an electronic resource is available in multiple presentations that may be generated from different underlying digital representations, e.g., images in TIFF or JPEG format, it is not necessary to acknowledge the condition.

Electronic Resources in Bibliographical References

With respect to bibliography notes, the term "bibliographical references" to include all kinds of resources, including electronic resources; do not give any special treatment to, or provide special mention of, the latter.

Many electronic resources are delivered as part of aggregators. Aggregator databases are forcing librarians to "color outside the lines". They bring up alternative solutions to the problem of scarce resources and point to a huge volume of work related to the bibliographic control of aggregator databases. This involves Aggregator-Neutral Record.

Aggregator-Neutral Record

Basically an aggregator-neutral record is one that is separate from the print that covers all versions of the same online serial on one record. There may be cases however, where a cataloger determines that because of substantial differences (e.g. in content or subject), another online "version" really represents a separate work, therefore a separate record is needed. The aggregator-neutral record has been defined for serials available by one or more providers. However, these records should not be that different from records for other online serials such as born-digital serials and free resources (e.g. government documents, free scholarly serials, etc.). The same serial titles are made available by multiple aggregators.

The appearance and coverage might differ among these aggregators. Recent trends have been for one aggregator to buy up another, or for publishers to pull their titles from an aggregation. Thus, maintaining separate records became very difficult and undesirable. By creating one record that can be used for all aggregations, records will not need to be updated or deleted to reflect such changes and far less maintenance will be required. The aggregator-neutral record will apply to all online serials distributed by one or more provider.

CHALLENGES AND ISSUES: CONCENTRATING ON E-RESOURCES

There are many challenges and questions related to the bibliographic control of electronic resources, and much room for research to understand how people discover them and what is the best way to provide access. The content of the information package is the most important factor when cataloguing. An e-resource that is primarily language material should be cataloged as a monograph, serial, or integrating resource, as appropriate. For example, a music score issued in electronic format should be cataloged as a score, not as an electronic resource. The computer/ electronic aspects of these materials are brought out with the addition of an 007 field to the record. The 007 field is mandatory for all electronic resources.

How can electronic information be accommodated when the cataloging rules are designed to describe physical items owned by and residing in libraries? How do libraries provide access to that information? Questions like these must be addressed before libraries move into the future and provide the patrons with information the way they are coming to expect it. Action is needed, and well-established rules and practices must be changed. It's easy to see that more and more library resources are coming to us in electronic format. It's less easy to figure out just how those resources should be handled when it comes to cataloging.

- Should cataloger make one catalog record or two when cataloger has both a print and an electronic version of an item?
- Should an electronic file be treated as a monograph or a serial?
- When tackling electronic resources should he catalog using MARC or some other protocol?

CATALOGING AND METADATA ISSUES FOR ELECTRONIC RESOURCES

The environment in which cataloging principles and standards operate has changed dramatically. The development of automated systems for the creation and processing of bibliographic data, the growth of large-scale shared cataloging programs, and emerging technologies have created multitude of opportunities to provide access to national and international academic library collections. However, economic pressures have also prompted libraries to try to simplify the cataloging process, using "minimal level" cataloging records in order to keep pace with the continued growth of publishing. Keeping in view several aspects, the Cataloging librarians have identified two significant needs:

1. to adapt existing [cataloging] codes and practices to accommodate change resulting from new forms of electronic publishing and the advent of networked access to information resources, and
2. to respond more effectively to an increasingly broad range of user expectations and needs.

Cataloging involves either the original or copy cataloging of all monographic materials. Copy cataloging includes finding the correct record on OCLC (out of multiple millions of records), determining if any record is of sufficient quality to be used as a copy cataloging record, modifying such record to meet standards, then sending the modified record to the Online Catalog. Original cataloging involves constructing a MARC (MAchine Readable Code) record from scratch, following the AACR2 rules, moving the newly created record from OCLC to the Online Catalog. München (1998) wonder how catalogers will guarantee the quality and relevance of bibliographic access within the exploding world of online materials. If so, what kind of bibliographic records will be required to meet the different uses and user needs?

The bibliographic data organization and structure for intellectual and physical access to the documents is also significant.

Regarding the source of information for cataloguing, AACR2 Rule 9.0B1 states:

The chief source of information for e-resources the resource itself. Take the information from formally presented evidence (e.g., title screen(s), main menus, program statements, initial display(s) of information, home page(s), the file header(s) including "Subject:" lines, encoded metadata (e.g., TEI headers, HTML/XML meta tags), and the physical carrier or its labels), including information that has been uncompressed, printed out, or otherwise processed for use. If the information in these sources varies in degree of fullness, prefer the source that provides the most complete information.

If the information required is not available from the resource itself, it may be taken from the following sources (in this order of preference):

- Printed or online documentation or other accompanying material (e.g., publisher's letter, "about" file, publisher's Web page about an electronic resource)
- Information printed on a container issued by the publisher, distributor, etc.

DRAFT INTERIM GUIDELINES FOR CATALOGING ELECTRONIC RESOURCES

For some time it has been the intent of the Cataloging Policy and Support Office (CPSO) to develop conceptual guidelines for the cataloging of electronic resources. The guidelines have been reviewed within LC by representatives of the units most directly concerned with cataloging electronic manifestations, particularly by the staff members from LC's special format divisions, who have been involved for some time with materials that LC is digitizing from its own collections. The purpose of the Draft Interim Guidelines was to establish an interim set of guidelines to be used for cataloging electronic resources in the Library of Congress based on a common conceptual context and a common terminology. The intent of the guidelines is to apply to resources of divergent character produced under varying circumstances and managed by different entities, a set of conventions for bibliographic control that will enable generalized, standard practice to the extent judged practicable in a diverse, dynamic environment. The guidelines then include:

1. policies on when to use multiple records and when to use a single record;
2. conventions developed especially for the single-record technique;
3. directions for indicating the existence of other physical formats;
4. directions related to electronic location;
5. directions relating to collocating records and linking them;
6. directions relating to identifying records related to specific projects.

The *Guidelines* are interim for the following reasons:

1. some of the copyright and collection development guidelines with respect to remotely accessed electronic resources are only now beginning to be formulated; the universe of material for which bibliographic control is to be applied will have a substantial impact on the resources available for this purpose and will in turn influence the nature of the conventions themselves (the larger the number of

materials to be controlled the less labor intensive the conventions to control them can be);

2. the dynamic nature of the environment of electronic resources is profoundly affecting the standards upon which current conventions of bibliographic control rest; it is necessary to monitor the changes that are developing in AACR2, in USMARC, and in such international activities as the *ISBD (ER): International Standard Bibliographic Description for Electronic Resources* and the IFLA study on the *Functional Requirements for Bibliographic Records*, and make adjustments accordingly;
3. experiments applicable to particular kinds of resources (e.g., serials and CONSER policies; the BEONLINE project for business and economic resources) were under way with evaluation of results and implications for policy guidelines still to be determined;
4. system considerations at LC are in a state of flux, particularly with the impending procurement of an Integrated Library System; hypertext links are still not available in the traditional interfaces to MUMS and SCORPIO; once this feature is more widely available, perceptions of which resources should be represented in the catalog and how data need to be depicted may change.

Fixed Field Values for Integrating Resources: TEXTUAL: MARC 008 values

Record Format	=	SERIAL	
Rec_Typ	=	a	Item is primarily textual
Bib_Lvl	=	i	Integrating resource
Date_Tp	=	c	Continuing publication
Date 1	=	[date]	If no date can be determined, use 199u or 200u
Date 2	=	9999	
Frequn	=	blank	Indeterminable frequency

Regulr	=	x	Completely irregular Frequn = u and regulr = u on copy is also acceptable when nothing is known of the frequency or regularity Note however: If there is an indication that the updating is done regularly (daily, weekly, etc.) or continuously, that frequency and its regularity should be coded.
Ser_Typ	=	w	Updating web site
or	=	d	Updating database
Repr	=	s	Electronic resource
S/L_Ent	=	2	Integrated entry (Latest title)

MARC 006 values:

TypeCode = m

FileType = d

NON-TEXTUALMARC 008 values:

Record format	=	MRDF	
Rec_Type	=	m	
Bib_Lvl	=	i	
Date_Tp	=	c	
Date 1	=	[date]	if no date can be determined use 199u or 200u
Date 2	=	9999	
FileType	=	b	computer software
	=	a	numeric data
	=	i	computer oriented multimedia
	=	j	online system or service
	=	m	combination

MARC 006 values:

TypeCode	=	s	continuing/seriality
Frequn	=	blank	indeterminable frequency
Regulr	=	x	completely irregular Frequn u and regulr = u on copy is

			also acceptable when nothing is known of the frequency or regularity Note however: If there is an indication that the updating is done regularly (daily, weekly, etc.) or continuously, that frequency and its regularity should be coded.
Ser_Typ	=	w	updating website
or	=	d	updating database
Repr	=	s	
S/L_Ent	=	2	Integrated entry (Latest title)

VARIABLE FIELDS FOR WEB RESOURCES:

006 m

Added to all web resources

007 cr mn

This is the most common coding. (c=electronic resource; r=remote access; blank=undefined; m=mixed color; n=no dimensions; blank=no sound). Other combinations are valid. For example: crbn = resource is in black and white (a pdf file, eg); crmna = resource has a sound component.

050/055

This information may prove useful in the future, so while cataloger should not add 050 or 055, leave them in (after a quick check for suitability) when he finds them.

090

If the record has an 090 with a suitable LC class no., change the 090 to 050 and retain. The second indicator should be set at "4." Shorten to base class number as above and delete series call numbers.

245 |a

Generally, transcribe the title as it prominently appears on the web page. Do not include such phrases as, "Welcome to..." or "Introducing..."

245 |b

Generally do not add unless it provides important imformation for access or clarifies the meaning of the main title.

245 |c

Transcribe |c only when the statement of responsibility appears prominently. Otherwise, include such statements in a 500 note as appropriate.

245 |h

[electronic resource] This GMD is mandatory.

246

It should be used as cataloger would search for book cataloguing for alternative or other titles. Generally, do not trace subtitles. Trace a title appearing in the HTML header if it is sufficiently different from the web page title to be important for access. (Use indicators 1 [blank] and: |iTitle in HTML header: . . .) If cataloger has copy or a citation that gives a different title from the one that appears on the screen, trace that title as an "other" title (|iAlso known as: . . .) unless cataloger has reason to believe that it is a former title and should be traced in the 247.

247

Use to record a former title of the resource. It should be used only when cataloger is sure that resource had this title in a former iteration. If cataloger knows when the previous title was used, the date(s) may be given in subfield f.

256 Electronic data

Do not add this field. Leave in record if it appears on copy and is correct.

260 |a, |b

Supply or verify publishing information as far as possible. Check all parts of the site, especially contact and/or "about" pages, as well as links to the home pages of sponsoring organizations. If cataloger cannot determine place, he should try at least to determine the country; [U.S] for example. Otherwise, use [s.l.]. If an individual is named as responsible for the site, and there is no named publisher, use the individual as the publisher.

260 |c

For integrating resources, dates are often difficult to determine. As a general rule, use the earliest date given, leaving it open. If cataloger cannot find a reasonably certain beginning date, do not code |c at all. Code an estimated date in the Date1 fixed field: eg., 199u.

300

Web resources do not have physical dimensions and therefore the 300 field is not used.

362

This field is used when the beginning date of the resource is not certain, but a probable date is known (for example, when cataloger has a copyright statement, such as 1996-2005). Note the probable date as: Began in 1996? Do not use if cataloger has a date in 260 |c.

500 Source of title

This note is mandatory in all cases. In order to simplify description, it is used : Title from Web page (viewed [date]) whenever the title in the 245 is from the opening screen of the site. Variations in this note are valid, if eg., the title is taken from a place (such as the HTML header, or the "about" page) that is not the opening screen. Title from opening screen of pdf file is a valid alternative for e-texts in pdf format.

500 Publication history

When cataloguing the electronic version of a book or article, add this note to indicate the date of the earlier publication; for example, Paper version published in [date]; or Reissue. Originally published in paper ...

505

Do not add to copy, except in cases where the contents are titles of separate documents or works. If on copy, check carefully, since the contents often change. Evaluate the contents to be sure that they really add useful information to the record. If not, delete.

516

This field is not usually necessary, but it may be used to bring out information that is not included elsewhere in the record. General statements such as "World Wide Web Resource" should be deleted. Do not add this field.

520 Summary

Evaluate these on a case by case basis to be sure that they really add useful information to the record by telling the user what the site contains. Add a summary only if cataloger can easily find concise information from the site itself. The introductory material and/or the "about" pages can be good sources of summary information.

530 Other formats

Note here any other formats in which the resource is available. For example, the existence of a paper or other version such as CD-ROM should be noted if this information is known: For example, "Also available in print format."

533 Electronic reproduction

This note may be used only when the resource is clearly a digital reproduction of a print original and not a new edition. When this field is used, the fixed fields and 260 information should be those of the original publication (as when cataloguing photoreproductions).

538 Mode of access: Internet

For consistency, always use Internet rather than World Wide Web.

538 System requirements

This field is only used when some extra components or plug-ins are required to access the resource. It is not necessary to add this note for the Adobe Acrobat reader. Add for other components such as QueckTime as appropriate.

590 Local Note

For any resource for which library has purchased access (NetLibrary, for example) always add this note with the text: Internet access available to library users only.

6XX

Subject headings are assigned for content as they are for books. Check the subjects on copy for both validity and appropriateness to the resource. Add additional subjects if they are needed/helpful for access. The subdivision "|xComputer network resources" is not a form subdivision and therefore should only be used for those site that *are about* computer network resources, such as subject-oriented collections of links to such resources. In other cases this subdivision should be deleted. The subdivision "Databases" may be used as a form subdivision as subject headings that are designations of the type of resource, such as "Web sites."

856

Must contain |u and a complete, working URL. There

may be other information given, such as a public note in |z. The value of these should be decided on a case-by-case basis. Indicators will normally be "40". Be sure to check and verify any differing values.

The URL should go directly to the title in the record, or occasionally to a search page from which the full-text is retrievable. In this case the URL should be prefixed with the subfield: |zSearch for this title in:|u

GUIDELINES FOR CODING ELECTRONIC RESOURCES IN LEADER/06

An electronic resource is a manifestation of a work that requires the use of a computer for access. Peripheral devices attached to the computer (such as a CD-ROM drive) may also be required. The manifestation's carrier is accessed either directly (e.g., via CD-ROM, etc.) or remotely (e.g., via the Internet). Items that do not require the use of a computer, such as audio CDs or movies on DVD-videodiscs, are excluded from this definition.

The *Leader/06 (Type of record)* character position in the *MARC 21 Format for Bibliographic Data* contains a one-character alphabetic code that differentiates MARC records created for various types of content and materials. The definition of code "m" (computer file) in Leader/06 was revised in June 1997 as a result of *Proposal No. 97-3R*. The new definition narrowed the choice of code "m" to the following types of electronic resources:

- computer software (including programs, games, fonts)
- numeric data
- computer-oriented multimedia
- online systems or services

Code "m" is defined as follows in the *MARC 21 Format for Bibliographic Data*:

m - Computer file

Code m indicates that the content of the record is for the following classes of electronic resources: computer software (including programs, games, fonts), numeric data, computer-oriented multimedia, online systems or services. For these classes of materials, if there is a significant aspect that causes it to fall into another Leader/06 category, code for that significant aspect (e.g., vector data that is cartographic is not coded as numeric but as cartographic). Other classes of electronic resources are coded for their most significant aspect (e.g. language material, graphic, cartographic material, sound, music, moving image). In case of doubt or if the most significant aspect cannot be determined, consider the item a computer file.

This revised definition stipulates that catalogers code electronic resources for the significant aspects of their content, as opposed to their carrier.

The Leader/06 determines which 008 code (*Fixed-length data elements - General information*) is used and the appropriateness and validity of other fixed data elements in a record.

Principles and Guidelines for Coding Fields 006, 007 and 008

The 008 field contains character positions that provide coded information about the record as a whole and about special bibliographic aspects of the item cataloged. This field is not repeatable. Field 006 (*Fixed-length data elements - Additional material characteristics*) permits coding for additional aspects of an electronic resource (including any computer file aspects) if the 007 and 008 fields do not adequately describe it. Some cataloging utilities and groups (such as CONSER) require the use of 006 fields under certain conditions. Sample records in this document include 006 fields for those who may wish to use this field.

Coding all of these positions involves making a series of decisions. Consider the following when deciding what code values to select:

- What are the primary characteristics of the content of the resource (as opposed to the physical format or carrier)? Look at the definitions of the various Leader/06 codes. Is the content primarily language material, notated music, cartographic material, a computer file, a musical sound recording, etc.?
- Does the resource match the Leader/06 definition of a computer file? If so, "m" (for computer file) goes in Leader/06, and the 008 field is coded for computer files. Position 008/26 contains the code for the type of computer file described in the record.
- If Leader/06 is coded "a" (*language material*), is the resource a monograph or a continuing resource? This determines the code in Leader/07 (*Bibliographic level*), which in turn influences 008 field coding (*Books* or *Continuing resources*). For other material types, the Leader/06 code determines 008 coding.
- Does the cataloger wish to add a 006 field to record characteristics that cannot be coded in the 008 field? Some electronic resources might need more than one 006 field. For others, a 006 field may not really add any additional information and could be left out.
- *Proposal No. 97-3R* specifies that a 007 field (*Physical description fixed field*) for electronic resources is mandatory regardless of the Leader/06 code value when the physical form of the resource is an electronic format in order to provide an explicit indication that the item is in an electronic format.
- Some combinations of 006, 007, and 008 fields may result in a certain amount of redundancy, in the sense that the same information about an electronic

resource might appear in more than one of these fields. Catalogers must decide whether the information added as a result of recording additional characteristics of an item justifies the redundancy.

CODING FOR DIFFERENT TYPES OF ELECTRONIC RESOURCES

Bibliographic database on the Internet

The record describes collections of bibliographic records retrieved via search software; the presence of such software does not change the content of the resource and does not mean that Leader/06 should be coded "m." The resource is primarily textual bibliographic data, so it is coded as *language material*. The type of computer file (006/09) is *bibliographic data.*

Collection of databases on the Internet

The record describes the system itself and not the content of individual databases. The type of computer file is *online system or service*.

Textual continuing resource

The resource is the equivalent of a print item, but in electronic form. The resource is coded as *language material.* If a 006 field for computer files/electronic resources is added, the type of computer file (006/09) depends on the content of the resource.

Textual continuing resource with search software

The resource is the equivalent of a print item, but in electronic form search software is included. The presence of such software and/or the location of the serial on the Internet does not necessarily change the content of the resource and does not mean that Leader/06 should be coded "m." The resource is primarily textual data and is coded as *language material*. If a 006 field for computer files/

electronic resources is added, the type of computer file (006/09) depends on the content of the resource.

Textual continuing resource received via email

The resource is the equivalent of a print item but is received via email from a news wire service. It is coded as *language material*. The type of computer file is *document*.

Textual document

The resource is the equivalent of a print item, but in electronic form. It is coded as *language material*. If a 006 field for computer files/electronic resources is added, the type of computer file (006/09) depends on the content of the resource.

Cartographic material in electronic form

The resource is non-manuscript cartographic material in electronic form. It is coded as *cartographic material*. The type of computer file is *representational*.

Still images

The resource is an electronic collection of graphic materials, such as drawings or photographic prints. Additional items, such as captions and other explanatory text or manuals, may be present, but the primary content is graphic and the resource is coded as *graphic material*. The type of computer file is *representational*.

Notated music

The resource is an online collection of sheet music in electronic form. It is coded as *notated music*. The type of computer file is *other*.

Census in textual form

The resource consists largely of numeric data, perhaps in tabular form, but is the electronic equivalent of a print item. It is coded as *language material*. The type of computer file is *document*.

Database containing manipulable numeric data

The resource consists largely of numeric data that can be manipulated. It is coded as a *computer file*. The type of computer file is *numeric data*.

Computer operating system

The resource consists of an ordered set of instructions directing a computer to perform certain operations. It is coded as a *computer file* in Leader/06 and the type of file is *computer program*.

Computer software

The resource consists of an ordered set of instructions directing a computer to perform certain operations. It is coded as a *computer file* in Leader/06 and the type of file is *computer program*.

Computer game

The resource is a game that allows multi-user play online. The type of file is *game*.

Internet search engine

It is coded as a *computer file*. The type of file is *computer program*. 006 fields may be added to bring out the "seriality" or any additional characteristics of the web site.

Web portal

The bibliographic record describes the system and its content. It is coded as a *computer file*. The type of file is *combination*. 006 fields may be added to bring out the "seriality" or any additional characteristics.

System or service on the Internet (includes E-commerce sites)

The resource has system-based user interaction that allows users to purchase various types of products or services. The bibliographic record describes the web site. It is coded as a *computer file*. The type of file is *online system or service*. 006 fields may be added to bring out the "seriality" or any additional characteristics of the web site.

Web site with significant audio and video content

The resource consists of several types of materials, including audio and video. Leader/06 is coded as a *computer file*. The type of file is *combination* since there is no one significant aspect. 006 fields may be added to bring out the "seriality" or any additional characteristics.

Streaming video

The resource is an electronic moving image. It is coded as a *projected medium* in Leader/06. The type of computer file is *combination*, as there are audio as well as moving images.

Streaming audio

The resource is a collection of sound recordings in electronic format. It is coded as either a *musical* or *non-musical* sound recording, depending on the content. The type of computer file is *sound*.

CATALOGING CD-ROMS

In current cataloging, bibliographic records for CD-ROMs are formatted based on their content-type (book, serial, visual material) rather than their carrier-type (computer data file). For example, RLIN assigns the bibliographic record to a file based on its content-type (On RLIN records, the second letter in the BLT fixed field.) In older cataloging, bibliographic records for CD-ROMs were always formatted as computer files; these records are likely to be in the RLIN MDF file. It is found that OCLC does not use separate file formats.

Descriptive Verification

The checklist is applicable to verify CD-ROMs not CDs (i.e., sound discs). It applies only to bibliographic records where the CD-ROM is the primary (as opposed to accompanying) material cataloged.

This checklist does NOT apply to situations:

- where a book is accompanied by a CD-ROM;
- where a serial issue is accompanied by a CD-ROM;
- where the CD-ROM is part of a mixed media kit.

Required Steps

Required fields must be added to the bibliographic record if the record was not cataloged by LC (consider records with 042 pcc to be LC). Prior to 1998, standards required all CD-ROMs to be **RT m** (computer data file). Effectively from 1998, record type is determined by the CD ROM's contents.

CD ROMs with contents such as computer software (e.g. Excel on CD ROM), numeric databases, computer oriented multimedia, and online systems or services (e.g. OCLC Passport on CD ROM) would continue to be coded m, unless that content is also a "significant aspect" of another category, in which case the cataloger should code for the category of the significant aspect. OCLC example is for map vector data; numeric (normally code m) but coded as map (e). For CD ROM contents that do not fall into the m categories, the cataloger should now code for the "significant aspect" (e.g. language material, graphic, cartographic material, sound, music, moving image).

Some important aspects for CDROMs

1. Computer files cover material encoded for manipulation by computer. These materials fall within the scope of Chapter 9 of AACR2 and, where applicable, the Guidelines for Bibliographic Description of Interactive Multimedia (ALA, 1994) for those institutions choosing to use these optional guidelines. Included are data (e.g., text, image, numeric, sound)

and software (e.g., spreadsheets, word processors, games) that may be stored on, or contained in, carriers available by direct access (e.g., CD-ROMs) or by remote access (e.g., Internet resources).

2. Applying the National Level Record (NLR) standard, code all bytes and fields designated by the NLR as mandatory, and supply any applicable bytes and fields designated by the NLR as mandatory-if-applicable. Depending on the individual automated system or bibliographic utility, part or all of the Leader and Directory and some variable control fields may be system supplied.
3. Title Variants: Use judgment in assessing each item and assign a complement of title variants which covers variations deemed important and coded as appropriate. The importance of title variant access information is intended to reflect individual cataloger's judgment and/or local institutional policy.
4. FOR DIRECT ACCESS FILES: Mandatory. Not applicable to remote access files.
5. Transcribe all series as found on an item in either a 490 or a 440 field. All traced series must be supported by a national level authority record. Untraced series need not be supported by a national level authority record. If a national level series authority record already exists for the series, follow the first tracing practice indicated on the record and record the series and tracing appropriately (i.e., in a 490 field, a 440 field or a 490/8XX pairing).
6. FOR DIRECT ACCESS FILES: Make a "System requirements" note according to Chapter 9 of AACR2. FOR REMOTE ACCESS FILES: Make a "Mode of access" note according to Chapter 9 of AACR2.
7. Make a note for the edition statement if it is not taken

from the source of the title proper. If using the Guidelines for Bibliographic Description of Interactive Multimedia, make a note according to the instructions in those guidelines.

8. FOR REMOTE ACCESS FILES: Make if material is available as a separate online file or physical document and that information is not already given in another note.
9. Minimally, supply a brief summary note if the content of the item is not obvious from the rest of the bibliographic record.
10. If appropriate, assign at least one or two subject access fields from an established thesaurus or subject heading system and/or genre/form list recognized by the USMARC Format.
11. Use judgment in assessing each item and assign a complement of added entries which cover primary relationships associated with a work (e.g., writer, programmer, principal investigator, producer, featured composer, animator and/or other artist). The inclusion and importance of added entries are intended to reflect individual cataloger's judgment and/or local institutional policy.
12. If applicable, assign at least one 856 field giving an electronic location of the item at the time of cataloging.

Guidelines for CD-ROMs that accompany materials in other formats

General : When a CD-ROM accompanies an item in another format (such as a book that has a CD-ROM with it), catalog the piece in-hand in its primary format and note the accompanying CD-ROM in the sub-field e of the collation area (300 field) to detail both the type of CD-ROM (optical, etc.) and the size of the CD-ROM in inches.

Copy cataloging: Follow what is found on the record. Do not add or expand the collation area (300 field). Refer poor quality member records and questionable entries to a librarian for a decision.

Original cataloging: A system requirements note (538) field is not required and is not current LC practice. Adding a 538 is an option. However, any information obtained from the CD-ROM that may be helpful to the reader should be indicated in the note area with added entries given as needed.

DATABASES

A database is a collection of logically interrelated data stored together in one or more computerized files, usually created and managed by a database management system. The data are encoded, and each file is designed with a high-level structure for accepting, storing, and providing information on demand. Typically, there is a set of definitions for the database that describe its various data elements and a set of codes to identify each element. The database may include the database management software that created the file, or it may include only the data.

Very early, prior to May 1996, the subdivision -Databases was regularly assigned as a form subdivision to any computer file other than executable software. In particular, it was often used in conjunction with other form subdivisions, for example -Directories-Databases, to indicate that a work was in electronic form. Since May 1996, the assignment of the subdivision -Databases has been limited according to the provisions of this instruction sheet.

1. The subdivision -Databases. Assign the free-floating form subdivision -Databases under subjects for a database as defined above. Do not assign the subdivision -*Databases* under subjects for computer files that are essentially textual in nature, such as articles, conference proceedings, literary works, form letters. These texts may be keyboarded through a word-processing program, or they may be digitized images of a print or microform format. Assign only the subject(s) appropriate to the textual material.

2. Cataloging from other than internal sources. Catalogers who do not or cannot load the file for cataloging purposes may make the determination that an item is a database based on these factors such as these:

- the item presents itself as a database.
- accompanying information describes the file as containing specific data elements that would lend themselves to discrete coding.
- accompanying information describes the data elements and their coding and structure.

In case of doubt, do not assign the subdivision -*Databases.*

3. Special cases. Do not use the subdivision -Databases for the following types of works:

- Computer files that have the structure of and present themselves as reference-type works, such as directories, bibliographies, catalogs, dictionaries, encyclopedias, indexes, or other similar types. Assign instead the pertinent form headings or form subdivision under subjects. (If one of these computer files is also a database, do not further subdivide by -Databases and do not assign another subject for the database.)
- Collections of non-textual data that are not specifically formatted and encoded for the purposes of manipulation of the data. Assign only the headings appropriate to contents of the files; do not assign the subdivision -Databases.

4. Works with computer files as accompanying materials. When a work being cataloged is accompanied by a computer file that constitutes at least 20% of the overall work and when the contents of the computer file are judged to be significant, assign the appropriate topical headings for the computer file.

5. Works about databases. To a work about databases in general, assign the appropriate topical headings, for example, Databases, or Relational databases. To a work about databases on a particular subject, assign as a topical subdivision the free-floating subdivision -Databases under the appropriate subject(s). To a work about a particular database, assign the name-title or uniform title for the database being discussed; in addition, assign, if appropriate, the same topical headings that were or would be assigned to an edition of the database itself.

Cataloging PDFs

LCRI 1.11A (for cataloging reproductions) states:

1. Transcribe the bibliographic data appropriate to the original work being reproduced in the following areas:
   - Title and statement of responsibility
   - Edition
   - Material (or type of publication) specific details
   - Publication, distribution, etc.
   - Physical description
   - Series
2. Give in a **single 533 note** all other details relating to the reproduction:
   - Format of the reproduction
   - Date of publication
   - Place and name of the agency responsible for the reproduction

- Date of the reproduction
- Physical description of the reproduction if different from the original
- Series statement of the reproduction (if applicable)
- Notes relating to the reproduction (if applicable)

For many PDF documents, cataloging copy is available. If copy is not available and library is able to determine that the PDF document exists also in print format, treat as a reproduction. Otherwise, catalog the PDF as a "born-digital" e-resources.

Born-digital PDF

If library cannot determine if the publication being cataloged exists in print, treat it as if it were available only online (i.e., "born digital").

GUIDELINES FOR INDIVIDUAL DATA ELEMENTS

Guidelines are given below to individual data elements to delineate a counterpart/subset/adjunct of an electronic manifestation that is remotely accessed:

1. **506 (Restrictions on Access Note):** It is unlikely there will be restrictions on access relating to the electronic manifestation. Should such occur, however, do not use this field; instead, mention them in the delineation in the 530 field.

2.516 (Type of Computer File or Data Note): Do not use this field.

3.530 (Additional Physical Form Available Note): For remotely accessed manifestations of tangible LC materials, a general reference to the Library of Congress Web site is sufficient, since the specific location is always given in an 856 field. For uniformity of presentation, the terminology is illustrated in the following examples to the extent practicable:

a. 530 ## $a Available also through the Library of Congress Web site under title: America's first look into the camera: daguerreotype portraits and views.

b. 530 ## $a Available also through the Library of Congress Web site under title: Color photographs from the FSA and OWI, ca. 1938-1944.

4. 538 (System Details Note): It is suggested to do not use this field. Ordinarily, it is not necessary to state explicitly that a browser or other client software is required to access Internet resources, since the protocols necessary should be obvious from the 856 field (e.g., mode of access is http). However, if a browser alone does not obtain access, state that additional requirement in the 530 delineation. Use judgment in stating any additional requirement, given the fact that the pace of technological change may rapidly make available tomorrow what is not available today. Requirements that are unlikely to be widely available are resources aimed at specialized communities in which the content is only available in a discipline-specific or industry-specific format (e.g., documents available in Postscript).

5. 555 (Cumulative Index/Finding Aids Note): For an electronic manifestation, the phrase "finding aid available in electronic form" is used. If a finding aid in electronic form is involved and it is the kind that incorporates actual material from the collection such that the finding aid itself becomes a remotely accessed electronic manifestation of the collection or a subset of it, describe this special condition in the delineation.

6. 710 (Added Entry - Corporate Name): If the resource being delineated is an LC collection or part of an LC collection to which access is desirable, provide the access through an added entry unless it would be the same as that of the 245 title in the collection-level record in which the delineation is being recorded.

7. 740 (Added Entry - Uncontrolled Related/ Analytical Title: When the electronic manifestation bears a title different from that of the tangible resource, provide uncontrolled title access through the title that differs. Do this by means of a 740 field with indicator values set to 0b/ . This is an exception to the general LC policy of providing title access through a controlled form (730).

a. 740 0# $a Documents from the Continental Congress and the Constitutional Convention 1774-1789. 740 0# $a Continental Congress and Constitutional Convention Collections.

8. 856 (Electronic Location and Access): For remotely accessed manifestations of tangible LC materials, this field must always be present. Use it to indicate the location of the electronic manifestation. The conventions applicable to this field are in a state of flux and will continue to change for some time to come.

9. 985 (Record History): The 985 field is available to identify the records in MUMS related to a particular project. Its use is optional except for American Memory projects. Do all notation in lowercase to facilitate input/update. If multiple unit/collection designations are involved, record each in a repeated 985 field.

10. 006 (Fixed-Length Data Elements - Additional Material Characteristics): It is suggested to do not use the 006 for computer file.

11. 007 (Physical Description Fixed Field): There is a need to provide access to the subset of records in the catalog that represents an electronic resource by means of a single data element. Therefore, when a remotely accessed electronic resource is delineated, include an 007 field in the record. Use value "c" (Computer file) in character position 0 and value "r" (Remote) in character position 1. Use a fill character (|) in the remaining character positions (2-5):

a. 007 ## $a cr | | | |

If more than one remotely accessed electronic resource is delineated, it is only necessary to provide a single 007 field. In the unlikely event that a single record in which delineation is used represents both directly and remotely accessed electronic resources, include a single 007 field for each different accessing mode:

b. 007 ## $a cr | | | | 007 ## $a co | | | |

OCLC-MARC CODING GUIDELINES FOR CATALOGUING E-RESOURCES

According to AACR2, 2005 Update, an electronic resource is: "Material (data and/or program(s)) encoded for manipulation by a computerized device. This material may require the use of a peripheral directly connected to a computerized device (e.g., CD-ROM drive) or a connection to a computer network (e.g., the Internet)." This definition does **not** include electronic resources that do not **require** the use of a computer, for example, music compact discs and videodiscs.

"Type of Record" Coding (Fixed Field "Type")

The definition of Leader/06 ("Type of Record") code "m" (Computer file) was revised and greatly narrowed, way back in June 1997 (LC Update No. 3 to *USMARC Format for Bibliographic Data*) to allow for the coding of electronic resources for the significant aspect of the content, rather than their physical form. Code "m" is now used only for the following general classes of electronic resources:

- Computer software (including programs, games, fonts)
- Numeric data
- Computer-oriented multimedia
- Online systems or services

Field 006

In records for electronic resources where the Type Code is not "m," OCLC mandates including the field 006 for the electronic aspects so that the "COM" search qualifier will continue to retrieve these materials. Remember to code the "File" value correctly, usually "d" for textual materials.

"Type" and "File" Coding

Keeping with the current definition of Type code "m," OCLC recommends the following choices of "Type" code and CF 006/09 and CF 008/26 "File" ("Type of Computer File") values for the following categories of electronic resources. In its definitions of certain values for the Computer File 008/26 ("File"), *MARC 21 Format for Bibliographic Data* clarifies coding for electronic resources that include search software. The presence of search software does **not** alter the basic intent of the resource and does **not** mean that the resource should be coded as software. If its primary purpose is, for instance, textual or bibliographic, it remains textual or bibliographic and is coded as such.

In the area of online systems and services, consider whether the system itself, for example, a library system providing an interface to several databases, or the content of the several constituent databases, is being cataloged. When cataloging the system itself, use "Type" code "m" and "File" code "j".

(A) Electronic data

(i) Electronic numeric data (If the resource consists of numeric data that can be manipulated, for instance a database of numeric data, use Type: m, File: a. If the resource consists of numeric data in tabular form equivalent to a non-manipulable print document, use Type: a, 006/File: d)

(a) Electronic census data (Type: m, File: a) or (Type: a, 006/File: d)

   (b) Electronic survey data (Type: m, File: a) or (Type: a, 006/File: d)

2. Electronic text data (Type: a, 006/File: d or e)
   (a) Electronic bibliographic database (Type: a, 006/File: e)
   (b) Electronic journal(s) (e.g., journals containing textual information) (Type: a, 006/File: d)
   (c) Electronic newsletter(s) (e.g., newsletters containing textual information) (Type: a, 006/File: d)
   (d) Electronic document(s) (e.g., other textual material) (Type: a, 006/File: d)
3. Electronic image data (Type: g or k, 006/File: c)
4. Electronic representational data (Type: e, f, g, k, c, or d, 006/File: c)
   (a) Electronic map(s) data (Type: e or f, 006/File: c)
   (b) Electronic music data (e.g., musical notation or scanned images of a musical score) (Type: c or d, 006/File: c)
5. Electronic sound data (e.g., MIDI files) (Type: i or j, 006/File: h)
6. Electronic font data (Type: m, File: f)

(B) Electronic program(s) (Type: m)

1. Electronic utility program(s) (Type: m, File: b)
2. Electronic application program(s) (Type: m)
   (a) Electronic CAD program(s) (Type: m, File: b)
   (b) Electronic database program(s) (Type: m, File: b)
   (c) Electronic spreadsheet program(s) (Type: m, File: b)
   (d) Electronic word processor program(s) (Type: m, File: b)

   (e) Electronic desktop publishing program(s) (Type: m, File: b)
   (f) Electronic game(s) (Type: m, File: g)
3. Electronic system program(s) (Type: m, File: b)
   (a) Electronic operating system program(s) (Type: m, File: b)
   (b) Electronic programming language(s) (Type: m, File: b)
   (c) Electronic retrieval program(s) (Type: m, File: b)

(C) Electronic data and program(s)

1. Electronic data and program(s) (e.g., several types of data and the software to process the data – unable to determine predominance; Web sites with significant audio and video) (Type: m, File: m)
2. Electronic interactive multimedia (Type: m, File: i)
3. Electronic online service(s) (e.g., bulletin boards, discussion groups/lists, collections of online databases) (Type: m, File: j)

"Form of Item" Coding

As part of the MARC 21 format changes implemented by OCLC in April 2000, a new code "s" was validated for the "Form of Item" fixed field, 008/23 and 006/06 in the Books, Serials, Mixed Materials, and Scores formats, and 008/29 and 006/12 in the Maps and Visual Materials formats. The code "s" was also implemented in the "Form of Item" fixed field, 008/23 and 006/06 for the Sound Recordings format. When cataloging an electronic resource that includes a significant aspect in any of these bibliographic formats according to current definitions, use "Form of Item" code "s" in the fixed field "Form" and/or in the "Form element of any 006 fields for that aspect, as appropriate.

Field 007

According to LC's Draft Interim Guidelines for Cataloging Electronic Resources, the computer file 007 is mandatory in any record representing an item whose carrier is a computer file.

Field 856

Cataloguer should be careful about the correct coding of the field 856 second indicator.

- "blank" is used when no information is provided about the relationship of the electronic resource to the bibliographic item described in the record. For instance, use "blank" when the subfield $u contains a URI that is no longer accessible but there is another 856 with a currently accessible URI. Display constant: None.
- "0" is used when the electronic location in the field is for the same electronic resource described by the record as a whole. Display constant "Electronic resource:" may be generated.
- "1" is used when the electronic location in the field is for an electronic version of the resource described by the record; an electronic version when the record is for a non-electronic version. The Library of Congress uses code "1" in conjunction with subfield $3 to indicate the electronic location of tables of contents. Display constant "Electronic version:" may be generated.
- "2" is used when the electronic location in the field is for an electronic resource that is related to the bibliographic item described by the record. In this case, the item represented by the bibliographic record is not the electronic resource itself. Use subfield $3 to further characterize the relationship between the electronic item identified in field 856 and the item represented by the bibliographic record as a whole.

- The display constant *Related electronic resource:* may be provided. Limit this use to electronic resources that have a specific bibliographic relationship to the resource described in the body of the record. This would include links to such resources as a finding aid for an archival collection or the Web site of a musical group on a bibliographic record for a sound recording. This would **not**, however, include Web sites that have merely a general subject relationship to the resource.

Because of OCLC's indexing needs and its electronic address checking software, however, it is suggested to leave URIs in field 856 subfield $u and adding an appropriate subfield $z note under the following circumstances:

- URI no longer works at all, does not redirect to a more current URI. 856 4 $u [Dead URI] $z This electronic address not available when searched on [Date]
- URI redirects (either automatically or with a forwarding link) to a new URI. 856 4 $u [Redirected URI] $z This former electronic address redirects to current address when searched on [Date]

In both of these cases, change the 856 Second Indicator to blank.

In cases where multiple URIs may be appropriate, they are recorded as following:

- Record a PURL and its corresponding original URL (both of which resolve to the same resource) in separate subfields $u in the same 856 field.
- For most other instances of multiple URIs, record them in separate 856 fields.

When the following characters appear in URIs, cataloger may now use the proper character or substitute the appropriate hex value. It is significant to not confuse these spacing characters with their long-valid non-spacing counterparts.

Character	*Hex Value*	*Note*
Spacing underscore	%5F	Because the spacing Underscore may cause problems with MARC output users may prefer to continue entering it with the hex value %5F.
Spacing tilde	%7E	
Spacing grave	%60	
Spacing circumflex	%5E	
Vertical bar or pipe	%7C	Continue to use the hex value for this character.

General Material Designation

The General Material Designation (GMD) "[electronic resource]" will now be used for items that are coded as Type "m." The GMD "[electronic resource]" is used for all records that would include the computer file 006 according to the OCLC guidelines, regardless of the Type Code.

URIs and LCRIs 9.7B and 21.3B for Remote Access Electronic Resources

Two Library of Congress Rule Interpretations, 9.7B and 21.3B, offer some guidance about how to deal with remote access electronic integrating resources and the disposition of the resource's Uniform Resource Identifier (URI). When the original URI is no longer accessible, but the resource (or a new iteration thereof) is now accessible at another URI, cataloger may edit the existing record to reflect this. When the original URI is still active but now represents an entirely different resource, rather than a new iteration of the original resource, he may create a new record for the new electronic resource. In cases where the cataloger is unable to edit, or prefer not to edit the existing record, he is encouraged to report the necessary changes to OCLC.

Separate Records Versus Single Record

Creating separate records for an item is preferable when both remote access electronic versions and tangible or direct access (including, but not limited to, print and other nonelectronic) versions exist. Cataloger may, however, find a single record approach is better for the local environment. OCLC recommends verifying the impact of these options with the local system vendor and other partners prior to implementation. Use of the term "nonelectronic" in the options that follow is meant as shorthand for any tangible resource (including print, videocassette, videodisc, CD-ROM, etc.) and is **not** meant to exclude, for instance, tangible resources that may have electronic aspects. In that light, elements of the recommendations may need to be adjusted to accommodate such aspects, for example, inclusion of fields 006 and/or 007.

Option 1: Separate records

Nonelectronic item

1. Select the workform based on the current definition of "Type" and the primary aspect of the item.
2. Do not input fields 006 and 007 and do not code "Form of Item" (008/23, 008/29, 006/06, or 006/12, depending on bibliographic format) for the electronic version.
3. Note the availability of the electronic version in field 530.

   Example: Available also on the Internet.
4. Add a 700-730 added entry field for the electronic version when the main entry differs.
5. Optionally, link to the electronic record with field 776.
6. Optionally, provide the location of any remotely accessible version(s) in field(s) 856. Use second indicator "1" when the address is for a version of the

resource other than the one described in the body of the entry, or "2" when the address is for an otherwise related resource.

Electronic item

1. Select the workform based on the current definition of "Type" and the primary aspect of the item.
2. Include field 006 for computer file, if Type is not "m."
3. Include field 007 for computer file.
4. Code "Form of Item" (008/23, 008/29, 006/06, or 006/12, as appropriate, depending on bibliographic format) for "electronic" (code "s").
5. Note the availability of the non-electronic version in field 530.

   Example: Also available in printed form.
6. Add a 700-730 added entry field when main entry for the non-electronic version differs.
7. Optionally, link to the non-electronic version using field 776.
8. Provide the location of any remotely accessible version(s) in field(s) 856. Use second indicator "0" when the address is for the resource itself, "1" when the address is for a version of the resource other than the one described in the body of the entry, or "2" when the address is for an otherwise related resource.

Option 2: Single record with a reference to the electronic item

Cataloger may create a record for the non-electronic version and add an annotation about the existence of and access to the electronic version. The non-electronic version is the primary version and the electronic copy is secondary.

1. Select the workform based on the current definition of "Type" and the primary aspect of the item.

2. Do not input field 006 for the electronic version.
3. Do not code "Form of Item"(008/23, 008/29, 006/06, or 006/12, depending on bibliographic format) for the electronic version.
4. Optionally, include field 007.
5. Note the availability of the electronic version in field 530.
6. Add a 740 added entry when the title for the electronic version differs.
7. Provide the location of any remotely accessible version in field 856. Use second indicator "1" when the address is for a version of the resource other than the one described in the body of the entry or "2" when the address is for an otherwise related resource.

Additional Separate Versus Single Record Considerations

If cataloger is cataloging an electronic item, he need not verify the physical existence of the non-electronic version or whether it has been cataloged. Similarly, when he catalogs a non-electronic item, he need not verify whether an electronic version exists. In both cases, he need not apply these guidelines, and cataloger may catalog the item as if no other version exists. Apply the input convention in this document if he has verification that electronic and non-electronic versions exist, and he wants to record the existence of both.

In all cases, cataloger may add references to electronic resources that are related to the item described in the body of the record when those references are thought to add value.

The CONSER Cataloging Manual: Module 31—Remote Access Electronic Serials (Online Serials) permits a single record for a non-electronic item to include information for the electronic version. OCLC's guidelines are currently compatible with CONSER's.

MARC21 coding in the single-record and separate record approaches compared for Single-record approach

In the *record for the original*:

- Code **008/22** ("form of original item") and **008/23** ("form of item") as correct for the original, not for the online version
- Note the availability of the online version in field **530**
- Add a **740** (2nd indicator blank) title added entry or 7XX author/title added entry when the title of the online version differs
- Provide the location of the online version in field **856**
- If a separate ISSN has been assigned to the online serial but a separate record doesn't exist, add field **776** with subfields $t and $x (and/or subfields $a and $s if appropriate)
- Optionally, an electronic resource **007** field may be added for the online version

Do not add an electronic resource **006** field for the online version. |

MARC21 coding in the single-record and separate record approaches compared for Separate record approach

In the *record for the original*:

- Note the availability of the online version in field **530**;
- Add a **730** title added entry or 7XX author/title added entry when the title of the online version differs
- Link to the online record with field **776**, and;
- Provide the location of the online version in field **856** (if not already present in the record).

In the *record for the online version*,

- Describe the digital version using all appropriate fields;
- Add a **730** title added entry or 7XX author/title added entry when the title of the original differs

- Link to the original version's record using field **776**, and;
- Give appropriate **856** fields

B. Separate records: the aggregator neutral record

The practices for the aggregator-neutral record were intended, as much as possible, to be applicable to all online serials, whether or not they are represented in e-serial packages, and whether or not they have a print counterpart. Certain elements may not be appropriate for some e-serials; for example, notes which refer to a print version would not be applicable to a serial which does not have a print counterpart.

The aggregator-neutral record does not contain information specific to any one particular provider, with the exception of citing the package and format upon which the record was based. Provider names are not added to uniform titles as qualifiers, given as name headings or mentioned in issuing body notes.

The aggregator-neutral record was developed after surveying CONSER and non-CONSER librarians on the need for an OPAC record representing the online version of a print title. Librarians told of problems with selecting and editing records from the national database to customize for local OPACs. They needed a simpler record, adaptable to local access methods through use of record sets, serials management systems, and databases that provide full text or citations to serial content.

Multiple document formats and access methods

Electronic serials may be issued in different "file" or "document" formats in order to meet the needs of users. Many online serials provide an HTML version to enhance online viewing and a PDF format to provide high quality printouts of articles. Graphic, sound, and video files may also be included as a part of an e-serial. A serial may be available in one, all, or a combination of these formats, and over time, the available formats may change. According to CONSER policy, do not create separate records for a serial offered in different file formats. CONSER policy is to create one record and make notes on file format; for common formats (HTML, XML, PDF) omit format information from the bibliographic description.

A. CONSER single record option (non-cataloging approach: giving access through the print/original record)

CONSER members may choose not to catalog online versions separately, but instead note the existence and electronic location of the online version(s) in the record for the printed serial (or, lacking that, in the record for another format, e.g., a CD-ROM serial). The following rules of thumb give advice on when the single-record approach is a viable choice, but do not prohibit application of the single-record approach in any case. The decision must be made by individual libraries, since it is not possible to require a library to catalog a particular online version and it is independently valid to note facts about an online version in the record for different versions. The principles behind the rules of thumb are: If the bibliographic record for the original version (print, CD-ROM, etc.) provides sufficient access for the online version, no matter what the differences are between the two, the single-record approach is a good alternative. If the desired access points for the online and the original version differ, separate records may be more useful. Separate records are always a permissible option.

- The single-record approach is considered most valid when the online version contains sufficient full-text to be a satisfactory substitute and has no significant additional content. That is, the single-record approach works best when the original and online versions can be considered equivalent manifestations.

- The single-record approach is also commonly applied when the online version lacks full-text or has only selected full-text from the original, and is therefore not considered to be an adequate substitute. The online site may not be considered worth cataloging separately in many such cases, so its existence and electronic location are noted on the record for the original, with appropriate indication of its relationship to the original version.
- Separate records are preferred when the online version has significant additional content not present in the original. The choice of a separate-record approach in such cases means that the versions are not considered equivalent and the difference of the online version from the original is significant to users.

Separate Records or Single Records? A mixed approach

As libraries catalog remote access journals (and other resources), library staff are confronted with what is often stated as an either/or choice: add the remote access electronic journal to the record for the print version of the same title or create a separate record. Each approach has its inherent advantages and disadvantages. The disadvantages of each approach make each approach unsatisfactory for readers and staff. The advantages of each approach make each approach desirable for readers and staff. Tradeoffs are inescapable. A somewhat oversimplified view of the tradeoff is one between simple records (i.e. separate records) with complex indexes (i.e. for multiple records differentiated by format) versus complex records (i.e. single records) with simple indexes (i.e. one index entry leads to multiple instances of the item in various formats).

For example, it was Yale Library policy to create a separate bibliographic record in Orbis for a remote access electronic journal and share these records with other libraries through the bibliographic utilities—OCLC and RLIN. They created a separate record whether or not the electronic journal has a print equivalent. Exception is made in two distinct cases.

Cataloging for Remote Access Electronic Serials

Cataloging remote access electronic journals is both an extension of traditional practice and an exploration of a new, rapidly changing environment for publishers, authors, readers, and librarians. Given the rate of change in the publishing environment and the media format for remote access electronic journals, the polices and practices are also likely to change. Remote access electronic serials are those serials available via the Internet and other networks. A remote access electronic serial is a continuing resource that is accessed "via computer networks." It is issued in a succession of discrete parts usually bearing numbering, and has no predetermined conclusion *(AACR2)*. This is in contrast to a direct access electronic resource which is issued on a physical carrier such as CD-ROM, floppy disk or diskette. The terms "electronic serial," "e-serial," "online serial," and "remote access serial" are used interchangeably for serials issued on the World Wide Web, via email, ftp, etc.

Though many online serials are "born-digital," created and existing only in a digital format, the majority of electronic serials cataloged by CONSER libraries are online versions of print publications available on the World Wide Web. Online versions are made available by many providers, including publishers, aggregators, distributors, vendors, secondary publishers, and libraries involved in digitization projects.

Cataloging online serials with AACR2 and MARC 21

Institutions use several methods to provide access to electronic serials; one method is to create *AACR2/MARC 21* records for online serials in the OPAC. Other methods include

A-Z listings of electronic resources and links to article and citation databases through link resolvers. New products and tools are evolving and institutions often use a combination of these, including OPAC records, to provide access to digitized content. Providing records for online versions of a resource in the OPAC is a way to allow users to find all related formats of the resource (e.g. print, CD-ROM, and online) in one place. OPAC users can find related records for a resource that has changed from print to online when both are cataloged. Searching for resources in the OPAC is enhanced with controlled name, series, and subject headings provided by catalogers. Links between OPAC records, serials management systems, citation databases and linking services enhance browsing of contents and delivery of journal articles. Since commercially packaged resources require subscription fees, it's appropriate to create bibliographic records associated with holdings and library acquisition records in order to track expenditures.

- Determine if the resource is a serial, integrating resource, or monograph.
- Decide whether the single record approach or a separate catalog record approach will be used.
- If a separate record is used, determine and record the basic bibliographic information in order to accurately identify and describe the serial.
- Determine the access points needed for retrieval of the catalog record.
- Determine and record the means by which the serial itself can be accessed online.

Integrating Resource or Monograph Versus Serial

The decision to code an electronic resource as a monograph or as a serial is a decision made separately from the Type Code decision. Note that for electronic serials where Type is not "a" or "m", two 006 fields will be necessary, one for the electronic aspects and one for the serial aspects. Apply the current AACR2 definitions of monograph and serial to electronic resources. Treat as serials (Bibliographic Level: s (or b)) only those continuing resources issued in a succession of discrete parts with no predetermined conclusion. The parts may constitute an issue, or in some cases, an individual article.

Applying the current AACR2R definitions may result in different manifestations receiving different cataloging treatment. A manifestation in print form, such as an annual directory, is cataloged as a serial whereas it is cataloged as an integrating resource when the directory takes on the form of an electronic file that is continuously updated. LC and CONSER adhere to current definitions, and OCLC recommends its users do the same. Remotely accessed electronic resources of a dynamic nature that are currently excluded from serial treatment are:

- Databases (including directories, A&I services, etc.)
- Electronic discussion groups (e.g., SERIALST)
- Electronic discussion group digests (e.g., AUTOCAT digest)
- Gopher servers (e.g., LC-MARVEL)
- Online public access catalogs (e.g., OCLC, RLIN)
- Online services (e.g., America Online)
- Web sites (e.g., the CONSER home page)

These electronic resources should be cataloged as integrating resources or monographs, as appropriate.

MARC 21 format and fixed field coding

Almost all electronic serials are textual in nature; therefore code "a" for "language material" in the leader/06 type of record code is used for most online e-serials. A continuing resource 008 field is used to code serial characteristics and an electronic resource 006 field is added to code electronic fixed field elements. The definition of type of record code "m" was changed in the late 1990s and some records coded "m" under the old definition may still exist on the utilities. CONSER catalogers convert them to type of record code "a" if appropriate. Additionally, serial format records for textual electronic serials are identified and distinguished by a code indicating that the item cataloged is in electronic form. Code "s" for "electronic" in the serial 008 was implemented in spring 2000 for "form of item" (008/23) and "form of original item" (008/22). It is used in the same way that codes for microfilm and microfiche are currently used in those 008 bytes.

ISSN for online serials

Recording the ISSN displayed on the serial is useful for searching and record matching on local systems, citation indexes, and full text databases. The centers of the ISSN Network currently assign separate ISSN to paper and online versions of a serial; however, not all online versions have been assigned a separate ISSN by the appropriate center. If separate ISSN have been assigned, sometimes ISSN for both the print and online versions are displayed on issues of the serial or in related pages on the serial's Web site. When print and online format ISSN are given (sometimes clearly labeled "print" and "E- ISSN"), record the ISSN for online version in $a of the 022 and record the ISSN for the print in $y of the 022. If the publisher appears to be printing the ISSN of the print instead of a separate ISSN for the online format, record the ISSN of the print in $y of the 022. If unsure which format the ISSN is for, record it in $y. If the serial does not print an ISSN but one format's ISSN, or both are known, they may be placed in the appropriate subfields of the 022.

LINKING RECORDS

General

Linking entry fields may provide additional access by means of indexing (currently, some, but not all, are indexed in LC). They also have the potential of supporting instantaneous navigating among records although that capability is not now available at LC. For linking among records, use the linking entry fields for the following reasons:

1. this technique is specifically designed for linking records, not for collocating *per se*;
2. when divorced from collocating, this technique supports flexibility because it frees the special format divisions from needing to ensure that main entry access in the bibliographic record for a collection be the same as the character string used for access purposes; for example:

   710 2# $a Continental Congress Broadside Collection (Library of Congress)

   773 0# $a United States. $b Continental Congress. $t Continental Congress broadsides $w (DLC) 90-898267
3. this technique facilitates the management of records for hierarchical groupings, especially in large collections.

Policy for Linking Records

As indicated previously, the focus on linking records is more a matter of managing records, providing additional access, and supporting navigation than it is a matter related to the cataloging of electronic resources *per se*. However, in the course of dealing with issues related to electronic resources, issues relating to linking have arisen that needed to be addressed. The overall policy for linking among records is as follows:

1. for general cataloging related to monographs and monographic component parts, do not link records except:
   a) for so-called "In analytics" in which the retrieval of the component part is dependent upon the physical identification and location of the host item or container (field 773);
   b) for a reproduction microform (link to the record for the original (field776));
2. for cataloging related to materials in special format divisions, the decision to link is at the discretion of the division or cataloging unit;

Guidelines for Linking Entry Fields

Use the following guidelines:

1) for monographs and monographic component parts, only use a linking entryfield when there is another record to which a record can be linked;
2) use field 773 (Host Item Entry) to express a vertical link; for example, in the record for a constituent unit, use field 773 to link to the record for the collection as a whole; in general, do not link from a larger bibliographic unit to a constituent unit (field 774);
3) use field 776 (Additional Physical Form Entry) to express a horizontal link; for example, between a record that represents a non-electronic tangible resource and its counterpart electronic manifestation).
4) always give in subfield $w the LCCN of the record being linked to;
5) use in the linking entry ,the bibliographic data constituting the main entry access of the record being linked to; use subfields $a and $t for a main entry(1XX)/title (240/245) combination; use subfield $t for entry under title (245).

CATALOGING REMOTE ELECTRONIC RESOURCES (MONOGRAPHIC & INTEGRATING) IN UNICORN

Tools

- Revised Chapter 9 of AACR2: Electronic Resources
- Revised Chapter 12 of AACR2: Continuing Resources
- Cataloguing Internet Resources : OCLC-MARC Coding Guidelines
- MARC21 manuals
- Integrating resources: a cataloging manual / prepared for the Program for cooperative Cataloging: http://www.loc.gov/catdir/pcc/bibco/irman.pdf
- CONSER Cataloging manual, Module 31, Spring 2004

Procedures

Before beginning to catalogue any Web resource, always verify that the URL is valid and active. This may be done by calling up the in-process record using either a title browse or keyword search and clicking on the 856; or, by copying and pasting the URL into the address box. The copy for Web resources varies a great deal, so always be sure to check it thoroughly and carefully. Be sure to look at the subject headings, not only to be sure that they are valid forms, but also that they are appropriate to the resource.

Determine the type of resource catalogers are cataloguing

Web resources may be integrating resources, monographs or serials.

Monographs

Are complete (even if part of something else) and static; that is, not intended to be updated or changed. Include digitized documents or texts,often reproductions of books essays, reports, etc. May be web sites that are complete and not intended to be updated, such as some online exhibitions. Look for indications of updating. Most pdf files are monographic, but monographs may be in either pdf or html format, or both. As a rule, treat pdf files as monographs. Monographs are catalogued on the MARC format workform.

Fixed Field (MARC 008) Values Monographs:

Record Format	=	MARC	
Rec_Typ	=	a	Item is primarily textual
Bib_Lvl	=	m	Monograph
Dat_tp	=	s	Single date of publication
Or		r	Reissue
Repr	=	s	Electronic Resource

MARC 006 Values:

TypeCode	=	m
FileType	=	d

REFERENCES AND NOTES

1. Calhoun, Karen. 2000. Redesign of traditional library workflows: Experimental models for electronic resource description. Invited paper for the Bicentennial Conference on Bibliographic Control for the New Millennium, Nov. 15-17, 2000. Accessed Nov. 28, 2001; *http://lcweb.loc.gov/catdir/bibcontrol/calhoun.html*
2. Calhoun, Karen, and Bill Kara. 2000. Aggregation or aggravation? Optimizing access to full text journals. *ALCTS Newsletter Online* 11, no. 4. Accessed Nov. 28, 2001; *http://www.ala.org/alcts/alcts_news/v11n1/gateway_pap15.xml*.
3. Campbell, D. Grant. 2000. Straining the standards: How cataloging Web sites for curriculum support poses fresh problems for the Anglo American Cataloging Rules. *Journal of Internet Cataloging* 3, no. 1:79-92.
4. *Journal of Internet Cataloging*. Published quarterly by Haworth Information Press.
5. Letarte, Karen. 2000. The school library media center in the digital age: Issues in the cataloging of electronic resources. *Journal of Internet Cataloging* 3, no. 1:13-40.

6. Li, Yiu-on, and Shirley W. Leung. 2001. Computer cataloging of electronic journals in unstable aggregator databases. *Library Resources & Technical Services* 45, no. 4: 198-211.

7. Ling-yuh, Pattie, and Bonnie Jean Cox. 1996. Electronic resources: Selection and bibliographic control. New York: Haworth Press, Inc.

8. Okerson, Ann. 2000. Are we there yet? Online e-resources ten years after. *Library Trends* 48, no. 4: 671-693.

9. Ward, David, and Diane VanderPol. 2000. Librarian, catalog thy work! Getting started integrating Internet resources into OPACs. *Journal of Internet Cataloging* 3, no. 4: 51-61.

10. Whiting, Peter C. 1999. The real world of integrating electronic resources into a Web OPAC at the University of New Mexico; workshop at the 1998 NASIG Conference. *The Serials Librarian* 36, no. 3-4:455-460.

11. http://www.und.nodak.edu/dept/library/Departments/abc/techhome.htm

12. *http://www.loc.gov/aba/cataloging/tools/*

13. *http://www.loc.gov/aba/*

14. *http://www.loc.gov/catdir/cpso/dcmb19.pdf*

15. *AACR2 2002 revisions impact on integrating remote access electronic resources http://www.loc.gov/catdir/pcc/ir/AACR2rev_dr02.ppt*

16. *AACR2 2002 revisions impact on loose-leafs http://www.loc.gov/catdir/pcc/ir/updatingll_02.ppt*

17. Ahronheim, Judy. *Judy and Magda's List of Metadata Initiatives http://www-personal.umich.edu/~jaheim/alcts/bibacces.htm*

18. ALCTS *http://www.lib.virginia.edu/alcts/ http://www.lib.virginia.edu/alcts/*

19. ALCTS. CC:DA. Task Force on the Harmonization of ISBD(ER) and AACR2. *Final Report (penultimate draft) : executive summary. 1999 http://www.library.yale.edu/cataloging/aacrer/tf-harm21.htm*

20. ALCTS. CC:DA. Task Force on Metadata and the Cataloging Rules. *Final Report*. 1999. *http://www.ala.org/alcts/*

organization/ccs/ccda/tf-tei2.html

21. ALCTS. CC:DA. Task Force on the Review of the IFLA Guidelines for OPAC displays. *Final Report.* 1999. *http://www.ala.org/alcts/organization/ccs/ccda/tf-opac2.html*
22. ALCTS. CC:DA. Task Force on Metadata. *Summary report, June 1999 http://www.ala.org/alcts/organization/ccs/ccda/tf-meta3.html*
23. ALCTS. CC:DA. Task Force on Rule 0.24. *Report to CC:DA, 1999 Annual. http://www.ala.org/alcts/organization/ccs/ccda/tf-024g.html*
24. Alves, Susana. *World Wide Web Site Evaluation for Information Professionals http://www.bf.rmit.edu.au/Dimals/rguides/website.htm*
25. American Association of Law Libraries, etc. *Principles for Licensing Electronic Resources http://www.arl.org/scomm/licensing/principles.html*
26. Anderson, Craig. *Cataloguing of Internet Resources http://www.yprl.vic.gov.au/yprl/catintres.html*
27. Arms, William Yeo. *Implementing Policies for Access Management http://www.dlib.org/dlib/february98/arms/02arms.html*
28. Association of Research Libraries and ARL Office of Leadership and Management Services, and Online Computer Library Center (OCLC). 1999 ARL/OCLC Strategic Issues Forum. *The Keystone Principles http://www.arl.org/training/keystone.html* ,
29. Auer, Nicole. *Bibliography on Evaluating Internet Resources*
30. Bailey, Charles W. *Scholarly Electronic Publishing Bibliography http://epress.lib.uh.edu/sepb/sepb.html*
31. Bailey, Charles W. *e Open Access Bibliography: Liberating Scholarly Literature with E-Prints and Open Access Journals* http://www.arl.org/pubscat/pubs/openaccess/ *http://info.lib.uh.edu/cwb/oab.pdf*
32. Calhoun, Karen. *Cataloging Procedures for Networked Electronic Resources.*
33. Calhoun, Karen and Bill Kara. *Aggregation or aggravation?*

Optimizing access to full-text journals http://ala8.ala.org/alcts/alcts_news/gateway_pap15.html

34. *Cataloging Remote Access Electronic Materials at Yale* http://www.library.yale.edu/cataloging/netinfo/

35. Chu, Heting. *Electronic Journals : Promises and Challenges for Academic Libraries*. 1999. http://phoenix.liu.edu/~hchu/ejournal.htm

36. *CIC-ARTFL Cataloging Project Manual* http://www.lib.uchicago.edu/Annex/TechSvcs/Cataloging/ARTFL/manual.html

37. CONSER *Cataloging Manual Module 31, Remote Access Computer Files Serials* http://lcweb.loc.gov/acq/conser/module31.html

38. CONSER *Cataloging Manual Module 33.18, Electronic Newspapers* http://lcweb.loc.gov/acq/conser/enewsppr.html

39. CONSER *Serials Cataloging Issues* http://www.loc.gov/acq/conser/issues.html

40. CONSER *Use of fixed fields 006/007/008 and Leader Codes in CONSER Records* http://lcweb.loc.gov/acq/conser/ffuse.html

41. CONSER Working Group. *Single vs. separate reocrds : draft report*. 1999 http://www.library.ucla.edu/libraries/cataloging/sercat/conserwg/conserwg.draft.htm

42. Council on Library and Information Resources. Select: Publications and resources; select: Reports. http://www.clir.org/pubs/reports/reports.html

43. *COUNTER* http://www.projectcounter.org/

44. In order to measure the úse of online resources in a more consistent way, COUNTER is an agreed to international Code of Practice governing the recording and exchange of online usage data.

45. *Criteria for cataloging selected remote access electronic resources* http://www.library.yale.edu/cataloging/netinfo/ecatselect.html

46. Davis, Renette. *Access Level Records for Internet Resources*

http://www.lib.uchicago.edu/staffweb/depts/cat/serials/access.html

47. Day, Elaine. *Managing Electronic Collections http://library.jmu.edu/libliaison/dayel/e-collect.htm*
48. Duke University Libraries. Cataloging Web Sites Task Force. *Report. http://staff.lib.duke.edu/catweb.htm*
49. Duranceau, Ellen Finnie. *Beyond Print: Revisioning Serials Acquisitions for the Digital Age http://web.mit.edu/waynej/www/duranceau.htm*
50. Dworaczek, Marian. *Electronic Sources of Information: a bibliography http://library.usask.ca/~dworacze/BIBLIO.HTM*
51. *Subject Index to Literature on Electronic Sources of Information http://library.usask.ca/~dworacze/SUBJIN_A.HTM*
52. Fattahi, Rahmatollah. *AACR2 and Catalogue Production Technology.* 1997 (JSC paper)
53. GPO *Cataloging guidelines : computer files no. 1A http://www.access.gpo.gov/su_docs/dpos/cgcomp01.html*
54. Grassian, Esther. *Thinking critically about World Wide Web resources http://www.library.ucla.edu/libraries/college/help/critical/index.htm*
55. Harken, Shelby E. *Cataloging Web Sites http://www.und.nodak.edu/dept/library/Departments/abc/webcat.htm*
56. Hawkins, Les. *Serials Published on the World Wide Web : Cataloging Problems and Decisions http://web.mit.edu/waynej/www/hawkins.htm*
57. Hawkins, Les and Hirons, Jean (2002). *Transforming AACR2: Using the revised rules in Chapters 9 and 12.* Available Sept. 6, 2002 *http://lcweb.loc.gov/acq/conser/aacr2002/A2slides.html*
58. Hirons, Jean. *AACR and MARBI Actions Relating to Integrating Resources* 2001. *http://www.loc.gov/acq/conser/integratingresources/*
59. Hirons, Jean. *Revising AACR2 to Accommodate Seriality :*

report to the Joint Steering Committee for Revision of AACR. 1999. *http://www.nlc-bnc.ca/jsc/ser-rep0.html*

60. Hsieh-Yee, Ingrid. *Cataloging & Metadata Resources http://slis.cua.edu/ihy/catmeta.htm*
61. Hunter, Karen. *ScienceDirect http://web/mit.edu/waynej/www/hunter.htm*
62. IFLA. *Digital Libraries: Cataloguing and Indexing of Electronic Resources http://www.ifla.org/II/catalog.htm*
63. IFLA. *Digital libraries: Electronic Journal and Text Archives http://www.ifla.org/II/etext.htm*
64. IFLA. *Digital Libraries: Metadata Resources http://www.ifla.org/II/metadata.htm*
65. IFLA. *Digital Libraries: Resources and Projects http://www.ifla.org/II/diglib.htm*
66. IFLA. *Licensing Principles http://www.ifla.org/V/ebpb/copy.htm*
67. IFLA. *Study on Functional Requirements for Bibliographic Records http://www.ifla.org/VII/s13/frbr/frbr.pdf*
68. International Coalition of Library Consortia (ICOLC). *Statement of Current Perspective and Preferred Practices for the Selection and Purchase of Electronic Information http://www.library.yale.edu/consortia/statement.html*
69. International Conference on Electronic Resources: Definition, Selection, and Cataloguing (2001 : Rome, Italy) *http://w3.uniroma1.it/ssab/er/en/program.htm*
70. *ISBD(ER) : International Standard Bibliographic Description for Electronic Resources.* 1997. *http://www.ifla.org/VII/s13/pubs/isbd.htm*
71. Jones, Wayne *Dublin Core and Serials: How Well do the DC Data Elements Describe E-serials? http://web.mit.edu/waynej/www/dublincore.htm*
72. Klemperer, Katharina, and Stephen Chapman. *Digital Libraries : a Selected Resource Guide http://www.lita.org/ital/1603_klemperer.htm*
73. Lagoze, Carl and Jane Hunter. *ABC ontology and model http://jodi.ecs.soton.ac.uk/Articles/v02/i02/Lagoze/*

74. *LC implementation of AACR2 2002 revisions http://www.loc.gov/catdir/pcc/ir/AACR2rev_ovrbt02.ppt*

75. *LIBLICENSE : licensing digital information : a resource for librarians http://www.library.yale.edu/~llicense/index.shtml*

76. Library of Congress. *Guidelines for the Use of Field 856 http://lcweb.loc.gov/marc/856guide.html*

77. Library of Congress. *MARC Standards http://www.loc.gov/marc/*

78. Library of Congress. *Online Resources for Serials Catalogers http://lcweb.loc.gov/acq/conser/resource.html*

79. Library of Congress. *Selection Criteria for Resources to be Included in the BEOnline Project*

80. Library of Congress. CPSO. *Draft Interim Guidelines for Cataloging Electronic Resources http://lcweb.loc.gov/catdir/cpso/dcmb19_4.html*

81. Library of Congress. CPSO. *Guidelines for Distinguishing Cartographic Materials on Computer File Carriers from other Materials on Computer File Carriers http://lcweb.loc.gov/marc/cfmap.html*

82. Library of Congress. Network Development and MARC Standards Office. *Guidelines for Coding Electronic Resources in Leader/06.* 1999. *http://lcweb.loc.gov/marc/ldr06guide.html*

83. Library of Congress. PCC Standing Committee on Automation (SCA). Task Group on Journals in Aggregator Databases. *Interim Report.* 1999. *http://www.loc.gov/catdir/pcc/aggupdrpt.html*

84. Library of Congress. PCC Task Force on Multiple Manifestations of Electronic Resources. *Final report* 2001. *http://www.loc.gov/catdir/pcc/tgmulerfinal.html*

85. *Licensingmodels.com : model standard licenses for use by publishers, librarians and subscription agents for electronic resources http://www.licensingmodels.com/*

86. *LinkBot information; a URL checker*

87. Machovec, George. *User Authentication and Authorization*

in a Networked Library Environment, Alliance Issues http://www.coalliance.org/reports/security.htm

88. Miller, Steven Jack (2002). *A prototype PCC training resource: a revision of a workshop given at LC on May 2, 2002* Available Sept. 6, 2002 *http://www.loc.gov/catdir/pcc/bibco/irtrng702.html*

89. Milstead, Jessica and Susan Feldman. *Metadata : cataloging by any other name. 1999. http://www.onlineinc.com/onlinemag/metadata/*

90. Myers, Nan. *PURLs: What do I need to know? Working with PURLs in your local catalog : list of resources.* 1999. *http://www.willamette.edu/~aweible/dlc/arlene.htm*

91. *NEWJOUR http://gort.ucsd.edu/newjour/search.html*

92. OCLC. *InterCAT : a catalog of Internet Resources*

93. OCLC. *Internet Cataloging Project http://www.oclc.org/oclc/man/catproj/catcall.htm*

94. Olson, Nancy B. *Cataloging Internet Resources : a Manual and Practical Guide http://www.purl.org/oclc/cataloging-internet*

95. http://www.loc.gov/marc/ldr06guide.html

96. http://library.princeton.edu/departments/tsd/katmandu/electronic/ercatpu.pdf

97. http://www.oclc.org/support/documentation/worldcat/cataloging/electronicresources/

98. *http://infopeople.org/workshop/instructor/61*

99. *http://www.oclc.org/bibformats/default.htm*

100. *http://www.oclc.org/support/documentation/worldcat/tb/246/*

101. *http://www.oclc.org/bibformats/default.htm*

102. *http://www.loc.gov/acq/conser/ffuse.html*

103. *http://www.loc.gov/acq/conser/Module31.pdf*

104. *http://ublib.buffalo.edu/libraries/units/cts/olac/capc/stnir.html*

105. *http://www.loc.gov/marc/856guide.html*

106. *http://lcweb.loc.gov/catdir/cpso/dcmb19_4.html*

107. *http://www.loc.gov/marc/856guide.html*

108. Pamela Cline-Howley, Suzanne Ellison, Charley Pennell, & Gary Tucker. *http://staff.library.mun.ca/staff/toolbox/remote.htm*

109. ALCTS/CCS/SAC/Subcommittee on Metadata and Classification. (1999a). Final report. {Electronic Resource}. Retrieved 09/23/2001 from http:// www.ala.org/alcts/organization/ccs/sac/metaclassfinal.pdf.

110. ALCTS/CCS/SAC/Subcommittee on Metadata and Subject Analysis (1999b). Subject data in the metadata record: Recommendations and rationale. {Electronic Resource}. Retrieved 09/23/2001 from http://www.ala.org/alcts/organization/ccs/sac/metarept2.html.

111. Breeding, M. (2000). Technologies for Sharing Library Resources. Information Today, 17(9):60-61.

112. *Brian E. Brewington , George Cybenko, Keeping Up with the Changing Web, Computer, v.33 n.5, p.52-58, May 2000* [doi>*10.1109/2.841784*]

113. Byrum, J.D. (2001). Challenges of Electronic Resources: State of the Art and Unresolved Issues. International Conference on Electronic Resources: Definition, Selection, and Cataloguing. {Electronic Resource}. Retrieved 09/23/2001 from http://w3.uniromal.it/ssab/er/relazioni/byrum_eng.pdf.

114. Calhoun, K. (2001). Redesign of Library Workflows: Experimental Model for Electronic Resource Description. In Sandberg-Fox, A. M., Proceedings of the Bicentennial Conference on Bibliographic Control for the New Millennium: Confronting the Challenges of Networked Resources and the Web. Washington, D.C.: Library of Congress. {Electronic Resource}. Retrieved 09/23/2001 from http://lcweb.loc.gov/catdir/bibcontrol/ calhoun_paper.html.

115. Chan, L. M. (2001). Exploiting LCSH, LCC, and DDC to retrieve networked resources: Issues and challenges. In Sandberg-Fox, A.M.,Proceedings of the Bicentennial Conference on Bibliographic Control for the New Millennium: Confronting the Challenges of Networked Resources and the

Web. Washington, D.C.: Library of Congress. {Electronic Resource}. Retrieved 09/23/2001 from http://lcweb.loc.gov/catdir/bibcontrol/ chan_paper.html.

116. Chaudhry, A. S., & Periasamy, M. (2001.). A study of current practices of selected libraries in cataloguing electronic journals. Library Review, 50(9):434-443.

117. Cline,N. M. (2000). Virtual continuity: The challenge for research libraries today. EDUCAUSE Review, 35 (5/6):22-28. {Electronic Resource}. Retrieved 09/ 23/2001 from http://www.educause.edu/ir/library/pdf/ERM0032.pdf

118. Cutter, C.A.(1904). Rules for a dictionary catalog. (4th ed.). Washington: U.S. Government Printing Office.

119. Landry, P.(2000). The MACS project: Multilingual access to subjects (LCSH, RAMEAU, SWD). International Cataloguing and Bibliographic Control, 30(3):46-49.

120. München, Saur (1998). Functional Requirements for Bibliographic Records: Final Report: IFLA Study Group on the Functional Requirements for Bibliographic Records. Deutsche Bibliothek: Frankfurtam Main. {Electronic Resource}. Retrieved 09/23/2001 from http://www.ifla.org/VII/s13/ frbr/frbr.pdf

121. Pitschmann, L. A. (2001). Building Sustainable Collections of Free Third-Party Web Resources. Washington, DC:Digital Library Federation. {Electronic Resource}. Retrieved 09/23/2001 from http://www.clir.org/pubs/ reports/pub98/pub98.pdf.

122. Tillett, B. B. (2001). Authority Control on the Web. In Sandberg-Fox, A. M., Proceedings of the Bicentennial Conference on Bibliographic Control for the New Millennium: Confronting the Challenges of Networked Resources and the Web. Washington, D.C. {Electronic Resource}. Retrieved 09/23/2001 from http://lcweb.loc.gov/catdir/bibcontrol/tillett.html.

123. USF Virtual Library Metadata/Cataloging Team (1999). Guidelines for cataloging USF electronic resources. Tampa, FL: University of South Florida Libraries. {Electronic Resource}. Retrieved 09/23/2001 from http://

www.lib.usf.edu/~jmichael/metadata_team.html.

124. Zyroff, E. (1996). Cataloging is a Prime Number. American Libraries, 27(5): 47-50.

125. Joint Steering Committee of the Anglo-American Cataloguing Rules. Available: http : / /www.nlc-bnc.ca/jsc/ .

126 Library of Congress. MARC Standards Office. Available: http://lcweb.loc.gov/ marc/index.html.

127. Program for Cooperative Cataloging. Available: http:// www.loc.gov/catdir/pcc.

9

CrossRef and Resource Identification in Electronic Environment

CrossRef was established in 2000. It is an independent membership association founded and directed by publishers with the aim to give the research community easier access to online publications. CrossRef's objective is to provide the most robust citation-linking network possible—across publishers, business models, and content types. It does not aggregate full-text content. Rather, it uses a system of "distributed aggregation" whereby full-text content is linked through a database consisting of publisher-provided metadata. To ensure that each link is persistent and accurate, CrossRef uses Digital Object Identifiers (DOIs) to permanently identify and track scholarly items on the web. Through CrossRef and DOIs, user can link to million of items from hundreds of publishers and societies. CrossRef integrates with the OpenURL and is completely access-model neutral.

CrossRef operates a technical service on behalf of its member publishers helping them establish URL links between their content and the content of other CrossRef publishers. CrossRef services require member's staff responsible for integrating with CrossRef's offerings to have some understanding of XML and Web technologies and to have a thorough understanding of their own production processes. While participating, following actions are expected:

- Build and operate the necessary systems on their side which compose the XML deposit files and submit them to CrossRef
- Regularly monitor their transactions with CrossRef, identify and correct errors or bring to attention problems arising due to a CrossRef system malfunction.
- Remain vigilant about updating the metadata for their DOIs, particularly the URL of the resource.
- Review the various CrossRef reports issued to members and correct any identified errors.

Publishers join CrossRef by completing and signing the membership agreement. Then they receive a DOI prefix, a user name and password to access the CrossRef system, and the general login to the members' area of the CrossRef web site. Libraries can open a no-fee library account for querying the CrossRef system. The affiliates can join depending upon the nature of the work they will be doing that utilizes CrossRef data or services. The researchers, authors and the public can lookup DOIs using their guest query form or simple text query service and include them when making references to scholarly publications

CrossRef and its DOIs primarily benefit the scholarly community by providing a somewhat invisible service behind the linking of references. While CrossRef's primary direct users are organizations Crossref does have in place several features intended for use by the general public and specifically researchers and authors. Using these tools, authors can retrieve DOIs for use in reference lists; and educators, researchers and librarians can retrieve DOIs to provide durable links in reading lists, bibliographies, and study guides. Guest query options can be used to retrieve DOIs for journal articles, books, and chapters. Researchers with a list of references can cut-and-pasted their bibliography into the Simple Text Query forms. The results will return the references and DOIs (if available), which can then be cut-and-pasted back into the source document. Researchers with unformatted bibliographic data can use the bibliographic metadata or author/title query to retrieve DOIs for journal articles, books, book chapters, conference proceedings, reports, standards, and other content types.

CrossRef offers secondary publishers and other affiliates the opportunity to identify, acquire, and capture DOIs for use in their internal systems or in products and services they offer to their customers. Depending upon the nature of the business (commercial Vs non-profit) and the application intended for metadata, there are a number of affiliate agreements offered by CrossRef with varying fee structures and metadata use restrictions. If someone is a database publisher, subscription agent, software vendor, or journal hosting/linking platform, he can join CrossRef by requesting, completing, and signing the affiliate agreement. CrossRef reviews his request to determine which agreement best applies.

Organizations and people work as CrossRef agents. CrossRef agents are journal hosting and/or linking platforms that support publishers' electronic content and interface with CrossRef on behalf of one or more publishers. In essence, agents serve as the CrossRef technical contact for their publisher clients and perform all deposit, querying and linking activities. CrossRef also offers special arrangement for other IDF Registration Agencies. This RA Affiliate agreement allows RAs' to act as agents on behalf of their publishing clients and to deposit metadata with CrossRef for DOIs registered by the RA.

OBTAINING A DOI PREFIX

Once any organization joins CrossRef, CrossRef assigns it a unique six-digit DOI prefix beginning with "10.". The organization does not need to get a DOI prefix prior to joining CrossRef nor pay a separate fee to the International DOI Foundation (IDF). Member organizations may also obtain multiple DOI prefixes upon request. It is important to know that once user associates an individual DOI with a particular content item, the DOI is permanently assigned to that content regardless of the owner. While specific publishers must assign DOIs using their unique prefix, ownership and control of individual DOIs can be transferred.

For example, if ownership of a journal passes from Publisher A to Publisher B, control of the DOIs for articles in that journal are given to Publisher B. Publisher B can update the metadata and URLs for those DOIs, but the DOIs themselves remain the same. Publisher A will continue to assign DOIs using its existing prefix, while Publisher B will use its own prefix to assign DOIs to other content it owns. Therefore, the prefix of a DOI does not reliably identify the publisher.

ESTABLISHING A DOI SUFFIX PATTERN

Before user can assign DOIs to articles or other content items, he must devise a DOI assignment scheme. CrossRef gives him a DOI prefix that user must use, but user can create his own pattern and system for suffixes. The DOI suffix has a very flexible syntax. It can be any alphanumeric string, consisting of a single node or multiple nodes. A node is a portion of a character string. A single node has no delimiters (periods, colons, pipes, and so on), for example: 123456. A character string with multiple nodes must include a delimiter (a period, colon, pipe, and so on) between each one, for example: 12.34.56. Each suffix must be unique within a prefix.

Users do not need to include any specific or descriptive information in the DOI. Such information forms the metadata associated with each DOI, which is submitted along with the DOI and URL. Existing identifiers can also be used for the DOI suffix, such as an ISBN, PII (personally identifying information), or existing internal numbering scheme.

Guidelines

- **Be concise** - The suffix should be made as concise as possible to facilitate human readability. DOIs will appear online and in print; users will also re-type DOIs.
- **Be unique** - A suffix must be unique within a given prefix.
- **Be case insensitive** - A suffix is case insensitive, so 10.1006/abc is the same as 10.1006/ABC.
- **Be consistent** - The suffix should reflect a consistent, logical system that can be easily documented and readily understood by employees of his organization, so that the task of assigning DOIs can be passed from one employee to the next. For example, user might want the suffix to include existing internal identifiers.
- **Avoid page numbers** - It is possible to use traditional bibliographic metadata (such as journal, volume, and page) in constructing DOI suffixes because both this metadata and the DOI are persistent. However, some issues need careful consideration before choosing such an approach. DOIs should be active as soon as articles appear online.
- **Use ISBNs for books** - The Association of American Publishers (AAP) recommends the use of ISBNs as the DOI suffix for electronic books and reference works. CrossRef follows these recommendations.

- **Only use approved characters** "a-z", "A-Z", "0-9" and "-._;()/"
- **Use one or more nodes** - User can use suffix nodes to reflect hierarchical information or levels of granularity. This is the scheme used by Academic Press, with resulting DOIs such as 10.1006/jmbi.1998.2354.
- **Make suffixes extensible** - DOI suffixes should be extensible. In the future, for instance, parts of articles, such as figures, graphs, and supplementary materials, might be assigned DOIs. Using the preceding Academic Press example, the second figure might be assigned this DOI: 10.1006/jmbi.1998.2354.f002.

How CrossRef works

CrossRef enables linking in scholarly content on a cross-publisher basis by providing two basic services:

1) Registration of a DOI with corresponding metadata that describes the item being identified.
2) A lookup service for finding DOIs. The first is necessary to allow for a uniform format in which to build Web links to the numerous participating content providers. This allows various publisher specific links (e.g. "http://publisher1.service.org/content/location/file.pdf" or "http://some. publisher.com/some_journal?article=page100. html") to be replaced with the standard form "http://dx.doi.org/10.1234/abcdef". The DOI also allows the content to be relocated without having to change the links that point to it, this is called persistence.

Following steps can be used:

1. Using a DOI prefix assigned by CrossRef, publishers create DOI names for content items. Before creating

any DOI name DOI Name Information and Guidelines should be reviewed. Then an XML file must be constructed and upload to the CrossRef system. When content is published online, the DOI name and metadata should be deposited with CrossRef as soon as possible (within 24 hours is preferable).

2. Members also submit the citations contained in each deposited content item to CrossRef. This way, the publisher can, as part of its electronic production process or online publishing system, add outbound links to any of an item's citations that point to content already registered in the CrossRef system. The member can also use DOI names to link references to their own content. It is an obligation of CrossRef members to link references using the DOI name.
3. Members then use the DOI names retrieved from CrossRef to create persistent outbound links to other members' content.
4. An end user reading the content on-line finds a DOI based link and clicks on it.
5. The user's browser first goes to the DOI central registry to retrieve the actual URL of the item

Then the user's browser is redirected to the publisher's site that contains the cited item as on DOI response page.

HOW DEPOSITING WORKS

Publishers can assign DOIs to a wide variety of content as identified in the categories listed below.

- **Journals** : DOIs may optionally be assigned to the journal itself, a specific volume or a specific issue. However, we strongly encourage the assignment of a DOI at the journal title level (journal title DOIs often use the ISSN as the suffix). DOIs should be assigned to all articles published within the journal and may be assigned to other content as well (e.g. book reviews, editorials etc.). Items that are part of an article which may benefit from having their own identifier can be registered as components and given a DOI unique from that of the article. These items include figures, tables or supporting data files.

- **Books :** DOIs are always assigned at the book title level and frequently at the chapter level as well. Books may also be deposited as part of a series in which case the series is assigned a DOI unique from the DOI of any volume within the series. Book deposits must have an ISBN for each volume title and an ISSN for each series title.
- **Conference proceedings :** Conference proceedings are quite similar to journals/articles with the major exception being the metadata includes information about the conference event as well as the proceedings title. Each papers within the proceedings a treated like a journal article.
- **Components :** Components are parts of some other content type which are to be given their own DOI. They require a parent DOI which may be the DOI of an article, journal, book, chapter, standard or any other DOI. Components may be deposited along with their parent or they can be deposited by themselves in a separate XML file.
- **Dissertations and thesis :** DOIs are assigned to each dissertation or thesis. DOIs are not assigned to an aggregation of this content type (e.g. if a collection of dissertations is published together it most likely would be deposited as a book).
- **Reports and working-papers :** This content type resembles books in many ways with the major difference being an ISBN is not required. DOIs need not

but are strongly encouraged to be assigned at the title level. Reports/working-papers may be published as part of a series in which case the series title is given a unique DOI and must have an ISSN. Volumes published with a series must also have an ISBN.

- **Standards :** Standards are assigned a DOI at the title level and may also have DOIs assigned to lower level "content-items". Standards published as stand alone publications do not need an ISBN but like reports if they're published in a series ISBNs and ISSNs are required. The metadata for standards differ primarily in the inclusion of additional designators along with the title which are commonly used when referring to a standard.
- **Database :** Databases are another top level construct which can be assigned a DOI. Lower level items within a database, called datasets, are each given a unique DOI and any database/dataset DOI may include components. This content type has been used to address a number of situations that do not easily fall into the other categories.

All deposits are made by uploading XML files to CrossRef. The basic process for depositing consists of these steps:

1. Determining the type of information for which user are assigning DOIs
2. Creating the XML file to upload. XML is based on the CrossRef deposit schema.
3. Verifying the XML.
4. Deciding whether user want to upload the file manually or programmatically.
   - CrossRef web interface (manual)
   - Java, Perl scripts or other program (programmatically)

5. Submitting the file(s).

The upload process is very basic and performs no data validation at the time of upload. The acknowledgment user receive at this step simply indicates that his file has been received. Each uploaded file then goes into a queue to wait processing which validates his XML using the Xerces parser. This step verifies that the XML is well formed and conforms to the rules of the CrossRef schema and performs certain logic checks on the data in the file.

After a deposit is processed, user receives an email indicating the results (in an XML format) which lists the status of each DOI contained in the file. Note that while many DOIs in a file may successfully get deposited, individual DOIs may fail. It is very IMPORTANT to examine these deposit logs and respond to any problems. During times of very heavy loads, jobs may take several hours to reach the top of the queue and large files can take an hour or more to process (a nice file size is under 150KBytes and no files bigger than 1.5MBytes are allowed). User can track his submission's progress and, if necessary request that CrossRef staff move it up in the queue.

Deposit rules: Most of the rules which govern the data allowed/required in a deposit are specified in the CrossRef schema (thus enforced via XML validation). A few rules are enforced by the software which processes the deposit.

1. DOIs may only contain the following characters: "a-z", "A-Z", "0-9" and "-._;()/"
2. Publication title ownership is enforced. This means that CrossRef recognizes a single publisher as owning a title and thus only DOIs using the prefix of that publisher may be assigned to the publication.
3. Timestamp. Every time a DOI is deposited it must be given a timestamp, the value of which must increment with subsequent updates. This value is a string of text

that gets interpreted as a number. The recommended format is YYYYMMDDHHMM (ex: 200810021422).

HOSTING CROSSREF DATA LOCALLY

CrossRef members and affiliates have the option of receiving a direct feed of all the data submitted to CrossRef, enabling local hosting of the data. Organizations that choose to host data locally pull it from CrossRef in XML and can take either all or a subset of the content delivered to CrossRef. Local hosting is for those organizations that want to retrieve DOIs within their local system without using the Internet to retrieve DOIs from CrossRef. Because the data is delivered in XML format, the organization must have an infrastructure to receive and load the information into its own system and databases.

Conditions for Local Hosting

- Local hosting is available to all CrossRef members and affiliates.
- Organizations that host locally are subject to the general membership terms and any specific terms for local hosting as determined by the CrossRef Board of Directors.
- Organizations that host locally are not allowed to resell the data provide a lookup service for other members' DOIs. There is no restriction on members providing a lookup service for their own DOIs.
- The annual administrative fee for local hosting is charged in addition to any other membership or deposit fees that may apply.
- Agents appointed by members are not eligible for local hosting.
- There are no individual DOI lookup charges for local hosting.

TECHNICAL INFORMATION ABOUT LOCAL HOSTING

The distribution of CrossRef metadata is accomplished via FTP of XML files from the CrossRef servers. FTP access to the file area is controlled by IP addresses and account authentication. There are two data model styles to choose from:

1. Model 1: Daily XML as deposited by member publishers

This is a legacy data distribution method which should not be adopted by any new local hosters. This method makes available on a daily basis the XML sent in by depositing publishers, minus any reference lists for a given article. These XML files are structured according to deposit Schema or to the older deposit DTD. In each file the publisher may be adding new DOIs or updating the metadata for DOIs deposited on an earlier date. The data in a single file may pertain to more than one journal. Each file (and possibly each DOI record in the file) will be marked with a timestamp. CrossRef only accepts the metadata if the timestamp has been incremented from the previously recorded value.

2. Model 2: 'lite-weight' and 'medium-weight' XML

The second model of XML provides the essential metadata and comes in two flavors, lite-weight' and 'medium-weight'. The medium-weight XML is structured according to an output data schema. This data is available via FTP from a directory tree on server. In the root level of the tree there are two folders, mdByTitle-lite and mdByTitle-medium. Each of these contains 12 additional folders as shown here:

day 0 day 1 day 2 day 3 day 4 day 5 day 6 full

week0 week1 week2 week3

Also in the lite-weight folder are six text files:

lastrundate_daily_books.txt

lastrundate_daily_confproc.txt

lastrundate_daily_journals.txt

lastrundate_weekly_books.txt

lastrundate_weekly_confproc.txt

lastrundate_weekly_journals.txt

Data is generated on a daily, weekly and monthly basis. Each day the prior day's DOI deposit activity (new or update) are written to one of the 'dayX' folders. The process rotates through the folders each week. Each week (on Saturday) the prior week's deposit activity is written to one of the 'weekX' folders. Again the process rotates through the folders. Once each four weeks (on the same week that 'week0' is populated) the entire metadata set (all DOIs for all journals) are written to the 'full' folder.

METADATA GUIDELINES

Nine easy steps to improve the quality of CrossRef's metadata and enhance CrossRef ability to optimize services:

1) Deposit article titles
2) Deposit all author names, not just the first author
3) Verify journal, book, and conference titles
4) Forward Linking publishers should deposit *all* references, including self-citations
5) Deposit "as crawled" URLs for Google
6) Deposit DOIs for supporting material, known as components
7) Deposit metadata and DOIs for all digitized backfile content
8) Check the Title List
9) Check the Failed Query Report

In order for CrossRef to optimize its citation linking capabilities and reliably provide a growing range of related services on behalf of its members, CrossRef needs to improve the overall quality and completeness of its metadata. A variety of data quality improvements are underway, but the most important factor remains the data deposited by member publishers. Below are new high-priority metadata guidelines:

- **Author names and article titles :** Although the CrossRef deposit schema specifies that some bibliographic metadata is optional for DOI registration purposes, CrossRef strongly encourages members to register comprehensive metadata for each DOI deposited. In addition to currently mandatory elements, include article title and given names and surnames of all authors for all articles.
- **Journal title :** Always verify the accuracy and completeness of journal title, volume, issue and page numbers prior to CrossRef registration. The depositor report at http://www.crossref.org/06members/51depositor.html now links to publisher-specific Missing Metadata Reports that pinpoint where deposits have been lacking requested metadata.
- **References.** For those publishers participating in Forward Linking, as well as those who would like CrossRef to provide their metadata to third parties such as search engines, user must supply complete references lists to CrossRef. There are two ways to do this (either within a metadata deposit or as a reference-only deposit. References lists should be complete: do not omit references that point to own publications.
- **As-crawled URL.** In its metadata proposal to publishers, Google is requesting that user provide "As-Crawled URLs" — that is, the URL Google actually crawls to index his full text. The CrossRef system now

supports registration of the as-crawled URL, utilizing the <collection> element of the existing schema.

- **Gaps in CrossRef coverage of online content:** Although CrossRef does not require registration of backfile content, in order for CrossRef to improve query matching rate and serve as a metadata delivery platform on behalf, all of digital content should be registered, including backfiles.
- **Components.** Supplemental or supporting information for a journal article, book chapter, or conference paper may be included as components. Components include figures, tables, images, video, audio and other data formats.

ACCESSING THE CROSSREF SYSTEM

Before a user can access the CrossRef system, he must join CrossRef, become an affiliate, or open a library account. CrossRef then sends user a login name (username) and password that lets him enter the CrossRef system, as follows:

1. Go to the CrossRef System at http://doi.crossref.org/ .
2. Enter login name and password.
3. Click Submit.

From the Home page, user can jump to the key areas and tasks in the CrossRef system. He can also click individual tabs to perform associated actions or view related information.

USING FREE DOI LOOKUP

The CrossRef free DOI lookup form allows users to retrieve DOI names using bibliographic metadata. This is a guest interface to the CrossRef system and is used for retrieving a DOI name for a single journal, article, book, chapter, conference proceeding, or paper. This interface is not intended for automated querying.

To use the Bibliographic metadata search form:

1. Access the free DOI lookup form
2. Select *Journal* if user is seeking the DOI for a journal or article. Select *Book/Conference Proceeding* if user is seeking the DOI for a book, chapter, conference proceeding, or paper.
3. Enter information about the content item. At minimum, user must supply either the first author's surname name or first page number.

   CrossRef recommends entering a journal's title and ISSN.
4. Select *Enable Multiple Hits* to allow the CrossRef system to return DOIs for items whose metadata closely resembles those in the query if it can't find an exact match.
5. Click Search.

To use the Article Title Search

1. Access the free DOI lookup form directly *or* by selecting For Publishers > Free DOI Lookup on the CrossRef web site.
2. Enter an author surname and article title into the available fields
3. Click Search.

Querying in CrossRef

Querying is the process of retrieving data from CrossRef and occurs in one of two modes:

- Metadata query: user knows the bibliographic data and wish to retrieve the DOI for the item
- DOI query: user has a DOI and would like to retrieve associated metadata

The majority of query transactions occur automatically by users who build systems that make simple HTTP GET requests to our server. CrossRef does provide interfaces for manual use which are useful for individual authors or researchers looking to find a specific article or by member's technical staff when trying to investigate a particular problem.

Some of these manual interfaces require no account login or other authorization for use. Individuals may freely use these services in an interactive manner. Automating access to these interfaces is not permitted. Performing automated access requires obtaining account registration with CrossRef.

Queries are formatted as either XML or pipe delimited text. XML queries allow more control over the matching process.

BATCH QUERIES

In situations where a large volume of queries need to be submitted CrossRef also supports a batch upload feature. Queries files in either an XML or piped format are uploaded to the CrossRef system where they will wait in a queue for processing. Files can contain either metadata or DOI queries (but not a mix). Users may request that their CrossRef account be configured so that the email results notice contains a link to the result file which would subsequently be downloaded by the user. This avoids problems associated with large email files.

QUERY RESULTS

User may request the system to return query results in the following formats.

- piped: metadata are returned delimited by the '|' character (this is the default format)
- xsd_xml: the original XML result format which contains basic metadata

- unixref: a more comprehensive dataset which includes all data exactly as submitted by the publisher*

It must be kept in mind that references for a given article (if deposited) are not returned to anyone other than the DOI owner.

Submitting simple text queries

The Simple Text Query allows users to retrieve DOI names for journal articles, books, and chapters by simply cutting and pasting a reference or reference list into the query box.

Interactive simple-text query form:

1. Access the simple text query form (CrossRef Web site, then select Simple Text Query under Technical resources)
2. Enter a reference using the preceding example as a guide.
3. Press Enter and enter another reference if needed. Repeat this step as necessary.
4. Select the *List All Possible DOIs per Reference* option to find all possible matches.
5. Click Submit.

Simple text query upload

An alternative approach to using the Simple Text Query is to upload a TEXT file containing a list of references. CrossRef will parse the file, process each individual reference and return a DOI if one is found. This service will NOT accept a full article in PDF, MSWord or any other document format. It expects to find only the list of references in a simple text file format (extension ".TXT").

Submitting interactive queries

This interface allows submitting piped or XML queries interactively and retrieve the results in various formats. It is particularly useful for technical analysis of problems/ concerns as it allows adjusting the XML properties of a query to determine why matches may not be occurring. The most useful properties to adjust are the enable-multiple-hits and the fuzzy control property "match=".

Metadata queries

1. Access the CrossRef system.
2. Click the Queries tab.
3. Click the Interactive Query Upload tab, if necessary.
4. Type queries (in either piped or XML format) in the box provided.

Sample XML query

Limit the number of metadata queries user enters in a single operation to less than 15 to reduce the chance of a timeout occurring.

5. Select the desired results format.
   - Default: currently piped
   - Piped: results returned in piped format
   - XML (legacy): a very basic XML format with no associated schema
   - XML (XSD): more sophisticated results structure (corresponding schema)
   - UNIXML: complete metadata as submitted by the publisher (corresponding schema)
6. Select the desired Area option (*Live* or *Test*).

   Each member account has a test area that can be used for trial uploads and queries. Each test area is isolated from other test areas. Queries into test area are matched against only metadata user previously submitted into the test area, not other publishers' metadata or 'live' metadata.
7. Select *Disable Fuzzy Matching* if user wants the

CrossRef system to return results only for exact matches.

8. Click Submit.

   When the CrossRef system is done processing the queries, it displays the results on the same page.

Sample results in piped format

How long the CrossRef system takes to process the queries depends on how many there are and how busy the system is at the time.

DOI queries

DOI queries are useful when user has a DOI and would like to examine its metadata.

1. Access the CrossRef system.
2. Click the Queries tab.
3. Click the DOI Query Upload tab.
4. Type the DOIs in the box provided, such as:

   10.1016/8756-3282(95)91695-4

   Limit the number of DOI queries user enters in a single operation to 15-20 to reduce the chance of a timeout occurring and interrupting his request.
5. Click Submit

When the CrossRef system is done processing the queries, it displays the results on the same page.

CrossRef system interface

The CrossRef system is built mainly to support automated transactions from the publishing and content delivery systems operated by members.

- Using HTTP to Query
- Using the Open Channel Interface (OCI)
- Using the OpenURL Query Interface
- Using the OAI-PMH interface

Using HTTP to Query

The most common method of submitting queries to CrossRef is to have an automated service interact with the CrossRef system using the HTTP interface. CrossRef strongly recommends that user groups between 5 and 20 queries into a single request. This helps reduce the network transaction load on CrossRef resources. These transactions use a simple HTTP GET request with the results being returned immediately to the caller. Queries may also be processed off line in batch mode.

Synchronous HTTP queries

Synchronous queries are performed using a URL with encoded parameters as follows:

http://doi.crossref.org/servlet/query?usr= <USERNAME> &pwd= <PASSWORD>&format= unixref&qdata=|Proc.%20Natl%20Acad.%20Sci.%20USA|Z hou|94|24|13215|1997|||

http://doi.crossref.org/servlet/query?pid= <USERNAME>:<PASSWORD>&id=10.1577/H02-043

where:

- **usr** is CrossRef-supplied login name.
- **pwd** is CrossRef password.
- **pid** is CrossRef-supplied login name and password.
- **format** is the desired results format (piped | xml | xsd_xml | unixref)

To place multiple queries in one request, include them in the qdata parameter separated by **%0A**, as shown here:

http://doi.crossref.org/servlet/query?usr= <USERNAME>&pwd= <PASSWORD>&qdata= |%20Natl%20Acad.%20Sci.%20USA|Zhou| 94|24|13215| 1997|||%0A|J.%20Mol.%20Biol.|Hagerman|260|||1996|||

Certain characters cannot be passed in a URL without

causing problems. The following table lists those characters that must be URL-encoded.

Character	Name	URL code
;	Semicolon	%3B
/	Slash, virgule, separatrix, or solidus	%2F
?	Question mark	%3F
:	Colon	%3A
@	At sign	%40
=	Equals sign	%3D
&	Ampersand	%26
lf	line feed	%0A

There are several drawbacks to submitting synchronous HTTP queries:

- A network connection is established every time an HTTP request is made. Even with HTTP keep-alive the web server disconnects the client after a short period of inactivity. The establishment of a connection with every query request can be expensive, especially for one-line queries.
- User authentication on the CrossRef side occurs with every HTTP request. Because most clients do not maintain a session with CrossRef, the cost in terms of CrossRef resources of establishing a session to enforce user access rights for every request is substantial.
- Users can overcome the first two drawbacks by submitting multiple queries within the same HTTP request where queries are separated by CRLF. However, this technique presents a different problem: queries are evaluated sequentially within the same thread, which means "hard-to-resolve" queries slow down other queries within the same batch. So even though users gain in terms of network connection and CrossRef authentication time, they lose the concurrence provided by submitting one-line queries.

Using the Open Channel interface

Open Channel interface (OCI) is a synchronous (while user waits) way to submit queries that offers significantly better performance than the normal HTTP interface. OCI operates much like a telnet session in that the system performing the queries connects to a special port on the CrossRef system, writes queries to the session, and the reads the results back.

USING THE OPEN URL QUERY INTERFACE

OpenURL Accounts

Using a login to access CrossRef's OpenURL Query Interface is required. CrossRef requests that users obtain and use a login to help monitor usage and deal with problems should they arise. OpenURL users who are already CrossRef members may use their CrossRef system account. Non-members may obtain a complimentary OpenURL account.

Metadata queries

CrossRef maintains an OpenURLQuery Interface that accepts metadata, searches to find a matching DOI, and redirects the user to the target of the DOI.

The OpenURL Query Interface can accept these parameters:

- **issn** - ISSN (not recommended)
- **stitle** - Short title, which may be supplied as an alternative to title
- **pid** or **sid** - CrossRef-supplied login name and password; in older forms, **sid** was used instead of **pid** (which is preferred)
- **redirect** - Set to **false** to return the DOI in XML format instead of redirecting to the target URL (the default is **true**)
- **multihit** - Set to **true** to return DOIs for more than one

content item if the CrossRef system does not find an exact match (the default is **false**)

DOI queries

CrossRef supports DOI queries formatted as OpenURL version 0.1 requests. This metadata includes identifiers (title and/or ISSN), first author, enumeration (volume issue page), and year, as shown here:

- **Open URL query :** http://www.crossref.org/openurl/?pid=username:password&id =doi:10.1103/PhysRev.47.777&noredirect=true
- **CrossRef query :** http://doi.crossref.org/servlet/query?pid=username:password&id=10.1006/jmbi.2000.4282

Like metadata queries, DOI query results are returned in XML format.

Using OAI-PMH

CrossRef operates an OAI-PMH service for the distribution of metadata to subscribers. This system is based on the OCLC version 2 repository framework and implements the interface. Access to CrossRef's service for retrieving DOI metadata is regulated by the IP address of a server which will be performing a harvest. The repository supports selective harvesting according to sets defined by the hierarchy of publisher, journal title, and year of publication. CrossRef service allows public access to two OAI verbs which allow for discovery of coverage information.

Many OAI requests are too big to be retrieved in a single transaction. If a given response contains a resumption token the user must make an additional request to retrieve the rest of the data. Note that resumption tokens remain viable for only 5 minutes.

Metadata Services - What data is available

CrossRef's Metadata Service is available based on

subscription. After an organization applies for subscription members of CrossRef may decide if they wish for their metadata to be included in distributions to the subscribing organization (knows as an opportunity to 'opt-out'). This may result in the subscribing organization being able to retrieve less than the full set of metadata available at CrossRef. Upon acceptance of an application the subscriber will supply CrossRef with two IP addresses from which they will be allowed to retrieve metadata. Any request received from these IP addresses will be filtered so as to exclude non-participating CrossRef member metadata. The two publicly available requests mentioned above are not subject to this limitation when the requests come from an IP address not assigned to a known subscriber. These two requests when received from a subscriber's registered IP addresses will only return data pertinent to that subscriber.

Initial data loads

The size of the CrossRef repository precludes using one OAI request to retrieve all the available data. Often a subscriber first obtains a list of the available sets using the ListSets request and then repeatedly submits ListRecords requests for each publisher. However, this approach can require a substantial amount of time. Upon request CrossRef staff can produce an archive of all the data available to a given subscriber which can then be downloaded via FTP.

Benefits for libraries

CrossRef, the official DOI registration agency for scholarly and professional publications, harnesses collaboration among publishers to provide the scholarly community with easier access to online research content.

The key benefits of the CrossRef DOI for libraries are:

- Truly persistent links
- Increases usage of acquired resources

- Expanded access to content not owned
- Enhanced localized linking
- DOI and metadata retrieval privileges at no cost to most libraries

There is no charge for most libraries to get a CrossRef account to retrieve DOIs or metadata. Through CrossRef, libraries can create links to CrossRef member publishers without signing bi-lateral linking agreements with each publisher and without having to track publishers' individual linking schemes. The CrossRef system also supports DOI re-direction for the purposes of localized linking within library holdings.

In most cases, information providers (publisher, database producers, etc.) will use CrossRef to add DOIs to their content and databases, so libraries will not need to use CrossRef for DOI retrieval alone. If libraries host local content, the content providers should add DOIs before delivering the content. Users browsing online content will see DOI links. Users can always look up DOIs at no charge at free query interface.

Considerations for DSpace Repositories

CrossRef encourages organizations which operate institutional repositories to assign DOIs to their original non-duplicative works. There are a few simple guidelines when the repository is a DSpace based system. DSpace and the DOI both utilize the Handle system for identifiers. When a DSpace repository is configured it must be registered with CNRI who provides the repository operator with a Handle prefix (typically a sequence of numbers). This is not a DOI prefix (also a sequence of numbers which begin with "10.").

In order to assign DOIs to DSpace items the repository must join CrossRef and be given a DOI prefix. Subsequently each item for which a DOI is desired is deposited with CrossRef using the CrossRef deposit schema. The DOI is best constructed as shown here:

THE-DOI = DOI-prefix / DSpace-prefix / Dspace-suffix

Example: 10.1575/1912/1099

CrossRef title records and ISSNs

When DOIs are deposited, the CrossRef system must assign the DOI to an internal title record. This is necessary to support query processing which is heavily dependent on matching query fields to a publication. Upon deposit, the XML publication title is used to determine if CrossRef already has a record for the publication. If needed a new title record is created, and then the DOIs in the deposit are assigned to that title. Title processing is a very simple 'string' compare thus an XML title using ampersand (&) would be considered unique from one using the word "and". ISSNs are also dealt with in a simple manner. Generally this is not a problem for the query match processing since the evaluation rules for a query are much more sophisticated and can overcome any confusion caused by such a condition. Further, the effected titles (e.g. the '&' Vs 'and') are typically related or are really the same publication.

In early 2006 CrossRef introduced a new query result format that solves this problem (format=unixref). Any query (XML or piped) that requests this format will be returned the exact data sent in by the publisher for that DOI. This results from the fact that the first ISSN is for an earlier version of this journal which has a different sub-title than the second ISSN.

DOIs are required for journal articles, conference papers and book titles but are optional for journal titles, volumes and issues and book chapters/entries and components. CrossRef is currently working on expanding the types of content it registers DOIs for to include theses and dissertations and database records.

DOI Ownership transfer

Once a DOI is assigned to a piece of content it should remain unchanged and only one DOI should exist for a given piece of content. When ownership of content changes from one publisher to another (at the moment this is most commonly a journal changing ownership), it is necessary to transfer the ownership of the DOIs. Typically, a CrossRef account can only be used to create/modify DOIs that have the same prefix as is associated with the user's account. The ownership transfer modifies this relationship so that a specific group of DOIs are marked as belonging to a prefix other than the prefix in the DOI. It is important to note that the DOI itself is not modified at all in this process.

In addition, the ownership transfer process allows to assign a new URL to the DOI redirecting it to the acquiring publisher's Web site. This shortcut is provided since the acquiring publisher may not always have the original XML for these transferred DOIs and therefore would be unable to easily perform an update.

Dealing with conflicts

Conflicts occur when two or more DOIs are deposited with CrossRef having the same exact metadata. The fields that must match exactly are:

journal | author | volume | issue | page | year | article-title

Omitting one or more fields in a deposit increases the chance of a conflict.

Deleting a DOI

DOIs are supposed to be persistent and are therefore very difficult to delete. In fact the CrossRef system has no "delete a DOI" function.

Special characters in deposits and queries

Special characters are those that are not part of the

ASCII or ISO 8859-1 (Latin-1) character sets. ASCII and Latin-1 characters can be represented in one octet (byte) of information and are displayed properly in almost all editors and viewers on most computer systems.

Using parameter passing

Parameter passing is a feature that allows data placed on an outbound DOI link to be passed along to the target publisher.

Digital Object Identifier DOI

The Digital Object Identifier (DOI®) System is meant for identifying content objects in the digital environment. DOI® names are assigned to an entity for use on the digital networks. These DOI names are used to provide current information, including where the digital objects (or information about them) can be found on the Internet. Information about a digital object may change over time, including where to find it, but it has unique feature that its DOI name will not change. This DOI System provides a framework for various functions such as persistent identification, managing intellectual content, managing metadata, linking customers with content suppliers, facilitating electronic commerce, and enabling automated management of media. DOI names can be used for any form of management of any data, whether it is commercial or non-commercial. The system is managed by the International DOI Foundation (IDF).

Using DOI names as identifiers makes managing intellectual property in a networked environment much easier and more convenient, and allows the construction of automated services and transactions.

DOI Facts

- DOI = Digital Object Identifier
- IDF = International DOI Foundation (operating and

governing organization)

- RAs = DOI Registration Agencies (members of IDF offering the system to customers who wish to assign DOI names)

Status: operational system

- Foundation launched to develop system in 1998; first applications launched 2000
- Currently used by c. 3,000 naming authorities (assigners), e.g., 2,600 publishers, EU documents, science data sets, etc.
- Approximately 40 million DOI names assigned to date
- Via 8+ RAs (international)
- Well established in professional information sector; best known application is

Scope

- *Digital Identifier* of an Object (not "Identifier of a Digital Object")
- Object = any entity (thing: physical, digital, or abstract)
  - Resources, parties, licences, etc.
- Digital Identifier = network actionable identifier ("click on it and do something")
- Initial focus on entities was documents/media e.g. articles, data sets
  - Now also moving into parties and licences
  - Extending to other sectors, such as Movie industry, Financial sector, Music, Newspapers.
- Extensible by design (as, e.g., URI): not intended as a publishing-only solution (digital convergence)
- International - e.g. in 2007 appointed China RA

What it does

- Provides an *actionable, interoperable, persistent* link
- *Actionable* - through use of identifier syntax and network resolution mechanism (Handle System®)
- *Persistent* - through combination of supporting improved handle infrastructure (registry database, proxy support, etc) and social infrastructure (obligations by Registration Agencies)
- *Interoperable* - through use of a semantically interoperable data model and grouping mechanisms

Governance

- IDF = operating and governing organization
- Provides the social infrastructure
  - e.g., obligations for persistence, back-up, in event of failure, etc.
- US "Not for profit" open membership (with membership fee)
- Federation of Registration Agencies makes up significant part of the IDF (possibly 100% eventually)
- Elected Board, working groups (including RA Working Group)
- No full time staff (contracted managing agent)

Business Model

- IDF receives membership fees from RAs, contracts technical operator
- RAs also pay operational fees to IDF's technical operator for registering and maintaining DOI names (sliding scale per volume)
- Assigners are customers of RAs
- RAs might have their own existing numbering scheme, existing communities etc. - which can be integrated

with a DOI Application not replaced by it (e.g., ISBN)

- RAs are *autonomous independent bodies*. They offer services to assigners using DOI names
  - RAs' business model with their customers is entirely autonomous
  - RAs only obligation to IDF is a licence/operating agreement
  - RAs may choose to put DOI names "under the hood"
- Inspired by bar code model, ISBN etc: assigner pays
- Some RAs are commercial; others are themselves member communities (e.g., CrossRef)

Technical Infrastructure

- *Handle System*: persistent identification in digital networks (devised by TCP/IP co-inventor)
- *Indecs*: principles of contextual ontology data model for associated metadata ("interoperability of data in e-commerce systems")
- Both used elsewhere: aim was not to re-invent the wheel

Standardization

- ISO: currently at DIS (Draft International Standard) stage. Final standard 2009
  - Through TC46/SC9 ("Information and Documentation"); IDF a liaison body to TC46 since its inception (historical reasons - connection with ISBN)
  - Syntax standardized through ANSI/NISO in 2000
  - Invited by TC46/SC9 to standardize the full DOI System
- URI (within info-URI scheme)

- Mechanism for, and emphasis on, enabling re-use of other existing identifier schemes, e.g., ISBN
- IDF is also the Registration Authority for the ISO MPEG 21 Rights Data Dictionary (which is NOT a part of the DOI System)

Relation to other schemes

- Strong focus on interoperability and on working with existing and new schemes
- Syntactic, semantic and community interoperability
- Use of DOI names by multiple RAs (through APs and Services)
- Involvement with key activities in the content sectors: ACAP, ONIX, ARK, PURL, info URI, URN, Open URL, GS1, MPEG-21, IETF, RDA, DCMI, FRBR, ITU-T Idm, ICSTI, CENDI, HSAC, indecs, CONTECS-DD (etc!)
- Adopt existing proven components
- Note potential confusion: the term "identifier" can mean several different things - not always clear like-for-like comparison (e.g. URI v ISBN...)

Intellectual Property Considerations

- IDF owns DOI®, a registered trademark for the system
- IDF does not have any patents (or patent applications) on DOI System
- IDF collectively licences appropriate technology from suppliers on behalf of members (CNRI Handle System global license, data dictionary tools, etc.)
- Patent Policy in place
- All RAs must sign RA agreement re use of DOI System
- Optional legal "Community of Interest" agreement to enable sharing of information on relevant patent issues - findings confidential to signatories

- IDF is a participant in the (related) CONTECS:DD ontology work, which has some patents

DOI® NAME

A DOI name - a *digital identifier* for any *object of intellectual property*. A DOI name provides a means of persistently identifying a piece of intellectual property on a digital network and associating it with related current data in a structured extensible way. A DOI name can apply to any form of intellectual property expressed in any digital environment. DOI names have been called "the bar code for intellectual property": like the physical bar code, they are enabling tools for use all through the supply chain to add value and save cost. A DOI name differs from commonly used internet pointers to material such as the URL because it identifies an object as a first-class entity, not simply the place where the object is located. The DOI name identifies an entity directly, not some attribute of an object (an address is an attribute of a thing, whereas the thing itself is a first class object). A DOI name also differs from commonly used identifiers of intellectual property such as standard bibliographic and related identifiers (ISBN, ISRC, etc) because it can be associated with defined services and is immediately actionable on a network. A DOI name is an implementation of the Internet concepts of Uniform Resource Name and Universal Resource Identifier.

Identification by a DOI name

A DOI name can be used to identify any resource involved in an intellectual property transaction. Intellectual property includes both physical and digital manifestations, performances and abstract works. An entity can be identified at any arbitrary level of granularity. DOI names can be used to identify, for example, text, audio, images, software, etc; and in future could be used to identify the agreements and parties involved. Intellectual property transactions don't necessarily involve money: DOI names can be used to identify free materials and transactions as well as entities of commercial value. A DOI name is an implementation of URI (Uniform Resource Identifier, sometimes called Universal Resource Identifier, IETF RFC 2396). It uses the Handle System for resolution of the identifier, and the indecs framework for metadata description. The syntax of the DOI name is specified by a NISO standard, (ANSI/NISO Z39.84).

While a DOI name can therefore be used like any other URI to identify "anything that has identity", the DOI System is a combination of components (identification, resolution, data model and policies) devised with the specific primary aim of identifying any "*intellectual property entity*". The initial focus of DOI System applications was "Creations" — that is, resources made by human beings, rather than other types of resource (natural objects, people, places, events, etc). However these other types of resource are also necessarily involved in intellectual property transactions, and so may be identified by DOI names where appropriate.

Formally, DOI scope is defined in terms of the indecs analysis: a DOI name can be assigned to any entity which is a Resource within the indecs model of e-commerce. This means the type of entity must be described in terms of attributes in the dictionary (e.g., media, mode, content, subject), and become an entry in the indecs Data Dictionary (iDD) used by the DOI System. The practical outcome of this is important and provides a pragmatic *functional specification*: a DOI name can identify any Resource, but the DOI System requires that the Resource is defined (technically and hence precisely) in terms of agreed public (iDD) attributes. The Data Model component of the DOI System uses the concept of a Kernel set of metadata. The kernel metadata as currently defined relates only to Creations, and a different kernel will need to be defined for fundamentally different Resources or entities such as parties, places or agreements. There is no problem in principle in doing this as the concepts are analogous; it may be a logical and necessary step (e.g. if a Registration Agency wishes to use DOI names to identify individual licence agreements, authors, consumers, etc).

Assigning a DOI name

A DOI name prefix (for example, 10.1000/) enables a registrant to assign many DOI names, by building on the prefix to construct a range of unique identifiers (10.1000/abc, etc). To obtain a prefix, one need to work either with a Registration Agency or, for experimental or prototype purposes, with the International DOI Foundation. Working with a Registration Agency (RA) brings with it the advantages of participation in a defined DOI System application with others. Several Registration Agencies have been appointed, and additional Registration Agencies will be appointed. RAs are free to set fees independently of the IDF. This allows a range of pricing and business models using third part registration agencies, in recognition of the fact that a simple model is not a "one size fits all" solution.

The DOI name syntax is a NISO standard, but allows the incorporation of any form of existing identifier. The DOI name suffix can be any alphanumeric string that the Registrant chooses. This can simply be a sequential number, or it can make use of an existing (legacy) identifier. The latter may often be administratively convenient for the Registrant. A check digit is not compulsory or necessary, but may be included. Identifiers such as URL and URI specifications, deriving from an Internet environment, do not have check digits: the underlying TCP/IP protocol they use has an error-correction component. Identifiers such as ISBN and similar bibliographic or documentation identifiers do have check digits: these acts as aids to readability or keyboard data entry in the absence of any automated protocol correction.

a. Allocating 2 DOI names to the same article

It is the intention that wherever practical only one DOI name should be assigned to a specified entity. However it is not impossible that multiple DOI names may be assigned. DOI names are assigned not by the IDF but by independent Registration Agencies operating under agreement with the IDF. Each RA assigns DOI names for a specific application. Thus it is possible that two DOI names could be assigned to the same material if that material is used in two different applications and the first DOI name is not known at the time the second is assigned. Such assignments are therefore not technically impossible but are deprecated. The two DOI names could, if it becomes known that they each refer to the same item, be linked by having one resolve to the other as an alias.

It is important to note that to make such an alias link it is imperative to ascertain that the DOI names do indeed refer to precisely the same entity. This can only be done by having the DOI name associated with appropriate declared metadata in a DOI Application Profile. Otherwise there is a risk that the two assigners intend (but have not made clear) the identifier to reference different entities: for example, the CrossRef DOI name referencing an article in abstract form, whereas a learning object application might reference a specific manifestation in one particular format. These are NOT the same entity.

Information about a DOI name is publicly available

Once a DOI name is assigned, anyone may resolve that DOI name without charge. At least some information will always be available on resolution. The information available on resolution depends on the Application Profile (AP) of the DOI name. DOI names can be associated with one of three categories of AP Public availability of information is as follows:

- **Zero AP :** no data other than a URL is registered and therefore only that is available.
- **Base AP :** the kernel metadata set (the minimum set of 6 elements, plus the DOI name value and the AP name) is registered with each DOI name within this AP.
- **Full APs :** these contain the kernel metadata set, plus other metadata values (which must be mapped to the DOI Data Dictionary). Whilst the AP *scheme* must be made available (so that users can determine which metadata fields are associated with the DOI name), the actual *values* of any metadata for each DOI name need not be; whether some or all of these are made available will be determined by the registrant or AP rules.

Need of a Registration Agency to assign DOI names

Registration Agencies (RAs) are established to provide services on behalf of specific user communities. CrossRef, for example, is providing citation-linking services for the scientific publishing sector, so publishers will choose CrossRef as their Registration Agency if they wish to use the specific service or services offered by CrossRef. Choosing an appropriate RA will give one access to DOI System services and implementations offered by the RA for that community. RAs may offer sectoral specialisms of this kind, which may have global application; or may offer regionally based services such as local language support.

If user cannot identify an appropriate Registration Agency able to meet the specific needs, the IDF will act as a "default" Registration Agency for the foreseeable future, to host registration of such DOI names until an appropriate Registration Agency can take over. It will not compete with RAs that have an established market position. Members of the DOI Foundation are organizations (not usually individuals). Membership requires payment of an annual subscription, which varies by category of membership. The International DOI Foundation is similar in some ways to other development organisations such as the World Wide Web consortium.

Comparing DOI

The International Standard Book Number (ISBN), in use by the book publishing industry for many years, is an example of a string of numbers that uniquely labels something. A DOI name Internet-enables such a string (Internet enabling in this context means resolution and then linkage to metadata). In effect the DOI System tackles two problems at once: (1) providing a label string if things don't have a common system right now; and (2) providing internet resolution for any label string at all. Although a DOI name is usually considered to be "An identifier (not a location) on digital networks for an entity", it in full is "a system for persistent and actionable identification and interoperable exchange of managed information on digital networks". So it's not only an identifier string for an object which may not have an existing identifier string; user could also have a DOI name which includes an ISTC, or an ISBN, or a GTIN, or anything else that is an existing identifier string or label or name for the entity. Early uses of DOI names have been for articles, chapters etc, but could be a lot more.

DOI name and system and various relations:

1. The relationship between a DOI name and other development efforts : The International DOI Foundation is a member of some standards organizations, and maintains a number of liaisons or alliances through memberships and/or exchange of information with others, which allow us to act as a collaborative interface in discussions on standards and infrastructure development across the spectrum of intellectual property and technology communities. This provides advantages both to members of the Foundation (who may otherwise not be able to participate in all of these discussions) and to the strategic partners (who deal with IDF as a common voice for the intellectual property community in this area). The IDF participates in the management and governance of two technology development activities where it is a major user: the Handle System, and the indecs framework. In addition the IDF has a number of other relationships with significant development and standards activities in many areas of intellectual property and technology. Some of these are specific to particular application areas, and are undertaken in order to seed activities and outreach from the DOI System to potential implementations.

2. The relationship between the DOI System and the Handle System : The DOI System is an application of the Handle System (a resolution system) to intellectual property. It is more than the Handle System: it adds to the Handle System an approach based on structured associated metadata, policies, procedures, business models and application tools. Initial implementations are now being supplemented by increasingly sophisticated value-added tools for metadata management and content management, which will use the Handle System multiple resolution function. The IDF participates in the management and governance of the Handle System, together with other stakeholders.

3. The relationship between the DOI System and the indecs framework : The DOI System is an implementation of the indecs metadata framework. In addition, IDF participates in the management and governance of the indecs framework, together with other stakeholders. IDF is one of the organisations which developed the original indecs framework and is now developing it further. The indecs approach is fundamental to the DOI System's design.

4. The relationship between DOI names and XML: The DOI System makes use of XML (eXtensible Markup Language), and XML is entirely compatible with DOI names. The expression of metadata in XML is recommended both for kernel metadata and for DOI Application Profile metadata extended from the kernel. The indecs data dictionary and the DOI® Resource Metadata declaration both allow the use of XML expressions, commonly used for metadata transport and messaging.

It seems likely that the relationship between DOI names and XML will grow over time. One obvious link is in developing DOI Application Profiles for the various emerging XML schemas for industry-specific uses, such as NewsML: when such a scheme has been developed, DOI names provide an obvious way of adding functionality (persistent identification, interoperable metadata mappings, multiple resolution framework, etc.) to that schema for practical uses. The linking of entities in XML is very different to the linking of entities with DOI names, as the two serve different, complementary purposes. XML entity resolution is concerned with the construction of an XML document or message; it exists to support the assembly of XML documents from components. DOI name resolution, on the other hand, deals with information about an identified entity and linkage of intellectual property entities and information about those entities. DOI names may of course be used to identify entities which are "marked up" in an XML schema; but not every tagged entity in an XML schema may merit a DOI name, unless there is a need for separate management of that entity (functional granularity). Several languages have been constructed using XML that support functions complementary to DOI name: e.g. XLink is a language that allows XML elements to be made into links, which specify relationship types and behavior characteristics between sets of resources; the Resource Description Framework is another language that can be expressed in XML and allows properties of an identified resource to be described. Although neither of these technologies is mainstream; they have similar characteristics to, and can be used with, DOI names. The IDF is actively pursuing such usages and monitors XML developments closely.

5. Relation with "Persistent identification" : The need for persistent identifiers is well recognized in many areas (particularly from the library, archives, and government communities), but the next step (adopting a practical implementation such as DOI names) is not yet so readily comprehended. There is a fundamental difference between recognizing the need for persistent identifiers through a technical scheme (like URN), and the practical implementation of this (which inevitably has associated costs but also associated added value: a DOI name is a URN and URI implementation). The key point is not about DOI name "versus" an alternative scheme; it is about technical versus business infrastructure, and the need for additional implementation work for the use of any persistent identifier. The implementation of persistent identifiers adds value, but necessarily incurs some costs (in number registration, infrastructure maintenance, and governance). There is a widespread recognition of the advantages of assigning identifiers; and a widespread misconception that an abstract specification (like a URN or URI) actually delivers a working system rather than a namespace that still needs to be populated and managed.

A common misperception is that user can have such a system at no cost. It is inescapable that a cost is associated with managing persistence and assigning identifiers and data to the standards needed to ensure long-term stability. If adding a URL "costs nothing", why should assigning a name? It is indeed possible to use any string; assigned by anyone, as a name — but to be useful and reliable any name must be supported by a social as well as technical infrastructure that defines its properties and utilities. URLs for example have a clear technical infrastructure, but a very loose social infrastructure (anyone can create them, with the result that they are unreliable alone for long term preservation use as they have no guarantee of stability let alone associated structured metadata). Product bar codes, Visa numbers, and DOI names have a tighter social (business) infrastructure, with rules and regulations, costs of maintaining and policing data and corresponding benefits of quality and reliability. Like any other piece of infrastructure, an identifier system (especially one which adds much value like metadata and resolution) must be paid for eventually by someone. The DOI name is designed to work with any business model, ranging from free assignment to assignment on a commercial basis.

6. Relation of the DOI System to DNS : The most common mechanism for resolution on the Internet is the Domain Name System (DNS): http as used in URL is a use of DNS. URLs are grouped by domain name and then by some hierarchical structure, originally based on file trees, now possibly unconnected from that but still a hierarchy. DOI names offer a more finely grained approach to naming where each name stands on its own, unconnected to any DNS or other hierarchy. This offers beneficial flexibility, especially over time, as the document origins reflected in that hierarchy lose meaning, such as a change in ownership which is reflected in DNS. In order to manage DOI names tools are created that allow more flexible management of sets of DOI names, in a more useful way than as a fixed sub-domain: a DOI name, DOI Application Profile and services can all be thought of as layers of abstraction which allow this. Functionality such as URL partial redirection and relative URLs make a lot of sense in the context of URLs. However since DOI names/Handles deliberately have a more finely grained approach to naming things, functionality such as partial redirection is dealt with through tools which capitalize on the finer granularity made available through DOI names.

7. Relation of the DOI System with physical identifier systems like RFID tags : Electronic product codes are identifiers which are articulated through Radio-Frequency Identifier tags or other means, and are assigned to physical goods; increasingly there are proposed applications which would relate such tags to digital networks for the look-up of associated data, such as the "internet of things" envisaged in the Auto-ID project. By definition, RFID tags are assigned to individual physical instances; in specifying intellectual property with a DOI name, it is essential to be able to interoperable name not only such physical manifestations but also digital manifestations and the underlying abstractions which they express.

DOI names allow an object to be uniquely, persistently identified and current state data about that object to be obtained on the internet. The DOI System's area of application is intellectual property — in any form. It is agnostic as to other uses of the identifier — product codes, bar codes, RFIDs, IP addresses, etc; the system is designed to offer persistence and interoperability for multiple functionalities. Thus DOI names can work with physical identifier strings, either by encapsulating the identifier string in some way or in conjunction with proposed specific identifier resolution mechanisms.

To be useful, electronic product codes will increasingly also be concerned with associated metadata, in product information databases. The principles of DOI System Data Model techniques are equally relevant to considerations of such associated data. Thus DOI names offer a way of articulating specific electronic product codes in a way that is interoperable with other systems.

Relevancy of the DOI System to rights transaction

Fundamental to rights transactions are the concepts of unique identification and appropriate structured metadata. DOI System implements the indecs approach, which has at its heart the concept of rights management. IDF has introduced the concepts of the DOI System and indecs into many digital rights management activities such as MPEG-21, OEBF, TV-Anytime, etc.

Developing a DOI System application

Applications can range from DOI names being a persistent redirection to a single URL (which is easily accomplished) to advanced applications and services. Multiple resolution and defined metadata related through the DOI System data model ensure interoperability; the starting point for such advanced applications is the registration of a set of metadata appropriate to the particular community use being conceived. The DOI System does not mandate a single metadata standard; someone may use any existing metadata standard; it does however require that for full interoperability the metadata set be mapped to the indecs Data Dictionary.

Association of Application Profile with a DOI name

Every DOI name is associated with one or more Application Profiles (APs). APs, which will themselves be identified by DOI names, are abstractions used to group DOI names into sets in which all DOI names of the given set, or AP, share a metadata schema, business rules for DOI name assignment, and other common characteristics. An AP consists of at least a set of structured metadata elements, plus some rules (policy, business and procedural rules, not all necessarily automated). APs are an aid to using DOI names, enabling all DOI names assigned to e.g. journal articles to behave in a consistent and predictable fashion that would necessarily differ from the characteristics and behaviour of DOI names assigned to e.g. recorded music. An Application Profile groups together characteristics not only of the type of identified entity (roughly what has been called the "genre") but also the intended usage, or application, of the DOI name.

The core elements of an AP will be a metadata schema and various business and procedural rules. The metadata elements common to all members of an AP will be defined through the use of the DOI Data Dictionary, which is an implementation of the indecs data dictionary developed as part of the ISO MPEG-21 process. Entities within this data dictionary will be assigned a unique iid (indecs identifier). In the DOI System implementation of the data dictionary, each iid will also be a DOI name (DOI.iid).

The DOI name/AP relationship can be in one of three states:

- Zero AP: no AP is associated with this DOI name. Most DOI names are currently in this state.
- Base AP: the only data associated with this AP is the kernel metadata (the minimum set of 6 elements, plus the DOI name value and the DOI System AP name).
- Full AP: the kernel metadata plus other metadata (which must be mapped to the DOI Data Dictionary) plus business rules and procedures plus any other common elements such as available services.

APs are intended, as are the other mechanisms, to serve as infrastructure for the coherent management and use of intellectual property. While they will be defined and maintained by communities of interest, probably as represented by IDF Registration Agencies, they may also serve as convenient mechanisms for associating third party services with classes of DOI names. Registries will be established for this purpose. The specific rules and procedures for relating a given AP to third party services will be determined by the creators of that AP. New APs must be approved by the IDF and centrally registered, to minimize duplication of effort and maximize interoperability.

Registration Agencies (RA) add value at various levels by offering services to registrants. There are two mandatory requirements for an RA using the DOI Data Model:

1. To declare the kernel metadata in a standard format
2. To map the full Application Profile to the DOI name standard data dictionary

Once an AP is defined, RAs can offer services in allocating DOI names within this AP, ensuring the AP information is completed, populating the DOI System with allocated DOI names, maintaining up to date records, etc.

Working on a practical development to use the DOI® System

IDF cannot design a solution to the specific problems: only user knows what he wants to achieve. The individual work necessary to build on top of the common infrastructure is done and financed by someone, or in collaboration with anyone else one wish. How much work is needed depends on what someone wants to do. The main tools are (1) handle resolution, and (2) semantic interoperability (metadata). The two tools are the data model framework, which defines the multiple resolutions; and the data dictionary, which defines the metadata in application profiles.

Depending on the depth of work needed, involvement with these technical experts is either free or by arrangement with them under IDF auspices. Others involve work for individual RAs. The cost of these has been charged to RAs at an agreed "IDF" consultancy rate. Where work is limited solely to the mapping and maintenance of an RA's terms to the iDD, Rightscom provides a service at a standard rate for RAs. However, it is common for an RA's iDD-related work and other ontology work to be highly integrated, and where this occurs, no clear separation of the activity, or a standard rate pricing, is possible as other commercial constraints may apply. An exemplar application was developed by IDF and some RAs. This is the Journal-RMD ("Resource Metadata Declaration"), an XSLT stylesheet designed to support the interchange of journal metadata between RAs, based on the existing schemas and requirements of three RAs. Its semantics are integrated with the iDD and it is proposed as a model for data interchange among RAs with other "RMDs" in future. Its development has been paid for by IDF and the participating RAs, and it is wholly owned by the IDF and its RAs.

RESTRICTION AND IDF: THE USAGE OF THE DOI SYSTEM

There are very few restrictions placed on DOI System applications. However they must abide by the rules of the IDF, and must be applications which respect appropriate legal frameworks of intellectual property such as those of the World Intellectual Property Organization. Some restrictions have been placed temporarily, designed to ensure that the system expands in a controlled way: for example, initial applications were restricted to single point resolution; DOI names are currently applied to any creation, but not yet to entities such as people and agreements. The mandate policy rules — for example that no consolidated data about use of a specific DOI name is made public or available to other than the registrant. They also mandate rules as to syntax and services.

RESOLUTION

The process in which an identifier is the input (a request) to a network service to receive in return a specific output of one or more pieces of current information (state data) related to the identified entity: e.g. a location (such as URL) where the object can be found. A name (or unique identifier) for a digital object enables that name to be resolved to one (or many) of several different pieces of data which may be associated with the digital object. Such pieces of data can be locations of the object, or services about the object, or any other defined piece of data. Resolution enables a single name (the identifier, DOI name) to be used persistently to manage the object, even if any of those pieces of data (like location) change. Resolution therefore (a) enables persistence and (b) enables multiple services to be directly associated with the DOI name.

Holding data in the resolution system and association with a DOI name

The core resolution system for all DOI names is the Handle System. Each DOI name is registered as a handle in the Handle System and associated with a set of typed values. These values are returned in response to a resolution request for a given DOI name. The values can be changed while the DOI name remains constant, giving the DOI name its basic qualities of being both actionable and persistent. DOI names, with the exception of certain special cases, are registered with a minimum of one value, of the type "URL". This can generally be thought of as 'location' but it really functions as the default value of the DOI name in the context of the web and may not actually be the location of the identified entity. For anything beyond the simplest DOI name, the declaration of an AP is an additional value within the handle record, with its own data type. The kernel metadata has as one element, "DOI ApplicationProfile," which will reference this same data.

The association of an AP with a DOI name may be sufficient, or may require additional data within the handle record. If services are associated with a given AP, for example, but the location of the service varies with DOI name, then the declaration of the AP may need to be accompanied by the location of the service specific to that DOI name. Similarly, two Registration Agencies (RAs) could share an AP but, in order to determine which RA had registered a given DOI name, the AP declaration would have to be accompanied by an indication of RA. The precise mechanisms for accomplishing these tasks will be defined by the AP. At a certain level of variability across DOI names within an AP, of course, it may be better to create an additional AP rather than stretch one to cover too many different cases. Functional requirements will determine which the case is.

Where data types require entities which are already defined within the DOI System Data Dictionary, the DOI.iid will be referenced. Data types will also be identified by means of DOI names.

The DOI® Data Model and its importance

The DOI Data Model comprises an interoperable structured data dictionary: the indecs Data dictionary (iDD) and a framework for applying it. The data dictionary component is designed to ensure maximum interoperability with existing metadata element sets; the framework allows the terms to be grouped in meaningful ways (DOI System Application Profiles) so that certain types of DOI names all behave predictable in an application through association with specified Services, This provides a means of integrating the features of Handle resolution with a structured data approach. DOI names need not make use of this data model, but it is envisaged that many will: any DOI name intended to allow interoperability is subject to DOI System Metadata policy, which is based on the registration of terms in the iDD.

The DOI Data Model uses the concept of a Kernel set of metadata which is related data about the object. Identifiers are simply names — names that follow a strict convention and are unique if properly applied, but names just the same. Unique identifiers are particularly valuable in machine-mediated commercial environments, where unambiguous identification is crucial. Some identifiers tell someone something about the thing that they identify – for example, since "ISBN" is the acronym of "International Standard Book Number", the identifier "ISBN 1-900512-44-0" can reasonably safely be assumed to identify a book (always assuming that ISBN rules have been correctly followed, which is not universally the case). However, to find out *which* book it identifies, it is necessary to consult metadata – the identifier links the metadata with the entity it identifies and with other metadata about the same entity. The Data Model is an integral part of making the identifier useful. Further, to be useful in the widest sense that metadata must be interoperable with other schemes. The Data Model approach used by the DOI System has no inherent commercial model.

DOI System stresses interoperability, resolution and metadata

The DOI System uses an interoperable structured data dictionary: the indecs Data dictionary (iDD). The DOI Data Model embraces both this data dictionary and a framework for applying it. The data dictionary component is designed to ensure maximum interoperability with existing metadata element sets; the framework allows the terms to be grouped in meaningful ways (DOI Application Profiles) so that certain types of DOI names all behave predictably in an application through association with specified Services. This provides a means of integrating the features of Handle resolution with a structured data approach. DOI names need not make use of this data model, but it is envisaged that many will: any DOI name intended to allow interoperability is subject to DOI System Metadata policy, which is based on the registration of terms in the iDD.

DOI name resolution allows identifier interoperability. An Application Profile is the hook into metadata semantic interoperability. The AP approach is built on indecs principles also adopted elsewhere such as ISO MPEG 21. DOI names resolve to one or more typed values in the Handle System and it is these typed values that determine client behavior. The predominant client at the moment is a proxy, or gateway, at dx.doi.org that takes normal http GETs, e.g., http://dx.doi.org/10.123/456 where the DOI name is 10.123/456, resolves the DOI name in the Handle System looking for URLs and returns those URLs to the originating web browser as http re-directs. This is how most DOI names currently implement a single level of indirection. Using a dedicated client, such as a plug-in for Acrobat, opens this up considerably, letting us use different data types for different purposes.

Current technologies on the Web and DOI

a. DOI names are designed for use in any digital networks, not just the World Wide Web, which is only one recent aspect of the evolution of digital networks and the use of digital objects within them. DOI names can be used in open or proprietary digital networks in broadcasting, multimedia systems, or indeed any conceptual framework. Even on the Web, only some aspects such as single redirection can be accomplished with some existing technologies. However no other current technologies offer the same packaged combination of multiple resolution; well-formed metadata; semantic analysis and mapping to metadata schemes; social infrastructure; and non-proprietary non-commercial operation supported by a wide range of content and technology providers.

Since identifiers like DOI names deliberately set out to provide advantages over existing, but widely deployed and implemented, mechanisms such as DNS and http, they need to be able to use those existing mechanisms. This is done via gateways into those existing widely implemented schemes. A gateway provides a means of accessing the functionality of one server through another.

b. DOI System metadata relation with the Dublin Core Metadata Initiative

Dublin Core aims to be an easy-to-create and maintain descriptive format to facilitate cross-domain resource discovery on the Web. "Qualified Dublin Core" supports the use of DC elements as the basis for extended but simple statements about resources, rather than as a foundation for more descriptive clauses. Complex descriptions may be necessary for some Web resources and for some purposes, such as administration, preservation, and reference linking. However, complex descriptions require more expressive data models that differentiate between agents, documents, contexts, events, and the like. This is achieved through the indecs model. While DC starts from a small group of "core" elements, and DOI Application Profiles include a small group of "kernel" elements, the two do not serve the same purpose. The kernel is derived from a comprehensive data model and has strict rules for mandating implementation. The Resource Metadata Declaration provides a tool set for extending metadata declarations to any desired set of entities, comparable therefore to DC-qualified but with the significant difference of a basis in an underlying comprehensive semantics to ensure consistency of all declarations for any purpose.

The DOI Data Model enables semantic interoperability between APs devised for any purpose (not only simple description but more complex events), so that "cross-domain" tools and applications can do so consistently and effectively. Such semantic interoperability will be required for widespread digital use of information from multiple sources.

c. Using a DOI name in a Web Browser

Applications using DOI names can be constructed on a web site with full functionality behind the scenes. For some applications, this may require additional functionality such as that supplied in the Handle System. DOI names are URIs (URNs) not URLs: they are names, not locations. Most web browsers support locations (URLs) but have limited functionality for names, though this is expected to improve substantially in the near future. However, DOI names are useable with browsers immediately.

d. Use of DOI name to locate specific local copy, which may have different access rights

The DOI System is for resolution of identifiers to global services. However it can be used with other complementary technologies, such as OpenURL, to allow the contextualization of requests to those services to local requirements. Registration Agencies such as CrossRef offer practical implementation of the DOI System with such local linking technology.

It is also possible to deal even with individual copies by identifying them by DOI names, though it may not always be appropriate. DOI names can be used to identify any resource: in CrossRef for example, the DOI name is allocated to the abstraction representing the article work. In other applications, different DOI names might be allocated to different formats, or even to individual instances.

e. Specifying format, DOI name registry: Abstract, HTML, PDF etc.

The assigner determines what a DOI name is resolved to. However, this needs a little more explanation. DOI names are assigned through RAs, and the RA does so in order to provide a service or application through persistent identification (e.g., CrossRef's reference linking service). Each RA will have its rules about what is resolved to from each DOI name its clients assign, in order to furnish that service.

For uses which are truly interoperable, it is recommended that the assigner of a DOI name must specify precisely what is being identified. Precisely here means through well-formed metadata. What is being identified need not be the same as what is resolved to. There can be no general rule which applies to all cases and each must be treated in context. Two digital entities are never the same in any absolute sense and can be considered copies of each other (the same) only in the context of some defined purpose.

f. Appropriateness of DOI names for use with non-public material such as a report that may never be published

The DOI System is designed principally for interoperability, which implies use by many users who aren't intimately connected. The key functionalities of the DOI System (persistence, interoperability, extensibility, efficiency, dynamic updating) may well be useful for internal systems. If users are going to manage information, then some level of identification and metadata is going to be necessary. Use of the DOI System can offer an off-the-shelf means of doing so by removing the need to develop a one-off solution which would not necessarily integrate with other systems, and make it very easy to make the document public later if this is appropriate. DOI "Restricted" Application Profiles are designed for applications where even the basic kernel is of a much restricted visibility and not for use outside of that application (e.g. applications in the defense and pharmaceutical research sector for example).

The benefits of the DOI System for Publishers, Intermediaries, and users

The DOI System offers a unique set of functionality:

- Persistence, if material is moved, rearranged, or bookmarked;

- Interoperability with other data from other sources;
- Extensibility by adding new features and services through management of groups of DOI names;
- Single management of data for multiple output formats (platform independence);
- Class management of applications and services;
- Dynamic updating of metadata, applications and services.

For users, these features provide the ability to:

- Know what someone have
- Find what someone want
- Know where it exists
- Be able to get it
- Be able to use it in a transaction

Claiming copyright and trademark on the DOI System

Persistence is a function of organizations not technology. The principle concern of a persistent organization is of continuing funding. The implementation of the DOI System adds value, but necessarily incurs some resource costs: in data management, infrastructure provision and governance, all of which contribute to persistence.

To make such a system work effectively requires protection of the assets within the system (1) from illicit exploitation, and (2) for assured quality control. Illicit exploitation would include someone calling something a DOI name when it is not part of the official system; this could be damaging to either or both the financial health (avoiding payment of an issuing fee) or the quality of the system (poor quality data). To prevent this requires the availability of legal remedies: specifically, the DOI System relies on copyright and trademark law to protect the DOI System brand and reputation. The DOI System is not a patented system; the IDF has not developed any patent claims on the DOI System and does not rely on patent law for remedy.

The underlying technologies used by the DOI System also have similar considerations. The Handle System is used by IDF under license from the Corporation for National Research Initiatives, who have certain intellectual property claims to protect the misuse of the Handle System; indecs intellectual property (IP) is assigned to, jointly and solely, IDF and EDItEUR and made available freely but under stated terms to others.

Popularity of the DOI System today

Several hundred different registrant organizations have so far allocated several million DOI names. Because the origins of the DOI System were in the text sector, an initial large implementation covering half of these registrants was from traditional print-publishing companies that have already established major online publishing programs. However the fundamental design of the system is applicable to any media or content. The IDF is working closely with many businesses in other sectors of the "content industries" to extend the application of DOI names to many other types of intellectual property.

DOI names can be used by anyone, independent of the applications that may have been originally devised by the registrant. Particular communities may develop applications which involve assigning DOI names not by the original publisher but by other parties appropriate to that sector of interest. DOI name users can be at any point in an information chain — intermediary, retailer, user, producer, agent, etc, in the same way as the physical bar code is useful to (and used by) a range of retailers, logistics companies, re-sellers etc even though the code is originally assigned by a manufacturer.

The DOI System can help to ensure smooth operation

in these supply chains by defining business rules for a particular DOI® Application Profile. These can state who in the supply chain is responsible for assigning a DOI name in that particular application: rules agreed and defined by the user community, not by the IDF. The DOI System can also help by creating automated links: if there are related DOI names in other Application Profiles a link can be made using multiple resolutions; if there are other forms of identifiers not in the form of DOI names, like SKUs, these can be carried as part of the metadata.

"DOI System Service"

A defined result from a defined action i.e., does X and the result will be Y. DOI System services perform specific functions when presented with data from Application Profiles. Services exchange data, share tasks, and automate processes over the Internet by using the information associated with a DOI name. The term was coined in analogy to "Web services": for DOI System applications on the Web, DOI System services would be Web Services. As a new class of Internet-native applications, web services promise to increase interoperability and lower the costs of software integration and data interchange: these aims are clearly identical to those of DOI name (and its underlying tools of resolution — Handle System — and metadata — indecs framework). Based on unambiguous rules, DOI System services make it possible for computer programs to communicate directly with one another and exchange data about intellectual property entities regardless of location, operating systems, or languages.

The combination of data typing through the resolution system, and interoperable metadata accessed through an Application Profile, provides a powerful set of tools for the creation of DOI System services.

Role of the International DOI Foundation

The IDF governs the DOI System, to ensure that all applications follow common rules. The system itself has several components: the technology is based on open agreed standards, while the infrastructure is defined by agreements between the various organizations which run the system, such as the Registration Agencies and the technology providers.

Joining the International DOI Foundation community allows someone to instantly leverage years of intelligent policies, standards development and other value-adds, yet not limit in any way the own autonomy or ability to organize/ create the own activities. The framework is open enough to leave tremendous room for a community's own autonomy, activities, and control. Working together rather than dividing efforts is a sensible way forward.

STANDARDS AND SPECIFICATIONS

1. ISO TC46/SC9 Standards

The DOI® System is currently being standardized through the International Standards Organization, ISO. In April 2008 the Committee Draft prepared by an international Working Group was approved, after voting by ISO's national bodies, for distribution as a Draft International Standard (DIS). In February 2009, ISO provided further editorial comments on that draft. A further revised draft was submitted to ISO on 2 April 2009. Depending upon the result of ISO activities and further voting, the final standard may be published in 2009 or 2010.

2. Internet Engineering Task Force (IETF) Request For Comments (RFC)

DOI is a registered URI within the info-URI namespace (IETF RFC 4452, the "info" URI Scheme for Information Assets with Identifiers in Public Namespaces). DOI names may be expressed as URLs through a proxy server. A URL is a URI that, "in addition to identifying a resource, [provides] a means of locating the resource by describing its primary access mechanism (e.g., its network 'location')."

The DOI System is an implementation of the *Handle System*. There are three Handle System RFCs:

- Sun, Sam; Lannom, Larry; Boesch, Brian. "*Handle System Overview*". RFC 3650, November 2003.
- Sun, Sam; Reilly, Sean; Lannom, Larry. "*Handle System Namespace and Service Definition*". RFC 3651, November 2003.
- Sun, Sam; Reilly, Sean; Lannom, Larry; Petrone, Jason. "*Handle System Protocol (Ver 2.1) Specification*". RFC 3652, November 2003.

3. ISO/IEC MPEG21 Standards

DOI names use a semantic data dictionary and the IDF is the formal Registration Authority of the MPEG21 Rights Data dictionary.

4. NISO Standards

The DOI syntax is a NISO standard.

RELATED TECHNOLOGIES

1. Handle System

DOI names are an implementation of the CNRI Handle System®, in which the term "DOI" is used instead of "handle" to describe the identifiers.

2. Indecs Data Dictionary

DOI names use a semantic data dictionary, the indecs data dictionary, which is based on work including the original indecs project and its further development into the MPEG21 Rights Data dictionary.

3. Persistent Identifiers

THE BENEFITS OF DOI LINKING VS. URL LINKING

1. Information-Based (Object-Based) vs. Location-Based

Whereas a URL only links to information by its location, the DOI links to the information successfully regardless of its location. Thus access to the information is "future-proofed" against any redesigns of the website, migrations of the information to other servers, outsourcing/insourcing of the content hosting, divestiture of the content to another company, etc.

2. Permanent, Persistent and Dynamic vs. Temporary and Static

URLs are temporary and static. Once the object is placed at a server location, the URL and all downstream web references pointing to that URL (e.g., search engine results, user bookmarks, links on other websites, etc.) are fixed. Thus, when the object is moved, the user's attempted link results in an "Error Message 404, File Not Found."

DOI-based links, on the other hand, by virtue of the underlying technology, are both permanent and dynamic such that the object owner can alter the URL at which the object is located without interfering with any of the existing web references. Thus, search engine results and bookmarks are never out-of-date and no 404 error messages result. Even if these links were hard-coded into downloaded files (e.g., via PDFs, Word documents, eBooks, etc.), printed onto paper, fixed onto CD-ROMs, etc., they still will link properly. In short, the DOI permanently represents the object itself, regardless of location, and the location can be changed with whatever frequency the owner wishes without disrupting the user experience.

3. Object-Based (at Any Desired Level of Granularity or Specificity or Deep-Linking) vs. Title-Based or More General

URLs often link only to a company home page, or section of a website, or some other general level of information. Even when they refer to an individual work of intellectual property (such as a book), they typically link only at the title level. Although URLs are capable of linking more "deeply" to a more specific item, they usually don't, partly because of the difficulty of maintaining unbroken links at such a detail level. But the DOI links to any level of "object," and/or to its component parts: entire book/individual chapters; music collection/individual tracks; any product/individual components; database record/individual fields; journal article/individual sections; software programs/individual routines; etc.

4. MultiLinking vs. Single Linking

Existing URL linking affords to the user only one location to which to be sent (routed), whereas DOI-based linking enables one-to-many linking ("MultiLinking"). A DOI-based link (or "MultiLink".) offers a menu of choices to any number of locations, services or related information - all established at the discretion of the object owner. In addition, downstream users of the DOI (e.g., via full content syndication, partner-based linking, etc.) can select from among the owner's MultiLink choices for the purpose of customizing their own applications to leverage the DOI and its infrastructure. Further, these downstream applications neither incur cost nor require maintenance. Further still, when users or organizations insert DOI links onto their websites, into their browser bookmarks or into their own documents, the DOI will retain its persistence concurrent with this DOI MultiLink feature, enriching the user experience by increasing functionality well beyond a URL.

Thus, a digital object provider has the ability via a single link to route users to as many locations for as many purposes as it might wish, all depending upon its own business strategies, sales and marketing efforts, customer service support, rights & permissions activities, etc. Further, downstream users of the DOI (including distributors, aggregators and retailers) also are enabled to adopt the routing options that best suit their needs, thus empowering each DOI adopter to derive his/her own value proposition by applying the DOI from the original object provider.

5. "Exporting" the Power of the Existing Website out to the Rest of the World

The own website already possesses rich and well-designed interlinking amongst the various products, including links to marketing information and other related info designed to convince consumers to buy or subscribe to the products. Now someone can exponentially leverage this existing investment in design and interlinking by exporting these interlinks wherever a DOI travels on the Internet. Someone can bring people back to the site and better still, directly to any/all deep links someone has already created, whenever a person encounters one of the DOIs anywhere in the world - not only on the own site, but in an email from a friend, in a downloaded document or music file or video clip, on a 3rd party website that one otherwise do not control, in a newspaper or magazine article, in reviews of all kinds (book/music/movie/product reviews), etc.

6. Improving the "Discoverability" and Exposure of the Content

Simply creating a web page does not guarantee that the rest of the world will find it, but registering a DOI ensures that it will be exposed to the outside world. Even the major Search Engines do not see or touch or index most web pages, especially those pertaining to actual published material, even though this represents the world's truly high-value, authentic, vetted, quality-assured, monetizable content. Most of these pages are invisible to Search Engines because they are locked behind subscription barriers, firewalls, or the proprietary search engines of individual websites. Registering a DOI, however, exposes the content's existence to the outside world, as well as guaranteeing much higher Search Engine rankings because the DOI exposes the interrelatedness of the content with other content via CDI's MultiLinking process.

7. Automated Link Lookup and Insertion vs. Manual Link Lookup and Insertion

Content owners who want to insert within their documents or onto their websites DOI hyperlinks that direct users to related (their own or others') content (e.g., intra- and/or inter-publisher citation linking), are able to insert DOI links into the appropriate places just as they can URLs today. The process of DOI lookup and insertion, however, can be fully automated and scaled for volume (e.g. to populate an entire magazine issue, a book's bibliography and footnotes, or an encyclopedia with external link-outs), whereas any URL-based interlinking process is entirely manual and thus limited in practical application due to time and cost.

REFERENCES AND NOTES

1. Arms, William Y. 2000. Automated Digital Libraries: How Effectively Can Computers Be Used for the Skilled Tasks of Professional Librarianship? *D-Lib Magazine*. 6(7/8). <http://www.dlib.org/dlib/july00/arms/07arms.html>
2. Berners-Lee, T.; Masinter, L., and McCahill, M. 1994. RFC1738: Uniform Resource Locators (URL). <http://search.ietf.org/rfc/rfc1738.txt?number=1738>
3. Caplan, Priscilla and Arms, William Y. 1999. Reference Linking for Journal Articles. *D-Lib Magazine*. 5(7/8).
4. Okerson, Ann and O'Donnell, James. 1995. Scholarly

Journals at the Crossroads; A Subversive Proposal for Electronic Publishing. Association of Research Libraries; Washinton DC. <http://www.arl.org/scomm/subversive/toc.html>.

5. http://www.crossref.org/
6. http://www.crossref.org/help/Content/01_About_ DOIs/About_DOIs.htm
7. http://www.crossref.org/help/Content/02_Getting_started/JoiningCrossRef.htm
8. http://www.crossref.org/help/Content/03_The%20CrossRef%20user%20interfaces/The%20CrossRef%20user%20interfaces.htm
9. Paskin, Norman and Lannom, Larry. 2000. From One to Many. <http://dx.doi.org/10.1000/190>
10. ONIX Web site <http://www.editeur.org/onix.html>.
11. Lagoze, Carl. "Keeping Dublin Core Simple - Cross-Domain Discovery or Resource Description?" *D-Lib Magazine*, January 2001 <doi:10.1045/january2001-lagoze>.
12. <http://www.dlib.org/dlib/july99/caplan/07caplan. html>
13. NISO. 2000. Report on the Meeting held July 24, 2000 at CNRI, Reston, Va. NISO/DLF/CrossRef Workshop on Localization in Reference Linking. <http://www.niso.org/CNRI-mtg.html
14. http://www.crossref.org/help/Content/04_Queries_and_retrieving/CrossRef%20Data%20Formats.htm
15. http://www.crossref.org/help/Content/05_Interfacing_with_the_CrossRef_system/Interfacing_with_the_CrossRef_system.htm
16. Psycoloquy open access journal, <http://psycprints.ecs.soton.ac.uk/>.
17. [Public] Public Library of Science, <http://www.publiclibraryofscience.org/>.
18. PubMed Central, <http://www.pubmedcentral.nih.gov/>.
19. Quint, B. (2002) "The Digital Library of the Future: CrossRef Search and QuestionPoint offer challenges to traditional services". *Information Today*, Vol. 19, No. 7, July/August.

<http://www.infotoday.com/it/jul02/quint.htm>.

20. Reference linking API, <http://www.cs.cornell.edu/cdlrg/Reference%20Linking>.
21. RefLinking demonstrator, <>.
22. NEC ResearchIndex, <http://citeseer.nj.nec.coma>.
23. http://www.crossref.org/08downloads/CR_Membership Agreement.pdf
24. http://www.crossref.org/02publishers/20pub_fees.html
25. http://www.crossref.org/help/Content/04_Queries_and_retrieving/Deposits/Deposits.htm
26. RoMEO project, <http://www.lboro.ac.uk/departments/ls/disresearch/romeo/index.html>.
27. InterParty Web site <http://www.interparty.org>.
28. Zaret, Elliot. "Internet Pioneer Urges Overhaul", Interview with Robert E. Kahn, CNRI. MSNBC, November 21, 2000. <http://www.doi.org/news/msnbc_rkahn_interview.pdf>.
29. Farber, Dan. "It's time to rebuild the Internet". *ZDNet Tech Update*, May 21,2003 <http://techupdate.zdnet.com/techupdate/stories/main/0,14179,2913761,00.html>.
30. [OAF] Open Archives Forum, <http://www.oaforum.org/index.php>.
31. [Nixon] Nixon, W. (2002) "The evolution of an institutional e-prints archive at the University of Glasgow". *Ariadne*, issue 32, July. <http://www.ariadne.ac.uk/issue32/eprint-archives/>.
32. [OAI-aggegator] OAI Aggregator 'Celestial', <http://celestial.eprints.org>.
33. [OAI-implementers] OAI-implementers discussion list, thread: XSD file for qualified DC, <http://www.openarchives.org/pipermail/oai-implementers/2002-June/000518.html>.
34. http://www.crossref.org/metadata_services_fees.html
35. http://www.crossref.org/02publishers/20pub_fees.html#local
36. http://www.crossref.org/help/Content/06_Maintaining

%20DOIs/Transferring_DOI_ownership.htm

37. Harnad, S. (1998) "The invisible hand of peer review". *Nature* [online] (c. 5 November). <http://helix.nature.com/webmatters/invisible/invisible.html>. Longer version: *Exploit Interactive*, issue 5, April 2000 <http://www.exploit-lib.org/issue5/peer-review>.

38. Harnad, S. (2001) "Research Access, Impact and Assessment". *Times Higher Education Supplement*, Vol. 1487, 18 May, p. 16.

39. Paskin, Norman. "On Making and Identifying a 'Copy'". *D-Lib Magazine*, January 2003 <doi:10.1045/january2003-paskin>.

40. http://www.crossref.org/04intermediaries/35request_mem.html

41. http://www.crossref.org/guestquery

42. http://www.crossref.org/SimpleTextQuery

43. http://www.crossref.org/help/Content/05_Interfacing_with_the_CrossRef_system/Using_OAI_PMH.htm

44. http://www.crossref.org/04intermediaries/35request_mem.html

45. Van de Sompel, Herbert and Hochstenbach, Patrick. 1999a. Reference Linking in a Hybrid Library Environment. Part 1: Frameworks for Linking. *D-Lib Magazine*. 5(4). <http://www.dlib.org/dlib/april99/van_de_sompel/04van_de_sompel-pt1.html>

46. Van de Sompel, Herbert and Hochstenbach, Patrick. 1999b. Reference Linking in a Hybrid Library Environment. Part 2:SFX, a Generic Linking Solution. *D-Lib Magazine*. 5(4). <http://www.dlib.org/dlib/april99/van_de_sompel/04van_de_sompel-pt2.html>

47. Van de Sompel, Herbert and Hochstenbach, Patrick. 1999c. Reference Linking in a Hybrid Library Environment. Part 3: Generalizing the SFX solution in the "SFX@Ghent & SFX@LANL" experiment. *D-Lib Magazine*. 5(10). <http://www.dlib.org/dlib/october99/van_de_sompel/10van_de_sompel.html> '

48. http://www.crossref.org/help/Content/Appendices/CrossRef%20Schema.htm

49. http://www.crossref.org/help/Content/04_Queries_and_retrieving/Deposits/Verifying_your_XML.htm
50. http://www.crossref.org/help/Content/03_The%20CrossRef%20user%20interfaces/Using_web_interface_to_deposit_files.htm
51. http://www.crossref.org/help/Content/05_Interfacing_with_the_CrossRef_system/Using_HTTP_to_POST.htm
52. http://xerces.apache.org/
53. http://www.crossref.org/help/Content/05_Interfacing_with_the_CrossRef_system/Tracking_submissions.htm
54. Van de Sompel, Herbert. July 2000. CrossRef – DOI – OpenURL – SFX demo using IDEAL metadatabase & enhanced DOI proxy. < http://www.sfxit.com/crossref/prototype1.html>
55. Van de Sompel, Herbert; Hochstenbach, Patrick and Beit-Arie, Oren. 2000. OpenURL syntax description. <http://www.sfxit.com/openurl/openurl.html>
56. Van de Sompel, Herbert and Hochstenbach, Patrick. 2000. Cookiepusher document. <http://www.sfxit.com/openurl/cookiepusher.html>
57. Van de Sompel, Herbert; Krichel, Thomas, Nelson, Michael L. and others. 2000. The UPS Prototype: An Experimental End-User Service across E-Print Archives. *D-Lib Magazine*. 6(2). <http://www.dlib.org/dlib/february00/vandesompel-ups/02vandesompel-ups.html>
58. *DOI Handbook* <http://www.doi.org/hb.html>.
59. http://www.crossref.org/schema/crossref_output3.0.1.xsd
60. http://www.publishers.org/digital/index.cfm
61. The Living Internet: Web Browser History. <http://livinginternet.com/?w/wi_browse.htm>.
62. And are still with us: "the rate at which once-valid links start pointing at non-existent addresses – a process called "link rot" – is as high as 16 percent in six months. That means that about one sixth of all links will break". Dowling, Thomas; "One Step at a Time", *Library Journal* Fall 2001, page 36.

<http://libraryjournal.reviewsnews. com/index.asp?layout=article&articleid= CA178131&publication=libraryjournal>.

63. "History of the Dublin Core Metadata Initiative" <http://dublincore.org/about/history/>.
64. Dekkers, Makx and Weibel, Stuart. "State of the Dublin Core Metadata Initiative, April 2003" *D-Lib Magazine*, April 2003, <doi:10.1045/april2003-weibel>.
65. "History of Google" <http://www.google.com/corporate/history.html>.
66. Green, Brian & Bide, Mark. (1997) "Unique Identifiers: a brief introduction". Book Industry Communication/EDItEUR <http://www.bic.org.uk/uniquid.html>.
67. Rust, Godfrey, and Bide, Mark. "The <*indecs*> Metadata Framework: Principles, model and data dictionary." 2000. <http://www.indecs.org/pdf/framework.pdf>.
68. International DOI Foundation Web Site <http://www.doi.org>.
69. Kahn, Robert E. & Wilensky, Robert. "A Framework for Distributed Digital Object Services". Corporation for National Research Initiatives (CNRI), Reston, Virginia, 1995. <hdl:4263537/5001>.
70. Pat. No. 6135,646 - System for uniquely and persistently identifying, managing and tracking digital objects - 10/24/00.
71. Paskin, Norman. "DOI: Current Status and Outlook". *D-Lib Magazine*, May 1999. [A summary of DOI progress as of mid-1999.] <doi:10.1045/may99-paskin> .
72. Paskin, Norman and Lannom, Laurence. "From one to many". International DOI Foundation, August 2000. <doi:10.1000/190>.
73. CrossRef Web Site www.crossref.org <http://www.crossref.org>.
74. HDL/DOI Plug-in for Adobe Acrobat and Acrobat Reader - Beta Version 1.0 <http://www.handle.net/hs-tools/adobe/download>.

75. Paskin, Norman. "Identification and Metadata". (To be published in *Digital Rights Management: Technical, Economical, Juridical, and Political Aspects in the European Union*), in the series "Lecture Notes in Computer Science" (Springer-Verlag, 2003) <http://www.doi.org/topics/drm_paskin_20030113_b1.pdf>.

76. Klimes, Ivan. "The science of science publishing"; *imi insights*, April 2003 1-4 <http://www.epsltd.com/IMI/IMI.htm> [subscriber access].

77. Spedding, Vanessa. "Journal Cross-Linking - The Web's potential untangled". *Research Information*, July 2002. <http://www.researchinformation.info/feature1a.html>.

78. http://www.crossref.org/guestquery

79. http://www.crossref.org/

80. http://www.crossref.org/help/Content/01_About_DOIs/Viewing_CrossRef_publishers_ and_titles.htm

81. Example:http://www.crossref.org/help/Content/05_Interfacing_with_the_CrossRef_system/Using_HTTP.htm

82. http://www.crossref.org/help/Content/03_The%20CrossRef%20user%20interfaces/The%20CrossRef%20user%20interfaces.htm

83. Vogt, Sjoerd. "Investigative Report: Resolving the Links"; *Information Today*, April 2003, Vol 20, Issue 4, p.25.

84. IDF Press release, April 2003: "Common Dictionary for DOI and ONIX tadata" <http://www.doi.org/news/030415 dictionarynews.pdf>.

85. De Soto, Hernando. *The Mystery of Capital: Why Capitalism triumphs in the west and fails everywhere else*. Basic Books 2000. <http://www.ild.org.pe/tmoc/cp1-en.htm>.

86. Caplan, Priscilla et al. "Linking to the Appropriate Copy: Report of a DOI-Based Prototype". *D-Lib Magazine*, September 2001. <doi:10.1045/september2001-caplan>.

87. Rosenblatt, Bill. "Enterprise Content Integration with the Digital Object Identifier: A Business Case for Information Publishers", June 2002. <http://doi.contentdirections.com/mr/cdi.jsp?doi=10.1220/whitepaper5>.

88. Hunter, Jane. "MetaNet - A Metadata Term Thesaurus to Enable Semantic Interoperability Between Metadata Domains." <http://archive.dstc.edu.au/RDU/staff/jane-hunter/harmony/jodi_article.html>.

89. DOI Registration Agencies: <http://www.doi.org/registration_agencies.html>.

90. MEDRA (multilingual European DOI Registration Agency) <http://www.medra.org/Content/project. htm>.

91. http://www.doi.org/welcome.html,

92. http://www.doi.org/registration_agencies.html

93. http://www.doi.org/

94. Worlock, David. "DOI: Starting a new Generation", *EPS Update Note*, 8th May 2003 <http://www.doi.org/news/EPS080503-DOIs.pdf>.

95. *Protecting Your Digital Assets: Technical Journal Publishers Lead the Way Using Digital Object Identifiers.* Patricia Seybold Group, 2003 <http://www.doi.org/topics/Protect_Digital_Asset.pdf>.

96. Rosenblatt, Bill. "Rights Expression Languages: The Key to DRM Interoperability"; *The Seybold Report*, Vol 2 No 24, April 2003 <http://www.seyboldreports.com/TSR/index.html>. [subscriber access]

97. Brooks, Ken. Publishing Dimensions, Inc. (personal communication)

98. IDF Press release, April 2003: "National Libraries Join International DOI oundation" <http://www.doi.org/news/030417-Library.html>.

99. ANSI/NISO draft standard for trial use (Z39.88-2003) May 1 - Nov 30 2003 <http://library.caltech.edu/openurl/PubComDocs/Announce/20030416-Announce-Trial.htm>.

100. NISO Committee AX Public Comments <http://library.caltech.edu/openurl/Public_Comments.htm>.

101. Bruning, Dennis. "Interview with Herbert van der Sompel, Creator of OpenURL/SFX"; *The Charleston Advisor*, Volume 4, Number 4, April 2003. <http://charlestonco.com/features.cfm?id=124&type=np>.

102. "OpenURL and CrossRef" <http://www.crossref.org/03libraries/16openurl.html>.

103. IDF "Alliances and Liaisons with Other Organizations" <http://www.doi.org/handbook_2000/governance.html#7.11>.

104. ANSI/NISO Standard Z39.84-2000. "Syntax for the Digital Object Identifier": <http://www.niso.org/standards/standard_detail.cfm?std_id=480>.

105. Nelson, Michael (Director Internet Technology and Strategy, IBM). "Industry Perspectives on the Future of the Cyberinfrastructure"; <http://www.dtic.mil/cendi/minutes/pa_1202.html>.

106. "Getting a Handle on Federal Information: Persistent Identification Using Handles" <http://www.dtic.mil/cendi/activities/01_29_03_handles_overview.html>.

107. Smith, MacKenzie, Barton, Mary, Branschofsky, Margret, McClellan, Greg, Walker, Julie Harford, Bass, Mick, Stuve, Dave, Tansley, Robert. "DSpace: An Open Source Dynamic Digital Repository", *D-Lib Magazine*, January 2003. <doi:10.1045/january2003-smith>.

108. CORES Standards Interoperability Forum Resolution on Metadata Element Identifiers <http://www.cores-eu.net/interoperability/cores-resolution/cores-resolution.pdf>.

109. Crossref

110. Anan, H. et al. (2002) "Preservation and Transition of NCSTRL Using an OAI-Based Architecture". *Proceedings of the Second ACM/IEEE Joint Conference on Digital Libraries*, Portland, Oregon, July. <http://128.82.7.99/ncstrl/p183-anan.doc>.

111. [Arc] Arc search service, <http://arc.cs.odu.edu>.

112. [Archon] Archon, <http://archon.cs.odu.edu>.

113. [Arms] Arms, W. Y. (2000) "Automated Digital Libraries: How Effectively Can Computers Be Used for the Skilled Tasks of Professional Librarianship?" *D-Lib Magazine*, Vol. 6, No. 7/8, July/August. <http://www.dlib.org/dlib/july00/arms/07arms.html>.

114. arXiv, <http://arxiv.org/>.

115. Atkins, H. (1999) "The ISI Web of Science - Links and Electronic Journals". *D-Lib Magazine*, Vol. 5 No. 9, September 1999. <http://www.dlib.org/dlib/september99/atkins/09atkins.html>.

116. Beit-Arie, O. et al. (2001) "Linking to the Appropriate Copy: Report of a DOI-Based Prototype". *D-Lib Magazine*, Vol. 7, No. 9, September <http://www.dlib.org/dlib/september01/caplan/09caplan.html>.

117. Bergmark, D. (2000) "Automatic Extraction of Reference Linking Information from Online Documents". Technical Report TR 2000-1821, Cornell Computer Science Department, November <http://www.cs.cornell.edu/cdlrg/Reference%20Linking/extraction.pdf>.

118. Bergmark, D. and Lagoze, C. (2001) "An Architecture for Automatic Reference Linking". *5th European Conference on Research and Advanced Technology for Digital Libraries (ECDL)*, Darmstadt, September. <http://www.cs.cornell.edu/cdlrg/Reference%20Linking/tr1842.ps>

119. BioMed Central, <http://www.biomedcentral.com/>.

120. Brin, S. and Page, L. (1998) "The Anatomy of a Large-Scale Hypertextual Web Search Engine". *Seventh International World Wide Web Conference*, Brisbane, April. <http://www7.scu.edu.au/programme/fullpapers/1921/com1921.htm>.

121. Brody, T., Carr, L. and Harnad, S. (2002) "Evidence of Hypertext in the Scholarly Archive". *Proceedings of HT'02, the 13th ACM Conference on Hypertext*, University of Maryland, June. <http://opcit.eprints.org/ht02-short/archiveht-ht02.pdf>.

122. Budapest Open Access Initiative, <http://www.soros.org/openaccess/read.shtml>.

123. Caplan, P. and Flecker, D. (1999) "Choosing the Appropriate Copy". *NISO News*, September. <http://www.niso.org/news/reports/DLFarch.html>.

124. Celestial, <http://celestial.eprints.org>.

125. Claivaz, J.-B. et al. (2001) "From Fulltext Documents to Structured Citations: CERN's Automated Solution". *HEP*

Libraries Webzine, Issue 5, November. <http://library.cern.ch/HEPLW/5/papers/2/>

126. Citebase, <http://citebase.eprints.org/cgi-bin/search>.
127. CogPrints, <http://cogprints.soton.ac.uk/>.
128. Crow, R. (2002) "The Case for Institutional Repositories: A SPARC Position Paper". Scholarly Publishing & Academic Resources Coalition, Washington, D.C., July. <http://www.arl.org/sparc/IR/ir.html>.
129. [DLF] Digital Library Federation, <http://www.diglib.org/architectures/testbed.htm>.
130. [Dublin Core] Dublin Core Citation Working Group, <http://www.dublincore.org/groups/citation>.
131. E-Prints UK, <http://www.rdn.ac.uk/projects/eprints-uk>.
132. Hellman, E. (2001) "Building a database for e-journals". Web4Lib Electronic Discussion, 17th October. <http://sunsite.berkeley.edu/Web4Lib/archive/0110/0175.html>
133. Van de Sompel, H. and Beit-Arie, O. (2001) "Open Linking in the Scholarly Information Environment Using the OpenURL Framework". *D-Lib Magazine*, Vol. 7, No. 3, March. <http://www.dlib.org/dlib/march01/vandesompel/03vandesompel.html>.
134. Velterop, J. (2002) "BioMed Central. What we do and what we don't do". American-Scientist-E-PRINT-Forum, August 14th. <http://www.ecs.soton.ac.uk/ ~harnad/Hypermail/Amsci/2228.html>.
135. Waters, D. J. (2001) "The Metadata Harvesting Initiative of the Mellon Foundation". *ARL Bimonthly Report*, No. 217, August. <http://www.arl.org/newsltr/217/waters.html>.
136. GQuery citation visualisation <http://www.cs.cornell.edu/cdlrg/Reference%20Linking/XGQuery.html>.
137. Hitchcock, S. et al. (1998) "Webs of Research: Putting the User in Control". *Internet Research and Information for Social Scientists (IRISS) 1998 Conference*, Bristol, March. <http://sosig.ac.uk/iriss/papers/paper42.htm>.
138. Hitchcock, S. et al. (1998) "Linking electronic journals:

Lessons from the Open Journal project". *D-Lib Magazine*, December. <http://www.dlib.org/dlib/december98/12hitchcock.html>.

139. Hitchcock, S. et al. (2000) "Developing services for open eprint archives: globalisation, integration and the impact of links". *Proceedings of the Fifth ACM Conference on Digital Libraries*, June (ACM: New York), pp. 143-151. <http://opcit.eprints.org/dl00/dl00.html>.

140. [Hunter] Hunter, K. (1998) "Adding Value by Adding Links". *Journal of Electronic Publishing*, Vol. 3, No. 3, March. <http://www.press.umich.edu/jep/03-03/hunter.html>.

141. Lawrence, S., Giles, C. L. and Bollacker, K. (1999) "Digital Libraries and Autonomous Citation Indexing". *IEEE Computer*, Vol. 32, No. 6, 67-71. <http://www.neci.nj.nec.com/~lawrence/papers/aci-computer98/>.

142. Liu, X. et al. (2001) "Arc - An OAI Service Provider for Digital Library Federation". *D-Lib Magazine*, Vol. 7, No. 4, April. <http://www.dlib.org/dlib/april01/liu/04liu.html>.

143. Garfield, E. (1955) "Citation Indexes for Science: A New Dimension in Documentation through Association of Ideas". *Science*, Vol. 122, No. 3159, July 15, 108-111. <http://www.garfield.library.upenn.edu/papers/science_v122(3159)p108y1955.html>.

144. <http://www.the-scientist.com/yr1996/sept/research_960902.html>.

145. SHERPA project, <http://www.sherpa.ac.uk/index.html>.

146. Simboli, B. and Zhang, M. (2002) "Citation Managers and Citing-Cited Data". *Issues in Science and Technology Librarianship*, Summer. <http://www.istl.org/02-summer/article4.html>.

147. Suber, P. (2002) "Momentum for eprint archiving". *Free Online Scholarship Newsletter*, 8th August <http://www.topica.com/lists/suber-fos/read/message.html?mid=1607391538&sort=d&start=38>.

148. TARDIS project, <http://tardis.eprints.org>.

149. GNU EPrints, <http://software.eprints.org>.

150. Harnad, S. (1996) "Implementing Peer Review on the Net: Scientific Quality Control in Scholarly Electronic Journals". In *Scholarly Publication: The Electronic Frontier*, edited by Peek, R. and Newby, G (Cambridge, MA: MIT Press), pp. 103-108. <http://cogsci.soton.ac.uk/~harnad/Papers/Harnad/harnad96.peer.review.html>.

151. [Mining] Mining the social life of an eprint archive, <http://opcit.eprints.org/tdb198/opcit/> and <http://opcit.eprints.org/ijh198/>.

152. <http://www.cogsci.soton.ac.uk/~harnad/Tp/thes1.html>. (extended version)

153. [Liu 2002] Liu, X. et al. (2002) "A Scalable Architecture for Harvest-Based Digital Libraries - The ODU/Southampton Experiments". *arXiv.org*, Computer Science cs.DL/0205071, May. <http://arxiv.org/abs/cs.DL/0205071>.

154.

155. [OAI sites] OAI registered sites, <http://www.openarchives.org/Register/BrowseSites.pl>.

156. Pace, A. K. (2002) "'Standard' Issue: Defining Standards and Protocols". *Computers in Libraries*, Vol. 22, No.8, September. <http://www.infotoday.com/cilmag/sep02/Pace.htm>.

157. Pentz, E. (2001) "CrossRef: A Collaborative Linking Network". *Issues in Science and Technology Librarianship*, Winter. <http://www.library.ucsb.edu/istl/01-winter/article1.html>.

158. Pinfield, S., Gardner, M. and MacColl, J. (2002) "Setting up an institutional e-print archive". *Ariadne*, issue 31, April. <http://www.ariadne.ac.uk/issue31/eprint-archives/>.

159. Powell, A. and Apps, A. (2001) "Encoding OpenURLs in Dublin Core metadata". *Ariadne*, issue 27, March. <http://www.ariadne.ac.uk/issue27/metadata/>.

160. Tennant, R., on *American Scientist September-98 Forum*, June 2002, <http://www.ecs.soton.ac.uk/~harnad/Hypermail/Amsci/2085.html>.

161. Van de Sompel, H. and Hochstenbach, P. (1999) "Reference Linking in a Hybrid Library Environment, Part 2: SFX, a Generic Linking Solution". *D-Lib Magazine*, Vol. 5, No. 4, April. <http://www.dlib.org/dlib/april99/van_de_sompel/04van_de_sompel-pt2.html>.

10

E-Resources and Licensing

Electronic information resources offer enormous benefits. Provide users faster, more convenient, 24-hour desktop access from home or campus, as well as special features such as hypertext links to related information, graphics, audio, video, and animation. These resources also offer benefits to libraries as they don't take up valuable space on library shelves. E-resources can't be stolen or destroyed. Depending on the license agreement, they allow more than one user to access information at the same time.

Significant portions of the libraries' collection money are spent on electronic resources. Almost every electronic book, database, and journal provided by the libraries is licensed. Each publisher's license agreement outlines specific terms and conditions under which the resources can be used. Within each library and campus, licenses go through several layers of review and negotiation before they are signed. Licensing e-resources allows libraries to provide access to many more titles than they could afford to purchase and shelve in paper format. These resources also provide superior indexing, retrieval, and access capabilities.

LICENSE AGREEMENT

A license agreement is a contract between an intellectual property owner (licensor) and a potential user (licensee). Unlike print resources, libraries do not own most e-resources. Instead, a license agreement is negotiated and signed with each owner which allows the library's users to access the electronic information for a specified amount of time for a specified fee.

Most e-resources licenses include detailed language that specifies who has the right to access the information, how the information may be used, stored, and transmitted, who is liable for violations or misuse of the information by library users, whether the information will be permanently accessible, and the charges for accessing the information.

DIFFERENCE BETWEEN LICENSE AND RIGHTS

License (ERMI): "Information from the legal document, a contractual agreement that defines the relationship between the grantor and the licensee and the terms and conditions of use for the product."

Rights (ODRL) : "Rights include Permissions, which can then contain Constraints, Requirements, and Conditions. Permissions are the actual usages or activities allowed.... Constraints are limits to these permissions.... Requirements are the obligations needed to exercise the Permission.... Conditions specify exceptions...."

FEATURES OF LICENSING AGREEMENTS

A. Common to Restrictions most license agreements : Although each license is unique, common restrictions found in licenses for digital information products include the following:

- The content may be used only for non-commercial educational, clinical, or research purposes.

- Individuals who are not affiliated with the library that has licensed the product may not use the content, or may use content only when physically at the library.
- Printing and downloading of e-resources are generally subject to copyright restrictions.
- Altering, recompiling, systematic or programmatic copying, reselling, redistributing or republishing of electronic content are typically prohibited.

B. Authorized user : The definition of an authorized user depends on the terms set out in the license of a particular electronic resource. Generally authorized users are the registered students, faculty, and staff of the institution purchasing the electronic resource. In many cases, authorized users also include members of the public who use the e-resource on library premises.

C. License agreement for a particular e-resource and specific terms : User can consult the reference staff to find out the specific terms in effect for a particular e-resource. Some distributors of electronic content publish general license terms on the website where the content is accessed. Others block activities that violate the license terms.

D. A breach of license terms and penalties : Each individual license details uses that constitute a failure to follow the license agreement and the penalties for such violations. Breach of contract may occur when unauthorized users access the electronic material, or when a user prints more pages than the contract allows. Penalties usually involve suspension or termination of access to at least the violator and possibly the University.

E. Proper user of Information : The library should include information on the legal use of electronic resources in class instruction sessions, on its website, and through instruction at the reference desk. The library should also monitor general usage trends of each electronic resource, while respecting rights of confidentiality of library users, and works in conjunction with electronic providers to identify possible violations of licensing agreements.

F. Violating a license agreement : Distributors of electronic content use various tools to monitor types of usage but not individual usage. They look for large-scale violations, such as systematic downloading of substantial portions of an electronic title. In these cases, whether the violations occur knowingly or unknowingly, the vendor will contact the library that holds the license and may suspend the university's access to the resource. In order to have access restored libraries must take sufficient measures, such as warning the offender or department, to satisfy the provider that appropriate action has been taken to prevent future violations.

G. Some e-resources available from home and others are not : License agreements require libraries to screen for status before allowing access. Some e-resources require passwords for authentication. The most common strategy for authentication is to register campus IP addresses and the official Internet identification numbers for computers located on each institution's secure network. If users access e-resources from a campus computer, the IP address is recognized and access granted. If users want to access e-resources from home, users may need to do so by going through a university computer with a recognized IP address. Users can do this by connecting through Virtual Private Networking (VPN), or by connecting through the campus modem pool or through the library's "proxy server." If users connect to the library's proxy server, it is needed to be aware that not every electronic journal title will be available full-text due to space limits on the server. Also, some publishers of electronic resources do not permit remote access and may limit use of their product to one building or one site. Some e-resources are only accessible via passwords available from the reference desk. License terms do not permit copying or downloading entire issues of a journal. This is also a violation of basic copyright principles. As a general rule, user can not e-mail full-text articles to unauthorized users.

LICENSING

When acquiring electronic resources, usually the Collection development or acquisition section should negotiate vendor licensing agreements in consultation with the appropriate subject specialists and Technical Service staff. Collection development and acquisition section maintains the file containing copies of all licensing agreements. Final responsibility for compliance with licensing agreements rests with the Head of acquisition section in consultation with the relevant members of the Libraries' committee, the Organization's Purchasing Department and the Organization's legal section, as may be necessary.

Information providers should employ a standard agreement that describes the rights of the libraries and their authorized users in readable and explicit. They should reflect realistic expectations about organization's ability to monitor use and discover abuse. Agreements should contain consistent business and legal provisions, such as indemnification against third party copyright infringement liability and the application of state laws.

Licenses should permit for use of all information for non-commercial educational, instructional and research purposes by authorized users. Authorized users are defined as all currently enrolled students, faculty, staff on or off campus, or visiting patrons located in the Libraries. License should include interlibrary loan permissions whenever feasible. Information providers should be able to link their access control mechanisms to organization's authentication infrastructure; access to their products should not require individual passwords and/or user IDs.

COMMON LICENSING ISSUES

- Negotiation (complexity, time, etc.)
- License terms supplant Copyright Law and Fair Use to determine:
  - Authorized users
  - Authorized use
- Need for "good faith" efforts to make users and staff aware of terms and live within them

ERMI Licensing Elements: Key Categories

- Administrative metadata
  - The parties
  - Period of license
  - The local contact
- Terms of use
  - Authorized users
  - Printing, downloading
  - ILL
  - Reserves, coursepacks
  - Other use restrictions
- Obligations of the parties
  - Warranties and indemnification
  - Breach remedies
  - Conditions of termination
  - Notice requirements
- Business terms (from license or acquisition)
  - Authorized sites

- Concurrent users
- Price, cancellation restrictions, price caps...
- Archival rights

The Common Problems

The problem is pervasive: when libraries acquire licensed electronic resources, they must comprehend, transmit, and inform others about the many financial, legal, and access aspects of these arrangements. The acquisitions and licensing processes are complex. Publishers transmit this information to libraries in a variety of paper and electronic formats, and the number of licensed electronic products that libraries are collecting is increasing rapidly. Such situations tend to spawn local, ad hoc fixes. By contrast, the some organizations' ERM has created a coordinated solution, developing the common specifications for the management of license agreements, related administrative information, and the internal processes associated with licensed electronic resources.

License Functions

- Communicate to End Users
- Permitted uses
- Restrictions
- Communicate to Staff
- ILL rights, reserve rights, confidentiality requirements
- Triggers and ticklers
- Product termination and renewal
- Contract termination and renewal
- Reporting
- Licenses permit access by alumni

Administration in ERMs

- Administrative

    - The parties
    - The license duration
    - The local contact
- definitions of authorized users
    - multi-site
    - remote
    - off-shore (permanent or temporary)
    - alumni access options
- definitions of authorized uses (with any limitations)
    - e-reserve
    - course-packs
    - classroom
    - ILL
- access method
    - IP
        - proxy server continuous access
    - password
    - both
    - conditions under which access to an address or the institution is blocked because of suspected abuse of download limits
- statistics
    - delivery mechanism
    - frequency
    - granularity
    - COUNTER compliant
- access to archive
    - post subscription
    - post vendor/publisher change

    - participation in archive services
    - participation in the Transfer Protocols
- trial access
    - length of trial
    - access method
        - IP
    - password
    - trial statistics
- availability (up-time)
    - compensation if >7 days unavailable
    - notice of scheduled downtime and negotiation of timing
    - 24x7 help desk
- price model
    - site licence or concurrent user
    - relationship to FTEs
    - based on institution or site
    - based on number in consortium
    - electronic-only price
    - relationship to current expenditure
    - method of calculation of current expenditure
    - central billing
    - adding/deleting titles
    - second & third year pricing
    - renewal schedule
- licence
    - consortial or institutional
    - jurisdiction
    - copyright

  - Conditions of termination
  - opt-out option for budget cut
  - Warranties and indemnifications
  - Breach remedies
  - Notice Requirements
- facilities for badging
  - institution-generated
  - vendor-generated
- content
- MARC records
  - availability
  - maintenance method
  - cost
- training
  - access to training materials
  - train-the-trainer
  - expanded access for training sessions (if concurrent user restrictions)
- customer service
  - turn around time for technical queries
  - turn around time for financial queries
  - regular updates on outstanding queries

License Data Exchange

- Library-vendor license exchange
- Standard license
- Final agreement with changes
- Exchange with consortial partners
- Communicate license data to external systems
- OPACs and portals

- Course management systems
- Migration to next generation ERMS

SOURCES OF LICENCE AGREEMENTS

Some of the Licensing models web site are also available. One can find a suite of standard licenses designed for the acquisition of electronic journals and other electronic resources. These contain the words needed to express most of the variables; publishers and librarians and the subscription will meet in negotiating licenses. There are four licenses such as Single academic institutions, Academic consortia, Public libraries, Corporate and other special libraries. These licenses were originally sponsored by and developed in close co-operation with major subscription agents: EBSCO, Harrassowitz, and Swets. Each of these international subscription agents has traditionally rationalized and eased the process of ordering journals from many publishers. The negotiation and management of licenses for electronic information is a natural expansion of this long-established activity. They have brought unparallelled experience of libraries and their needs to these licenses.

Without the huge effort that has already gone into licensing during the 1990s, these licenses would not have been possible. The starting point was the UK's PA/JISC model license, jointly developed by publishers and librarians from the Publishers Association and the Joint Information Systems Committee of the Higher Education Funding Councils. It was a vital source of format, concepts and model provisions. The US *Principles for Licensing Electronic Resources* from the American Library Association et al, and the *Statements of Current Perspectives* from the International Coalition of Library Consortia were both important sources of ideas, as were the LIBLICENSE web site and many publishers' individual licenses.

These model licenses deal with contentious issues: These do not prescribe the outcome of those negotiations, but are designed to account for the varying needs of different types of customer, requirements and policies of different publishers. They contain a range of variables, so that the clause appropriate to each situation can be selected in compiling the license. These are the result of consultation in with librarians, publishers and subscription agents These are international in scope but local in nature. Scholarly publishing is truly international in its scope. But licenses have to take account of local circumstances and local legal requirements. These models have been written to express clearly and succinctly what has been negotiated. They contain optional clauses that may vary depending on the country, state or province where the license is to operate. The licenses will be updated when there are new requirements, products or business models to deal with. They have been widely adopted by publishers and are familiar to librarians. They still cover all the issues that are likely to arise in respect when licensing journals. Since these are in the public domain so permission is not needed to use them. They have been placed there by the sponsoring subscription agents to benefit the community. They are intended to help publishers, subscription agents and libraries to create agreements that express what they have negotiated.

RE-NEGOTIATION OF CONTRACTS

- **Basic model.** Members should consider whether the current model works and should essentially be retained, or whether a different model should be sought.
- **Conditions for the entry of new subscribers.** Access to the agreement should be available for non-participants.

- **Additional consortial discounts for the addition of new subscribers.** The current model should be examined to see whether improved conditions may be obtained for increasing the size of the participating group.
- **Multi-year agreement.** The length of the agreement should be reviewed.
- **Price cap.** The price cap is likely to be the most important element for renegotiation.
- **Content change management.** Experience of the current agreement may highlight changes to the way titles are added and removed from a journals package.
- **Timing.**

FURTHER DEVELOPMENTS

Publishers and librarians are well into their second decade of experience with e-resources. Many new and transformed business models are operating in the electronic resource market, many of which are subscription models of various types. Early subscriptions for electronic content almost always incorporated the use of license agreements as a mechanism for defining the purchase transaction and also the usage rights of the subscribers. Many publishers and librarians developed a presumption that license agreements were a legal necessity of e-resource transactions. This assumption has occasionally been challenged, and recent observations suggest that a surprising number of publishers have been offering electronic publications without the use of a license agreement.

Recently a systematic examination of the assumed license agreement requirement has been made, and now it has been possible to create a new option for organizing the relationship between publishers and librarians for electronic resource transactions. SERU (the Shared Electronic Resource

Understanding) is a tool available to libraries and publishers who are comfortable forgoing a license agreement in an e-resource transaction.

Various efforts made by agencies

Very early, the READI project (1994) (Rights for Electronic Access to and Delivery of Information) offered guidance on agreements and contract negotiation to the licensing community. This groundbreaking effort by the Coalition for Networked Information was based on conversations with a range of stakeholders. It laid out a set of contract elements appropriate for electronic resource license agreements. Six library organizations released "Principles for Licensing Electronic Resources" in 1997. It was a consensus document that presented six principles that libraries expect publishers to honor in preparing license agreements. The Association of Research Libraries also developed a series of workshops that educated many librarians and publishers about licensing principles and practice. Liblicense was launched by Yale University library with support from the Council on Library and Information Resources. This influential project provided a forum for ongoing discussion around licensing issues and substantially improved licensing practice through the development and promotion of model agreements and standard definitions for many common license terms.

Publisher organizations also developed model agreements and licensing principles. Probably the most visible was the work of John Cox. The STM Library Relations Committee commissioned Cox to produce a white paper, "Publisher/Library Relationships in the Digital Environment." The white paper emphasized the need for cooperation and the creation of a mutual understanding between publishers and librarians. The efforts to create standard agreements have been successful in creating shared understanding of common license terms for electronic publications. There efforts assisted in many areas in moving libraries and publishers toward mutual agreement on many issues.

As publisher and library experience with licensing blossomed, the fundamental limitations of a license agreement approach also became clearer. The inability of either libraries or publishers to fully adopt standard agreements presents problems that are not easily resolved. It has become apparent that there is no single agreement a publisher can offer that all libraries can accept. As Linda Beebe from the American Psychological Association observed, "Increasingly, institutions are required by university regulations or state law to add very substantive clauses before they can sign a license. Issues include liability, indemnification, governing law, security, and perpetual access among others". Equally, there is no standard agreement a library could offer that would be agreeable to all publishers, and inevitably any publisher would have to review each library's license terms.

License negotiation requires considerable resources for license management. Reaching coming to agreement cannot be done without the elapse of significant amounts of time, delaying payment for publishers and access for libraries. When agreements are confined to a limited number of expensive information products, the resources and delays incumbent in the process may be acceptable conditions for doing business. Scholarly publishing has always involved a multitude of small enterprises, and research libraries, must acquire publications from publishers of all sizes and kinds. For many e-resource transactions, the costs of license agreement negotiation can conceivably approach the costs of content production. For libraries faced with hundreds or even thousands of transactions annually, the resources needed to manage agreement negotiations for each transaction substantially erode the resources available for purchasing content.

Working Without a License Agreement

Increasingly, publishers and librarians have questioned whether the benefits of license negotiation outweigh the costs for all e-resource transactions. Rick Anderson observed that license agreements are not a legal requirement of e-resource transactions but rather a chosen instrumentality. Publishers such as the OECD (Organization for Economic Co-operation and Development) have as a matter of policy used license agreements only when required by a library.

Once it is acknowledged that e-resource transactions can legitimately take place in the absence of an agreement, it requires diverse set of practices involving some mechanism for enhancing mutual trust and cooperation between libraries and publishers. The willingness of some publishers to make minimal use of license agreements is also in the air. Public discussions challenging the assumption that universal use of agreements is inherent in e-resource sales, suggest that both publishers and librarians have reached a level of trust where new approaches can be considered.

During 2005 and 2006, many publishers and librarians wanted to find a way to manage e-resource transactions without engaging in license negotiation. Appropriate and inappropriate use of materials has been an arena where publishers and librarians have frequently struggled in finding common ground in license negotiation. An even more dynamically evolving arena has perhaps been that of preservation, archiving, and access rights to archived content. The library community is struggling in expressing its concerns about how license agreements do or do not address preservation rights beyond those inherent in copyright law. Widely available mechanisms for electronic resources are relatively recent developments, and there is still significant variability in the level of engagement by libraries and publishers in current. Audit programs to establish broader trust in license were also in development. While, in principle, there is clearly shared consensus on the importance of preservation, the relative immaturity of present preservation systems makes it difficult to clearly express shared expectations.

Various XML and License Information

- Originally considered a schema for the entire data dictionary, but
- Significant overlap with existing and *emerging* schemas.
- Limited functionality.
- Need of licensing
- Area of considerable concern and current interest.
- Significant commercial activity in defining and schematizing.
- Limited library activity in defining and schematizing.

Uses for License Data Exchange

- Licensing elements actionable in an ERM system
- Convey appropriate license restrictions.
- Show or hide resources depending on availability to certain groups.
- Prompt staff for action
- Exchange with consortial partners
- License feeds from vendors

ERMI License Terms

- Fair Use Clause Indicator
- Citation Requirement Details
- Display
- Digitally Copy
- Print Copy
- Scholarly Sharing
- Distance Education
- ILL Print or Fax
- ILL Secure Electronic Transmission
- ILL Electronic
- Course Reserve Print
- Course Reserve Electronic / Cached Copy

- Electronic Link Permission
- Course Pack Electronic
- Course Pack Print
- Walk-in Users
- Remote Access
- Authorized Locations
- Authorized User Groups

ERMI License ≠ ODRL Rights Expression

- Many similarities in function and specifics
- ODRL is extensible, non-proscriptive
- ERMI licensing needs more generic rights statements
- ERMI needs more specific rights statements
- ODRL requires explicit permission assertions (silence=prohibition)

"ODRL pictures the contracts which define the relationships as a series of checkboxes rather than a complex legal document written in somewhat creative English."

Loss of Libraries

- Inability to distinguish prohibitions from silence leads to loss of much useful data
- "silence=denial" means extra work to identify and explicitly state all assumed permissions
- The "assumed permissions" extensions don't mesh with ODRL processing model
- Extensions increase validation demands
- Concern that ERMI usage may be incorrectly used to limit users' activities

Coins of Libraries

- Uses existing rights expression language
- Avoids creation of library-specific metadata standard
- Helps build momentum for open ODRL
- Helps bridge human license reading into actionable computing values

- Builds a crosswalk between ERM systems and DRM applications

XML Investigation

- Find, extend, or create a genuine *licensing* metadata exchange scheme
- Creative Commons license via RDF

Unlike Digital Rights Management (DRM) technology, which tries to restrict use of digital works, Creative Commons is providing ways to encourage permitted sharing and reuse of works.

THE SIGNIFICANCE OF LICENSING FOR E-RESOURCES

As digital content entered the market, contract law was almost immediately pitted against copyright as both publishers and librarians grappled with the reality that contracts trump copyright. Electronic delivery raised the possibility that new business models could be created that parsed previously bundled uses of content. The new possibilities for selling limited rights to use content immediately engendered interest in using contracting approaches to library sales. In addition, almost all early digital content was expensive to produce and consequently expensive to purchase. It was perhaps inevitable that the first generation of electronic resource products were licensed to libraries using negotiated agreements. Uncertainty was high on both sides of the sales counter and the negotiations involved in sales, easily extended beyond price into user rights, site definitions, applicable law, indemnification, and a host of other issues.

Despite the fairly obvious appeal of license agreement-based sales, some of the problems created when buying and selling by using an agreement paradigm were apparent even in the earliest days. The process of license negotiation is time consuming and resource intensive, requiring significant expertise by both participants in any balanced negotiation. At first, both the publishing and library communities faced steep learning curves. Great efforts were made by a variety of individuals and organizations to educate stakeholders and to create and promulgate best practices.

REFERENCES AND NOTES

1. CEIRC (CAUL Electronic Information Resources Committee). Vendor Check-list) (*http://www.caul.edu. au/datasets/checklist-vendor-negotiations.doc*)
2. American Association of Law Libraries, American Library Association, Association of Academic Health Sciences Libraries, Association of Research Libraries, Medical Library Association, and Special Libraries Association. 1997. Principles for Licensing Electronic Resources. Place Published. <*http://www.arl.org/sc/licensing/licprinciples.shtml*>.
3. Anderson, Rick. 1999. To License or Not to License — That Really Ought to Be the Question — Of the many changes that the electronic information revolution has brought to library acquisitions, perhaps none is as significant as the licensing agreement. *Against the Grain* 11 (2):68-72.
4. Beebe, Linda. 2005. Licensing electronic products at the American Psychological Association. *Serials Librarian* 48 (1/2):175-184.
5. Collins, Maria. 2007. SERU: An Alternative to Licensing—An Interview with Selden Durgom Lamoureux. *Serials Review* 33:122-128.
6. Cox, John. 2000. Model generic licenses: cooperation and competition. *Serials Review* 26 (1):3-9.
7. Davis, Trisha L. 1997. License agreements in lieu of copyright: Are we signign away our rights? *Library Acquisitions: Practice and Theory* 21 (1):19-28.
8. http://www.dlib.org/dlib/november07/hahn/11hahn.html#Davis

9. Farb, Sharon. 2006. Libraries, licensing and the challenge of stewardship. *First Monday* (7), *<http://firstmonday.org/issues/issue11_7/farb/index.html>*.

10. Kenney, Anne R., Richard Entlich, Peter B. Hirtle, Nancy Y. McGovern, and Ellie L. Buckley. 2006. E-Journal Archiving Metes and Bounds: A Survey of the Landscape. In *CLIR pub 138*: Council on Library and Information Resources.

11. Luther, Judy. 1999. Licensing electronic resources to libraries - An ARL workshop for publishers. *Against the Grain* 11 (1):67, 70.

12. Ogburn, Joyce. 2001. A look back at licensing. *Against the Grain* 13 (4):90-91.

13. Okerson, Ann. 1999. The LIBLICENSE project and how it grows. D-Lib Magazine (9), *<doi:10.1045/september99-okerson>*.

14. Huang, K.T. (1998). Capitalising on intellectual assets, in: J.W. Cortada & J.A. Woods, eds., *The knowledge management yearbook 1999-2000*, pp. 346-366. Boston, MA: : Butterworth Heinemann.

15. Johnston, R. & Rolf B. (1998) Knowledge moves to centre stage. *Science Communication* 20(1), 99-105/li>

16. Knowledge management: big challenges, big rewards. (1999) Framingham, MA: CIO.com Available at: http://www.cio.com/sponsors/091599_km_1.html [Site visited 6th September 2002]

17. Marwick, D. (2001). Knowledge management technology. *IBM Systems Journal*. 40(4), 814-830 Available at: http://researchweb.watson.ibm.com/journal/sj/404/marwick.html [Site visited 6th September 2002]

18. Narayanan, V. K. (2001). *Managing technology and innovation for competitive advantage*. Englewood Cliffs, NJ: Prentice Hall

19. Nonaka, I. (1991) The knowledge creating company. *Harvard Business Review*, 69, 96-104

20. Nonaka, I & Konno, N. (1998). The concept of "ba": building a foundation for knowledge creation, in: J.W. Cortada & J.A.

Woods, eds. *The knowledge management yearbook 1999-2000*, pp. 37-51. Boston, MA: Butterworth Heinemann.

21. Nonaka, I. & Takeuchi, H. (1995) *The knowledge creating company: how Japanese companies create the dynasties of innovation*. Oxford: Oxford University Press.

22. Polanyi, M (1958) *Personal knowledge: towards a post-critical philosophy*. Chicago: University of Chicago Press.

23. Polanyi, (1966) *The tacit dimension*. New York, NY: Doubleday.

24. Prusak, L. (1999). What's up with knowledge management? A personal view, in: J.W. Cortada & J.A. Woods, eds. *The knowledge management yearbook 1999-2000*, pp. 3-7. Boston, MA: Butterworth Heinemann.

25. Ruggles, R.L., ed. (1997a). *Knowledge management tools*. London: Butterworth-Heinemann.

26. Ruggles, R.L. (1997b). Knowledge tools: using technology to manage knowledge better. Cambridge, MA: Cap Gemini Ernst & Young, Center for Business Innovation. Available at: http://www.cbi.cgey.com/pub/docs/KnowledgeTools.PDF [Site visited 1st September 2001]

27. Schultz, C. (2000). Agencies, companies turn to knowledge management. *Washington Technology*, 15(3) Available at: http://www.washingtontechnology.com/news/15_3/tech_features/1296-

28. RLG. 2005. *An Audit Checklist for the Certification of Trusted Digital Repositories*. Mountain View, CA: RLG.

29. Schottlaender, Brian. 1998. The development of national principles to guide librarians in licensing electronic resources. *Library Acquisitions: Practice and Theory* 22 (1):49-54.

30. Ubell, Robert, and Mark Tesoriero. *Negotiating Networked Information Contracts and Licenses: READI (Rights for Electronic Access to and Delivery of Information)*. Coalition for Networked Information, November 15, 1994. <*http://www.cni.org/projects/READI/guide/*>.

31. Waters, Donald J. *Urgent Action Needed to Preserve*

Scholarly Electronic Journals, October 15, 2005 <*http://www.arl.org/bm~doc/ejournalpreservation_final.pdf*>.

32. http://www.licensingmodels.com/

33. http://www.dlib.org/dlib/november07/hahn/11hahn.html#2

11

Open Access and E-Resources

World wide researchers publish their results to establish their own claim to the research and to enable other researchers to build upon them. In the case of journal, only the richest institutions have been able to afford a reasonable proportion of all the scholarly journals published and so learning about and accessing such articles have not always been easy for most researchers. Open Access comes as a breather for this. The World Wide Web provides the platforms for researchers to make their research results available to anyone, anywhere, at any time. This applies to journal articles regardless of whether or not their library has a subscription to the journal in which the articles were published as well as to other types of research output such as conference papers, theses or research reports. This is known as Open Access.

'Open access' (OA) means that a reader of a scientific publication can read it over the Internet, print it out and even further distribute it for non-commercial purposes without any payments or restrictions. At the most the reader is in some cases required to register with the service in question, which for instance can be useful for the service providers in view of the production of readership statistics. The use of the content by third parties for commercial purposes is, however, as a rule prohibited. Thanks to the open availability the linking from reference lists to OA publications is substantially facilitated, since the reader does not encounter barriers such as use licenses, and each reference is only a mouse-click away. In general, the author keeps almost complete copyright and can also publish the material elsewhere.

The Internet is a superb channel for the free distribution of information in the public domain. Science as a social institution has also always had as an ideal the open sharing and critique of information. Thus there is a much stronger case for open access to scientific content than, for instance, for the use of Open Source methods in the development of information technology applications not to mention free downloading of music files from subversive third parties, that is counter to the legitimate interest of the producing artists. A related development is also the posting of teaching resources for free on the Internet, a phenomenon for which the label 'OpenCourseWare' has been used.

The best-known subject-specific repository, for high-energy physics, was founded in 1991. Such repositories typically aim at the parallel publishing of material, which is being written for other outlets (such as conferences or traditional journals), allowing earlier and more efficient dissemination. Subject-specific repositories have emerged in research areas where traditions for the exchange of preprints have existed prior to the Internet and where the speed of publication is an essential factor. The guiding principle of such electronic archives is that researchers themselves upload article manuscripts, conference papers etc., into the repositories. Thus, very low maintenance costs can be achieved. The custodians of the repositories usually only check that totally irrelevant material is not deposited. Papers in a repository are available globally much earlier, than, for instance, the finally published versions of the manuscripts in paper-based journals. In areas like computer science this can be a significant benefit.

The Open Access research literature is composed of free, online copies of peer-reviewed journal articles and conference papers as well as technical reports, working papers etc. Most of the cases have no licensing restrictions on their use by readers. They can be used freely for research, teaching and other purposes. The Budapest Open Access Initiative (www.soros.org/openaccess/) defines Open Access as:

"By 'open access' to this literature we mean its free availability on the public internet, permitting any users to read, download, copy, distribute, print, search, or link to the full texts of these articles, crawl them for indexing, pass them as data to software, or use them for any other lawful purpose, without financial, legal, or technical barriers other than those inseparable from gaining access to the internet itself."

There are various misunderstandings about Open Access. It is not self-publishing, nor a way to bypass peer-review and formal publication, nor is it a kind of second-class, cut-price publishing route. It is simply the means to make research results freely available online to the whole research community.

The four most important OA channels are electronic, refereed, scientific periodicals, research-area-specific archive (e-print) servers (sometimes called subject-specific repositories), institutional repositories of individual universities, and self-posting on authors' home pages. OA scientific periodicals have been founded since the early 1990s, usually as individual efforts. Almost as a rule, such journals are electronic only, because of the need to minimize costs, but in some cases it may be possible to have a paid subscription to a paper version. OA journals are usually funded largely by the voluntary work of the involved editors and direct or implicit grants (the free usage of the host university's Web servers could be seen as a subsidy). In more recent years a number of efforts to publish OA journals on a larger scale have emerged. Their business plan is usually to finance the operations through author charges. A variety of OA journals are also traditional subscription journals, which become freely available in electronic form after a delay of, typically, six months to a year. Open Access can be provided in following ways :

1. A researcher can place a copy of each article in an Open Access repository.
2. He can publish articles in Open Access journals.
3. A researcher may place a copy of each article on a personal or departmental website. These routes to Open Access ensure that far more users can access such articles than if they were hidden away in Closed Access (subscription-based) journals.

The first two constitute much more systematic and organized approaches than the third and maximize the chance of other researchers locating and reading articles.

INSTITUTIONAL REPOSITORIES

While explaining, it can be said that institutional repositories are digital collections of the outputs created within a university or research institution. The purposes of repositories may vary such as, some universities have teaching/ learning repositories for educational materials. In most cases they are established to provide Open Access to the institution's research output. There are over 1300 repositories around the world at the beginning of 2009. Over the past three years the number has been growing at an average rate of one per day. The statistics on numbers and where they are can be found in the Registry of Open Access Repositories (ROAR: http://roar.eprints.org/) and in the Directory of Open Access Repositories (OpenDOAR http://www.opendoar.org/). There is also a map showing where they are at Repository66 (*http://maps.repository66.org/*). The experiences from the first ten years of experimenting show that it is much harder to change the "system" than originally envisaged. In a few years hundreds of scientific journals adhering to the OA principles were launched, but of these roughly half have already disappeared and many only publish a few articles per year. There are, nevertheless, some success stories, such as *First Monday*, which on the first Monday of every month publishes papers on Internet research. It is possible to maintain subject-specific repositories with minimal costs and in some domains these have acquired a prominent position. The best known of these is arXiv, in which researchers during its eleven year old history have deposited 225,000 publications from the fields of physics, mathematics, and information technology. Despite such success stories it had become clear by the turn of the millennium, that the enthusiasm and collaborative spirit of researchers involved in OA efforts was not, alone, enough to offer viable competition to the traditional subscription based delivery channels.

Objectives of Institutional Repositories

1. To serve all types of content; not just text-based items
2. To be compatible with Archive
3. Enabling metadata and content to be harvested by other institutions
4. Reduce maintenance costs, due to the migration to open source and a single management interface
5. Improve prospects for long-term preservation of the content
6. Opens up the outputs of the institutions to the world

7. Maximizes the visibility and impact of these outputs as a result
8. Showcases the university to interested constituencies - prospective staff, prospective students and other stakeholders
9. Collects and curates digital outputs
10. Manages and measures research and teaching activities
11. Provides a workspace for work-in-progress, and for collaborative or large-scale projects
12. Enables and encourages interdisciplinary approaches to research
13. Facilitates the development and sharing of digital teaching materials and aids
14. Supports student endeavors, providing access to theses and dissertations and a location for the development of e-portfolios

Advantages of a Repository to an Institution

Repositories represent a certain basic cost to an institution but there are ways of minimizing this. The sustainability of a repository depends in large amount on how much effort is needed to fill it. A repository that is filled by self-archiving - that is, by researchers depositing their own articles - is far less costly to an institution than one where the library does all the depositing work. Ideally, deposit activity should show a reasonably steady pattern throughout the year. The way to ensure that researchers deposit their work regularly is to have a proper Open Access policy which requires them to make their work Open Access. It must explain why this is important for them and the institution. A repository has the following purposes and benefits for an institution:

- The OAI-PMH allows a single gateway to search and access many repositories

- subject-based portals or views
- subject-based classification and search
- institutional storage and support
- Practical reasons
- use institutional infrastructure
- integration into work-flows and systems
- support is close to academic users and contributors

Repositories adhere to an internationally-agreed set of technical standards that means that they expose the metadata (the bibliographic details such as author names, institutional affiliation, and date, titles of the article, abstract and so forth) of each item in their contents on the Web in the same basic way. In other words, they are 'interoperable'. This common protocol to which they all adhere is called the open Archives Initiative Protocol for Metadata Harvesting (OAI-PMH). The contents of all repositories are then indexed by Web search engines such as Google and Google Scholar, creating online Open Access databases of freely available global research. As the level of self-archiving (the process by which authors deposit their work in repositories) grows the Open Access corpus will represent an increasingly large proportion of the scholarly literature. Because Google and the other Web search engines index the content of repositories, anyone with internet access can find themselves arriving at an article or dataset in a university or research institution's repository via a Web search. But there are other ways that repositories are used, too. Users may search a particular repository if they know a specific researcher works at that institution. Or they may follow a link from another researcher's website or blog. Although these specific 'referrals' are not uncommon, by far the most common way for searchers to arrive in a repository is through a Web search engine such as Google. This underlines how important these informal 'world research databases' that the Web search engines have created are for repositories and their institutions.

Repository use

- Access to material
- Citation analysis
- Overlay journals
- Review projects
- Evidence based work
- Data-mining
- Cross-institutional research group virtual research environments: It creates. . . *Services built on top*
- RAE-like submissions, activities and management
- Archival storage
- Facilitate industrial links
- Career-long personalised work spaces
- Putting stuff in, getting stuff out
- Deposit
- Create a description of the eprint
- Attach a copy
- Put into an institutional repository

Discovery

- use search engines
- subject-based portals
- find similar material within subject

Institutional repositories present a rather different picture from current OA journals and subject-specific repositories. University libraries have considerable funds at their disposal and are used to outsourcing part of the work in building their information technology infrastructure. They also take a long-term perspective in the setting up of institutional repositories. For instance, already in the planning stages, they need to take into account the periodic necessity to upgrade the storage media and the storage formats. In addition to scientific publications universities also have a need to systematically organize the Web-based educational material produced by the faculty.

When institutions start planning for such systems they are likely to use one of the following solutions or perhaps combinations of these:

- Plan for joint national collaboration platforms
- Use well-proven open source applications
- Buy the software from outside information technology consultants
- Outsource the whole service to commercial publishers

CONTENTS OF INSTITUTIONAL REPOSITORIES

1. Article from peer-reviewed journal and conference proceedings

The primary type of content in repositories is the peer-reviewed journal literature. A collection of the journal articles published from an institution, (provided in Open Access through the repository), gives the research programme worldwide visibility and increases its impact. Individual authors also enjoy the same increased visibility for their work and concomitant impact.

2. Research data

Now that research data are increasingly created in digital form, repositories are the places where authors can deposit the data that underpin their final articles. More and more research funders are requiring their grant-holders to make their data Open Access. It is possible once they have analysed and published their findings from the data. This is in order that other researchers can use the data to verify results, to compare with their own data or to re-use in some way to generate new data and knowledge. Datasets may be of many types such as spreadsheets, photographs, audio files, video files, representations of artwork, diagrams, charts and so on. They may even be 'complex objects', that is, combinations of several types of data.

3. Monographs and books

Most institutional repositories also contain books or chapters. Books are often written for monetary gains and in such cases authors may be reluctant to deposit them for free in a repository. In these cases it is still important for the book to be deposited, with the metadata (title, author, synopsis, publisher details, etc) on display, but the text may be 'hidden' from viewers. The metadata visible means that the book is counted in the institution's assessment procedures. Its existence is known to would-be readers and it can be located by Web search engines. The evidence is accumulating; however, sales of the book frequently rise. This is because the visibility in the repository is raising awareness of the book and promoting it to an audience which is then likely to buy the book if it seems relevant to their work.

4. Other content types

As well as the types of content described above, institutional repositories frequently contain theses, dissertations and other research-related outputs such as presentations.

- Preprints
- Postprints
- Datasets
- Learning objects
- Videos
- Sound files

Linkage between these objects

- Theses
- Dissertations
- Royalty publications
- Conference papers
- Technical reports
- Grey literature

Examples of Institutional Repositories

- OpenDOAR - The Directory of Open Access Repositories, from Project SHERPA
- ROAR - Registry of Open Access Repositories, from the University of Southampton

Linking service to OA repositories

Link resolvers are extremely effective tools that offer appropriate means of obtaining primary documents from licensed e-journals, open access journals, library print holdings and through Interlibrary Loan requests. Link resolver software and services have been deployed in many types of organizations all over the world. However, link resolvers have not been offering satisfactory article-level resolution for Open Access documents that have been accumulated in repositories and in institutional repositories (IR). One approach to providing access to documents in repositories is to offer search links targeting services such as Google Scholar and OAIster that harvest records from many repositories. However, this is unsatisfactory for the following reasons:

- Until the actual search is executed, the existence of a matching OA document is uncertain, and at the present time, such documents are only occasionally found.
- At present, Google Scholar and OAIster cannot be searched precisely by using article identifiers such as

the DOI, or by article descriptors such as the ISSN, volume, issue, and page.

- The link resolver should search the items registered in IRs and display a link to the repository version only when usable documents are found. When this mechanism is achieved, the following effects are obtained:
- The researcher will be able to obtain the OA document easily through the link resolver even when the affiliated organization has not subscribed to the electronic journal.
- By improving the visibility of material collected in the repository, the results of the research will be used and cited more widely.

To implement the mechanism by which the resolver only displays usable items, libraries must accumulate the metadata (DOI, ISSN, title, volume, issue and page, etc.) for each repository in a machine-readable format. A central service provider is needed to collect the necessary metadata from each repository and enable searching from a link resolver.

OPEN ACCESS REPOSITORIES

1. PubMed Central (PMC)

PubMed Central is a free digital archive of biomedical and life sciences journal literature at the U.S. National Institutes of Health (NIH). It is developed and managed by NIH's National Center for Biotechnology Information (NCBI) in the National Library of Medicine (NLM). With PubMed Central, NLM has taken the lead in preserving and maintaining access to the electronic literature. PubMed Central aims to fill the role of a world class library in the digital age. NLM believes that giving all users free access to the material in PubMed Central is the best way to ensure the durability and utility of the archive as technology changes over time.

PubMed Central follows in the footsteps of other highly successful and useful services that NCBI has developed for the worldwide scientific community such as GenBank, the genetic sequence data repository, and PubMed, the database of citations and abstracts to biomedical and other life science journal literature. GenBank, and the tools provided by NCBI for searching and manipulating its contents, have been a boon to molecular biologists and have helped advance developments in the field. PubMed is the database of choice, for researchers and clinicians alike, to locate relevant articles and, it link directly to a publisher's site for the full text in many cases.

Participation by publishers in PubMed Central is voluntary, although participating journals must meet certain editorial standards. Journals are encouraged to deposit all their content in PMC so that the archive becomes a true digital counterpart to NLM's extensive collection of print journals. NLM has *digitized* earlier print issues of many of the journals that are in PMC. Although immediate free access to all content is most desirable, a journal may delay release of its full text in PMC for some period of time after publication. A journal is guaranteed access to a copy of its deposited data upon request, at no cost. PubMed Central does not claim copyright on any material deposited in the archive. Copyright remains with the journal publisher or with individual authors, whichever is applicable.

The value of PubMed Central, in addition to its role as an archive, lies in what can be done when data from diverse sources is stored in a common format in a single repository. GenBank has proven the advantages of collecting DNA sequences in a central repository with a common format. With PubMed Central, one can quickly search the entire body of full-text articles and locate relevant material regardless of its source. It also makes it possible to integrate the literature with a variety of other information resources such as sequence databases and other factual databases that are available to scientists, clinicians and everyone else interested in the life sciences.

Most journals now have online publishing operations and there is a growing tendency to publish material online only. This literature must be preserved in a form that ensures unrestricted access to it over the longer term. This is what NLM has undertaken to do. They invite all journals to join those that have already committed to creating this resource for people all over the world. PubMed Central began operating in February 2000 with content from two journals: *PNAS: Proceedings of the National Academy of Sciences* and *Molecular Biology of the Cell*. The currency and age of material in PubMed Central varies by journal. Many journals make their content available in PMC as soon as it is published. Others may delay release of content in PMC for anywhere from a few months to more than a year after publication. Most journals provide free access to full text in PMC within a year of publication. Journals that deposit their articles in PMC fall into one of three categories.

For several hundred journals, PMC has the complete contents of each issue, starting with the first issue. For the older journals in this group, the back issues of a journal (generally, anything prior to the late 1990s) are available as digitized (scanned) copies of the original print journal. For a smaller group of journals, PMC has complete issues and volumes for recent years. For still other journals, PMC does not contain any complete issues, e.g., just those that are the result of NIH-funded research, or those that the journal has published as open access articles. In all three categories, PMC contains a journal's final published version of the respective articles. The *PMC Journal List* includes information about what content is available from each journal, as well as links to that content. In addition to the articles from these journals, PMC contains author manuscripts of selected articles from several thousand other journals

Connection between PubMed Central (PMC) and PubMed

PubMed is a database of citations and abstracts for millions of articles from thousands of journals. It includes links to full-text articles at several thousand journal web sites as well as to most of the articles in PubMed Central. PubMed Central (PMC) is an electronic archive of full-text journal articles, offering free access to its contents. PMC contains nearly 2 million articles, most of which have a corresponding entry in PubMed.

PubMed does not have citations for certain types of PMC material, such as book reviews, that are considered out of scope for PubMed. These items constitute a small portion of the total PMC collection and there are no plans to include them in PubMed. In addition, articles added to PMC via the *Back Issue Digitization* project may be in PMC for several months before equivalent citations appear in PubMed. Citations and links for these articles are added to PubMed one journal at a time, after all the back issues for that journal have been added to PMC.

Participation

Participation in PMC is open to any life sciences journal that meets NLM's standards for the archive. A journal must qualify on two levels: the scientific quality of the publication and the technical quality of its digital files.

Types of material are deposited in PubMed Central

PMC strives to collect and preserve everything that is published in a participating journal. It has a cover-to-cover digital copy of the early issues of a journal that came into PMC through NLM's digitization program. For more recent material, which a journal must supply in XML or SGML form, PMC accepts any editorial content that can be represented accurately with the *NLM Journal Publishing XML DTD* or a compatible DTD. The editorial content" refers to articles and article-like items, including book reviews, news items and obituaries. PMC also accepts journal cover images and accompanying captions. In general, a participating journal must deposit in PMC the final, published version of an article as it appears on the journal's own web site. However, in the instance where PMC serves as the repository for a funding agency's access program, PMC will accept an author's final, peer reviewed manuscript of an article. Journals also contain administrative content such as Few, if any, journals have it in XML form. PMC is developing XML tagging guidelines so that the administrative content can be included in the PMC archive as well.

OTHER OPEN ACCESS REPOSITORIES

American Communication Journal : The American Communication Journal (ACJ) is the premier online scholarly refereed journal dedicated to the study of communication. The ACJ is published by the American Communication Association.

arXiv.org e-Print archive : ArXiv is an e-print service in the fields of physics, mathematics, non-linear science, computer science, and quantitative biology. The contents of arXiv conform to Cornell University academic standards. arXiv is owned, operated and funded by Cornell University, a private not-for-profit educational institution. arXiv is also partially funded by the National Science Foundation.

BioMed Central : BioMed Central is an independent publishing house committed to providing immediate open access to peer-reviewed biomedical research.

Citebase Search : Citebase Search is a semi-autonomous citation index for the free, online research literature. and contains articles from physics, maths, information science, and (published only) biomedical papers.

CiteSeer.IST Scientific Literature Digital Library : A search engine that finds PostScript and PDF research articles on the web, focusing on computer and information science.

Cogprints : This is an electronic archive for self-archive papers in any area of Psychology, Neuroscience, and Linguistics, and many areas of Computer Science (e.g., artificial intelligence, robotics, vison, learning, speech, neural networks), Philosophy (e.g., mind, language, knowledge, science, logic), Biology (e.g., ethology, behavioral ecology, sociobiology, behaviour genetics, evolutionary theory), Medicine (e.g., Psychiatry, Neurology, human genetics, Imaging), Anthropology (e.g., primatology, cognitive ethnology, archeology, paleontology), as well as any other portions of the physical, social and mathematical sciences that are pertinent to the study of cognition.

FindArticles : FindArticles gives free access to millions of articles from thousands of top publications.

Directory of Open Access Journals : This site covers free, full text, quality controlled scientific and scholarly journals in multiple subjects and lauguages.

Journal of Medical Internet Research(JMIR) : All articles are accessible FREE of charge (as HTML file). In addition, PDF files for members are available.

Open Access Journals in the Field of Education : This site is owned by the American Education Research Association Special Interest Group (AERA SIG) Communication of Research and provides electronic journals that are scholarly, peer-reviewed, full text and accessible without cost.

The Directory of Open Access Repositories (OpenDOAR) : The OpenDOAR service is being developed to support the rapidly emerging movement towards Open Access to research information. This will categorise and list the wide variety of Open Access research archives that have grown up around the world.

Reading on Line : It is offered as an archived collection.

Google Scholar : Google Scholar provides a simple way to broadly search for scholarly literature. Searches can be performed across many disciplines and sources: peer-reviewed papers, theses, books, abstracts and articles, from academic publishers, professional societies, preprint repositories, universities and other scholarly organizations. Google Scholar helps to identify the most relevant research across the world of scholarly research.

Harvey Project : An international collaboration of educators, researchers, physicians, students, programmers, instructional designers and graphic artists working together to build interactive, dynamic human physiology course materials on the Web. Materials produced by the Harvey Project will be made freely available to any educational institution.

Journal of Digital Informationv(JoDI) : A peer-reviewed Web journal supported by Texas A and M University Libraries.

University of California eScholarship Repository : The repository is a service of the eScholarship initiative of the California Digital Library. Research and scholarly output included here has been selected and deposited by the individual University of California units.

University of Nevada Collection of Free Electronic Journals : Free Electronic Journals lists by Unviersity of Nevada, Reno Library.

PLoS Biology : PLoS Biology is a peer-reviewed, open-access journal published by the Public Library of Science (PLoS), a non-profit organization committed to making scientific and medical literature a public resource.

PLoS Medicine : PLoS Medicine provides an open-access venue for important, peer-reviewed advances in human health.

Dspace Digital Repositories Lists : A listing of worldwide institutions' instructional repositories which adopted Dspace technology...

OAlster : OAlster is a project of the University of Michigan Digital Library Production Service. The goal is to create a collection of freely available, previously difficult-to-access, academically-oriented digital resources that are easily searchable by anyone. User can search wide variety of collections from a wide variety of institutions.

Stanford Encyclopedia of Philosophy : An academic encyclopedia, produced by philosophy scholars

Yahoo's Free Full Text : FreeFullText.com provides direct links to over 7000 scholarly periodicals which allow some or all of their online content to be viewed by ANYONE with Internet access for free (though some may require free registration).

OPENDOAR (DIRECTORY OF OPEN ACCESS REPOSITORIES)

*Open*DOAR is a project to list and categorise academic open access research repositories. The aim is to provide a comprehensive and authoritative list of such repositories for end-users who wish to find particular archives or who wish to break down repositories by locale, content or other measures. *Open*DOAR will also provide listings to third-party "service providers" - typically search services who wish to use the categorised lists within their service. This will increase the accessibility and use of the content of these repositories, which will benefit the authors of the research material and the researchers who wish to find it. *OpenDOAR* is being developed and maintained by the University of Nottingham as part of a portfolio of work in Open Access and repositories under the SHERPA umbrella. *Open*DOAR was started and initially developed by the University of Nottingham, UK, and the Lund University , Sweden. The project is being funded by the Open Society Institute (OSI), the Joint Information Systems Committee (JISC), the Consortium of Research Libraries (CURL) and SPARCEurope.

A multiplicity of Open Access research archives have grown up around the world, mushrooming in recent years in response to calls by scholars, researchers and open access advocates to provide open access to research information. Beyond these basic listings there is a need to move from cumulative lists to a more structured information service, cataloguing and describing repositories. Users need to know the scope and comprehensiveness of the information they find and be given features which facilitate the use of that information.

Repositories need to be categorised with clear information on their policies regarding tagging peer-reviewed/non-peer-reviewed material, their subject coverage, the constituency they draw on for content, their collection and preservation policies, etc. Where this information does not exist, repositories should be encouraged to provide it as a means to further improve their visibility and the use of the content that they hold. Therefore there is a need for a dependable listing of the academic e-print research repositories that are available world-wide, to underpin the outreach of the Open Access movement. *Open*DOAR has been set up to provide this service.

Scope

*Open*DOAR maintains a comprehensive and authoritative list of institutional and subject-based repositories. Much valuable work has already been conducted in listing repositories in different countries and *Open*DOAR is building on this existing knowledge. *Open*DOAR is therefore primarily a service to enhance and support the academic and research activities of the global community.

Users of the service are able to analyse repositories by location, type, the material they hold and other measures. This key point about *Open*DOAR is that this information is of use not only to users wishing to find original research papers but also for third-party service providers, like search engines or alert services, who need easy to use tools for developing tailored search services to suit specific user communities.

Aims

*Open*DOAR aims to:

- Survey the growing field of academic open access research repositories and categorise them in terms of locale, content and other measures.
- Produce a descriptive list of open access repositories of relevance to academic research.
- Provide a comprehensive and authoritative list for end users wishing to find particular types of, or specific repositories.
- Deliver a comprehensive, structured and maintained list with clear update and self-regulation protocols to enable development of the list.
- Play a prominent international role in the organisation of and access to open access repository services.
- Support Open Access outreach and advocacy endeavours within institutions and globally.

OPENDOAR - COUNTRIES AND ORGANISATIONS

- *Africa*
- *Asia*
- *Australasia*
- *Caribbean*
- *Central America*
- *Europe*

- *North America*
- *South America*

Opening further

*Open*DOAR is not in competition with OAI registration, since the service intends to categorise repositories in ways that are not supported by normal OAI registration. Indeed the current registration protocol requires complete repository details to a level which some find problematic and for this, and other, reasons there are open access repositories which have not registered with OAI. *Open*DOAR is actively searching for repositories to list and hopefully offers a straightforward registration process that will ensure that there will be significantly fewer omissions.

Repositories registered or included within *Open*DOAR will be more visible and will naturally have their contents more easily found by researchers. While search services can be aware of repositories for metadata harvesting through a basic list or register, with rapidly expanding numbers of sites individual repositories and pieces of content will become harder to find amongst a larger number of search results.

With *Open*DOAR allowing for repository listing by the content types it contains or the constituency it serves, a greater level of precision can be given to the searching process. In this way there is an increased chance for end-users to find a particular repository or for a search service to clearly flag an individual eprint or piece of research.

Open Access Journals

Open Access journals are peer-reviewed journals whose articles may be accessed online by anyone without charge. Some, mainly those published from a university department or with substantial subsidy, make no author or page charges. Others levy a charge for publishing an article, turning on its head the traditional model where a library pays for access to the contents of a journal through a subscription.

This charge may be paid by the author(s) but in most cases it is financed by a research grant or institutional funds. The institution may already have taken the decision to pay for Open Access articles to be published, or grant-awarding body may have adopted this as one of its policies. Many publishers now offer their authors the option of paying a publication charge to make a particular article open access, even if the remainder of the journal is only available on subscription. A comprehensive list of Open Access journals in all subject areas is maintained by the University of Lund. At the start of 2009, the list contains over 3800 journals. Many of these Open Access journals have impact factors and are indexed by the Institute for Scientific Information for its Web of Knowledge/Web of Science service. There is accumulating evidence that shows that research articles that have been selfarchived are cited more often than those that have not. A bibliography of studies on "The effect of open access and downloads ('hits') on citation impact" is maintained by the Open Citation Project. Making research publications Open Access means that research has much more impact than before. Moreover, the research cycle - where work is published, read, cited and then built upon by other researchers - is enhanced and accelerated when results are available on an Open Access basis. Academic institutions are also finding open access repositories valuable in generating management information and reports on their research programmes and in raising awareness of their research profile.

THE LEGAL ASPECTS

In the case of traditional journals, typically published by commercial publishers or learned societies, the author usually grants the publisher a rather exclusive copyright, in return for the services that the publisher renders the author. It must be stressed that contrary to what proponents of OA often state, authors do not give away the product for free.

Instead, they trade their papers without specific payment in exchange for the services that the publisher renders them (peer review, quality labelling, marketing, and dissemination). The fact that some publishers have charged page charges to authors in addition to charging subscribers is one indication of this. The surrender of copyright is so total that, the author is usually forced to ask written permission from the publishers to publish copies of his own papers as part of his thesis (the thesis is usually published as a monograph by his own university and is mainly distributed for free).

Many copyright forms grant the author the right to limited distribution of copies to colleagues. The emergence of the Internet has brought into light a particular problem, concerning the non-commercial distribution by posting copies on the Web. In many of the copyright forms which publishers ask authors to sign, this area is not properly addressed and constitutes a grey zone.

Open access journals, on the other hand, have, from the start, adopted a rather liberal approach reminiscent of the licensing schemes used by the open source programming community (often referred to as 'copyleft'). As a rule the author retains the copyright to the work. What the open access journals typically are interested in is that the paper, if made available elsewhere in the exact format of the journal, is attributed to primary publication in the journal, and also that no one (except the author) can resell the content. The copyright issue does not constitute an obstacle for the proliferation of open access journals. Currently used copyright agreements for OA journals are quite satisfactory from both the author's and the journal's viewpoint.

SUBJECT-SPECIFIC REPOSITORIES

A strong impulse for subject-specific repositories was the long lead-time between submission of a draft manuscript and the publication of the full paper. In some areas of science, such as high-energy physics, a tradition of scientists exchanging preprints on paper already existed and the new repositories just developed this mechanism further. The name preprint server describes this function.

One of the problems with low cost subject-specific repositories is that, because of the high number of papers in the successful ones, the managers of the service have no resources to check the legality of the papers posted. It is at the discretion of authors to remove papers once they have been accepted for publication, if they have signed copyright agreements, which prohibit keeping the copies on the server. On one hand the situation resembles that of the controversial music server Napster, on the other hand there are significant differences. The biggest difference is that, in the case of scientific publications, it is the author of the work who voluntarily puts up a copy on the server, not a third party.

Institutional Repositories

In the early stages institutional repositories will get their initial content from works of the faculty for which the university itself or the authors retain the copyright, such as PhD theses and working paper series of departments. These entail no legal problems. In the longer run, however, the critical mass of institutional repositories depends on the inclusion of the best work of each university's faculty that is the journal papers published elsewhere. From a legal viewpoint this constitutes a challenge, since university administrations will be very careful not to be break any copyright contracts, in contrast to individual researchers posting copies of their work on their home pages quite carelessly in spite of possible legal obstacles.

The Further Tasks

General awareness of the advantages of open access publishing is naturally a prerequisite for scientists choosing to use OA channels both for primary and secondary publishing and much remains to be done to achieve this. The recent rapid increase in the number of national and international conferences devoted to this theme is promising, but these conferences are mainly attended by the publishing and library community, not the content authors who are in the key position. Branding is extremely important from a marketing viewpoint, and in this respect it is interesting to follow the success or failure of attempts such as BioMed Central and the Public Library of Science. A key issue for efficient indexing of open access material is the success of the OAI-Protocol for Metadata Harvesting. Its widespread adoption would enable the setting up and in particular filling up with content of OA harvesting services, which would provide good access points worldwide for OA material. The enthusiasm and iconoclastic spirit of the early days of open access is now changing into a more realistic search for sustainable business models, and a better understanding of the formidable barriers to overcome. The marketplace, both on the supply side and the demand side, will decide the issue in the coming years.

REFERENCES AND NOTES

1. Björk, B.-C. & Hedlund, T. (2003). Scientific publication life cycle model (SPLC). In S.M. de S. Costa, J.Á Carvalho, A.A. Baptista, and A.C.S. Moreira (Eds.) *From information to knowledge: Proceedings of the 7th ICCC/IFIP International Conference on Electronic Publishing held at the Universidade do Minho, Portugal 25-28 June 2003*. http://elpub.scix.net/data/works/att/0317.content.pdf
2. Björk, B.-C., Turk, Z. (2000). How scientists retrieve publications: an empirical study of how the Internet is overtaking paper media. *Journal of Electronic Publishing*, 6(2). Retrieved 11 December 2003, from http://www.press.umich.edu/jep/06-02/bjork.html
3. ArXiv, <http://arxiv.org/>.

4. RePEc, <http://repec.org/>.

5. Davis, P. M., and Connolly, M. J. (2007). Institutional repositories: evaluating the reasons for non-use of Cornell University's installation of DSpace, *D-Lib Magazine*, *13*(3/4) <*doi:10.1045/10.1045/march2007-davis*>

6. Khoo, M. (2005). Tacit user and developer frames in user-led collection development: the case of the digital water education library, *Proceedings of JCDL*, ACM Press, 213-222.

7. Lynch, C. A. (2003). Institutional repositories: essential infrastructure for scholarship in the digital age, *ARL Bimonthly Report*, vol. 226, 2003. Available at <*http://www.arl.org/resources/pubs/br/br226/br226ir.shtml*>.

8. Crow, R. (2002). The case for institutional repositories: A SPARC position paper, *ARL Bimonthly Report*, vol. 223, 2002. Available at <*http://www.arl.org/bm~doc/instrepo.pdf*>.

9. Lynch, C.A. and Lippincott, J.K. (2005). Institutional repository deployment in the United States as of early 2005," *D-Lib Magazine*, *11*(9). Available at <*doi:10.1045/september2005-lynch*>.

10. Humboldt Bay Community home page. <*http://dscholar.humboldt.edu:8080/dspace/handle/2148/209*>.

11. California State University Accessible Technology Initiative. <*http://www.calstate.edu/Accessibility/index.shtml*>.

12. California State University Accessible Technology Initiative, Instructional Materials. <*http://www.calstate.edu/accessibility/instructionalmaterials/index.shtml*>.

13. California State University Accessible Technology Initiative, Web Accessibility Deliverables and Timeline. <*http://www.calstate.edu/accessibility/webaccessibility/deliverable_timeline.shtml*>.

14. Humboldt Digital Scholar Submission Guidelines. <*http://dscholar.humboldt.edu:8080/dspace/help/HDS_Submission_Guidelines.htm*

15. Electronic Theses. <*http://dscholar.humboldt.edu:8080/dspace/help/Electronic_theses.htm*>.

16. DSpace Format Support. <*http://libraries.mit.edu/dspace-mit/build/policies/format.html*>.

17. IEEE Standard for Learning Object Metadata: <*http://ltsc.ieee.org/wg12/*>.

18. Google Scholar, <http://scholar.google.com/>.

19. Guédon, J.C. (2001). In Oldenburg's long shadow: librarians, research scientists, publishers, and the control of scientific publishing, In *Creating the digital future. Association of Research Libraries. Proceedings of the 138th Annual Meeting, Toronto, Ontario May 23-25, 2001.* Washington, DC: Association of Research Libraries. http://www.arl.org/arl/proceedings/138/guedon.html

20. Gustafsson, T. (2002). *Open access - en empirisk undersökning om fritt tillgängliga vetenskapliga journaler på Internet.* Unpublished Master's thesis. Svenska Handelshögskolan, Informationsbehandling, Helsinki.

21. Office of Fair Trading (2003). The market for scientific, technical and medical journals: a statement by the OFT, Sept. 2002. London: Office of Fair Trading. http://www.oft.gov.uk/NR/rdonlyres/ efvqwtvbz6bqcpm5 vcfexjlnbl7l tb5anbnu7kuri5bhmfwx34kjdjni4qgpivcokr jdmugt4l6ic4kbokoji6a7xgg/oft396.pdf

22. Norman, D.A. (1988). *The psychology of everyday things.* Basic Books, New York.

23. Bailetti, J.A. and Litva, P.F (1995). Integrating customer requirements into product designs, *Journal of Product Innovation Management, 12* (1), 1995, pp. 3-15; Pruitt, J., and Adlin, T. (2006) *The persona lifecycle: keeping people in mind throughout product design.* Morgan Kaufmann: San Francisco.

24. Nielsen, J. and Norman, D. (2000). Usability on the web isn't a luxury, *Information Week,* January 2000. Available at: <*http://www.informationweek.com/773/web.htm*>; Temkin, B and Hult, P. (2005). Usability flaws of financial service web sites, *Forrester Research,* July 2005. Available at: <*http://www.forrester.com/Research/Document/Excerpt/0,7211,37302,00.html*>.

25. Pruitt, J. and Adlin, T. (2006). *The persona lifecycle: keeping people in mind throughout product design.* Morgan

Kaufmann: San Francisco.

26. OpenArchives Initiative (2003). *The Open Archives Initiative protocol for metadata harvesting. Version 2*. OpenArchives Initiative. http://www.openarchives.org/OAI/openarchives protocol.html

27. Björk, B.-C.(2001). Open source, open science, open course ware. In H. Penttilä (Ed.), *Architectural Information Management, eCAADe 19th Conference, Helsinki University of Technology, Department of Architecture, Espoo 2001*, (pp. 13-17). Helsinki, Helsinki University of Technology. http://www.hut.fi/events/ecaade/E2001presentations/01_01_bjork.pdf

28. Goode, R. (2003). *Open access initiative from Oxford Journals*. Oxford: Oxford University Press. (Press release.) http://www.eurekalert.org/pub_releases/2003-08/oup-oai080703.php

29. Open Citation Project. (2003). Core metalist of open access eprint archives. Open Citation Project. http://opcit.eprints.org/explorearchives.shtml

30. OAIster, <http://oaister.umdl.umich.edu/>.

31. AIRway Project, <http://airway.lib.hokudai.ac.jp/>.

32. 1CATE, <http://openly.oclc.org/1cate/>.

33. Parks, R. (2002). The Faustian grip of academic publishing. *Journal of Economic Methodology*, **9**(1), 317-335

34. RoMEO. Rights MEtadata for Open archiving Project. http://www.lboro.ac.uk/departments/ls/disresearch/romeo/

35. Shapiro, C and Varian, H. (1999). Information rules: a strategic guide to the networked economy. Boston, MA: Harvard Business School Press.

36. Walker, T.J. (1998). Free Internet access to traditional journals. *American Scientist*, **86**(5), 463-471.

37. Ferreira, M. E. A., Rodrigues, E. E. A., Baptista,A. A., and Saraiva, R. E. A. (2008). Carrots and sticks: some ideas on how to create a successful institutional repository, *D-Lib Magazine*, *14*(1/2), *<doi:10.1045/january2008-ferreira>*

38. Mercer, H. E. A., Rosenblum, B., & Emmett, A. (2007). A multifaceted approach to promote a university repository: the University of Kansas' experience, *OCLC Systems & Services*, *23*(2), 190-203

39. Thomas, C., and McDonald, R. H. (2007). Measuring and comparing participation patterns in digital repositories, *D-Lib Magazine*, *13*(9/10), *<doi:10.1045/september2007-mcdonald>*

40. Xia, J. (2007). Assessment of self-archiving in institutional repositories: across disciplines, *Journal of Academic Librarianship*, *33*(6), 647-654.

41. [12] Pruitt, J. and Adlin, T. (2006). *The persona lifecycle: keeping people in mind throughout product design*. Morgan Kaufmann: San Francisco.

42. Competition Commission. (2001). Reed Elsevier plc and Harcourt General, Inc: a report on the proposed merger. London: Competition Commission. (Cm5184) http://www.competition-commission.org.uk/rep_pub/reports/2001/457reed.htm

43. Cox, J. (2003). Value for money in electronic journals: a survey of the early evidence and some preliminary conclusions. *Serials Review* **29**(2), 83-88. Retrieved 11 December, 2003 from http://dx.doi.org/10.1016/S0098-7913(03)00041-8 [Note - Science Direct site, subscription necessary.]

44. Frazier, K. (2001). The librarians' dilemma - contemplating the costs of the 'Big Deal'. *D-Lib Magazine* **7**(3). http://dx.doi.org/10.1045/march2001-frazier

45. Ginsparg, P. (1996). *Electronic publishing in science*. Paper presented at a Conference held at UNESCO HQ, Paris, 19-23 February, 1996, during session *Scientist's View of Electronic Publishing and Issues Raised*, Wednesday, 21 February, 1996. http://arXiv.org/blurb/pg96unesco.html

46. Pruitt, J and Adlin, T. (2006). *The persona lifecycle: keeping people in mind throughout product design*, Morgan Kaufmann: San Francisco, p. 11.

47. Cooper, A. (1999). *The inmates are running the asylum.* Morgan Kaufmann: Indianapolis.

48. Eisenberg, B. (2005). Measuring personas for success, *Clickz Solutions for Marketers*, August 2005. Available at: <*http://www.clickz.com/experts/crm/traffic/article.php/3524941*>

49. Sinha, P. (2003). Persona development for information-rich domains. *Proceedings of the Conference on Human Factors in Computing Systems*, 2003, pp. 830-831

50. Grudin, J. and Pruitt, J. (2002). Personas, participatory design and product development: an infrastructure for engagement. *Proceedings of the Participatory Design Conference*, 2002, pp. 144-161.

51. Lawrence, S. (2001). Online or invisible? *Nature*, **411**(6837), 521. http://www.neci.nec.com/~lawrence/papers/online-nature01/

52. Massachusetts Institute of Technology. (2001). MIT to make nearly all course materials available free on the World Wide Web. *MIT News*, 4.4.2001 http://Web.mit.edu/newsoffice/nr/2001/ocw.html

53. Odlyzko, A. (1998). The economics of electronic journals. *Journal of Electronic Publishing*, **4**(1). Retrieved 11 December, 2003 from http://www.press.umich.edu/jep/04-01/odlyzko.html

54. Bates. (2007). Attitudes tó the rights and rewards for author contributions to repositories for teaching and learning. *ALT-J: Research in Learning Technology*, *15*(1), 67.

55. Adams, A., Blandford, A., and Lunt, P. (2005) Social empowerment and exclusion: a case study on digital libraries. *ACM Transactions on Computer-Human Interaction*, *12*(2), p. 198.

56. Weatherley, J. and Davis, L. (2006). How science web sites are using DLESE search web services to extend value to their users. *Proceedings of the 6th ACM/IEEE-CS joint conference on Digital libraries*, 381

57. Weatherley, J. (2005). A web service framework for embedding discovery services in distributed library

interfaces. *Proceedings of the 5th ACM/IEEE-CS joint conference on Digital libraries*, 42-43.

58. Krafft, D. B., Birkland, A., and Cramer, E. J. (2008). Ncore: architecture and implementation of a flexible, collaborative digital library. *Proceedings of JCDL*, 313-32; Lagoze, C., Krafft, D. B., Payette, S., and Jesuroga, S. (2005). What is a digital library anymore, anyway? *D-Lib Magazine*, *11*(11). Available at: <*doi:10.1045/november2005-lagoze*>.
59. Wells, A. (1999). *Exploring the development of the independent, electronic, scholarly journal*. Unpublished Master's thesis, University of Sheffield, Sheffield. http://panizzi.shef.ac.uk/elecdiss/edl0001/index.html
60. HUSCAP, <http://eprints.lib.hokudai.ac.jp/index.en.jsp>.
61. SUZUKI Masako and SUGITA Shigeki, "From Nought to a Thousand: The HUSCAP Project", *Ariadne*, Vol. 49 (October 2006), <http://www.ariadne.ac.uk/issue49/suzuki-sugita/>.
62. DSpace, <http://www.dspace.org/>.
63. Kvændrup, H.M.. (2003). *Fremtidens forskningspublicering - et nordisk samarbejde*. Copenhagen: Biblioteksstyrelsen. [22] Goodwin, K. (2002). Getting from research to personas: harnessing the power of data, *Cooper Newsletters*, November 2002. Available at: <*http://www.cooper.com/content/insights/newsletters/2002_11/getting_from_research_to_personas.asp*>.
64. Metadata: Technology: DSpace Federation, <http://dspace.org/technology/metadata.html>.
65. Next-Generation Scientific Information Resources Infrastructure, <http://www.nii.ac.jp/irp/index-e.html>.
66. http://www.opendoar.org/faq.html
67. Miaskiewicz, T., Sumner, T., and Kozar, K.A. (2008). A Latent Semantic Analysis methodology for the identification and creation of personas, *Proceedings of CHI 2008*, ACM Press, 1501-1510.
68. Thomas, C., and McDonald, R. H. (2007). Measuring and comparing participation patterns in digital repositories, *D-*

Lib Magazine, *13*(9/10) *<doi:10.1045/september2007-mcdonald>*,

69. McDowell, C. A. (2005). Evaluating institutional repository deployment in American academe since early 2005: repositories by the numbers, part 2, *D-Lib Magazine*, *13*(9/10). Available at *<doi:10.1045/september2007-mcdowell>*.

70. Xu, H. (2007). The current situation of faculty participation in institutional repositories - a study of 40 DSpace implementations supporting IRs. *Proceedings of the 70th Annual Meeting of the American Society of Information Science & Technology, Joining Research and Practice: Social Computing and Information Science*, Volume 44 (October 19-24, 2007).

71. Greig, M. E. A. (2007). Repositories and copyright: major hurdle or minor obstacle?, *ALISS Quarterly*, 3(1), 16-19; Swan, A. and Brown, S. (2005). Open access self-archiving: an author study, *Technical report, unspecified, external collaborators, JISC, HEFCE*. Available at: *<http://eprints.ecs.soton.ac.uk/10999/>*

72. Watson, S. E. A. (2007). Authors' attitudes to, and awareness and use of, a university institutional repository, *Serials*, *20*(3), 225-230.

73. ARL Joint Task Force for Library Support for E-Science (2007). *Agenda for Developing E-Science in Research Libraries: Final Report and Recommendations to the Scholarly Communication Steering Committee, the Public Policies Affecting Research Libraries Steering Committee, and the Research, Teaching, and Learning Steering Committee*. Available at: *<http://www.arl.org/bm~doc/ARL_EScience_final.pdf>*.

74. Krevit, L.E.A. and Crays, L. (2007). Herding cats: designing DigitalCommons @ the Texas medical center, a multi-institutional repository. *OCLC Systems & Services*, 23(2), 116-124.

75. Open access repo

76. ArXiv, *<http://arxiv.org/>*.

77. RePEc, *<http://repec.org/>*.

78. Google Scholar, <*http://scholar.google.com/*>.

79. OAIster, <*http://oaister.umdl.umich.edu/*>.

80. AIRway Project, <*http://airway.lib.hokudai.ac.jp*>.

81. Davis, P. M., and Connolly, M. J. L. (2007). Institutional repositories: evaluating the reasons for non-use of Cornell University's installation of DSpace. *D-Lib Magazine, 13*(3), <*doi:10.1045/10.1045/march2007-davis*>.

82. Cooper, A. and Reimann,, R.M. (2003). *About face 2.0*, Wiley Publishing: Indianapolis.

83. Norman, D.A. (1988). *The psychology of everyday things.* Basic Books: New York.

84. Goodwin, K. (2002). Getting from research to personas: harnessing the power of data, *Cooper Newsletters*, November 2002. Available at: <*http://www.cooper.com/content/insights/newsletters/2002_11/getting_from_research_to_personas.asp*>.

85. Miaskiewicz, T., Sumner, T., and Kozar, K.A. (2008). A Latent Semantic Analysis methodology for the identification and creation of personas, *Proceedings of CHI 2008*, ACM Press, 1501-1510.

86. W. Crawford. *MARC for library use: understanding integrated USMARC* (2nd ed.). 1989. K. Hall & Co. Boston, MA, USA.

87. W. Nejdl, B. Wolf, C. Qu, S. Decker, M. Sintek, A. Naeve, M. Nilsson, M. Palmér, T. Risch. EDUTELLA: a P2P networking infrastructure based on RDF. *Proceedings of the 11th international conference on World Wide Web*. 2002. Honolulu, Hawaii, USA, pages 604-615.

88. S. Ceri, G. Gottlob, and L. Tanca. *Logical Programming and Databases*. 1990. Springer, New York, NY.

89. H. Van de Sompel, M. L. Nelson, C. Lagoze, S. Warner. Resource Harvesting within the OAI-PMH Framework, *D-Lib Magazine*, Volume 12, Number 12, December 2004, <*doi:10.1045/december2004-vandesompel*>.

90. <*http://www.chiariglione.org/mpeg/*>.

91. Swan, A. and Brown, S. (2005). Open access self-archiving:

an author study, *Technical report, unspecified, external collaborators, JISC, HEFCE*. Available at: <*http://eprints.ecs.soton.ac.uk/10999/*>.

92. CATE, <*http://openly.oclc.org/1cate/*>.
93. HUSCAP, <*http://eprints.lib.hokudai.ac.jp/index.en.jsp*>.
94. SUZUKI Masako and SUGITA Shigeki, "From Nought to a Thousand: The HUSCAP Project", *Ariadne*, Vol. 49 (October 2006), <*http://www.ariadne.ac.uk/issue49/suzuki-sugita/*>.
95. DSpace, <*http://www.dspace.org/*>.
96. Metadata: Technology: DSpace Federation, <*http://dspace.org/technology/metadata.html*>.
97. Next-Generation Scientific Information Resources Infrastructure, <*http://www.nii.ac.jp/irp/index-e.html*>.
98. Humboldt Digital Scholar. <*http://dscholar.humboldt.edu:8080/dspace/*>.
99. DSpace Mailing Lists. <*http://www.dspace.org/feedback/mailing.html*>.
100. Handle System® homepage <*http://www.handle.net/*>.
101. California State University ScholarWorks. <*http://www.calstate.edu/UIAS/ScholarWorks.html*>.
102. Registry of Open Access Repositories (ROAR). <*http://roar.eprints.org/*>.
103. SHERPA/RoMEO. <*http://www.sherpa.ac.uk/romeo.php*>.
104. Zthes, <*http://zthes.z3950.org/cql/*>.
105. SRW: Search/Retrieve Web Service is described in the SRU Version 1.1 Archive at <*http://www.loc.gov/standards/sru/sru1-1archive/srw.html*>.
106. The SRU Via HTTP SOAP specification is at <*http://www.loc.gov/standards/sru/specs/transport.html#soap*>.
107. XQuery, "An XML Query Language", is a W3C standard. The current specification, version 1.0, is at: <*http://www.w3.org/TR/xquery/*>.
108. The MODS (Metadata Object Description Schema) version 3.3 schema is at: <*http://www.loc.gov/standards/mods//v3/mods-3-3.xsd*>.

109. E. Duval, E. Forte, K. Cardinaels, B. Verhoeven, R. Van Durm, K. Hendrikx, M.W. Forte, N. Ebel, M. Macowicz, K. Warkentyne, F. Haenni. The ARIADNE Knowledge Pool System: a Distributed Digital Library for Education, *Communications of the ACM*, 44(5):73-78, May 2001.

110. IMS Global Learning Consortium: <*http://www.imsglobal.org*>.

111. The Dublin Core Metadata Initiativa: <*http://dublincore.org/*>.

112. MPEG-7: <*http://www.chiariglione.org/mpeg/standards/mpeg-7/mpeg-7.htm*>.

113. F. Van Assche, E. Duval, D. Massart, D. Olmedilla, B. Simon, S. Sobernig, S. Ternier and F. Wild. Spinning interoperable applications for teaching & learning. *Journal of Educational Technology & Society*, 9(2):51-67, April 2006. Special Issue: Interoperability of Educational Systems.

114. C. Lagoze, H. Van de Sompel, M. Nelson, S. Warner. *The Open Archives Initiative Protocol for Metadata Harvesting - Version 2.0* <*http://www.openarchives.org/OAI/openarchivesprotocol.html*>.

115. K. Verbert and E. Duval. Evaluating the ALOCOM Approach for Scalable Content Repurposing. *Second European Conference on Technology Enhanced Learning (ECTEL) - Creating new learning experiences on a global scale*, 17-20 September 2007, Crete, Greece.

116. R. Sanderson, J. Young, R. LeVan, SRW/U with OAI, Expected and Unexpected Synergies, *D-Lib Magazine*, Volume 11, Number 2, February 2005, <*doi:10.1045/february2005-sanderson*>.

117. E. Duval, S. Ternier, F. van Assche (eds). *Learning Objects in Context, special issue of International Journal on E-Learning*, Vol. 5, No.1, <*http://go.editlib.org/p/21768*>, 2006.

118. D. Massart. The EUN Learning Resource Exchange (LRE). *The 15th International Conference on Computers in Education (ICCE2007) Supplementary Proceedings*, volume 1, pages 170-174, November 2007.

119. CQL: Contextual Query Language (SRU Version 1.2 Specifications). Last accessed 12 November 2007 at <*http://www.loc.gov/standards/sru/specs/cql.html*>.

120. J.-N. Colin and D. Massart. LIMBS: Open source, open standards, and open content to foster learning resource exchanges. *Proceedings of The Sixth IEEE International Conference on Advanced Learning Technologies, ICALT'06*, pages 682-686, Kerkrade, The Netherlands, July 2006. IEEE Computer Society, Los Alamitos, California.

121. B. Simon, D. Massart, F. Van Assche, S. Ternier, E. Duval. *A simple query interface specification for learning repositories*. CEN Workshop Agreement (CWA 15454).

122. F. Van Assche, D. Massart, (eds). *The EUN Learning Resource Exchange Metadata Application Profile Version 3.0*. Last accessed November 13, 2007 at <*http://fire.eun.org/LRE-AP-3.0.pdf*>.

123. D. Massart. LRE-QL: Introducing an *LRE Context Set For The Federated Discovery of Learning Resources*. July 2007. Last accessed November 13, 2007 at <*http://fire.eun.org/QueryingTheLRE.pdf*>.

124. The XML Path Language: <*http://www.w3.org/TR/xpath*>.

125. S. Ternier, F. Neven, M. Macowicz, N. Ebel. Web services for Learning object Repositories - the ARIADNE Knowledge Pool System. *12th International World Wide Web Conference*, Budapest, Hungary, pages 203-204.

126. J. Broisin, P. Vidal, M. Meire, and E. Duval. Bridging the Gap between Learning Management Systems and Learning Object Repositories: Exploiting Learning Context Information. In *ELETE 2005*, IEEE Computer Society, p. 478-483, Lisbon, July 2005.

12

Digital Information, the Public Domain and Digital Copyright

The World Intellectual Property Organization solicits studies in an expanding field of activities ranging from the Internet, health care, all aspects of science and technology, literature and the arts, patent systems and access to drug care, genetic resources, traditional knowledge and folklore. Intellectual property such as licensed software is clearly protected by several legal mechanisms such as patents, copyright (among the most important forms of intellectual property) or trade secrets. Faced by digital piracy and illicit copying, proprietary software producers in addition frequently restrict or limit use, for example, by anti-copying measures such as copy bars.

Some do not accept restrictions on the free utilization of intellectual property, e.g., in countries where piracy is openly justified or covertly condoned, sometimes arguing that poverty prevents their paying high prices for imported materials, or even that it represents redress for colonial exploitation. The physics of piracy of the intangible are different from the physics of the tangible'. Are they in the wrong, ethically speaking? This is a very fundamental point but is beyond the present scope. It serves to illustrate, however, that there are a number of unresolved problems in the borderlands of law and ethics.

There can be a never ending debate on the status of public domain. Whether the public domain is a virtual wasteland of undeserving detritus or the font of all new creation has always been a matter of intellectual yet legal concern. Those who adhere to the former perspective do not worry about "threats" to this domain any more than they would worry about scavengers who go to garbage dumps to look for abandoned property. Adherents of the latter view are, interestingly enough, not of one mind about "threats" to this domain. Some believe that propertizing value residing in the public domain might produce social benefit, while others regard propertization itself as the main threat to the public domain. These views: such as some of what is in the public domain is detritus; some of what is valuable in the public domain might be better utilized if propertized to some degree; other parts of the public domain need to remain open and unownable as sources for future creations are significant in the context.

PUBLIC DOMAIN : PRESENT STATE IN THE DIGITAL ENVIRONMENT

The impact of the convergence of the technologies of computing and telecommunications on societies, economies and universities, will undoubtedly be profound. Like other major shifts in communications the full effect will probably not be known for generations. The pace of change, which is unprecedented and bewildering, can blind us to the fact that we are still at the dawn of this new era. Most of what there is to know about how to realize the great promise of the new technologies is still unlearned. The territory is unmapped, and any reports from the frontier can only provide partial and provisional information to guide those who follow us.

The public domain seems an undifferentiated blob of unnamed size and dimensions. The public domain focuses on one or a small number of its component parts or traits. The public domain consists, of a vast and diverse assortment of contents. The public domain is, different sizes at different times and in different countries. Sometimes the public domain grows. Sometimes it shrinks, as when the European Union promulgated a directive requiring EU member states to protect the contents of databases. The public domain has some murky areas, too.

Access may be interpreted restrictively to refer only to the open versus closed access of users to library materials. Here the trend has been from closed to open access almost everywhere except in archival and research collections or the library systems of totalitarian states. Yet, in the context of information ethics, access has a far wider application than libraries. Internationally, the digital divide among and within, countries is probably the most obvious aspect of the access issue. Some see the digital divide as one of the most serious ethical problems internationally in the information age. The public domain are several categories of content that are widely enough usable. For practical purposes, they seem to be part of the public domain. This includes much content that is protected by copyright law. This content is widely available to the public, as when it is posted on publicly accessible websites available to all comers without fee or apparent restrictions on use. Also outside the public domain, in theory, are such things as open source software; a penumbra of privileged uses under fair use, experimental use, and other rules that permit unlicensed uses and sharing of information to take place. There are standards that are licensed without payment of royalties. There are some works whose intellectual property rights are on the verge of expiring and arguably some creations about to be made (a new computer programming language or the solution to a longstanding mathematical problem) that, once they exist, will be part of the public domain.

PUBLIC DOMAIN INFORMATION: CATEGORIES AND COUNTRIES

Publication of scientific content has been one of the areas to benefit most from the emergence of the Internet. A scientific publication, as an information good, can easily be delivered electronically to the end user. Scientists already have the necessary equipment and skills to access the material in their normal work environment, and have been forerunners in the use of the Internet for communication. In the near future scientists worldwide will access most of the texts they read over the World Wide Web. In addition to traditional publications, there are many other ways in which scientific communities can use information technology and the Internet to enhance their communication and collaboration processes, such as e-mail discussion lists, databases of observation data, the sharing of models and programming code etc.

Various categories of public domain information are akin to regions of that nation. The contents of each category are akin to the cities or villages within that region that, in turn, have populations of various sizes. Mapping the public domain and contiguous terrains is useful for several reasons. First, it can help in an assessment of the likely impacts of certain developments, such as the digitization of information and the development of global digital networks. Second, the map can be a tool for calibrating the extent to which a particular legal or policy initiative may affect the public domain, it can affect either in a positive or negative way. Some legal and policy initiatives have broader and more serious potential impacts than others. Third, it can contribute to an analysis of which among the contents of the public domain are detritus (e.g., grocery lists) and which gems (e.g., Mozart symphonies), which are among the constitutionally core elements of the public domain (e.g., scientific principles), and which of the public domain's contents will be most harmed if propertized (e.g., information).

The open archives and open source movements are consistent with the IFLA core value of free access to information, which is fully subscribed to by most professional library associations. Yet as has been argued elsewhere, free access to information and the freedom of expression are ideals which under certain conditions, e.g., emergencies or war, can be legally proscribed even in democratic societies. Major individual rights in democratic societies are the right to life and safety, the right of free consent, right to private property, right of free speech and fair treatment. Much here depends on who we claim these rights for. If these are those on the *other* side of the digital divide—the vast majority of the world's present population of 6.4 billion—who are still not online, it would seem that both consequentialist-utilitarian and deontological ethical theory condone the open archives and open source movement.

The digitization of information can have a very positive impact on the effective existence of the public domain is readily apparent. To the extent scientific data is either collected in or transposed into digital form. It can then be shared and processed more readily than if it remained in paper from. The existence of global digital networks means that scientists from around the world can share data sets and conduct experiments. It may lead to further discoveries that will contribute to further growth of the public domain. Similarly, digitization of information, and posting of information on the Internet makes the information more widely accessible than print equivalents. This makes the public domain more effective and robust in serving that part of the public interested in such information. Digitization of information and the existence of digital networks do not, necessarily enhance the public domain. Firms may be able to attain meaningful exclusive control over digital information that is in the public domain, both in theory and in law, through technological access controls or licensing or both. There are certain inevitable questions.

In parallel to the developments, pioneering scientists have jumped on the opportunity offered by the Internet for bypassing the costly intermediaries in the publishing process. During the 1990s several e-print archives as well as a few hundred peer-reviewed, electronic, scholarly journals emerged. The common denominator for these is that they offer free access to the electronic product. This has become known as "open access publishing". The experiences of this first wave of pilots demonstrate that the barriers for changing the commercially oriented communication system were greatly underestimated. Because of such barriers the impact of open access on the total volume of scientific publishing is still negligible.

Do these technical controls or licenses diminish the public domain? Printed forms of these materials are, still widely available without license or technical restrictions. They may be a resource for further digitization projects having a non-proprietary character. Even those who care deeply for the continued existence of the public domain in information would have to admit that no firm could justify undertaking the very substantial expense of digitizing public domain information and building a database of these contents and software tools to enable effective use of the database without some way to recoup these expenses, as through some exercise of exclusive control over the resource.

Concern about restrictions imposed by proprietary

databases of information has, generated a variety of initiatives to "free" information from these constraints. Organization themselves have undertaken to publish information on the websites. Some for-profit firms provide open Internet access to digitized information without charge in the hopes of attracting users to their sites. In these and other initiatives, digitization of the information and the availability of digital networks have been essential components of the strategy for effectively contributing to an enhancement of this facet of the public domain. This characterization of the transaction affects rights that copyright law confers on owners of copies of copyrighted content (e.g., to make backup copies of software, to modify software, and to sell or otherwise redistribute software).

Many software licenses restrict the right to reverse engineer computer programs, even though this activity would be acceptable under trade secrecy and copyright law as a means to get access to information that may be part of the public domain. However, by conferring rights on compilers to control the use or extraction of all or a substantial part of a collection of information that is the product of substantial investment. The technical measure widely used to protect DVD movies, for example, does not enable fair uses to be made. Indeed it does not even permit users to skip through commercials included on the disk. Once technical protection measures are embedded in hardware, hacking to release public domain information or to enable fair or other privileged uses will become much more difficult than at present. More likely, is legislation applicable to some electronics equipment, but not (yet) as to computers. This addresses a key problem for the content industry. Manufacturers of consumer electronics equipment want to make products that customers will be eager to buy. At the same time customers prefer technologies that enable them to copy and share digital content. Efforts, such as the Secure

Digital Music Initiative (SDMI), are not easy to bring to fruition because of the content industry has very different interests than the consumer electronics industry.

A person who makes reasonable uses of protected information which the licensor claims are breaches of the license can at least argue that the license term interferes with intellectual property policy and should be preempted, is a misuse of intellectual property rights, is a fair breach of the license, or is unconscionable. A legal challenge to a technical measure interfering with reasonable uses is, unlikely to succeed or be cost-effective. Some scholars have endorsed "selfhelp" measures by users to preserve the public domain or have argued for changes so that anti-circumvention protections would only be available to copyright owners who had escrowed keys to unlock technical protections so that prospective fair users could get access to them. Although the reasons for their preferences may differ, their goals may converge sufficiently to make them allies in insisting on greater control over the online environment. This would diminish the digital public domain.

ONGOING STRATEGIES

Scientists have created a variety of digital public domain resources, including libraries of reusable code and databases of scientific and technical information in digital form. There are also available on the Internet. The Library of Congress has not undertaken digitalization projects of historically significant parts of the Library's collection. It has also convened a group to consider strategies for digital preservation of information. Both have very substantial and positive implications for the digital public domain. Entrepreneurial individuals have also taken advantage of the Web to make available a wide array of materials that are protected by copyright. Some material is available on open websites with few or no restrictions on copying or distribution. This includes articles written by academics posted on their home pages, pre-print archives of articles enabling scientists to share the latest learning in their fields, electronic journals, newsgroups, web resources on the poster's favorite topic, and MP3 files of music posted. Some have created a vast nonprofit digital archive of the Internet and World Wide Web so that researchers can investigate certain things this includes growth of web over time, changes occurred in the languages used on the Web over time. It also discerns into what proportion of Web content is taken down or put up in units of time, just to name a few researchable questions. A very substantial amount of high quality free content is available on the web. Even sites of profit-making entities, post a large volume of high quality information on the Internet.

Among the most interesting developments that contribute to the digital public domain, is open source or "free" software. Open source software contributes to the public domain because its licenses require that source code instructions be publicly available. All of the know-how embodied in the program will thus be accessible. Open source licenses encourage follow-on innovation, open source contributes to ongoing learning and it enhances the public domain. Open source software is not itself in the public domain. Rather, it invokes intellectual property rights as the basis for a licensing strategy aimed at preserving a digital commons the program's developer wished to establish for it. From the standpoint of many open source developers, dedicating a program to the public domain is a suboptimal strategy for achieving open source objectives because proprietary derivatives can be made of public domain programs. Those who breach the terms of an open source license by making a proprietary derivative program will be deemed infringers of the underlying intellectual property rights in the program. They can be enjoined from this form of free-riding on open source development. Open source licenses use property rights to preserve and maintain a commons in an existing intellectual resource. The initial subject matter of open source development was software. Currently some efforts are being made to adapt open source licenses to other subject matters, such as digital music. As admirable as open source may as an example of a strategy for preserving and extending the digital commons, there is also value of preserving a public domain from which proprietary derivatives can be made. An inducement to the creation of new works from the public domain is the incentive of copyright protection for the derivative work.

As worthy of attention as risks to the public domain, so are risks to investments in developing high-value digital information products. The marginal cost of reproducing and distributing digital information may be zero (or nearly so), but initial development costs may still be high, as may be costs of transforming the digital information into marketable form and then of marketing it. While some hoped that advertising would provide a sustainable revenue stream through which digital content providers could recoup investments, this seems a less viable long-term strategy after the dot.com bust. With a good business model, intellectual property rights may be much less important. The digital information market is quite unstable right now in part because no one is sure what business models are viable for distributing digital information via global networks.

INTERNATIONAL COPYRIGHT PROTECTION

Most public domain information to date has been individual efforts created by single academics and groups of academics, often managing the information on a part-time basis. Hence, the information technology infrastructure of these resources is quite varied, ranging from rather rudimentary, static HTML-versions to quite sophisticated database driven systems, depending on the skills and resources of the creators. The platforms have seldom been bought from outside companies or larger publishers. One of the drawbacks of these systems is that they are very vulnerable, in case the person in charge for some reason or other stops working with the information. Copyright protection rules are fairly similar worldwide, due to several international copyright treaties, the most important of which is the Berne Convention. Under this treaty, all member countries must afford copyright protection to authors who are nationals of any member country. This protection must last for at least the life of the author plus 50 years, and must be automatic without the need for the author to take any legal steps to preserve the copyright. In addition to the Berne Convention, the GATT (General Agreement on Tariffs and Trade) treaty contains a number of provisions that affect copyright protection in signatory countries.

The exception is for materials put to work under the "fair use rule." This rule recognizes that society can often benefit from the unauthorized use of copyrighted materials when the purpose of the use serves the scholarship, education and an informed public.

Often, it's difficult to know a proposed use to be fair. The fair use statute requires to consider the following questions in deciding this issue:

- Is it a competitive use? (In other words, if the use potentially affects the sales of the copied material, it's usually not fair.)
- How much material was taken compared to the entire work of which the material was a part? (The more someone takes, the less likely it is that the use is fair.)

The method of using information material is an important aspect. How was the material used? Using material to help create something new is considered a fair use.

Criticism, comment, news reporting, research, scholarship and non-profit educational uses are most likely to be judged fair uses. Uses motivated primarily by a desire for a commercial gain are less likely to be fair use.

What types of creative work does copyright protect?

Copyright protects works such as poetry, movies, CD-ROMs, video games, videos, plays, paintings, sheet music, recorded music performances, novels, software code, sculptures, photographs, choreography and architectural designs. To qualify for copyright protection, a work must be "fixed in a tangible medium of expression." This means that the work must exist in some physical form for at least some period of time, no matter how brief. Virtually any form of expression will qualify as a tangible medium, including a computer's random access memory (RAM), the recording media that capture all radio and television broadcasts, and the scribbled notes on the back of an envelope that contain the basis for an impromptu speech. In addition, the work must be original – that is, independently created by the author. It doesn't matter if an author's creation is similar to existing works, or even if it is arguably lacking in quality, ingenuity or aesthetic merit. So long as the author toils without copying from someone else, the results are protected by copyright. A work must be the result of at least some creative effort on the part of its author.

Copyright shelters only fixed, original and creative expression, not the ideas or facts upon which the expression is based. Allowing authors to monopolize their ideas would thwart the underlying purpose of copyright law, which is to encourage people to create new work.

Copyright does not protect scientific, historical, biographical facts or news of the day. Any facts that an author discovers in the course of research are in the public domain, free to all. For instance, anyone is free to use information provided that that they express the information in their own words. Facts are not protected even if the author spends considerable time and effort discovering things that were previously unknown.

In the complicated scheme of copyright laws, the application of law to a particular work depends on when that work is published. A work is considered published when the author makes it available to the public on an unrestricted basis. It is possible to distribute or display a work without publishing it, if there are significant restrictions placed on what can be done with the work and when it can be shown to others. If author authorizes posting of the essay on the Internet, however, it would likely be considered published.

INFORMATION ON INTERNET

People are posting vast quantities of creative material on the Internet. This material that is available for downloading by anyone who has the right computer equipment. The information is stored somewhere on an Internet server, is fixed in a tangible medium and potentially qualifies for copyright protection. Whether it does, qualify depends on other factors that user had no way of knowing about, such as when the work was first published, which affects the need for a copyright notice, whether the copyright in the work has been renewed whether the work is a work made for hire which affects the length of the copyright and whether the copyright owner intends to dedicate the work to the public domain.

DIGITAL PRESERVATION AND COPYRIGHT

If all information in the world was written on clay tablets, carved into marble, or written on paper its preservation would be greatly simplified. Today, however, much of the information being produced is digital, and digital formats are notoriously fragile. Either the media on which the information is stored becomes unreadable, or the hardware and software needed to read the work becomes obsolete. To preserve analog information resources, it is often sufficient to house them in a benign environment. Digital preservation starts with copying. Good preservation practice requires much more, including making multiple copies of files. Digital documents may need to be changed from WordStar to WordPerfect to Word format, or perhaps even converted to PDF or XML format. In copyright law, copying is known as "reproduction," and it's one of the exclusive rights of the copyright owner. The right to publicly display a work is also an exclusive right of the copyright owner, as is the right to make an adaptation, known as a "derivative work."

EXEMPTION

Fortunately, while there is no general exemption for preservation activities in copyright law, there are exemptions that can help individuals and especially libraries and archives legally preserve expressive works for the future. In the absence of a specific exemption, one can always consider fair use as a defense when making a preservation copy. Even before user start looking for exemptions in the copyright law; it is always a good idea to check first to determine if an item really is copyrighted. Most digital information is copyrighted as soon as it is created. But there are exceptions. Digital copies of public domain works may themselves be in the public domain. User also doesn't need to worry about legal restrictions on preservation if he owns the copyright in the work.

ARCHIVING COMPUTER PROGRAMS

If the digital file, someone is interested in saving, is a computer program, can help. This law states that in spite of the copyright owner's exclusive rights, it is permissible to make a copy for archival purposes of a copyrighted computer program. Acomputer program is defined in the law as "a set of statements or instructions to be used directly or indirectly in a computer in order to bring about a certain result." The law allows to make a copy of the WordStar program (if someone legally owns it), and even adapt it to run on Windows XP or Linux machine (if user can), but not share the file with anyone else. The section only applies to the computer program itself. It does not authorize the reproduction or adaptation of documents created with WordStar when the copyright in those documents is owned by someone other than user.

LIBRARIES AND ARCHIVES MAKING PRESERVATION COPIES

Libraries and archives have additional preservation options under law. One of the few good things included in the Digital Millenium Copyright Act (DMCA) was a provision that explicitly allows libraries and archives to make up to three copies of a work for preservation purposes. The items being preserved can be in any format (text, images, sound, etc.). The copies can not be digital, as long as they are not distributed digitally nor made available to the public in a digital format outside the premises of the library or archives.

In order to take advantage of the exception, libraries and archives must follow certain ground rules. They must be either open to the public or allow access to non-affiliated researchers. The copying cannot be for "direct or indirect commercial advantage". The library or archives must own a legal copy of the original item; and any copies made must carry with them a notice of copyright. If the work is unpublished, preservation copies can be made for the purpose of preservation or security. If the work is published, preservation copies can be made to replace an original that is "damaged, deteriorating, lost, or stolen, or if the existing format in which the work is stored has become obsolete." The law stipulates that a format is obsolete "if the machine or device necessary to render perceptible a work stored in that format is no longer manufactured or is no longer reasonably available in the commercial marketplace." The library or archives must also conduct a reasonable investigation to confirm that an unused copy cannot be obtained at a fair price. If digital copies are made, access to the digital version must be limited to the premises of the library or archives.

FAIR USE PRESERVATION BY INDIVIDUALS AND LIBRARIES

The protection of intellectual property also benefits workers in many industries that are not linked directly to the creation or invention but benefit from its protection. These include employees of sound recording companies, video recording companies, software producers, the book industry and others that are involved in the various production stages of protected works.

Intellectual property refers to the ownership of information; hence the laws that regulate intellectual property are first and foremost property laws. What distinguishes intellectual property from other property is that intellectual property is characterized by the lack of tangible form. Because intellectual property is intangible, it needs to be defined in such a way that will allow it to be protected. Intellectual property laws are intended to encourage originality by preserving ownership rights and setting terms for the copying and duplicating of original works. Intellectual property laws apply to four types of intangible property: patents; trademarks; copyrights; and trade secrets.

Mary Minow provides a highly readable overview of fair use in "*How I learned to love FAIR USE...*" At the heart of the fair use exemption is the assessment of the four factors that constitute fair use: **P**urpose of the use, **N**ature of the work, **A**mount or substantiality used, and **M**arket impact (**PNAM**). It is likely that most preservation copying would meet

Minow's PNAM test. As Robert Oakley has noted about preservation copying in general:

Virtually everyone views preservation copying as socially beneficial. It is consistent with the Constitutional purposes for copyright since the preservation of printed knowledge is necessary for the progress of science and the useful arts.

If preservation is being done for non-commercial, socially beneficial reasons, it seems likely that the "Purpose" factor would lean towards fair use. The nature of digital works, the second fair use factor, can vary greatly, but Congress seems open to preserving a wide variety of material when preservation is at stake. The "Nature" factor, then, might also support a fair use.

The third factor, the Amount and substantiality copied, might normally weigh against a finding of fair use, since the item is being copied in its entirety. The extent of permissible copying varies with the purpose and character of the use. Obviously, if the purpose is to preserve a work, then the entire work must be copied. The amount copied is appropriate for the purpose, and so a court might even find this use fair. The fourth factor, the Market impact of making of a preservation copy, is likely to be the most important in any fair use assessment, and unfortunately it is almost impossible to guess how a court might rule on this. Purchasing a copy of a work does not give the right to copy it onto new media or transform it into new formats into perpetuity. Individuals, like libraries copying, must first determine if an unused copy can be purchased before a preservation copy can be made?

PRESERVING THE INFORMATION ON WORLD WIDE WEB

In general Copyright infringement occurs whenever copyrighted material is copied from or posted to a website without authorization from the copyright owner.

1. Posting Information on a Website

Posting involves a user sending information from the user's computer to the website (sometimes referred to as "uploading"). Once posted, others can view or copy the material. Below is an example of a "click to accept" agreement intended to prohibit unauthorized postings.

Uploading Restrictions

User agrees not to post:

- *any materials protected under copyright, trademark or trade secret laws unless with the express authorization of the owner; or*
- *any material likely to defame or invade the privacy of any individual.*

User agrees to indemnify the owners of the site and their affiliates and employees from any liability (including attorney fees) related to User's violation of this agreement.

2. Taking Information from a Website

A user may take information from the website and transfer it to the computer. This is typically done either by downloading or by copying. Many sites are set up for users to download material. Shareware sites, allow users to download software they want by clicking on a downloadable file, which will then be transferred onto the user's computer. Another way of obtaining material from websites is simply by selecting text, copying and pasting it into a word processing document on the user's computer. Though this is not downloading, but the effect is the same. The user has obtained material from the website and copied it onto his computer.

a. Copying : If a website doesn't offer material to download at the site, the main concern isn't whether it will infringe someone else's copyright, but whether users will copy the material without permission. Particularly if the site contains copyrightable works by outside authors. One common method is to prominently display a copyright notice on some or all of Web pages clearly stating the copyright.

To deal with the fact that many users may copy information anyway, one option is to accept this fact and include in his copyright notice a prohibition on any commercial use of the material. In addition, he can require that the copyright notice must always be included with the material, so anyone who reads it knows who created it. Many webmasters are willing to accept some limited copying by users for personal use, especially if the copies show who originally generated the material.

b. Downloading : The concept of unauthorized downloading may seem strange, considering that most sites that offer files for download are obviously consenting to the download. However, even if downloads are specifically allowed from a site, he still may have concerns over unauthorized uses of the downloaded material. For example if he offers free material for download at his site, he may want to prohibit users from selling the material, and limit their use to personal use. If the user violates the restriction, he may be able to sue for breach of contract. Even if the agreement is not enforceable, its presence may defeat a claim of innocent infringement by the user.

COPYRIGHTING THE SOFTWARE

When software developer/programmer doesn't put that little © on his work, he automatically get a copyright the instant his work of expression becomes fixed in a tangible medium. Theoretically, this means that he owns the copyright, and no one may copy, distribute, display or make adaptations of the work without his permission. The problem comes if someone infringes on his copyright. Then, suddenly, the protection is no longer automatic. It's up to him to file a lawsuit in court and to convince the judge to order the other party to stop the infringement and compensate him for his losses. What's more, even though he owns the copyright, he can't file his lawsuit unless he has registered the copyright with the Copyright Office. Until he registers, there's nothing he can do to stop the infringement.

REGISTRATION OF COPYRIGHT

The timely registration can help. That's because an infringer who knows that creator could recover substantial statutory damages in court may be more willing to negotiate and settle out of court. Of course, if what someone is publishing probably has no value to anyone but creator, he may want to just place a copyright notice on the material. If his work is valuable enough to publish, it's valuable enough to register. Registering a copyright registration is a simple process. Registering requires some basic information about the work, including:

- the title of the work
- who created the work an when, and
- who owns the copyright.

Web site permissions

Most information found on the Web is automatically copyrighted when created. The groups that want to preserve Web pages, however, are often not the copyright owners of those Web pages. We can presume that the copyright owner has granted an implied license to allow people to copy a Web page to a local machine and display it there; after all, if they did not want people to be able to read a page which in the Web environment means making a temporary copy on his local machine, they would not have put the document up on the Web.

The most ambitious attempt to preserve the Web, the Internet Archive and its "Wayback Machine," allows retrieving outdated Web pages from multiple points in time.

The Internet Archive has attempted to bolster a possible fair use defense in a number of ways. First, it allows Web page producers to "opt out" of the archives. It does this by offering instruction on how to use a "robots.txt" file to prevent its crawlers from retrieving new pages. Presence of a "robots.txt" file will also prevent Wayback Machine users from accessing previously harvested pages. In addition, under certain conditions, the Internet Archive will remove material from its holdings. The Internet Archive's willingness to respect the wishes of those copyright owners who want to limit and control the reproduction of their copyrighted works reduces the Archive's risk of infringement suits. At the same time, it diminishes the utility of the archive as a whole by excluding important parts of the Web.

The opportunities for inexpensive publishing on the Web have made "publishers" out of everyone who posts material online. While Web technology has made publishing more accessible to everyone, it's also brought potential copyright disputes to the masses. Copyright infringement occurs whenever copyrighted material is transferred to or from a website without authorization from the copyright owner. Transferring information to and from a website can be done in a few ways. A user can take information from a website by copying or downloading. Any time copyrighted information is transferred to or from a website without authorization from the owner, the owner may have a copyright infringement claim against the copier, the website or both. A link takes a user from one website page to another simply by clicking on a word or image. Although permission is not needed for a simple word link (also known as a "hypertext" link), it is required when the link comprises a trademark from the linked site. Some other types of links known as framed links also require permission.

There are Five Ways to Stay Out of Trouble regarding websites.

1. Assuming It's Protected
2. Reading and following Click-Wrap Agreements
3. Remove Unauthorized Material
4. Investigating Claims Promptly
5. Seeking Permission in care of doubt

CONNECTING TO OTHER WEBSITES

One of the central features of the Web is the ability for each Web page to offer quick connections to other Web pages in the click of a button. There are a few different ways that websites connect with one another, each with different legal implications in the permissions context.

1. Linking and Framing

Two common ways, websites connect to other sites are linking and framing.

a. Linking : Most often, a website will connect to another in the form of a link. A link is simply a specially coded word or image that when clicked upon, will take a Web user to another webpage. A link can take the user to another page within the same site (an "internal link"), or to another site altogether (an "external link").

Permission is not needed for a regular word link to another website's home page. If a dispute ever arises regarding linking, it can be squared away by having the linked site sign a linking agreement giving permission for the link.

b. Framing : Besides external links, another way to access other sites is by framing. Framing is a lot like linking in that creator codes a word or image so that it will connect to another Web page when the user clicks on it. What makes framing different is that instead of taking the user to the next page, the information from that page is imported into the original page and displayed in a special "frame." Technically, when user is viewing framed information his computer is connected to the site doing the framing – not the site appearing in the frame. Framing is generally unpopular with websites whose content is framed at another site (unless they have agreed to it). Websites who frame the content of other sites are often seen as stealing the other site's content. It must be kept in mind that some forms of framing are perfectly legal. For instance, many sites use frames as a way of organizing their own content. Unless he knows a site won't object and preferably have their agreement in writing, he should proceed very carefully if he wants to frame other websites' content.

2. Linking Agreements

The purpose of a linking agreement is to avoid a dispute. If a webmaster is confident that a link will not create a dispute, then a linking agreement is probably not necessary.

However, the following types of links may create disputes:

1. Image links, particularly where the image is a trademark from the linked site
2. Deep links that bypass the site's homepage links that result in framing, and
3. Inlining links that only pull certain elements from a site, such as an image.

The permission may be informal, such as a written statement from the distant site stating, "You have permission to link to our website's homepage using the words [insert the words in the link]. " Or, you can use a longer agreement that covers the terms more specifically.

a. Explanation for Linking Agreement

- In the introductory section, insert the name of the company or person that owns the source site. The source site is the site where the link is located—that is, the starting point for the link. Once the link is clicked the user is taken to the destination site. Insert the URL (Web address—for example, www.address.com) for each site.

- In the next section, choose hypertext link or image link (or both if necessary). A hypertext link is a word link (usually viewed as color highlighted text). An image link should be described. If it is a trademark of the destination site, ask the destination site to supply it (usually in a GIF or JPG format).
- The Grant section permits the use of the link and related trademarks or images. The statement, "Any goodwill associated with the Source Site's trademarks automatically vests in the Destination Site" is a requirement of trademark law. It guarantees that the destination site preserves its trademark rights.
- The optional section entitled "Standards and Notification" is a further assurance sometimes required by a destination site that the source site won't operate in an unlawful manner or change the link dramatically. It offers the option of instant termination. Even if this section is not included, the Destination Site can probably force the removal of the link if it desires.
- Both parties should sign the agreement. Many of the miscellaneous provisions included in legal agreements, such as dispute resolution, are not included in order to keep the agreement lean and make it appealing for a quick signature.

b. Linking Disclaimers : To minimize liability for any activities that occur when a visitor is taken to a linked website, a webmaster may want to include a disclaimer on the home page. A disclaimer is a statement denying an endorsement or waiving liability for a potentially unauthorized activity. A sample disclaimer appears below.

Linking Disclaimer

By providing links to other sites, [name of site] does not guarantee, approve or endorse the information or products available at these sites.

A disclaimer is not a cure-all for infringement. If a disclaimer is prominently displayed and clearly written a court may take it into consideration as factor limiting damages.

EDUCATIONAL GUIDELINES ON FAIR USE

The proposed guidelines may give idea of what may be permissible.

1. Digital Copying

Under proposed guidelines, educators can digitize analog images (non-digital photographic prints or paintings). Digitizing is traditionally accomplished by scanning a printed photo. In this process, an analog image (that is, a three dimensional printed photograph or slide created by a non-computer photo processing method) is converted into a digital format known as binary code. This digital format is stored in a computer file. Under the proposed guidelines, educators can digitize a lawfully acquired analog image for educational use unless the image is readily available in usable digital form at a fair price. Under the proposed guidelines, an educational institution may use digital thumbnail images created from analog images for inclusion in a searchable catalog used by the institution. A thumbnail is a small scale, typically low resolution, digital reproduction which has no commercial or reproductive value. An educational institution may display images digitized under the proposed guidelines through its own secure electronic network, provided that notice is included stating that the images shall not be downloaded, copied, retained, printed, shared, modified or otherwise used, except as provided in the educational use guidelines.

2. Use of Digitized Images

Under proposed guidelines, an educator may display a digital image prepared from an analog image if the display is for educational purposes such as face-to-face teaching or research and scholarly activities at a nonprofit educational institution. An educational institution may compile digital images for display on the institution's secure electronic network to students enrolled in a course given by that educator for classroom use, after-class review or directed study. Educators, scholars, and students may use or display digital images in connection with lectures or presentations in their fields, including uses at non-commercial professional development seminars, workshops and conferences.

3. Preparation of Multimedia Works

There are extensive proposed guidelines for the creation and use of multimédia works. Multimedia works include any combination of music, text, graphics, illustrations, photographs and audiovisual imagery combined into an integrated presentation, along with accompanying projection and playback equipment. In general, students and instructors may create multimedia works for face-to-face instruction, directed self-study or for remote instruction provided that the multimedia works are used only for educational purposes in systematic learning activities at nonprofit educational institutions. Instructors may use their multimedia works for teaching courses for up to two years after the first use.

There are also certain "portion limitations." An educational multimedia presentation may include:

- up to 10% or 1,000 words, whichever is less, of a copyrighted text work. For example, an entire poem of less than 250 words may be used, but no more than three poems by one poet, or five poems by different poets from any anthology.

- up to 10%, but in no event more than 30 seconds, of the music and lyrics from an individual musical work.
- up to 10% or three minutes, whichever is less, of a copyrighted motion media work (for example, an animation, video or film image).
- a photograph or illustration may be used in its entirety but no more than five images by an artist or photographer may be reproduced. When using photographs and illustrations from a published collective work, no more than 10% or 15 images, whichever is less. Or,
- up to 10% or 2,500 fields or cell entries, whichever is less, from a copyrighted database or data table may be reproduced. A field entry is defined as a specific item of information, such as a name or Social Security number in a record of a database file. A cell entry is defined as the intersection where a row and a column meet on a spreadsheet.

Only two copies of an educational multimedia project may be made, only one of which may be placed on reserve. An additional copy may be made and only be used or copied to replace a copy that has been lost, stolen or damaged. If an educational multimedia project is created by two or more people, each creator may retain one copy for the educational purposes described in the proposed guidelines. Permission is needed for uses that are commercial or go beyond the limitations in the proposed guidelines.

USE IN ACADEMIC ENVIRONMENT

Online access to licensed e-resources (e-books, e-journals, bibliographic databases and other digital resources) are governed by the Terms of Use as per the Institutional license agreement between the Library and the respective publishers. The e-resources are licensed for the non-profit educational use of the Institute. Copyright law in addition to individual license agreements also governs use of these e-resources. It may be noted that publishers do watch pattern of use (particularly downloads) of these resources. Any misuse will be identified by the publisher precisely as to from which local system (its IP and MacAddress), the date & time and the number of articles / records viewed / downloaded etc. Any breach to the License agreement (misuse) would result in denying of online access to the resource by the publisher. Therefore libraries/academic institutions are requested to adhere to the following guidelines with respect to access and use of e-resources usually;

ALLOWED:

- Viewing / downloading of a small number (one or two) articles from an e-journal / one or two chapters from an e-Book is allowed.

NOT ALLOWED

- Systematic / Programmatic downloading (eg. more than a few contiguous articles from an issue, continuous downloading from a particular journal etc) and storing of journal articles and downloading of a complete book and storing the same in his system hard-disk is not permitted.
- Downloading and electronically forwarding of articles.
- Any outsider / visitor to access e-resources from his system or any system in his Lab.

GOOD PRESERVATION PRACTICES: LEGAL ASPECTS

Good preservation practice has often existed in a legal gray area. Libraries usually made three copies when microfilming long before the law gave explicit permission for the practice, and many radio programs have been saved only because individuals systematically taped them from the air, without the permission of the copyright owner. Digital preservation resides in an even murkier legal gray area because of the fundamental need to copy digital information (one of the exclusive rights of the copyright owner) in order to preserve it. In addition, there is greater interest in preserving works that user may not own, particularly web pages. The lack of legal certainty, however, should not prevent individuals and libraries from undertaking the socially beneficial task of preserving digital information. The law explicitly authorizes some preservation actions (especially if the materials are not made digitally available to others), and a strong fair use defense can be built outside the library or archives.

REFERENCES

1. June Besek, "Copyright issues relevant to the creation of a digital archive: a preliminary assessment" (Washington, D.C.: Council on Library and Information Resources and the Library of Congress, 2003) <*http://www.clir.org/pubs/reports/pub112/contents.html*>
2. Adrienne Muir, "Copyright and licensing for digital preservation" Library and Information Update, June 2003 < *http://www.cilip.org.uk/update/issues/jun03/article2june.html*>
3. Dwayne Buttler and Kenneth Crews, "Copyright Protection and Technological Reform of Library Services" in Tomas Lipinski, ed., Libraries, Museums, and Archives: Legal Issues and Ethical Challenges in the New Information Era (Lanham, Maryland: Scarecrow Press, 2002)
4. Peter Lyman and Hal Varian, "How Much Information 2003?" <*http://www2.sims.berkeley.edu/research/projects/how-much-info-2003/*>
5. *17 U.S.C. § 106(1)*
6. http://www4.law.cornell.edu/uscode/17/106.html
7. *17 U.S.C. § 106(5)* http://www4.law.cornell.edu/uscode/17/106.html

8. http://fairuse.stanford.edu/Copyright_and_Fair_Use_Overview/chapter0/0-b.html

9. *http://fairuse.stanford.edu/Copyright_and_Fair_Use_Overview/chapter0/0-a.html*

10. *http://www.law.cornell.edu/uscode/html/uscode17/usc_sec_17_00000117——000-.html*

11. Hefter, L.R. & Litowitz, R. D. (1995) *Protecting Intellectual Property* . Washington DC: United States Information Agency. *http://www.usinfo.org/trade/bg9515e.htm*

12. *http://www.law.cornell.edu/uscode/html/uscode17/usc_sec_17_00000108——000-.html*

13. http://fairuse.stanford.edu/primary_materials/legislation/dmca.html

14. http://fairuse.stanford.edu/commentary_and_analysis/2003_11_hirtle.html

15. Rabina, Debbie L. (2001) "Information ownership is Israel: a reality of 'being pushed into the corner'," *Information Research*, 6(4) Available at http://InformationR.net/ir/6-4/paper110.html

16. *17 U.S.C. § 105 http://www4.law.cornell.edu/uscode/17/105.html*

17. *17 U.S.C. § 102; Feist v. Rural Telephone Serv.*, 499 U.S. 340 (1991). *http://www4.law.cornell.edu/uscode/17/102.html*,, http://www.law.cornell.edu/copyright/cases/499_US_340.htm

18. *17 U.S.C. § 102(b)* http://www4.law.cornell.edu/uscode/17/102.html

19. In *Bridgeman Art Library, Ltd. v. Corel Corp.*, 36 F. Supp. 2d 191 (S.D.N.Y. 1999), *http://www.law.cornell.edu/copyright/cases/36_FSupp2d_191.htm*

20. Brett I. Miller, "Recent Lessons from the Courts: The Changing Landscape of Copyright in a Digital Age," *RLG DigiNews* 4:2 (April 2000) <*http://www.rlg.org/preserv/diginews/diginews4-2.html#feature*>

21. *17 U.S.C. § 101* http://www4.law.cornell.edu/uscode/17/101.html

22. *17 U.S.C. § 108(a)* http://www4.law.cornell.edu/uscode/17/108.html

23. *17 U.S.C. § 108(b)* http://www4.law.cornell.edu/uscode/17/108.html

24. *17 U.S.C. § 108(c)* http://www4.law.cornell.edu/uscode/17/108.html

25. Mary Minow, "How I Learned to Love FAIR USE... or how to bring a $300,000 lawsuit down to $0 if you're a library, archive, or nonprofit educational institution" <*http://fairuse.stanford.edu/commentary_and_analysis/2003_07_minow.html*>. See also Mary Minow, "Library Digitization Projects and Copyright" <*http://www.llrx.com/features/digitization.htm*>.

26. Robert Oakley, Copyright and Preservation: A Serious Problem in Need of a Thoughtful Solution (Washington, D.C.: Council on Library and Information Resources, September 1990) <*http://www.clir.org/pubs/abstract/pub11.html*>.

27. For example, 17 USC § 108 exemptions do not apply to "a musical work, a pictorial, graphic or sculptural work, or a motion picture or other audiovisual work other than an audiovisual work dealing with news" unless the material is being preserved, at which point the nature and format of the material ceases to matter.

28. *Campbell v. Acuff-Rose Music* 510 U.S. 569 (1994) *http://www.law.cornell.edu/copyright/cases/510_US_569.htm*

29. http://fairuse.stanford.edu/commentary_and_analysis/2003_11_hirtle.html#_ftn12

30. *http://www4.law.cornell.edu/uscode/html/uscode17/usc_sec_17_00000107—-000-.html*

31. http://fairuse.stanford.edu/commentary_and_analysis/2003_11_hirtle.html#_ftn13

32. House Report on the new copyright law, H.R. Rep. No. 94-1476, quoted in U.S. Copyright Office, Reproductions of Copyrighted Works by Educators and Librarians (Washington, D.C, 1995): p. 10 <*http://www.copyright.gov/circs/circ21.pdf*>

33. Mark A. Greene, "Floods, Flashsite, and Fond Delusions: Archiving the Web," Spectra, the Journal of the Museum Computer Network 25:3 (Spring 1998), 10-14.

34. <*http://www.loc.gov/minerva/collect/elec2000/*>

35. <*http://september11.archive.org/*>

36. <*http://searchclinton.archives.gov/*>

37. World Trade Organization. (1994). *Trade-related aspects of intellectual property rights*. Geneva: World Trade Organization. Retrieved 8 January, 2005 from http://www.wto.org/english/docs_e/legal_e/27-trips_01_e.htm

38. <*http://www.archive.org/*>

39. http://fairuse.stanford.edu/commentary_and_ analysis/2003_11_hirtle.html#_ftnref23

40. <*http://www.netarchive.dk/*>

41. <*http://nwa.nb.no/*>

42. The Oakland Archive Policy: Recommendations for Managing Removal Requests And Preserving Archival Integrity, Dec. 13-14, 2002. <*http://www.sims. berkeley.edu/research/conferences/aps/removal-policy.html*>

43. Ebay User Agreement <*http://pages.ebay.com/help/community/png-user.html*>

44. Andrew Charlesworth, Legal Issues Relating to the Archiving of Internet Resources in the UK, EU, USA, and Australia: A Study Undertaken for the JISC and Wellcome Trust, version 1.0, 25 February 2003, p. 44. < *http://www.jisc.ac.uk/uploaded_documents/archiving_l egal.pdf*>

45. *17 U.S.C. § 1201* http://www4.law.cornell.edu/uscode/17/1201.html

46. Rulemaking on Exemptions from Prohibition on Circumvention of Technological Measures that Control Access to Copyrighted Works, 28 October 2003 <*http://www.copyright.gov/1201/*>

47. *http://fairuse.stanford.edu/Copyright_and_ Fair_Use_Overview/chapter6/6-b.html*

48. Vaagan, R. (Ed.). (2002). *The ethics of librarianship: an international survey*. Munich: International Federation of

Library Associations and K.G.Saur Verlag. (IFLA Publications No. 101)

49. Vaagan, R. (2004). Ethical issues raised by the electronic information environment. *Proceedings of the annual conference of the Library Association of Ireland and the Chartered Institute of Library and Information Professionals* (CILIP) Ireland (in press in *An Leabharlann*)
50. Vaagan, R. and Holm, S. (2004). Professional values in Norwegian librarianship. *New Library World*, **105**(1200/1201), 213-217.
51. Yourdon, E. (2002). *Byte wars: the impact of September 11 on information technology*. Upper Saddle River, NJ: Prentice Hall.
52. Zwass, V. (2003). Ethical issues in information systems. In *Encyclopedia of Library and Information Science* (2nd ed.) vol. 2. (pp. 1054-1062). New York, NY: Marcel Dekker.
53. http://fairuse.stanford.edu/Copyright_and_ Fair_Use_Overview/chapter0/0-f.html
54. *http://fairuse.stanford.edu/Copyright_and_Fair_Use_Overview/index.html*
55. *http://fairuse.stanford.edu/commentary_and_analysis/2003_11_hirtle.html#_ftn26*
56. http://fairuse.stanford.edu/Copyright_and_Fair_Use_Overview/chapter6/6-c.html
57. *http://fairuse.stanford.edu/Copyright_and_Fair_Use_Overview/chapter7/7-c.html*
58. *http://www.library.iisc.ernet.in/e-Resourcesaccess.html*
59. *http://fairuse.stanford.edu/commentary_and_analysis/2003_11_hirtle.html#_ftn31*
60. Erik Smith, "Around the Dial Web Battle Is Latest Episode in Old-Time Radio Serials One firm is carrying on the fight to enforce copyrights, much to the dismay of collectors and Internet users." Los Angeles Times, 2/16/2001.

APPENDICES

APPENDIX 1 : GLOSSARY FOR E-RESOURCES

A

AACR2

See Anglo-American Cataloguing Rules

Abstract

A brief summary of a work which describes enough to allow a reader to decide whether or not it has the information sought. It also contains keywords and/or terms used to index the work so that it can be retrieved.

Abstract Service

See Service Expression.

Access management

It is a kind of control of access to material in digital libraries. Sometimes it is called terms and conditions or rights management.

Access point - A name, term, code, etc., through which a bibliographic or authority record or reference is searched and identified.

See also Authorized access point, Controlled access point, Name, Uncontrolled access point, Variant form access point

ACM Digital Library

A digital library of the journals and conference proceedings published by the **Association for Computing Machinery.**

Acquisitions

Activities related to obtaining library materials through purchase, exchange, or gift.

Additional access point

An access point that may be used in addition to the essential access points to enhance the retrieval of bibliographic or authority records.

See also Essential access point.

Administrative metadata

Metadata used in managing and administering information resources, e.g., location or donor information. It includes rights and access information, data on the creation and preservation of the digital object.

AGLS

Australian Government Locator Service

Agent

A person (author, publisher, sculptor, editor, director, composer, etc.) or a group (family, organization, corporation, library, orchestra, country, federation, etc.) or an automaton (weather recording device, software translation program, etc.) that has a role in the lifecycle of a resource.

See also Author, Creator

Aggregator

A company that provides digitized access to the content of many different serials and other resources, often from a variety of different publishers. Aggregators may also be called by other terms, including but not limited to: distributors, vendors, or secondary publishers. Aggregators provide access to digitized material through a searchable database. Generally the collections that aggregators produce fall into two different categories: those that provide access to complete issues of serials and those that contain the text of selected articles from serial issues.

Aggregator database

The searchable collection of digitized material produced by an aggregator.

Aggregator-neutral record

A catalog record representing all versions of a resource made available by multiple online providers.

ALA

American Library Association.

ALISE

Association of Library and Information Science Education.

Alexandria Digital Library

A digital library of geospatial information, based at the University of California, Santa Barbara.

Anglo-American Cataloguing Rules (AACR2)

The dominant bibliographic standard regulating cataloging in the English-speaking world. It represents a set of rules for the standard description of and access to all materials which a library holds or to which it has access.

American Standard Code for Information Interchange (ASCII)

A scheme that provides standard numeric values to represent letters, numbers, punctuation marks and other characters. The use of standard values allows computers and computer programs to exchange data.

Annotation

A note which accompanies an entry in a bibliography, which tells what the item is about. It differs from an abstract in that it need not necessarily be a summary of the contents. It can be objective, evaluative, or promotional, depending on the purpose of the bibliography.

Anonymous FTP (File Transfer Protocol)

Allows retrieval of electronic resources from a remote site without requiring a user ID or password.

Applet

A small computer program that can be transmitted from a server to a client computer and executed on the client.

API

Application Program Interface - A method by which an application program (a complete program that performs a specific function directly for the user) can access the computer's operating system.

Application

A term referring to a deployed ICT software system or program designed to carry out tasks or solve problems specific to a given use or requirement. In the e-Framework, an application can be either an Application System or an Application Service.

Application Profile (1)

Customization of a standard(s) (*de facto* or *de jure*) or specification(s) for a community. The customization may be through the specification of constraints on how features are used (or not used), through the definition of extensions, or through definitions of how elements of the standard(s) are interpreted and used within the community. Note that a standard or specification can be used as a generic term for any *de facto* standard, *de jure* standard, or specification.

Application profile (2)

In DCMI usage, an application profile is a declaration of the metadata terms an organization, information resource, application, or user community uses in its metadata. In a broader sense, it includes the set of metadata elements, policies, and guidelines defined for a particular application or implementation. The elements may be from one or more element sets, thus allowing a given application to meet its functional requirements by using metadata elements from several element sets including locally defined sets. For example, a given application might choose a specific subset of the Dublin Core elements that meets its needs, or may include elements from the Dublin Core, another element set, and several locally defined elements, all combined in a single schema. An application profile is not considered complete without documentation that defines the policies and best practices appropriate to the application.

Application Service

A term referring to an application that is a Service Implementation. A machine-to-machine interface to the implementation of a service genre or service expression, possibly composed with infrastructure service implementations.

Application System

A term referring to an Application deployed for end-users.

Appropriate values

Best practice for a particular Element or Qualifier may vary by context.

ASP

Application Service Provider - A company that offers organizations access over the Internet to applications and related services that would otherwise have to be located on site at the organization's premises.

Archival Collections and Primary Source Databases

Included here are indexes to primary documents (e.g., Index to 19th Century American Art Periodicals), databases or collections of documents, lists of archival collections or libraries. Also included are the websites for archival collections, museums or libraries if those websites provide access to actual content. If the resource listed provides access to the actual document (rather than just a reference to a document), it will be designated as "Full text" or there will be a further designation under "Image/Sound type". A single title that provides a significant run of unique, high quality content not available through any other database will be included in here.

Archives

Collections with related systems and services, organized to emphasize the long-term preservation of information.

The Archives Hub

The Archives Hub enables inter-networked delivery of collection and multi-level archival finding aids (JISC-funded service)

Ariadne: Ariadne is an electronic and print newsletter for librarians and information scientists.

ARL

Association of Research Libraries

Art and Architecture Thesaurus

A controlled vocabulary for fine art, architecture,

decorative art, and material culture, a project of the J. Paul Getty Trust.

Article Databases

Included here are indexes to articles published in journals and magazines. Indexes to newspapers are not generally listed here unless magazines are also indexed by the database. Indexes to single titles are not generally listed here unless the title is generally accepted by the professional community to be "reference-like". Book chapters, proceedings, patents, government documents, dissertations, etc. may be indexed in some resources but the main focus must be on articles.

Databases of research reports are listed under Article Databases. Journal "platforms" that provide portals to journals produced by one publisher, Blackwell Synergy) will not generally be included. If the platform is popular and/or commonly used by patrons to access articles, it will be included. If the platform/publisher covers a specific discipline or subject area, then it will also be listed.

Artifact

It is a physical object in a library, archive, or museum.

ASCII

American Standard Code for Information Interchange. A standard character-tonumber encoding scheme used widely in the computing industry. The term "ASCII" is also used to refer to electronic files that consist only of plain text.

Atlases, Maps and Gazetteers

Included here are atlases, collections of maps, aerial photos and other cartographic resources. They may be thematic or subject oriented or political. Also included are gazetteers and other resources that provide geographic information.

Athens

Athens system created and operated by NISS, provides access management for subscription services supplied by publishers and subscription agents. Athens is a service of EduServ (JISC-funded service)

Attribute

Characteristic of an entity. An attribute can be inherent in an entity or externally imputed.

Audience

Dublin Core element to record a class of entity for whom the resource is intended or useful. A class of entity may be determined by the creator or the publisher or by a third party.

Author

A creator responsible for the intellectual or artistic content of a textual work.

See also **Creator**

Authority control

A set of rules or procedures that assist in the maintenance of consistent forms of names or terms within a database.

Authority file

A collection of authority records.

Authority record

A record that identifies an entity (agent, work/expression, or subject) and can be used to facilitate access to the authorized access point for that entity or the display of any access point for the entity.

Authorized access point

The preferred controlled access point for an entity, established and constructed according to rules or standards.

See also Access point, Controlled access point

Authorized access point for the work/expression

The preferred form of name for a work/expression, with or without the name of the creator(s) or other identifying elements, through which its manifestations are linked/grouped together for searching/access purposes.

See also Name of the work/expression

Automatic indexing

Creation of catalog or indexing records using computer programs.

B

Basic Semantics Register

An ISO Standard ISO/TS 16668:2000 which identifies and defines semantic components for use in data exchange.

Behaviour

A named, defined function or capability provided by a service via its interface. Behaviour is implemented through operations on data models.

Best practice

Guidance and documentation to describe and standardize the use of metadata elements that best support a community's needs.

Bibliographic description

A set of bibliographic data identifying a bibliographic resource.

Bibliographic instruction (BI)

In academic libraries, classes for students on how to use the library. In elementary and high schools, teaching library skills is more commonly used

Bibliographic record

The set of data elements that describe and provide access to manifestations and identify related works and expressions.

Bibliographic resource

An expression or manifestation of a work or an item that forms the basis for bibliographic description. A bibliographic resource may be tangible or intangible.

Blog

A Web site (or section of a Web site) where users can post a chronological, up-to-date | entry of their thoughts. Basically, it is an open forum communication tool that, depending on the Web site, is either very individualistic or performs a crucial function for a company.

Boolean searching

Methods of information retrieval where a query consists of a sequence of search terms, combined with operators, such as "and", "or", and "not".

Born-digital

An adjective describing a document that was created and exists only in digital format.

Browsers

Software programs for reading hypertext documents. Browsers are mounted locally either on site for terminal mode or on the user's PC. Netscape, Internet Explorer, and Lynx are examples of hypertext browsers used to view World Wide Web documents. Netscape and Internet Explorer are graphical browsers, Windows- or Mac-based; Lynx is a text-only terminal mode browser. They all allow a user to read and follow hypertext links specified in a document. They vary in their ability to handle graphic or sound files.

BSR

Basic Semantics Register

Business Process

A process, workflow, or set of operations used in support of the (business) requirements of a domain, delivering results for the user. Note that 'business' does not imply commerce.

C

Cache

A temporary store that is used to keep a readily available copy of recently used data or any data that is expected to be used frequently.

California Digital Library

A digital library that serves the nine campuses of the University of California.

Carrier type - a designation that reflects the format of the storage medium and housing of a carrier in combination with the type of intermediation device required to view, play, run, etc., the content of a resource.

Cartographic material

Any material representing the whole or part of the earth or any celestial body at any scale; cartographic materials include, two- and three-dimensional maps and plans (including maps of imaginary places); aeronautical, navigational, and celestial charts; atlases; globes; block diagrams; sections; aerial photographs with a cartographic purpose; bird's-eye views (map views); etc.

Case-sensitive

Lower and upper case letters are not treated as if they were interchangeable; e.g. 'a' is not the same as 'A'.

Catalog

A collection of bibliographic records created according to an established set of rules.

CEN

European Committee for Standarization (Comité Européen de Normalisation; Europäisches Komitee für Normung) "CEN is contributing to the objectives of the European Union and European Economic Area with voluntary technical standards which promote free trade, the safety of workers and consumers, interoperability of networks, environmental protection, exploitation of research and development programmes, and public procurement."

CGI (Common Gateway Interface)

A programming interface that enables a web browser to be an interface to information services other than web sites.

Classification (1)

A logical scheme for arrangement of knowledge, usually by subject. Classification schema are alpha and/or numeric; for example, Library of Congress Classification, Dewey Classification, Universal Decimal Classification.

Classification (2)

See Service Classification.

Classification (3)

An organization of library materials by a hierarchy of subject categories.

Client

A software application that works on user's behalf to extract a service from a server somewhere on the network.

CNI (Coalition for Networked Information)

Coalition for Networked Information, sponsored by ARL

and several educational organizations; concerned with information policy, with special attention to copyright and intellectual property issues

Collection

1. A real or virtual set of two or more works combined or issued together.
2. A real or virtual set of bibliographic resources held or created by a given institution.

Complex object

Library object that is made up from many inter-related elements or digital objects.

Compression

Reduction in the size of digital materials by removing redundancy or by approximation; lossless compression can be reversed; lossy compression can not be reversed since information is lost by approximation.

Computer file.

See Electronic resource.

Concept

An abstract notion or idea.

Constraint

A restriction on behaviour or interaction. Constraints may be imposed for technical, policy, or other reasons, e.g., accessibility, scope, ease of evolution, efficiency, extensibility.

Content type

A designation that reflects the fundamental form of communication in which the content is expressed and the human sense through which it is intended to be perceived. Content type reflects attributes of both work and expression.

Continuing resource

A bibliographic resource that is issued over time with no predetermined conclusion. Continuing resources include serials and ongoing integrating resources.

Controlled vocabulary

A prescribed set of consistently used and carefully defined terms. A set of subject terms, and rules for their use in assigning terms to materials for indexing and retrieval.

Contributor

The Dublin Core element used to designate the entity responsible for making contributions to the content of the resource. Examples of a Contributor include a person, an organization or a service. Typically, the name of a Contributor should be used to indicate the entity.

Controlled access point

An access point recorded in an authority record to control the different names, forms of names, terms, or codes for the same entity and to clearly identify it.

Controlled access points include authorized or preferred forms as well as those designated as variant forms. They may be:

- based on personal, family, and corporate names,
- based on names (i.e., titles) for works, expressions, manifestations, and items,
- consisting of a combination of two names, as in the case of a name/title access point representing a work that combines the name of the creator with the preferred title of the work,
- based on the terms for events, objects, concepts, and places,
- based on identifiers such as standard numbers, classification indicia, etc.

Other elements may be added to the name *per se* (e.g., dates) for the purpose of distinguishing between entities with identical or similar names.

See also Access point, Authorized access point, Name, Uncontrolled access point

Conventional name

A name, other than the official name, by which a corporate body, place, or thing has come to be known.

Conversion

Transformation of information from one medium to another, including from paper to digital form.

Copy cataloging

The process of adapting an existing catalog record prepared by another library or agency

CORBA

A standard for distributed computing where an object on one computer invokes an Object Request Broker (ORB) to interact with an object on another computer.

CORE

A project from 1991 to 1995 by Bellcore, Cornell University, OCLC, and the American Chemical Society to convert chemistry journals to digital form.

Corporate Body

An organisation or group of persons and/or organisations that is identified by a particular name and that acts, or may act, as a unit.

Coverage

The Dublin Core element used to designate the extent or scope of the content of the resource. Coverage will typically include spatial location (a place name or geographic co-ordinates), temporal period (a period label, date, or date range) or jurisdiction (such as a named administrative entity). Recommended best practice is to select a value from a controlled vocabulary, and that, where appropriate, named places or time periods be used in preference to numeric identifiers such as sets of co-ordinates or date ranges.

CPM

Cost Per Thousand - An industry standard measure for ad impressions. Email has a relatively low CPM compared to other marketing channels (Note: "M" represents thousand in Roman numerology).

CRM

Customer Relationship Management - The methodologies, software, and Internet capabilities that help a company manage customer relationships in an efficient and organized manner.

Creator

A person, family, or corporate body responsible for the intellectual or artistic content of a work.

See also Author

Creator (2)

The Dublin Core element used to designate the entity primarily responsible for making the content of the resource. Examples of a Creator include a person, an organization, or a service.

Crosswalk

A table that maps the relationships and equivalencies between two or more metadata schemes. Crosswalks or metadata mapping support the ability of search engines to search effectively across heterogeneous databases

CSS (Cascading Style Sheets)

System of style sheets for use with HTML, the basis of XLS.

CSTR (Computer Science Technical Reports project)

A DARPA-funded research project with CNRI and five universities, from 1992 to 1996.

D

DANTE

Delivery of Advanced Networking to Europe a not-for-profit company providing academic and research network links to most European countries.

DARPA (Defense Advanced Research Projects Agency)

A major sponsor of computer science research in the U.S., including digital libraries. Formerly ARPA.

Data Sources

A term referring to something that has a representation, is owned, controlled (by policy) and is uniquely identified.

Data type

Structural metadata associated with digital data that indicates the digital format or the application used to process the data.

Date

The Dublin Core element used to designate the date associated with an event in the life cycle of the resource. Typically, Date will be associated with the creation or availability of the resource.

Database Management System

A database system that provides possibilities for users to connect.

DCAPS

Dublin Core Application Profile" is a declaration specifying which metadata terms an organization, information provider, or user community uses in its metadata. By definition, a DCAP identifies the source of metadata terms used - whether they have been defined in formally maintained standards such as Dublin Core, in less formally defined element sets and vocabularies, or by the creator of the DCAP itself for local use in an application. Optionally, a DCAP may provide additional documentation on how the terms are constrained, encoded, or interpreted for application-specific purposes."

DCMES

Dublin Core Metadata Element Set. See Dublin Core.

DCMI

See Dublin Core Metadata Initiative

DCMI recommendation

A DCMI recommendation is a human-readable document that may define one or more DCMI terms.

DCMI term

A DCMI term is a DCMI element, a DCMI qualifier or term from a DCMI-maintained controlled vocabulary. Each DCMI term is defined in a DCMI recommendation and is identified by a Uniform Resource Identifier (URI) within a DCMI namespace.

DCMI term declaration

A DCMI term declaration is the machine-processable representation of one or more DCMI terms, expressed in a schema language.

DCSV

See Dublin Core Structured Value

DES (Data Encryption Standard)

A method for private key encryption.

Description

The Dublin Core element used to designate a textual description of the content of the resource.

Descriptive cataloguing

The part of cataloguing that provides both descriptive data and nonsubject access points.

See also Subject cataloguing.

Descriptive metadata

Metadata that supports the discovery of an object.

Design

A description (typically represented in a collection of documents in different forms) used by developers as the basis to convert a concept into an artifact.

DIALOG

Major vendor of online databases.

Digital object

An item as stored in a digital library, consisting of data, metadata, and an identifier.

Digital signature

A cryptographic code consisting of a hash, to indicate that data has not changed, that can be decrypted with the public key of the creator of the signature.

Digital tourist

An inexperienced searcher in the digital environment who does not possess knowledge of community- specific vocabularies. The Dublin Core provides a rudimentary vocabulary, or "pidgin language" for information discovery when exploring new digital territories. Coined by Ricky Erway at the Metadata Workshop on Metadata for Networked Images, September 24-25, 1996.

Direct access (Electronic resources)

The use of electronic resources via carriers (e.g., discs/disks, cassettes, cartridges) designed to be inserted into a computerized device or its auxiliary equipment.

Digital Object Identifier

DOI was developed by the International DOI Foundation as a system for identifying and exchanging intellectual property in the digital environment. It provides a mechanism to link a searcher to digital content and facilitates copyright management.

Discovery software

A computer application designed to simplify, assist and expedite the process of finding information resources.

Dissertation and Thesis Databases

Included here are resources that list masters' theses and doctoral dissertations. Some resources are geographically specific, specific to an institution or department, or subject specific. Some databases include the full-text or information on how to acquire the actual dissertation. Most include an abstract.

Distributed computing

Computing systems in which services to users are provided by teams of computers collaborating over a network.

D-Lib Magazine

A monthly, online publication about digital libraries research and innovation.

DNS

Domain Name Server (or system) - An Internet service that translates domain names into IP addresses.

Document Type Definition (DTD)

In SGML or XML, a formal description of the components of a specific document or class of documents. DTDs provide a formal grammar used for machine processing (parsing) of documents expressed in SGML or XML. A DTD description includes:

- The containers or elements that make up the document; e.g., paragraphs, headings, list items, figures, tables, etc.
- The logical structure of the document; e.g., chapters containing sections, etc.
- Additional information associated with elements (known as attributes); e.g., identifiers, date stamps, etc.

Document-like object (DLO)

Originally defined as an entity that resembles a document from the standpoint that it is substantially text-based and shares other properties of a document; e.g., electronic mail messages or spreadsheets. The definition was expanded at the 3rd DC workshop to refer to any discrete information resource that are characterized by being fixed (i.e., having identical content for each user). Examples include text, images, movies, and performances.

DOI

See Digital Object Identifier

dot.syntax

A mechanism for refining the meaning of the element in HTML; for example, <METANAME="DC. Title.Alternative" CONTENT="*Title*">

Domain

A core referring to a problem area, business *specialty area, or supporting area.*

Download

To transfer a copy of a file from an Internet server to one's own computer.

DTD

See Document Type Definition

Dublin Core

The Dublin Core is a metadata element set. It includes all DCMI terms (that is, refinements, encoding schemes, and controlled vocabulary terms) intended to facilitate discovery of resources. The Dublin Core has been in development since 1995 through a series of focused invitational workshops that gather experts from the library world, the networking and digital library research communities, and a variety of content specialties.

Dublin Core Metadata Initiative

The Dublin Core Metadata Initiative is the body responsible for the ongoing maintenance of Dublin Core. DCMI is currently hosted by the OCLC Online Computer Library Center, Inc., a not-for-profit international library consortium. The work of DCMI is done by contributors from many institutions in many countries. DCMI is organized into Communities and Task Groups to address particular problems and tasks. Participation in DCMI is open to all interested parties.

Dublin Core Simple

See Simple Dublin Core

Dublin Core Structured Values

DCSV recognizes two types of substrings: labels and values. A label is the name of the type of a value, and a value is the data itself. A value that is comprised of components, i.e. a value which has its own label and value, is called a structured value. Punctuation supports the parsing of the DCSV.

Dublin Core Terms

See DCMI term

Dumb-down Principle

The qualification of Dublin Core Elements is guided by a rule known colloquially as the Dumb-Down Principle. According to this rule, a client should be able to ignore any qualifier and use the value as if it were unqualified. While this may result in some loss of specificity, the remaining term value (minus the qualifier) must continue to be generally correct and useful for discovery. Qualification is therefore supposed only to refine, not extend the semantic scope of an Element.

E

EAD

See EAD (Encoded Archival Description)

EDINA

EDINA provides a library of data, information and research resources (JISC-funded national datacentre)

Electronic information resource

An information resource that is maintained in electronic, or computerized format, and may be accessed, searched and retrieved via electronic networks or other electronic data processing technologies (e.g., CD-ROM)

Electronic journal

An online publication that is organized like a traditional printed journal, either an online version of a printed journal or a journal that has only an online existence.

Electronic mailing list

Internet software that automatically processes commands in an email forum environment. It provides for automatic mailing of electronic serial issues to subscribers and handles messages sent to and from discussion lists.

Element

An element is a property of a resource. As intended here, "properties" are attributes of resources – characteristics of a resource, such as a Title, Publisher, or Subject. Elements are formally defined terms which are used to describe attributes and properties of a resource.

Element refinement (qualifier)

Qualifiers make the meaning of an element narrower or more specific. An element refinement is a property of a resource which shares the meaning of a particular DCMI Element but with narrower semantics. In some application environments (notably HTML-based encodings), Element refinements are used together with elements in the manner of natural-language "qualifiers" (i.e., adjectives). However, since element refinements are properties of a resource (like elements), element refinements can alternatively be used in metadata records independently of the properties they refine. In DCMI practice, an Element refinement refines just one parent DCMI property.

Electronic resource

Material (data and/or program(s)) encoded for manipulation by a computerized device. This material may require the use of a peripheral directly connected to a computerized device (e.g., CD-ROM drive) or a connection to a computer network (e.g., the Internet).

Email (electronic mail)

A system whereby a computer user can exchange messages with other computer users (or groups of users) via a communications network utilizing a standardized protocol. Some electronic journals are available via electronic mail subscriptions, either through an electronic mailing list or by direct email from the distributor of the serial.

Embedded metadata

Metadata that is maintained and stored within the object it describes; the opposite of stand-alone metadata.

Emulation

Replication of a computing system to process programs and data from an early system that is no longer available.

Encoded Archival Description

An SGML DTD that represents a highly structured way to create digital finding aids for a grouping of archival or manuscript materials. The standard is maintained in the Network Development and MARC Standards Office of the Library of Congress (LC) in partnership with the Society of American Archivists.

Encoding scheme

An encoding scheme provides contextual information or parsing rules that aid in the interpretation of a term value. Such contextual information may take the form of controlled vocabularies, formal notations, or parsing rules. If an encoding scheme is not understood by a client or agent, the value may still be useful to a human reader. There are two types of encoding schemes: Vocabulary Encoding Schemes and Syntax Encoding Schemes

Encryption

Techniques for encoding information for privacy or security, so that it appears to be random data; the reverse process, decryption, requires knowledge of a digital key.

Entity

Something that has a unitary and self-contained character, something that has independent or separate existence, an abstraction, ideal concept, object of thought, or transcendental object. Examples of types of entities in FRBR and FRAD include the products of intellectual or artistic endeavour (work, expression, manifestation and item); the agents responsible for creating that intellectual or artistic content, for producing and disseminating the content in physical form, or for maintaining the custody of the product (person, family, corporate body); or the subject of intellectual or artistic expression (work, expression, manifestation, item, person, family, corporate body, concept, object, event, place).

Entities and elements

In a mark-up language, entities are the basic unit of information, including character entities; elements are strings of entities that form a structural unit

Essential access point

An access point based on the main attributes and relationships of each entity in bibliographic or authority records, which ensures retrieval and identification of those records.

See also Additional access point

Event

An action or occurrence.

Expression - The intellectual or artistic realization of a work.

Extensible

Having the potential to be expanded in scope, area or size. In the case of Dublin Core, the ability to extend a core set of metadata with additional elements.

Extensible Markup Language (XML)

A subset of Standard Generalized Markup Language (SGML), a widely used international text processing standard. XML is being designed to bring the power and flexibility of generic SGML to the Web, while maintaining interoperability with full SGML and HTML.

Fair use

A concept in copyright law that allows limited use of copyright material without requiring permission from the rights holders, e.g., for scholarship or review.

Federated digital library

A group of digital libraries that support common standards and services, thus providing interoperability and a coherent service to users.

Field, subfield

An individual item of information in a structured record, such as a catalog or database record.

Fielded searching

Methods for searching textual materials, including catalogs, where search terms are matched against the content of specified fields.

File (Electronic resources)

A basic unit in which electronic resources are organized and stored. Electronic resources can contain one or more files.

See also Electronic resource.

Finding aid

A textual document that describes holdings of an archive, library, or museum.

Firewall

A computer system that screens data passing between network segments, used to provide security for a private network at the point of connection to the Internet.

First sale

A concept in copyright law that permits the purchaser of a book or other object to transfer it to somebody else, without requiring permission from the rights holders.

Format

The Dublin Core element used to designate the physical or digital manifestation of the resource.

Formal Model

A term referring to the overall technical description of the elements, the overall process used to build and document these elements and the processes used to translate these elements into designs and deployed applications within the domains.

FRBR

Functional Requirements for Bibliographic Records is a conceptual model to describe bibliographic entities, their relations and attributes within IFLA (International Federation of Library Associations). The complete work is available at http://www.ifla.org/VII/s13/frbr/frbr.htm

Framework

A collection of cooperating Service Genres within a Domain. A vocabulary of components (e.g., service genre, service expression and reference model) used to model concepts and behaviours within a domain or to create a particular type of infrastructure (system or environment). Associated with the vocabulary is the grammar or language used to describe how the elements are combined or constrained to create systems and environments. Note that the grammars and languages are used to describe the reference models and service descriptions.

Freeware

A free computer program usually made available on the Internet or through user groups.

FTP (File Transfer Protocol)

A protocol that defines how to transfer files from one computer to another; also the access method used to move files from a remote location to a local site for use. To retrieve files, the user initiates an FTP session by logging into a remote host computer, changing to the desired directory, and retrieving the files.

Full text searching

Methods for searching textual materials where the entire text is matched against a query.

G

Gateway

A computer system that transfers data between normally incompatible applications or networks. It reformats the data so that it is acceptable for the new network (or application) before passing it on. This is a hardware or software set-up that functions as a translator between two dissimilar protocols. A gateway can also be the term to describe any mechanism providing access to another system.

General material designation

A term indicating the broad class of material to which an item belongs (e.g., sound recordings).

Genre

The class or category of an object when considered as an intellectual work.

GIF

A format for storing compressed images.

Glossary

An alphabetized list of terms with definitions often created by an organization to reflect its needs. Normally lacks hierarchical arrangement or cross references. Also known as a term list.

GMD

See General material designation

Google

A web search program that ranks web pages in a list of hits by giving weight to the links that reference a specific page.

Gopher

A pre-web protocol used for building digital libraries, now largely obsolete.

Graphics Interchange Format (GIF)

The dominant graphics format on the Web, limited to 256 colors. GIFs provide sharper black & white images than JPEGs.

Granularity

The level of detail at which an information object or resource is viewed or described.

H

Handle

A system of globally-unique names for Internet resources and a computer system for managing them, developed by CNRI; a form of URN.

Harvest

A research project that developed an architecture for distributed searching, including protocols and formats.

Harvester

A harvester is a client application that issues OAI-PMH requests. A harvester is operated by a service provider as a means of collecting metadata from repositories. (http://www.openarchives.org/OAI/openarchivesprotocol.html#harvester)

Hash

A short value calculated from digital data that serves

to distinguish it from other data.

HayStack

An MIT project to develop to personal management systems that would all individuals to organize their information objects, such as email, web pages, documents, images, calendars. The information can be categorize and create relationships that are meaningful for themselves.

HighWire Press

A publishing venture, from Stanford University Libraries, that provides electronic versions of journals, on behalf of learned and professional societies.

Hit

1. An incoming request to a web server or other computer system.
2. In information retrieval, a document that is discovered in response to a query.

Home page (e-serials)

The hypertext document that serves as the "preface" for a service or publication mounted on the World Wide Web. It is normally an introductory screen that provides general information about the institution maintaining the site, or a publication or group of publications available. Hypertext links are included to access specific documents or files archived at the site.

Host computer

A computer, also called a node, that directly provides service to a user.

Host name

The address of the host computer on which a remote-access electronic resource resides.

HTML (Hypertext Markup Language)

A subset of Standard Generalized Markup Language (SGML). The language in which World Wide Web documents are written.

HTML header

Refers to the HEAD element of HTML source code specifications. The HEAD element contains information about the current document, such as the TITLE element and keywords that may be useful to search engines, and other data that is not considered document content. The TITLE element can be displayed separately from the document in the browser title bar.

HTML header title

The title displayed in the title element of the HTML HEAD portion of an HTML document, sometimes used interchangeably with Source code title.

See also Source code title.

Hypertext Markup Language (HTML)

The standard text-formatting language for documents on the World Wide Web. HTML text files contain content that is rendered on a computer screen and markup, or tags, that can be used to tell the computer how to format that content. HTML tags can also be used to encode metadata and to tell the computer how to respond to certain user actions, such as a mouse click. For more information, see http://www.w3.org/MarkUp/.

HTML source

The underlying source code for an HTML document. It includes HTML elements such as the HEAD, BODY, TITLE, and other coding which gives information about the document and/or determines how a document is displayed in a browser.

Hyperlink

A network link from one item in a digital library or web site to another.

Hypertext Transfer Protocol (http)

Method of presenting information in which selected words or other document elements, when chosen, execute automatic links to related documents or files. The linked documents on the World Wide Web may contain graphics, sound, or even moving images.

I

IBSS

International Bibliography of the Social Sciences Jointly funded by JISC and the ESRC.

ICPSR (International Consortium for Political and Social Science Research)

An archive of social science datasets, based at the University of Michigan.

Identifier (1)

An unambiguous name for a digital Resource.

Identifier (2)

The Dublin Core element that is an unambiguous reference to the resource within a given context. Recommended best practice is to identify the resource by means of a string or number conforming to a formal identification system.

IETF

Internet Engineering Task Force

IEEE LOM

Institute of Electrical and Electronics Engineers Learning Object Metadata

Image and Sound Databases

Included here are image and sound databases which provide access to works of art, news and film archives, cultural artifacts, design collections, advertising, historical broadcasts, manuscripts and photographs.

IMAP

Internet Message Access Protocol - A protocol used to retrieve email messages. Most email clients use either the IMAP or the POP protocol.

IMS

See Instructional Management Systems

IMT

Internet Media Type

Implementation

Service Implementation.

Imprint

A note on a book's title page or its reverse or at the end of the book, giving the publisher's or printer's name, time and place of publication.

Instructional Management Systems (IMS)

Instructional Management Systems Global Learning Consortium. A global coalition of academic, commercial and government organisations, working together to define the Internet architecture for learning. IMS is an initiative of EDUCAUSE. The funded service JISC-CETIS was established to provide information on IMS standards and initiatives.

INDECS

See INDECS (Interoperability of Data in D-Commerce Systems)

Indexing

The process of evaluating information entities and creating terms that aid in finding and accessing the entity. Index terms may be in natural language or controlled vocabulary or a classification notation.

Indexing program

Computer software used to order things; frequently used to refer to software that alphabetizes some or all of the terms in one or more electronic documents.

Indicator

One of two character positions at the beginning of each variable data field in a USMARC record containing values that interpret or supplement the data found in the field.

Information discovery

General term covering all strategies and methods of finding information in a digital library.

Information Environment

The aim of the Information Environment is to help provide convenient access to resources for research and learning through the use of resource discovery and resource management tools and the development of better services and practice. The Information Environment aims to allow discovery, access and use of resources for research and learning irrespective of their location.

Information industry

Used by librarians to lump vendors of online databases, jobbers, producers of materials and automated systems acquired by libraries, etc.

Information resource

Any entity, electronic or otherwise, capable of conveying or supporting intelligence or knowledge; e.g. a book, a letter, a picture, a sculpture, a database, a person.

See also DLO.

Information retrieval

Searching a body of information for objects that match a search query.

Instantiation

An identifiable occurrence or occasion of something; in the case of Dublin Core, a specific occurrence of an information resource.

Integrating resource

A bibliographic resource that is added to or changed by means of updates that do not remain discrete and are integrated into the whole. Integrating resources can be finite or continuing. Examples of integrating resources include updating loose-leafs and updating Web sites.

International Organization for Standardization

ISO was established in 1947 as a worldwide federation of national standards bodies from some 130 countries.

Internet

The world-wide "network of networks" that are connected to each other, using the IP protocol and other similar protocols. The Internet provides file transfer, remote login, electronic mail, news, and other services.

Internet 2

Internet2 is a development project funded by over 100 American universities to develop leading edge Internet applications and the next version of the Internet Protocol (IP).

Internet Commons

The global Internet environment, collection of

information-bearing repositories whose data can be accessed through the Internet.

Internet RFC series

The technical documentation of the Internet, provided by the Internet Engineering Task Force. Internet Drafts are preliminary versions of RFCs.

Internet Engineering Task Force (IETF)

The IETF is responsible for solving short-term engineering needs of the Internet. It has over 40 Working Groups.

Internet Media Type (IMT)

A set of terms that describe types of resources on the Internet. Used as an encoding scheme for the Format element in Dublin Core. http://www.isi.edu/in-notes/iana/assignments/media-types/media-types

Interoperability

The ability of different types of computers, networks, operating systems, and applications to work together effectively, without prior communication, in order to exchange information in a useful and meaningful manner. There are three aspects of interoperability: semantic, structural and syntactical.

Interoperability Qualifiers

Additional metadata used either to refine the semantics of a Dublin Core metadata element's value, or to provide more information about the encoding scheme used for the value.

Intranet

Contrary to the public Internet, an intranet is a private network inside a company or organization.

Intute

Intute is a free online service providing you with access to the very best web resources for education and research. The service is created by a network of UK universities and partners.

IP (Internet Protocol)

The most important of the protocols on which the Internet is based. It allows a packet to traverse multiple networks on the way to its final destination. Often, this is used in conjunction with TCP (Transmission Control Protocol), as in TCP/IP.

IP address

The Internet Protocol or numeric address of a computer connected to the Internet. It consists of four numbers separated by periods.

IPR

Intellectual Property Rights

ISO

See International Organization for Standardization

ISP

Internet Service Provider - A company that provides access to the Internet, including the World Wide Web and email, typically for a monthly fee.

Item

A single exemplar of a manifestation.

J

JANET

Joint Academic NETwork· This links all higher education institutions, Research Council sites, many FE colleges and other bodies with a legitimate interest in working with the higher education and research community.

Java

A programming language used for writing mobile code, especially for user interfaces, developed by Sun Microsystems.

JavaScript

A scripting language used to embed executable instructions in a web page.

Joint Photographic Experts Group (JPEG)

A standard for compressing digital images. The advantage of JPEG is that it uses compression to make graphics files smaller, making them faster to transfer and view over the World Wide Web. More than 16 million color hues are available. Better than GIF for color photographs. The disadvantage is some loss of image quality due to data loss during compression. For more information see http://www.jpeg.org/

JSTOR

A subscription service, initiated by the Andrew W. Mellon Foundation, to convert back runs of important journals and make them available to academic libraries.

K

Key

A digital code used to encrypt or decrypt messages. Private key encryption uses a single, secret key. Dual key (public key) encryption uses two keys of which one is secret and one is public.

Key heading

In Sears subject headings, a heading that serves as a model of subdivisions for headings in the same category.

Key title

The unique name assigned to a continuing resource by the ISSN Network and inseparably linked with its ISSN. The key title may be the same as the title proper; or, in order to achieve uniqueness, it can be constructed by the addition of identifying and/or qualifying elements such as name of issuing body, place of publication, edition statement, etc.

L

Lexicon

A linguistic tool with information about the morphological variations and grammatical usage of words.

Lexis

A legal information service, a pioneer of full-text information online.

Link resolver

Server software that accepts citations to articles and other items (often formatted according to OpenURL standard) and uses a context sensitive link to connect users to designated target resources such as full-text repositories, A&I, and citation | databases, online library catalogs, and other Web resources and services.

Literal

A literal or "appropriate literal" is the value of any given metadata entity that can be either a hyperlink or a string value (literal). A literal affords a great deal of flexibility and power, but increases complexity. Metadata should as well include an appropriate literal that reflects the base value of the metadata entity.

M

Manifestation

The physical embodiment of an expression of a work.

A manifestation may embody a collection of works, an individual work, or a component part of a work. Manifestations may appear in one or more physical units.

MARC

MARC (Machine-Readable Cataloging Record)

Mark-up language

Codes embedded in a document that describe its structure and/or its format.

Medline

An indexing service for research in medicine and related fields, provided by the National Library of Medicine.

MELVYL

A shared digital library system for academic institutions in California; part of the California Digital Library.

MeSH (Medical Subject Headings)

A set of subject term and associated thesaurus used to describe medical research, maintained by the National Library of Medicine.

Message

A unit of data sent from one Service Implementation or Service Instance to another.

Messaging

Transmission of messages through a network via protocols.

META tag

The HTML element used to demarcate metadata on a Web page. <META> </META>.

Metadata

In general, "data about data;" functionally, "structured data about data." Metadata includes data associated with either an information system or an information object for purposes of description, administration, legal requirements, technical functionality, use and usage, and preservation. In the case of Dublin Core, information that expresses the intellectual content, intellectual property and/or instantiation characteristics of an information resource.

Metadata record

A syntactically correct representation of the descriptive information (metadata) for an information resource. In the case of Dublin Core, a representation of the Dublin Core elements that has been defined for the resource. The majority of metadata records and record fragments in this document are presented in HTML syntax.

Metadata schema registry

A publicly accessible system that records the semantics, structure and interchange formats of any type of metadata. A formal authority, or agency, maintains and manages the development and evolution of a metadata registry. The authority is responsible for policies pertaining to registry contents and operation. See also http://www.dlib.org/dlib/may02/wagner/05wagner. html

METS (Metadata Encoding & Transmission Standard

Metadata Encoding & Transmission Standard

Migration

Preservation of digital content, where the underlying information is retained but older formats and internal structures are replaced by newer.

MIME

See Multipurpose Internet Mail Extensions

Mirror site

An alternative URI for accessing an electronic

resource. A mirror site might provide users in a particular geographic location better access than other URIs associated with the resource.

MODS

See MODS (Metadata Object Description Schema)

MRDF

Machine-readable data file (e.g., the census data tapes).

Multipurpose Internet Mail Extensions

The standard for attaching files to Internet e-mail messages. Attached files may be text, graphics, spreadsheets, documents, sound files, etc.

N

Name

A character or group of words and/or characters by which an entity is known; includes the words/characters designating a person, family, corporate body; the terms by which concepts, objects, events, or places are known; as well as the title given to a work, expression, manifestation, or item. Used as the basis for an access point.

See also Authorized access point, Controlled access point, Variant form access point

National Information Standards Organization

NISO, accredited by ANSI, develops and promotes technical standards used in a wide variety of information services.

Namespace

A DCMI namespace is a collection of DCMI terms. Each DCMI namespace is identified by a URI. An XML namespace [XML-NAMES] is a collection of names, identified by a URI reference [RFC2396], that are used in XML documents as element types and attribute names. The use of XML namespaces to uniquely identify metadata terms allows those terms to be unambiguously used across applications, promoting the possibility of shared semantics. DCMI adopts this mechanism for the identification of all DCMI terms. For example, the namespace for Dublin Core elements and qualifiers would be expressed respectively in XML as:

xmlns:dc = "http://purl.org/dc/elements/1.1/
xmlns:dcterms = "http://purl.org/dc/terms/

The use of namespaces allows the definition of an element to be unambiguously identified with a URI, even though the label "title" alone might occur in many metadata sets. In more general terms, one can think of any closed set of names as a namespace. Thus, a controlled vocabulary such as the Library of Congress Subject Headings, a set of metadata elements such as DC, or the set of all URLs in a given domain can be thought of as a namespace that is managed by the authority that is in charge of that particular set of terms.

Name of the work/expression

A title of a work/expression, with or without the name of the creator(s), with or without identifying elements added, recorded to control variant titles of different manifestations of the same work/expression.

See also Authorized access point for the work/ expression

NCSTRL (Networked Computer Science Technical Reports Library)

An international distributed library of computer science materials and services, based at Cornell University.

Netlib

A digital library of mathematical software and related collections.

NSF (National Science Foundation)

U.S. government agency that supports science and engineering, including digital libraries research.

Networked resource

An object that is available electronically via a network.

NISO

See National Information Standards Organization

O

Object

A material thing.

OAI

See Open Archives Initiative

OAI-PMH

See Open Archives Initiative Protocol for Metadata Harvesting

OCLC

See Online Computer Library Center

ONIX

ONline InformationeXchange

Ontology

A hierarchical structure that formally defines the semantic relationship of a set of concepts. Used to create structured / controlled vocabularies for the discovery or exchange of information. A thesaurus, like the AAT is an example.

Online Computer Library Center (OCLC)

The major source of cataloging data for libraries around the world; located in Dublin, Ohio, US. For more information, see http://www.oclc.org/.

OPAC (online public access catalog)

An online library catalog used by library patrons.

Open Archives Initiative

"Develops and promotes interoperability standards that aim to facilitate the efficient dissemination of content. The Open Archives Initiative has its roots in an effort to enhance access to e-print archives as a means of increasing the availability of scholarly communication" For more information see http://www.openarchives.org/organization/index.html.

OpenURL

A method for describing resources and associated resources that are referenced in a network environment. It defines the mentods for transporting these descriptions between networked systems. NISO standard NISO Z39.88-2003 (still in draft). The Standard has been issued in two parts and it available for comment through California Institute of Technology http://library.caltech.edu/openurl/Public_Comments.htm

Open Archives Initiative Protocol for Metadata Harvesting

The Protocol "provides an application-independent interoperability framework based on metadata harvesting. There are two classes of participants in the OAI-PMH framework: Data Providers administer systems that support the OAI-PMH as a means of exposing metadata; and Service Providers use metadata harvested via the OAI-PMH as a basis for building value-added services.," For more information see http://www. openarchives.org/organization/index.html.

Open Source

Any software whose code is available for users to look at and modify freely. Linux is the best-known example.

Open Standard

A standard (*de jure* or *de facto*) or specification, developed collaboratively through an open, consensus-building process, that is platform independent, vendor neutral, extensible, reusable, publicly accessible, and not encumbered by royalties, licenses or constraints on use and implementation.

Operating system

A program that manages all other programs in a computer, such as Windows or Unix.

Outsourcing

An arrangement where one company provides services to another company that would otherwise have been implemented in-house.

OWL

Web ontology language (http://www.w3.org/TR/owl-features/). OWL is a language for describing ontologies and schema. It can specify concepts and their relationships. OWL/XDD (XML declaration description) allows a means to express complex rules and constraints.

P

Parsing

Parsing may be divided into parts: lexical analysis and semantic parsing. Lexical analysis divides strings into components based on punctuation or tagging. Semantic parsing then attempts to determine the meaning of the string.

Pattern heading

A subject heading that serves as a model of subdivisions for headings in the same category. Subdivisions listed under a pattern heading may be used whenever appropriate under other headings in the same category.

PDF

Portable Document Format. The file format of documents viewed and created by the Adobe Acrobat Reader, Acrobat Capture, Adobe Distiller, Adobe Exchange, and the Adobe Acrobat Amber Plug-in for Netscape Navigator. This file format was developed to standardize formatting of documents that are used on the Internet.

Persistent Uniform Resource Locator

An approach to the URL permanence problem proposed by OCLC. A PURL is a public alias for a document. A PURL remains stable, while the document's background URL will change as it is managed (e.g. moved) over time. A PURL is created by a Web administrator who is registered as a PURL "owner" and who maintains a mapping of the PURL to a current and functioning URL. A PURL is a form of URN.

Person

An individual or a single identity established or adopted by an individual or group.

Place

A location. Reference - No longer used in the Principles. *See* Variant form access point

Policy

A constraint on the Behaviour *of an* Service Implementation *(and its service instance)*.

POI (PURL-based Object Identifier)

A specification for resource identifiers that are described by metadata 'items' in OAI-compliant repositories. POI are based on the PURL system [POI]. "Because POIs conform to the URI specification, they can be used unmodified in DC metadata and LOM." See http://www.ukoln.ac.uk/metadata/dcmi-ieee/identifiers/ and http://www.ukoln.ac.uk/distributed-systems/poi/

Preservation

Actions taken to prevent the deterioration of library materials and to save their intellectual content

Property

A property is a specific aspect, characteristic, attribute, or relation used to describe a resource. Dublin Core metadata elements are properties. (http://dublincore.org/documents/2003/04/02/dc-xml-guidelines/)

Provenance

Dublin Core element used for making statements of any changes in ownership and custody of the resource since its creation that are significant for its authenticity, integrity and interpretation. The statement may include a description of any changes successive custodians made to the resource.

Publisher

The Dublin Core element used to designate the entity responsible for making the resource available. Examples of a Publisher include a person, an organization, or a service. Typically, the name of a Publisher should be used to indicate the entity.

PURL

See Persistent Uniform Resource Locator

Principle

A fundamental rule that applies to a large number of situations.

Protocol

A mutually-determined set of formats and procedures governing the exchange of information between different kinds of computers.

Provider

A general term used throughout this module to refer to any company, publisher, or aggregator enabling access to digitized text.

Provider (Service Implementation)

A Service Implementation (or its service instances) used by other service implementations that provides the functionality and behaviour of the provider.

Q

Qualifier

"Qualifiers" is the generic heading traditionally used for terms now usually referred to specifically as Element Refinements or Encoding Schemes. A qualifier must follow the Dumb-Down Principle. There are two broad categories of qualifiers: Encoding schema and Element refinement.

Qualified Dublin Core

Qualified Dublin Core includes an additional element, Audience, as well as a group of element refinements (also called qualifiers) that refine the semantics of the elements in ways that may be useful in resource discovery

Query

A textual string, possibly structured, that is used in information retrieval, the task being to find objects that match the words in the query.

R

RDF

See Resource Description Framework.

RDF Site Summary

RSS was created and popularized by Netscape for their personalized portal site. Rich Site Summary (RSS) is a lightweight XML application designed to exchange headline metadata between news content providers and portals.

Record

A record is some structured metadata about a resource, comprising one or more properties and their associated values.

Record terminator

A symbol used to signal the end of a USMARC record

Reference Model

A service-oriented description of a collection of processes and workflows supporting at least one application, domain or business process.

Registry

A system to provide management of metadata elements. See also metadata schema registry The DCMI Registry Working Group (WG) is the development of a metadata registry providing authoritative information regarding the DCMI vocabulary and the relationship between terms in that vocabulary.

Relation

The Dublin Core element used to designate Areference to a related resource. Recommended best practice is to reference the resource by means of a string or number conforming to a formal identification system.

Relationship

A specific connection between entities or their instances.

Remote access (electronic resources)

The use of electronic resources via computer networks.

Request for Comment (RFC)

A Request for Comment (RFC) is the process of establishing a standard on the Internet. Discussion of the proposed standard on the Internet is facilitated by the Internet Engineering Task Force (IETF). Once approved, the standard receives a unique number which identifies it; e.g., RFC See http://www.isi.edu/rfc-editor/ and http://www.ietf.org/rfc.html

Requestor (Service Implementation)

An application or service implementation (or its service instances) that interacts with other (provider) service implementations (or their service instances) requesting that the providers perform some function for the requestor.

Resource

A resource is a term that can have many meanings depending upon context. Often, but not always, it can be a synonym for "data sources". More generally, it can refer to anything that can be uniquely identified. A resource is anything that has identity. Familiar examples include an electronic document, an image, a service (e.g., "today's weather report for Los Angeles"), and a collection of other resources. Not all resources are network "retrievable"; e.g., human beings, corporations, and bound books in a library can also be considered resources.

Resource Description Framework (RDF)

The basic language for writing metadata; a foundation which provides a robust flexible architecture for processing metadata on the Internet. RDF will retain the capability to exchange metadata between application communities, while allowing each community to define and use the metadata that best serves their needs. For more information see http://www.w3.org/RDF/

Resource discovery

The process through which one searches and retrieves an information resource.

Resource Type

See Type.

Resource Description

See Description.

Resource Identifier

See Identifier

RFC

See Request for Comment

Rights

The Dublin Core element used to provide a link to information about rights held in and over the resource. Typically a Rights element will contain a rights management statement for the resource, or reference a service providing such information. Rights information often encompasses Intellectual Property Rights (IPR), Copyright, and various Property Rights. If the rights element is absent, no assumptions can be made about the status of these and other rights with respect to the resource.

RightsHolder

Dublin Core element used to record a person or organization owning or managing rights over the resource. Recommended best practice is to use the URI or name of the Rights Holder to indicate the entity.

Rights Management

See Rights

RLIN

Research Libraries Information Network, the

bibliographic utility which serves primarily very large university libraries

ROADS

Resource Organisation And Discovery in Subject based services. A UK funded project whose aim is to develop discovery software for Internet resources.

S

Schema or scheme (plurals schemas or schemata; schemes)

In general terms, any organization, coding, outline or plan of concepts. In terms of metadata, a systematic, orderly combination of elements or terms. In terms of DCMI term declarations represented in XML or RDF schema language, schemas are machine-processable specifications which define the structure and syntax of metadata specifications in a formal schema language. In terms of an encoding scheme, is a set of rules for encoding information that supports a specific community of users.

See also Encoding scheme.

Scheme

See schema

SCORM

Sharable Content Object Reference Model

Search engine

A utility capable of returning references to relevant information resources in response to a query.

Semantic interoperability

Ability to search for digital information across heterogeneous distributed databases whose metadata schemas have been mapped to one another. It is achieved through agreements about content description standards; for example, Dublin Core, Anglo-American Cataloging Rules.

Semantic Web

A term coined by Tim Berners-Lee which views the future Web as a web of data, like a global database. The infrastructure of the Semantic Web would allow machines as well as humans to make deductions and organize information. The architectural components include semantics (meaning of the elements), structure (organization of the elements), and syntax (communication).

Semantics

Significance or meaning. In the case of Dublin Core, the significance or intended meaning of individual metadata elements and their components.

SGML (Standard Generalized Markup Language)

A standard for formatting textual documents so that they can be read by different document processing tools.

Server

Software that allows a computer to offer a service to another computer. Other computers contact the server program by means of matching client software. Also, the computer on which the server software runs is often called the "server." It acts as a central information source and provides services to programs in the same or other computers. The term can either refer to a particular piece of software, such as a WWW server, or to the machine on which the software is running.

Service

A general operational capability.

Service Description

A term referring to an informal narrative and graphical description of a Service Genre or a Service Expression presented in a normative format. It documents all aspects and characteristics of the service genre or service expression.

Service Expression

A term referring to a specific set of functionality and behaviours described in terms on interfaces, messages, standards and technologies; a specialisation of a single service genre by specification of exact interfaces and standards used.

Service Expression Definition

A term referring to a machine-processible definition or specification of the interface to a Service Expression and the semantics of the service expression. It defines the message formats, datatypes, transport protocols, and transport serialisation formats that should be used between the Requestor Service Implementation and the Provider Service Implementation. Formats, datatypes, protocols, etc., should be based on defined standards and specifications. The service expression definition represents an agreement governing the mechanics of interacting with the service expression.

Service Implementation

Operational code providing the complete functionality specified in a Service Expression Definition; a component of the computational infrastructure that implements the functionality defined by a Service Expression; a computational resource.

Service Implementation Design (Specification)

Software specification used to guide development and programming of a Service Implementation, derived from a Service Expression Definition. The design is created by selecting and specialising elements from the service expression description, combined with design choices and the addition of constraints imposed by a particular community or by the technologies that will be used to implement and develop the service implementation.

Service Oriented Approach (soa)

A software design methodology using networks of loosely-coupled, communicating services.

Service Oriented Architecture (SOA)

Software architecture for a Service Oriented Approach (soa) implemented using a particular technology, e.g., CORBA, Web Services. SOAs enable domain-oriented operations through message exchange within a network of services. Services and messages have platform-independent formal definitions, based on open standards. They define standard interfaces and protocols to encapsulate information tools as services that clients can access without knowledge or control of their inner workings. Note that soa is a generic concept. SOA is that concept implemented using a particular technology, typically Web Services.

SICI

Serial Item and Contribution Identifier (ANSI/NISO Z39.56-1996 Vers. 2) A numeric notation to identify serial issues and articles uniquely regardless of their distribution medium (paper, electronic, microform).

Simple Dublin Core

The fifteen Dublin Core elements used without qualifiers, that is without element refinement or encoding schemes. Sometimes referred to as Dublin Core simple.

SMTP

Simple Mail Transfer Protocol - A protocol used to send email on the Internet. SMTP is a set of rules regarding the interaction between a program sending email and a program receiving email.

SOAP

A protocol that uses XML for the exchange of structured information, that is messages, in a distributed environment. See http://www.w3.org/TR/soap12-part1/

Software agent

A computer program that carries out tasks on behalf of another entity. Frequently used to reference a program that searches the Internet for information meeting the specified requirements of an individual user.

Source

The Dublin Core element used to designate a reference to a resource from which the present resource is derived. The present resource may be derived from the Source resource in whole or part. Recommended best practice is to reference the resource by means of a string or number conforming to a formal identification system.

Source code

The form in which a computer program or Web site is written. On the Internet, for example, the source code for a Web page could contain any of the following languages: HTML, JavaScript, Java, or SGML.

Source code title

Generally refers to the title element appearing in the underlying source code of a document.

Spatial

An element refinement of Coverage. Spatial characteristics of the intellectual content of the resource.

SSA

Society of American Archivists

Standard Generalized Markup Language (SGML)

A non-proprietary language/enabling technology for

describing information. Information in SGML is structured like a database, supporting rendering in and conversion between different formats. Both XML and later versions of HTML are instances of SGML.

Stand-alone metadata

Metadata that is created, maintained and stored independently of the object it describes. The opposite of embedded metadata.

State

The representation of a resource (attributes, values, properties) at some point in time.

Streaming media

Audio and video files transmitted on the Internet in a continuous fashion.

Structured value

See Dublin Core Structured Value

Structural interoperability

Is achieved through data models for specifying semantic schemas in a way that they can be shared; for example, RDF.

Structural metadata

Structural metadata defines the digital object's internal organization and is needed for display and navigation of that object.

Sub-element

See element refinement

Subject

The Dublin Core element used to describe the content of the resource. The element may use controlled vocabularies or keywords or phrases that describe the subject or content of the resource.

Subject cataloguing

The part of cataloguing that provides subject heading/ terms and/or classification.

See also Descriptive cataloguing

Subject Headings

An alphabetical list of words or phrases that represent a concept that is under authority control, e.g., the Library of Congress Subject Headings.

Surrogate content

Metadata as a substitute for an actual resource.

Switching language

A mediating language used to establish equivalencies among various indexing languages. Dublin Core has been viewed as a switching "language" between various metadata schemas.

Syntactic interoperability

Achieved by marking up our data in a similar fashion so we can share the data and so that our machines can understand and take the data apart in sensible ways; for example, XML, EAD and MARC.

Syntax

The form and structure with which metadata elements are combined. In the case of Dublin Core, the form and structure of how metadata elements and their components are combined to form a metadata record.

Syntax Encoding Schemes

Syntax Encoding Schemes indicate that the value is a string formatted in accordance with a formal notation, such as "2000-01-01" as the standard expression of a date.

T

TAP

A project developed at Stanford, TAP seeks to create a web of "machine-readable" (XML, RDF) data, not just human readable (HTML) data. A server which is queried for information about people or subjects, will collocate documents about people and concepts.

Taxonomy

In general terms, systematic classification according to principles or general laws. In digital terms, automated classification of documents in a hierarchy based on information gathered by a metacrawler. May refer to a classification of DCMI terms. A classification system such as Library of Congress Classification is an example of a taxonomy.

Technical metadata

Metadata that documents the creation and the digital characteristics of the files.

TEI

See Text Encoding Initiative

TCP (Transmission Control Protocol)

One of the protocols on which the Internet is based (a connection-oriented reliable protocol). Often used in combination with IP (Internet Protocol) as in TCP/IP.

TCP / IP

Transmission Control Protocol / Internet Protocol - This is the protocol that defines the Internet. TCP / IP was originally designed for the unix operating system, but is today available for every major kind of computer operating system.

Telnet

The Internet protocol for remote terminal connection

service. Telnet allows a user at one site to log in and interact with a system at another site just as if the user's terminal were connected directly to the remote computer.

Temporal

An element refinement of coverage. Temporal characteristics of the intellectual content of the resource.

Text Encoding Initiative (TEI)

An international project to develop guidelines for the preparation and interchange of electronic texts for scholarly research as well as a broad range of other language industry uses. The TEI DTD is an SGML Document Type Definition for encoding literary works.

Thesaurus

A structured vocabulary make up of names, words, and other information, typically including synonyms and/or hierarchical relationships for the purpose of cross-referencing in order to organize a collection of concepts for reference and retrieval. A controlled vocabulary of terms or concepts that are structured hierarchically (parent/child relationships) or as equivalences (synonyms), and related terms (associative). See also Subject headings and glossary. A thesaurus is a taxonomy.

Thesaurus of Geographic Names

The TGN is a controlled vocabulary containing around 1,000,000 names and other information about places. It includes physical features and administrative entities, such as cities and nations. The emphasis in TGN is on places important for art and architecture.

Title

The Dublin Core element used to designate the name given to the resource. Typically, a Title will be a name by which the resource is formally known.

Title bar

The colored bar at the top of each window that displays the program and file names.

Title screen (Electronic resources)

In the case of an electronic resource, a display of data that includes the title proper and usually, though not necessarily, the statement of responsibility and the data relating to publication.

Type of carrier

See Carrier type

Type of content

See Content type

U

Uncontrolled access point

An access point that is not controlled by an authority record.

See also Access point, Controlled access point

Uniform title

No longer used in the Principles.

See Authorized access point for the work/expression

ULAN

See Union List of Artist Names

Unicode

A universal encoding scheme designed to allow interchange, processing and display of the world's principal languages, as well as many historic and archaic scripts. Unicode supports and fosters a multilingual computing world community by allowing computers using one language to "talk" to computers using a different language. A registered trademark of Unicode, Inc.

Unicode Transformation Format, 8-bit (UTF-8)

A temporary form of Unicode that is well suited for routing data through systems that are not designed for Unicode, such as some email servers and Web clients. UTF-8 is an attractive way of storing multilingual data on the Internet, without requiring full Unicode compliance.

Uniform Resource Identifier

The syntax for all names/addresses that refer to resources on the World Wide Web.

URI

Uniform Resource Identifier. Provides a standard syntax for locating files using existing Internet protocols as in a Uniform Resource Locator (URL) or by resolution of a Uniform Resource Name (URN).

Uniform Resource Locator (URL)

A technique for indicating the name and location of Internet resources. The URL specifies the name and type of the resource, as well as the computer, device and directory where the resource may be found. The URL for Dublin Core Metatdata Initiative is <http://dublincore.org/>.

URL. (2)

Uniform Resource Locator. Location information of an electronic resource expressed in a standardized format, which allows for electronic resources to be sent and received automatically. The World Wide Web uses the URL as the basis of linking to other files and documents around the Internet. A URL can be identified by a protocol such as "http."

Uniform Resource Name (URN)

A URI (name and address of an object on the Internet) that has some assurance of persistence beyond that normally associated with an Internet domain or host name.

Uniform Resource Name. (2)

A URI that has an institutional commitment to persistence, availability, etc. A particular scheme, identified by the initial string "urn:", that is intended to serve as a persistent, location-independent, resource identifier.

Union Lists of Artists' Names (ULAN)

Union List of Artist Names. A controlled vocabulary of artists' names and biographical and bibliographic information produced by the Getty Vocabulary Program.

Usenet News

Separate from the Internet but available with many Internet accounts, it's a worldwide set of over 12,000 bulletin boards, called "newsgroups." Software called a "newsreader" is used to read and post.

Userid

Sometimes called "user name," userid is short for "user identification." This precedes the @ sign in an email address.

USMARC

See MARC

UTF-8

See Unicode Transformation Format, 8-bit.

V

Variant form access point

A form of name not chosen as the authorized access point for an entity that may be used to access the authority record for the entity or be presented as a reference or link to the authorized access point.

See also Access point, Controlled access point, Name

Variable field

A field with variable length in a USMARC record.

Virtual hosting

A Web server hosting service that replaces a company's need to purchase and maintain its own Web server and connections to the Internet.

Virtual library

Access to electronic information in a variety of remote locations through a local online catalog or other gateway, such as the Internet

VLE

Virtual Learning Environment

W

WAIS

An early version of Z39.50, used in digital libraries before the web, now largely obsolete.

Warwick Framework

An architecture for the interchange of metadata packages, or "containers"; designed to satisfy the need for competing, overlapping, and complementary metadata models.

Watermark

A code embedded into digital material that can be used to establish ownership, may be visible or invisible to the user.

Web crawler

A web indexing program that builds an index by following hyperlinks continuously from web page to web page.

Webmaster

A person who manages web sites.

Web Service

As defined by the W3C, "a software system designed to support interoperable machine-to-machine interaction over a network. It has an interface described in a machine-processible format (specifically WSDL). Other systems interact with the web service in a manner prescribed by its description using SOAP messages, typically conveyed using HTTP with an XML serialisation in conjunction with other Web-related standards."

Web Service Definition

A service definition for a web service; a WSDL document.

Workflow

The paths through a networked structure of tasks and activities; the steps in a Business Process

World Wide Web (WWW)

A hypertext-based system for locating and accessing Internet resources which presents materials to the user in the form of interlinked documents (which can include text, images, and digitized sound).

World Wide Web Consortium (W3C)

An international industry consortium founded in October 1994 to lead the World Wide Web to its full potential by developing common protocols that promote its evolution and ensure its interoperability. For additional information see http://www.w3.org/Consortium/.

WWW

See World Wide Web

W3C

See World Wide Web Consortium

Work

A distinct intellectual or artistic creation (i.e., the intellectual or artistic content.).

Weblog

See Blog.

X

XML

Extensible Markup Language. XML is a pared-down version of SGML, designed especially for Web documents. It enables Web authors and Web developers to create their own customized tags to provide functionality not available with HTML.

Z

Z39.50

A NISO (National Information Standards Office) standard protocol for metadata -'information describing an information resource, such as a dataset. Consistently defined metadata permits rapid and effective browsing of a wide range of data resources, an essential requirement for efficient use of electronic resources distributed across a network. This protocol that allows a computer to search collections of information on a remote system, create sets of results for further manipulation, and retrieve information; mainly used for bibliographic information.

Index